THE
COMPLETE GUIDE TO
PAINTBALL

THIRD EDITION

NEW YORK

THE
COMPLETE
PAINT

Written by Steve Davidson, Pete "Robbo" Robinson, Rob "Tyger" Rubin, and Stewart Smith

Special Contributions by Jerry Braun, Durty Dan, and Sarah Stevenson

Photographed by Peter Field Peck

Illustrations by Mark Smith

GUIDE ^{TO}
BALL

The Complete Guide to Paintball
Third Edition

Written by Jerry Braun, Steve Davidson, Justin Owen, Pete "Robbo" Robinson, Rob "Tyger" Rubin, and Stewart Smith
Special Contributions by Durty Dan and Sarah Stevenson
Photographed by Peter Field Peck
Illustrations by Mark Smith
Conceived by Andrew Flach
Researched by Tracy Tumminello

Adaptations of "Getting Started," "Rules to Play By," and "Common Mistakes," courtesy of splatterzone.com

The Complete Guide to Paintball
A GETFITNOW.com Book

Hatherleigh Press/GETFITNOW.com Books
An affiliate of W.W. Norton & Company, Inc.
5-22 46th Avenue, Suite 200
Long Island City, NY 11101

Visit our website: www.getfitnow.com

All Hatherleigh Press titles are available for bulk purchase, special promotions, and premiums. For more information, please contact the manager of our Special Sales Department at 1-800-528-2550.

Library of Congress Cataloging-in-Publication Data

The complete guide to paintball / written by Jerry Braun ... [et al.] ;
special contributions by Jerry Braun, Druty Dan, and Sarah Stevenson ;
photographed by Peter Field Peck ; illustrations by Mark Smith.-- 3rd ed.
    p. cm.
  ISBN 1-57826-173-2
1. Paintball (Game) I. Braun, Jerry.
  GV1202.S87C64 2004
  796.2--dc22
                            2004009614

Photographed with Canon® cameras and lenses on Fuji® and Kodak® print and slide film
Text design and composition by edn Design
The text is set in Agenda
Cover photos by Rigo Ramirez © JT USA 2004
Cover designed by Deborah Miller

Printed on acid-free paper
10 9 8 7 6 5 4 3 2 1
Printed in Canada

"A friend of ours found this gun in an agricultural catalogue that was used by cattlemen to mark cows. It wasn't long afterwards that we bought two of these things and had ourselves a little duel. After it was over, we just knew we had stumbled upon something great."

- Hayes Noel

Acknowledgments

The editors and publisher are grateful to the following individuals for their assistance and encouragement in the publication of this book.

Jerry Braun and Paintball Sports International, for their endless help and support.

Cousins Paintball, for the use of their field in Medford, NY for our photo shoots. Paul Sattler, Fred Dorski, and Elio Napolitano, for giving so generously of their time and knowledge.

Jay Tavitian, and everyone at Oceanside Paintball, for showing us the time of our lives.

Sarah Stevenson, Karen Barber, and the entire 2 Die 4 team for their knowledge, enthusiasm and determination.

Cleo and Paul Fogal, for sharing their home, their field, and their story with us.

Mike Henry, Jim Lively, and Colin Thompson, for always leading us in the right direction.

NY Dogs, a great bunch of guys and a terrific team of paintball players. It was an honor playing with them.

Glenn Palmer, for always lending his assistance and equipment so willingly to this project.

Graham Easton, for helping outfit us for this paintball adventure.

Dawn and Bill Mills, of warpig.com for all their guidance and assistance.

Guy Cooper of Pro Star Sports, for his informative "Paintball Field Operator's Guide."

Steve Dunn and Extreme Adventures Canada, for the use of their Flak Jacket. It helped make Peter's job a little less painful.

National Paintball Supply, for the use of Squeegee Man.

The entire Wild Geese team, and especially Ralph Torrell, for sharing with us his extensive paintball gun collection.

Jim Della Constanza, for making Skyball such an enjoyable tournament.

Matthew Howard, for all his assistance with our Australian paintball directory.

We would also like to thank the following companies for generously loaning us equipment.

ADCO, Brass Eagle, Diablo, Diggers, JT, Kingman International, Lapco, Palmer's Pursuit Shop, Pro-Team Products, R. P. Scherer, Sheridan, Smart Parts, Soft Boards & Barriers Co., Tippmann Pneumatics, WDP, and Zap.

To everyone in the paintball industry – the players, manufacturers, field owners, distributors, and fans. We couldn't have written this book without your help and support. Thank you!

Contents

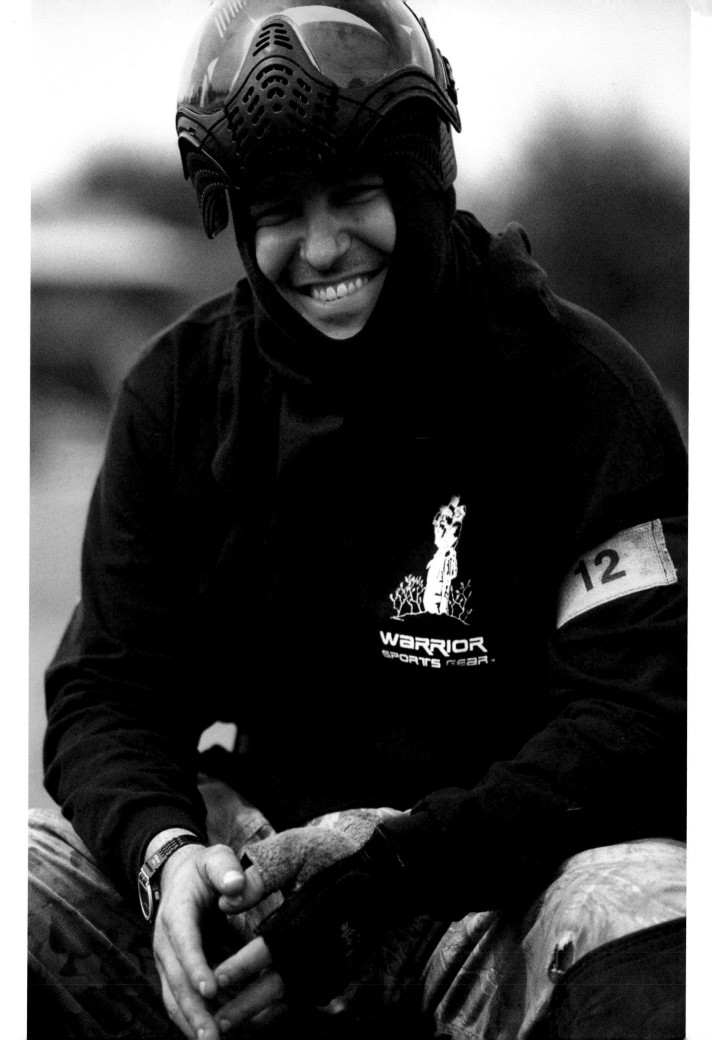

WHO IS THIS BOOK FOR?

This book is for everyone who plays or is interested in playing paintball. Everyone will appreciate the scope of this first edition; it is as much a tribute to the diversity within the game and its players as it is a guide. Regardless of your skill level, this book holds something for you.

We cover the fascinating history of the game (with firsthand accounts from its originators!), and the basic rules of the game (and descriptions of exciting variations on the paintball theme!). We offer in-depth equipment and gun information, and include essential tactical insights, as well as a thorough glossary and resource guide. Beginners and novices take note: Insights from the best players in the world make this book an ideal starting point for those of you serious about adding new dimensions of fun and excitement to your hobby and becoming great at this game.

For those of you who have played for a few years or are seasoned veterans, check out this book's authoritative analysis of guns and air systems, articles on advanced strategy, exclusive input on injury prevention stretches from former Navy SEAL, Stewart Smith, discussion of accessories, and comprehensive listing of international resources for both playing and purchasing equipment.

Our authoritative sections on the physics of paintball and guidelines for cleaning your gun correctly are among many gems in this book. We're sure that you'll find our interviews with great players both enlightening and useful in your search for competitive advantages. Motivated to elevate your game to the next level and beyond? Read on!

And then, of course, there are the pictures—visually arresting, dynamic shots taken by Peter Peck, who was himself "shot" innumerable times garnering these photographs. If you just love the game and want a book that captures the action, look no further.

Although we have attempted to be comprehensive, we realize that this volume is not the last word on the sport. For example, such luminaries as Jerry Braun, Bob Long, Jim Lively, and Dawn and Bill Mills of warpig.com gave of their time and shared insights that made this book possible. We would have loved to include more from them. We did not cover scenario games, a paintball format that we learned early on truly merits its own book. That said, we believe that we're off to a strong start. In the interest of ensuring that future editions raise the bar, we encourage you to contact us with your feedback about aspects of the game we ought to cover for the first time or in greater depth.

WHO IS PAINTBALL FOR?

For those of us who play paintball and love it, the question is what are you looking for in a game?

The answers that lead directly to paintball are listed below

If these are your answers, welcome home! This game is for you. Otherwise, you should read on. You just may want to change your mind.

I want fast-paced, totally immersive action.

There isn't a single, true standstill in paintball play, nor is there a moment where you don't feel like something is at stake. You are on offense and defense constantly, and your objectives require you to be alert and decisive—not hyper, mind you, just in the flow of the game. Opponents lurk around every corner and paintballs travel at up to 300 feet per second. You need to survive, but be willing to make a coordinated sacrifice to win the game for your team. Your teammates count on you to act with caution and precisely controlled aggression from one moment to the next. You can hear your competition moving toward you. You see paintballs flying and hear them splat against trees or barriers. You slide forward on your knees, dive behind a tree, cover your teammates' advance, celebrate victory after a hard-fought contest. Guaranteed to render "first-person, shoot'em-up, networkable computer simulations" a permanent second choice, paintball is the premiere action game.

I want a vigorous mental challenge as well as a rigorous physical one.

This is a thinking person's game. A lapse in concentration leads to elimination. If you're indoors, you may choose tactics based on speedy deployment with constant movement and firing in support of advances. If you're outdoors on a wide open field, you may want to split your force in two and converge on the enemy from opposite directions. To win at this game consistently, you and your team must use appropriate tactics while communicating (that means speaking and listening) coherently, and thinking quickly to adapt to the unexpected. It takes maturity to act as an individual without losing sight of your role in a team effort. It takes intelligence and quick decision making to prevail in the hair-raising scenarios that paintball presents.

I want a game I can play.

Except for the newborn, paintball is for everyone! The rules are straightforward, there are games and formats for every skill level, and the costs of playing are affordable. You can play the game with family and friends, with your church group, with corporate colleagues, or even go on your own simply to meet people who share your passion for intense, team-oriented sports. Whether things go well or not during your game, you will form a unique bond with whomever you play. And you can't make friends of strangers any faster than by playing paintball with them. It's safe to say that paintball is an unparalleled social experience, and open to all comers.

I want to be the best at whatever game I play.

If you put in the time and energy, form a great team, train together regularly, and have a little luck, you can become a professional paintball player, experience a tempo of game play that is unsurpassed, and vie for national and international championships against the best players in the world. For some, being a weekend warrior is enough. Others play for the thrill of victory, and seek out ever higher levels of competition. Paintball serves up plenty of opportunities for everyone. How far you go in this sport is largely up to you.

Whether you played tag or hide-and-seek when you were younger or yesterday, this game, in any of its manifestations, represents the most thrilling experience of competition you are likely ever to experience. Add to that the extraordinary comraderie you invariably develop with teammates, and you have one of the best games ever invented!

PAINTBALL IS FOR YOU!

Everybody wants to experience adventure—a highly intensified, dramatic realization of acting heroically and skillfully to attain a goal. We seek a sense of mission, of honoring our values, of taking advantage of opportunities that present themselves in our professional and romantic lives. Paintball is a microcosm of the adventure we experience each day. It crystallizes the sense of drama we seek to lend meaning to our choices and actions. Paintball taps into your imagination—*what if my life hinges on what I choose to do in the next moment?* Paintball provides a rapid succession of such moments that lead to an unparalleled gaming experience that is both universal and highly personal for every player. For those of you looking for a game that is more than the sum of its parts, here it is. Seize it!

WHO ARE WE?

The authors and interviewees are among the finest and most influential men and women ever involved with the game of paintball. For them, paintball is a passion of one sort or another. They share in common a singular devotion to the widespread enjoyment of this game, and that is why we sought their involvement with this endeavor. We think you'll be thrilled with the results.

The publisher of this book is a multifaceted multimedia company that perceived a unique opportunity to present an authoritative text on the subject of paintball to the game's growing base of enthusiastic participants, among whom we count ourselves.

GETFITNOW.com is an imprint of The Hatherleigh Company, Ltd. committed to developing multimedia health and fitness products for consumers of all ages. We believe that leading a healthy life-style can and should be a source of enjoyment and fulfillment. Paintball combines vigorous physical activity and tactical thinking in a way that we find irresistably fun.

You should go play this game as soon as possible.

—AWC

PART 1

WELCOME
to the Game of
PAINTBALL

Genesis of the Game

WHAT IS PAINTBALL REALLY ABOUT?

Paintball is an extraordinarily simple game in its basic form. A couple of people alternately hunt and evade one another, until one person or a team emerges triumphant over another. The victor is the first to achieve an objective or the last left standing. Yes, the game uses sophisticated technology, which is constantly evolving as people come up with new paintball accessories and gun mechanisms, and the specific objectives vary according to game designers' imaginations. But the basic game remains the same.

No matter what version of the game you find yourself most attracted to, its essence is constant. What is paintball's essence? The answer is two-fold.

Paintball is a Game

Paintball is, in the final analysis, one of many games people play with balls. In what is basically an advanced version of tag, the balls—gel-encased, water soluble goo—are propelled at up to 300 feet per second by a special, gas-powered gun. You *eliminate* (tag) opponents when paintballs you or your teammates shoot hit and break on them. Simple, right? And, as with any game, the whole point of it is to have a good time in a competitive context. Like football, basketball, and baseball, elements of paintball require players to acquire and practice certain skills. Like these other games, it has rules, some hard and fast and others that are subject to interpretation. It shares in common with more free form activities, like skateboarding and surfing, built-in enthusiasm for innovation, personal style, fast-thinking, and highly individualistic approaches. As the people who played the first game did, anyone can come up with their own version of the game. Once

Smart-thinking, alert and precise action, and good fortune lead to victory

with other people—family, friends, coworkers who are our team members. There is no escaping the fact that however well we may do on our own, we lead more fulfilling lives when we spend time in meaningful pursuits with others who share our values and goals.

Especially in America, with our culture of "manifest destiny," and the "American Dream," we are hard-wired with an optimistic and moral sense that people should put forth their best effort, go for it, "just do it," when it comes to just about everything in life. We attach importance not only to our goals, but how we achieve them.

**Be honest. Don't lie.
Be considerate. Don't be violent.
Follow the rules. Don't cheat.
Be creative. Don't be predictable.
Have fun. Don't have a negative outlook.
Be a team player. Don't be egotistical.
Be resilient. Don't ever give up.**

you're equipped with the essential safety equipment, there is enormous room for having your own kind of fun with this game.

Paintball is About Survival

Paintball is also more than just a game. At its most exhilarating moments, it is an intensified version of what people do everyday. With varying degrees of success, we're all avoiding and confronting obstacles on our way to reaching goals. This is the case whether you're in school or pursuing a career, a man or a woman, regardless of your beliefs or ethnicity.

We're all survivors. We all have goals that we're in different stages of reaching. We take risks. We learn from our mistakes and get back into the fray. We improve at the skills necessary to meet daily objectives and lifelong dreams. We do all of this

Of course, these are things all people value, not just Americans. They work for everybody in all situations. But it is no accident that paintball was created in America.

Paintball captures the essence of the basic struggle of every living being. Staying in the game is the most obvious metaphor for staying alive. And winning is about being great at surviving while vanquishing foes in fair play.

The game of paintball creates a situation in which the only way to survive is to act in manner that balances precise aggression with caution. You attain objectives by taking risks that you have a good chance of handling.

Being great at paintball requires you to learn how to take great risks and succeed.

Welcome to the Game of Paintball

It is also a very physical game, and to play it well means executing moves quickly and dynamically. The height of game play is achieved by mastering basic techniques and tactics, improvising effectively, working well with a team, and being fit.

The notion of paintball as a test of survival skills is what inspired its progenitors, Hayes Noel and Charles Gaines.

BIG QUESTIONS

A little less than 20 years ago, these two very close friends discovered a way to test ideas they had debated extensively during their relationship. *Are we born with all the resources we need to survive, or do we learn how to survive in response to our environment? Are survival skills learned in one context portable to other contexts? How does a person's tolerance for risk affect his ability to prevail in adverse conditions? What is the relationship between honesty and survival?* To address these tremendous questions, Noel and Gaines devised a game they called, simply, "survival." Today, we know that game as paintball. When you play, give a moment's thought to the questions this game was first invented and played to resolve. What are your answers? You can learn more about what the founders were thinking in their interviews in this book.

FROM "THE NATIONAL SURVIVAL GAME" TO TODAY

Seizing a unique opportunity to turn the game into a profitable business model, Noel and Gaines teamed up with a friend, Bob Gurnsey, and started selling marking guns and paint, and access to fields where people could get together to play the survival game. The first guns—"Splatmasters"—were made by the Nelson Paint Company, which actually had the guns manufactured under contract by the Daisy Manufacturing Company Incorporated. They made up rules for simple games like Capture the Flag and Total Elimination. This was the birth of the first paintball franchise, The National Survival Game, and what would grow to a 800 million dollar industry.

Soon other franchises emerged that started to experiment with new kinds of team games. New technologies and the development of unique paintball products dramatically accelerated the evolution of multiple paintball formats, from recreational play to scenario games, from amateur tournaments to professional, international championships.

The game has undergone dramatic changes over the years. If you look closely, however, you'll see that its essence has survived.

—AWC

Walking through the woods one day...

The actual genesis of the game really started in my mind on a walk through the woods of Virginia with a friend of mine who lives in Charlottesville and has a farm there. We were walking through the farm and he was talking about hunting wild buffalo. I'm not a hunter myself, but I was enthralled by his story. He was talking about hunting buffalo in Africa and how he was in these bulrushes and couldn't see the beasts but could hear them, about having to be aware of wind direction, about the feelings he had experienced in this extreme scenario.

I was really caught up in the thrill and the excitement and the high that he clearly had felt doing that kind of thing. The severity of the situation he was describing, the notion of survival being boiled down to a few decisive moments, just blew me away. This was 1976 and I was 35 years old. I said, "Why don't we just stalk and hunt each other on the way back to the house?" I'd done this as a kid, playing cowboys and Indians and things. But somehow the context of his story made me feel like more was at stake, and I had this remarkable adrenaline rush. I didn't forget it when I returned to New York City where I lived for 15 years making my living trading the markets on the American Stock Exchange.

I used to go to New Hampshire about once every two months to see Charles Gaines, who's one of my best friends, as well as a big outdoorsman, hunter, writer... a guy just totally at home in the wilderness.

Charles said something like, "You know, if I ever got you in the woods you'd be dead meat in a second." So we began a conversation and then sort of a debate over almost a year and half about surviving in the wilderness and what qualities it would take.

I told him that if I could survive in the Wall Street jungle, I would survive in any jungle. Charles thought this was nonsense, but I was convinced that survival skills were transportable across environments. For example, to my way of thinking tolerance for risk-taking, aggressive and defensive tendencies, a tempo of decision making and action are things that one masters in order to excel in any context. Charles believed that survival skills were inextricably linked to context, and could be learned or acquired in one environment without the benefits accruing to experiences in others. So I could be great on Wall Street, but would be devoured in the forest. Needless to say, this was a great debate.

We'd read Richard Connell's "The Most Dangerous Game" in high school and stuff like that always really turned us on. And then we were in the midst of this debate for over a year and half, and gradually over the course of our conversations we tried to devise good survival tests. And maybe with that story kicking around subconsciously somewhere in there, we developed a sense that we needed a hunting game to test our theories.

But we really never could come up with anything, until a friend of ours, George Butler, found this paintball gun in an agricultural catalogue that was used by cattlemen to mark cows. It wasn't long afterwards that we bought two of these things and had ourselves a little duel. After it was over, we just knew that we had stumbled upon something great. Almost right away we were talking about the potential for games based on survival using this kind of gun.

—Excerpt from interview with Adam W. Cohen

Hayes Noel currently trades the markets in Santa Cruz, CA, where he lives with his wife and two children.

PAINTBALL AT GROUND ZERO

Hayes Noel

ADAM COHEN: So who won that first duel?

HAYES NOEL: [Laughs] Charles did. He's a much better shot than I am. In fact, he shot me directly in the ass. [Laughs] I was wearing a bathing suit. We didn't have goggles or any protective gear, but what did we know. We were just thrilled to be doing this finally. I shot at him first and missed. Then he got me in the butt. His shot raised a little welt, which stung for a while. As far as I was concerned, that just made it more realistic.

We could see right then that we had the tool we needed to play this kind of hunting game that we wanted, because it wasn't like these tomato wars that they have in New Hampshire or Vermont. These guns were fairly accurate and could really tag you from quite a distance away. So they were sort of like guns without the danger of guns.

Not long after the duel, we played a little stalking game out in one of the wooded fields around his house. I was ecstatic because I knew that now we could play these awesome games whenever we wanted.

So then Bob Gurnsey got involved in it when we started to formulate the rules and an idea of the game. The three of us spent another six months arguing about the rules, and how a large-scale competitive version of the game would be structured.

We had decided to invite 9 different people that we knew to join us and play this game. The participants were from all over the country, people who were successful in whatever they had undertaken to accomplish. For example, we invited a guy from Alabama, who was one of the best wild turkey guides and hunters in the sport. We had two guys who had been long-range reconnaissance patrol leaders in Vietnam. Among the others were a lawyer or two, a doctor from Chicago, a movie producer from Los Angeles, and the outdoor writer for Sports Illustrated who had been cleared to do an article on the game.

The mix of people was exciting. Some were local New Hampshire friends of Charles. The man who eventually won, Richard White, was a local lumber man and deer hunter.

Anyway, we took this 80 acre cross-country ski area, filled with second growth woods. You could see through it. There were trails and it was clear enough that you could move pretty well through these woods. We marked off the boundaries of the space and appointed a responsible friend of ours to be head judge.

So we had these four flag stations. In each flag station there were 12 flags of the same color, one for each player. So there was one flag station with 12 blue flags just hanging out in the open and others with 12 green flags, 12 yellow flags, and 12 red flags. Each flag station had a judge with a whistle.

At 10 o'clock in the morning, we positioned people at equal distances apart along the circumference of the area. Some guy fired a shotgun and it started.

The first person to go in and get one flag of each color and get back out without being shot won the game as soon as he reached the home base where the head judge was waiting. We didn't know how long it would take. Everybody had a different color paint, so you could tell who shot you by color. And if you got any paint on you at all, even splatter from a hit on a tree, you were out. That's not the way it's done now, but that was the way that we did it then. Everybody was cammoed up and looked really intense. I'm certain that observers would be simultaneously a little bothered and titillated by the militant look. We weren't striving for that. We were just wearing what made sense to wear when you're running around in the woods trying not to be seen.

At the beginning of the game, everybody had maps. And as I said, we had a judge with a whistle at each flag station. These judges blew their whistles every 15 minutes so that the non-woodsmen who couldn't read the map that well had a way of gauging their progress toward a given flag.

ADAM: What are some examples of strategies that you saw?

HAYES: One obvious strategy involved running full speed to the station you were closest to at the outset of the game, and then shooting every person who approached it. The idea was that once you shot 11 people you knew there was nobody else and you could just walk through the woods and get the other flags. This would be rational, but very risky.

Another strategy was just to wait. Remember, we didn't know how long it would take for everything to work out, and nobody wanted to get eliminated early. After waiting, you could move and feel relatively confident that your opponents weren't behind you. This was less risky.

Another strategy was to hunt everybody down, play aggressive until there was nobody left—definitely the riskiest approach. There were a lot of different ways to play it.

ADAM: What was your strategy?

HAYES: Well, I was in really good shape. I knew that I would not get tired, no matter how long the game took. My strategy was to walk the perimeter, basically run around our field of 80 acres.

Since I was running along the boundary, I only had to worry about one side of me. When I got close to where a flag station was, I followed a straight line to it, and then returned along the same path. I knew I was unlikely to encounter someone where I had just been.

And it turns out there was not a lot of activity around the flag stations; the bottom line is that 80 acres was probably way too big for the game.

But we didn't know that. I was doing well. I actually got three flags before anybody did. But then I couldn't find the fourth flag station [*laughs*], and as I wandered around looking for it, I ended up getting in a fire fight with a doctor, Bob Carlson, who was this intensely aggressive guy. He was having fun trying to shoot everybody. I don't think he even got a single flag. In general, the more shooting fights you go into, the greater your chance of elimination. He eliminated me. Anyway, that was my strategy. And it was just totally exciting.

As it turned out, the illusion of danger was so real, it was the most exciting thing I had ever done. Every cell in my body was turned on. After the first 15 minutes, every breeze that blew something was like an alarm bell; you didn't know if it was somebody behind you, around you, above you. I mean it was a whole new level of excitement.

And it ended up that the game was over after about two and a half hours and I'd say at least nine or ten of the people were out of it at that point, or had been shot. The guy who ended up winning it had been in the woods all his life. Richard White never fired a shot at anybody, and he was never shot at the whole time. He just walked through the woods and kept himself out of trouble.

ADAM: How did this outcome inform your debate?

HAYES: The conclusion you can draw from the first game is essentially that the less aggressive you are, the better off you are. But that needs to be qualified. The guy who won was not taking a riskless strategy. He went for the flags. He just avoided firefights.

ADAM: He was on offense, but cautious.

HAYES: Yeah, he was invisible. I don't think we really settled the debate. But we did know that this game was amazing. Bob and Charles and I knew that this was fun. Bob pushed this more than anybody, but we all knew that we were onto something that many people were going to want to do.

I mean, it would just turn people on when they read this Sports Illustrated article. We decided to start some type of operation, a company, to try and promote this game and make a business out of it, basically.

ADAM: So that's really how the first game went, and led directly to the formation of your company.

HAYES: That's pretty much the idea and origin of the first game and the experience playing it. It was unique for everybody, you know. Charles and everybody there had a different experience. For some people, like myself, I took it pretty seriously and I was really into it.

We played in June of 1980, and in November of '80, the Sports Illustrated article came out.

ADAM: Not soon after this experience, you started a paintball company.

HAYES: That's right.

ADAM: Tell us about how you made that happen.

HAYES: Sure. Bob and I flew out to the Nelson Paint Company that made the paintball gun and sought an exclusive contract with them to sell the guns to us and nobody else except cattlemen.

We knew there were people who wanted to play the National Survival Game. It wasn't called "paintball" back then. We named the company after the game as we'd named it, and we called the various scenarios we promoted survival games. Paintball is probably a better name, but that came later.

We flew out to their Michigan headquarters, and we asked them, "How many markers [paintball guns] did you sell last year?" Bob and I didn't have any idea of what their business was like. The paintballs were made by a company called R.P. Scherer that makes vitamins and gelatin capsules. They sold the paintballs to Nelson. Nelson just made the guns to try and sell paint. It was just a product they had.

So anyway, they responded, "Oh, we sold about 700 last year." And we said, "If you give us this price, we can guarantee sales of 2000." I literally just picked a number. It turned out in the first year we sold about seven or eight thousand. Nelson couldn't keep up with our orders. We didn't know whether we'd be a mail order firm or how it would work out. We ended up authorizing people to set up deals for fields and resell our merchandise.

Guys from Atlanta would call and say, "I'd like to start a paintball company. I'll buy 30 guns." So instead of selling guns to individuals, we'd sell 25 to a guy who was going to rent them out to people to play.

Eventually, areas around the country were covered by people who owned franchises, and we wouldn't sell guns to anybody else within their area. For the first two or three years, we were the only show in town.

Then, people found out about Nelson. Nelson began selling to them at the original retail price. We couldn't control that after a while.

ADAM: How was business?

HAYES: Incredible. Sales skyrocketed. We turned a profit after about six months. Most startup companies take two or three years to show a profit. These days you've got Internet companies that don't make anything but vaporware but are worth millions and billions. We were legitimately successful from the start.

We were never as confident as we probably should have been. We were preoccupied with the image thing, how the game was perceived.

ADAM: I've heard that the game's militant look was a publicity problem from the start.

HAYES: Unfortunately, yes. For instance, during the early going, I went to Chicago. The Donahue Show had called and wanted us to talk about what we were doing. Local news shows, anybody who had heard about it, they all wanted to come cover us, because it was kind of controversial and looked really violent. Of course, it really wasn't, but they were selling their story, and it made good copy and dramatic pictures.

I went out to Chicago for the Donahue Show, and then did a segment of Nightline with Ted Koppel in New York.

So, I talked a little bit to the Donahue producer about the game, and we sent them a gun. I really wanted Donahue to shoot me on the set, inside the studio, at point blank range. I figured that it would take something that dramatic, that looks cool and would make clear to people that paintball wasn't really dangerous, to soften people's impression of the game. Donahue wouldn't do it. Instead, he invited me and an "anti-violence" psychologist for a debate format. The psychologist thought any G.I. Joe toys and stuff like that were problematic. They also had a woman and her son who had played the game. There were four of us on the show.

Donahue came in and said, "Now listen, this is not like school, you don't have to raise your hands, it's going to be over in 15 minutes. If you guys have anything to say, you'd better say it." Then he said, "When I open the show, I'm going to shoot a police target." He didn't want to shoot me, so he planned to use a police target instead.

So we go into the studio and there's the live audience ready to go. I know there's a psychologist who's going to try and do me in, so I'm kind of nervous. Donahue's ready to fire away at this silhouette type target that you might see that police shoot at. It was a white, paper silhouette hanging on the back stage curtain.

I said, "Wait a minute. Hey! You can't do that. The paintball will go right through that paper target." And he said, "Oh yeah, you're right." So he got somebody behind the curtain to hold a blackboard up behind the thing. But then he said [Laughs], "Tonight we have the survival game. Is it a game or is it more than a game?"

Then he turned and shot this thing and it sounded like a cannon going off. [Laughs] And it went right through the paper target. [Laughs] It looked as though he could have shot it with a 38 caliber handgun. I mean, the hole looked just like what a bullet would make.

Then the paintball broke when it hit the curtain, and it was red paintball exploding on that white backdrop.

ADAM: So that was kind of bad. [Laughs]

HAYES: [Laughing] I said, "I know this looks really bad," to myself, and I got pretty uptight. Donahue went and rubbed his finger around the hole like it was a wound or something. He looked at me right in the face and said, "This scares the shit out of me." Just like that.

Well, I knew I was in trouble right there. At the opening of the show, Donahue said, "Well, we just shot the paintball, and I think I'd rather play this game in armor, than with goggles." The woman ended up shooting me on the show, and that was fine. But still, at the end of the show, the audience gets to ask questions, and some woman said, "I just don't even understand what this is all about."

ADAM: How did Nightline go?

HAYES: You wouldn't believe it. They had Ted Koppel doing a live interview with a guy named Frank Camper, who ran a mercenary school in Alabama. About four months earlier, a Pakistani airline flying into England had blown up and people had gotten killed. They had traced some of the terrorists back to this Frank Camper guy. So they presented this information, and then Koppel asked Camper if he ever killed anybody. Frank Camper looks right at the camera and says, "Yeah. Yeah, I have."

So they were saying, "Hey, look, this is what's going on in America. We've got terrorist training bases and now look what people are starting to do for recreation. Look at the games they're playing."

They showed pictures of people playing the paint-ball game out in the woods, and they really tried to do a number on us. Anyway, that was on a Saturday night. Well, Monday morning in the office we got about 200 calls. [*Laughs*] "Where can I play this game. It looks great! It looks like fun."

After that we started to relax a little bit about the image. But we were always concerned about it. So anyway, the acceptance of it, it just really grew and it started evolving. And then other companies started making paintball guns and just like any business, rival manufacturers and stuff crept up and the industry took off.

ADAM: We've heard that the industry is up to 800 million dollars in total revenue.

HAYES: Yeah. So it's a really big business. And whether it's going to continue to grow and so forth will be interesting to see.

ADAM: To hear you talk about it sounds like it was a game that on some basic level everybody was playing. All kids play one form of tag or another, and hide-and-seek.

HAYES: Right.

ADAM: You guys sort of tapped into this whole idea of using the paintball gun instead of make-believe or fruit. You formalized the game, gave it a new instrument and more mature format. But it's still a game that human beings just play, because they are naturally excited by the chase and the hunt.

HAYES: Yeah, I mean, you can ask any kid why he plays cops and robbers or cowboys and Indians. It's a raw, primal thing that never goes away.

In order to become a business, the game had to evolve from the individual game, which is far and away the most interesting in my opinion. The game we played where every individual was against every other individual was the ultimate. It became a game where teams played against other teams. When you play it that way in smaller fields, you shoot more paint.

So the name of the game is selling guns and selling paintballs. We were always against that. Let me clarify. We weren't against the idea of the team game, because from a business respect, that made more sense. But we opposed the virtual extinction of the individual game. Unfortunately, it just doesn't work as well from a business standpoint.

ADAM: What do you think about the game as it is played today?

HAYES: I was at this convention recently, they were debating whether they should have a rate of fire where the gun can't shoot more than 20 balls a second. Twenty balls per second? I think it's crazy, but if that's what the market demands.... It's still the same game underneath. It's just become something totally different on the surface.

The more you start to make it look like war, the more worried I get about the game's image.

I talked to Charles at length and we both agree. The industry needs to make the game visually pleasing. To make it viewer friendly for TV.

My opinion is that the flight of the ball is what's pleasing to see in any sport. If you watch people watching a tennis match, they don't watch the players, they watch the ball. And in football, you know you love to watch a pass spiraling through the air and the receiver running under it. You would never watch a guy drive or putt a golf ball, if you couldn't see the ball.

So the challenge for paintball is to make the ball visible in a way that pleases the senses of the person watching it. I mean, it's totally uninteresting otherwise. Charles and I sort of both worked up this idea about how to make paintball visually pleasing. But it would involve slowing the game down, slowing the paintball down, making it bigger, playing an individual game rather than a team game.

And it wouldn't affect the game at the field level, they could still play the tournaments and have the 20 balls a second and these things that they do. They'd sell a lot of paintballs at the field level.

However, in order to get sponsorship and TV revenue and live gate revenue, in order to put asses in the seats, so to speak, you have to make it viewer friendly. Right now, it's not a viewer friendly sport. And so you look at the magazines that come out and this and that, and all the advertisers are basically people who are producing products that people who play the game use and I think the only people that buy the magazines are people who play the game.

Whoever gets paintball on TV will make as much money as all the people selling all the paint and guns that exist today.

But, you know, that's not where they're at right now. They want to sit around and debate about whether to shoot 23 balls or ten balls. And to a certain extent they're not wrong to do so. 14-year-old boys want the best paintball gun money can buy for Christmas, and that's the market they're serving.

ADAM: Any final thoughts on the game, your sense of its essence, what you love about it?

HAYES: Have you seen "Life is Beautiful?"

ADAM: Yes, I have.

HAYES: That character was a survivor. I thought it was a great movie, that it dealt with the holocaust from the standpoint of a survivor. I felt the movie was about the perseverance of an individual in the face of this total horror. His humor, his resilience, his creativity, his courage-he was a total survivor. And I'm not saying that people who didn't survive somehow didn't measure up. Obviously, not. It's just that here was this guy doing everything he could to save his family. And at any moment, his luck could have run out, but he made sure that as far as he had anything to do with it, could have any control over what might happen, his son would live. And even though he

dies, he wins. That guy would have won our first game.

ADAM: Interesting.

HAYES: I don't even know why I'm bringing this up, except to say, that really, to me, this survival game is about whoever does well in the individual game. I'm not trying to be too heavy about it, but you know, a guy from the hills of Tennessee or a guy on Madison Avenue in New York is just as likely to have the qualities of a survivor as not.

This was an extraordinary man who, however he did it, faced this horror, dealt with it, and saved his genes. I don't know, I just thought it was very moving, a great movie.

So I wouldn't say a country or city boy is a better survivor than the other.

ADAM: It's the individual.

HAYES: Absolutely.

ADAM: Got it. Do you ever actually get together with these guys and just play the survival game, because just listening to you talk, it's hard to picture you enjoying the team approach much.

HAYES: No, I never did it in a recreational way. And honestly, to be on the floor of the American Stock exchange...

The thing is I used to love to play poker, and once I started trading the market by myself, I never played poker anymore. I know better than anybody who I know of what risk is. I get to take 50 risks a day if I want to. Or 20 risks or 10 or five. I get to practice what it feels like all the time. This is an important thing about survival games.

This wasn't initially why I wanted to start paintball, but it was very clear to me that because of the illusion of danger that you create in the game, it allows people to feel what it feels like to take risks.

ADAM: People don't usually like that feeling,

but they're enticed by it.

HAYES: No, they don't like it at all. It's the same feeling whether you're falling in love or whether you're making a commitment, a real commitment to something or whether you're taking a financial risk. People don't really like that feeling.

At some point, you have to learn that on the other side of risk is growth and not death. It's one of T.S. Elliot's points in "The Wasteland." Between the thought and the action falls the shadow— between the conception and realization falls the shadow. The shadow is the personal fear that people feel, the anxiety they feel, and it's a physical feeling, in all of these things. I think it's an actual physical anxiety that people feel. You need to practice getting through that.

So I don't really play paintball anymore. Except for that first game, the survival game, which was so new. But I do "play" every day.

ADAM: Understood. Thank you for your time, Hayes.

HAYES: You bet.

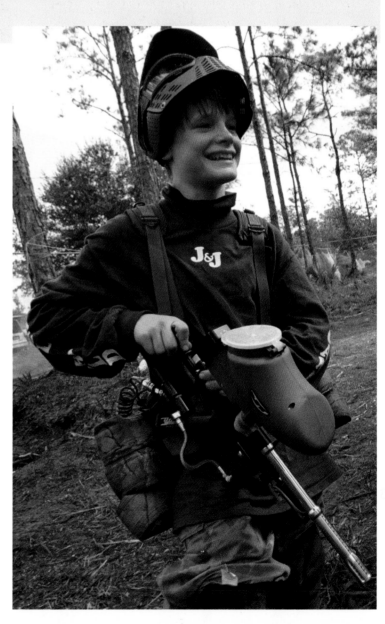

The Attraction of Paintball

Jerry Braun

A Game for Children of All Ages

Stop and think about the very first games you ever played. There are two games most of us played as children. One of them was Follow the Leader. The other one was a primal hunt and chase game, such as tag or hide-and-seek. You can be Chinese, you can be Venezuelan, you can be American, you can be Aleutian, you can be anyone from anywhere in the world. These are games you have played, the ones you started with, the ones you associate with being a child bursting with energy.

Remember when you were a kid playing hide-and-seek? Your heart would be in your mouth because your friend was three feet away from you and was just about to find you out. You felt that the world was going to come to an end if you were discovered. Remember playing tag? There was always a safe spot, but you'd leave it and run as hard as you could in order not to get tagged. Sometimes you'd run behind an obstacle to gain time. The exhilaration of not being found or tagging another player is what you experience playing paintball. That is why it is so appealing.

Now, some of us pretend it isn't so, but human beings, like most animals, have predatory instincts. Look at the very first games played by kittens and puppies, they are primal hunt-and-chase games. They stalk each other, bat at and chew on each other. Basically, they playfully attack one another. Pure play is nature's way of teaching survival. Playing paintball triggers the same kinds of responses in humans, except that we don't have to learn how to "go for the jugular" to survive the way animals do. So our enjoyment of games like paintball is a little different than theirs.

Jerry Braun, 4th from left in back row, at Skyball 1999, Toronto, Canada.

People talk about the game being violent. No doubt the images of adults brandishing guns looks intimidating and suggests violence. The basic characteristics of violence—the use of force to destroy or hurt others and a chaotic lack of structure that promotes reckless and dangerous behavior—are simply nowhere to be found in paintball. The objectives never involve hurting people, and the rules are clear and enforced. Nothing like the bench-clearing brawls that occur in professional baseball or hockey ever occurs in amateur or professional paintball.

When you first play the game, it elicits emotions in you that you may not have experienced since you were 3 years old. It's a sophisticated game of tag, except that it doesn't involve physical contact, incorporates teamwork, and frequently involves objectives beyond eliminating your opponent . And the pure joy you see on the faces of kids playing tag, that's what paintball provides. That's why people who play it once usually come back for more.

PAINTBALL'S PIERCING TRUTHS

Charles Gaines

ADAM COHEN: Do you think the skills that you acquire and develop by playing paintball are applicable to everyday real-life experiences?

CHARLES GAINES: Absolutely! More to the point, I think the survival game, as it was played back when Hayes [Noel] and I played it, is illuminating for anyone who plays it. Unlike Hayes who held that people are born with certain survival skills, I think that for the most part, we learn them based on our will to immerse ourselves in an environment and discover it. And so the game is a way of finding out about yourself...if you want it to be. I can't say too much about the game as it's played today, because I haven't played it recently and it's definitely changed. But I imagine from what I read about it and hear about it, that at the very least, the game's essential experience still heightens your awareness of yourself as a survivor in a specific context. Your ability to win is related to your receptiveness to the details and the nuances of your surroundings and your response to the scenario you're in. So I do believe that it's true that you can take lessons learned in the midst of playing any version of paintball, and apply those to improving your everyday life.

ADAM: Knowledge is power, and what you learn in paintball is often very personal knowledge. In terms of risk-taking, in terms of learning about how you function under pressure, in terms of making quick decisions, in terms of communicating with others effectively. You agree?

CHARLES: It's true. The survival game is like a little paradigm for real life. You know, it's more this way with the original game. After all, we play life as individuals, not as a team, regardless of our social experience. I mean, you can be part of a team in a business or family, but we're all individuals and we play life that way. Each of us has to make decisions

and live with the consequences of acting on them.

I believe that the initial game, the every-man-for-himself format, was more paradigmatic of life than the team game. But, of course, both of them are nice paradigms. The point is always to succeed at what you're trying to do. And either alone or as part of a team, you have to act.

ADAM: The responsibility is still on each individual in the team game. Especially at the pace that the team game is played today, "teamwork" is really driven by individual actions that are more implicitly than explicitly coordinated.

CHARLES: That's how the initial paradigm plays out in today's game. Of course, in life, you're trying to make something of yourself. You're trying to succeed at making money or becoming happy or famous or all of these things. And accomplishing these things means taking steps. In the survival game, you're trying to succeed at a very limited task. You know, in the case of the team game, you go in and grab the other team's flag. In the case of the individual game, the way we played it, you grab all four flags and get out without being put out of the game. These are great metaphors for staying alive that are impossible to ignore, especially for first time players.

If you're smart about it, you bring to both the game and your life who you really are. You don't try to fake it. In other words, the people who got put out the quickest and the easiest in the game when I played it were people who were trying to be something other than what they were, the one who pretended to have talents and skills that they didn't actually own. Being good at this game means being willing to play within yourself.

ADAM: Like a baseball pitcher in a clutch situation, you shouldn't throw a pitch you can't handle.

CHARLES: Exactly. But then you learn new

pitches and start working them in as you get better at them. I think that may be the deepest and most piercing truth that overlaps playing paintball and playing at real life. All we know after a certain age in life is that the only way to achieve success is to be who we are, to rely on our real strengths, not our perceived or dreamed about strengths. And to play honestly. That was one of the things that we learned very early on about the game.

Now, I don't know if any of these things relate as profoundly anymore to the current game. I just literally don't know. I haven't played it and I don't even know how it's played. I hope it's the case. But the original game, the reason it was so resonant and the reason it was so much fun for us, was that it was so clear from the very beginning that we were doing something that really was alive with these metaphorical implications we're talking about now. You really teach yourself something about who you are, where you are, and something about the condition of life.

ADAM: Awesome. I completely understand what you mean. It's basically the kind of experience you have when you're faced with an extreme challenge and you have to rely on yourself to succeed.

CHARLES: That's it.

ADAM: And you know in that moment that whether or not you succeed is going to require you to keep your cool, keep focused, and simultaneously go for it. I mean it's a higher level of alertness. For me it comes in situations where I've been in sports competitions, or acting on stage, or speaking in public. Anytime I'm pushing myself.

CHARLES: Right. And so much of it has to do with timing, which is another thing that you learn in life. You can make the same choice at two different times and one time you'll be successful and the other time it'll cost you big time.

ADAM: Right. Having spoken with a number of people who are in the game now, I can say, that it has lost this sort of philosophical edge. I wouldn't say the game itself isn't enjoyable as it's being presented now. It's just not what it was for you guys, an experiment, playing with ideas of survival. It's a business now, a diversion, recreation, entertainment. You have any comments on that.

CHARLES: Yeah. That's the way I perceive it to be. And it's one of the reasons for my sort of inattention to the game in its present version. But I bet that the idea of surviving is still a factor, still part of the attraction of the game.

I mean, as far as I'm concerned, we who founded it had it at its very best. After we invented it, we started playing on a regular basis, both the individual game and more and more the team game. We had a field that we rented out, or borrowed. My kids played it, and my wife played it once and [Bob] Gurnsey's kids played it and we had our children out there acting as field judges. We'd make whole weekends out of this thing. And it was just joyous and wonderful. Good, simple fun with friends and family.

We'd have people come up from New York and out from Los Angeles to play the game. They would play it for the first time and immediately "grok" it and see how cool it was. I had my friend P.J. O'Rourke up to play it and he loved it.

It was great because it started as our little secret game. And then we introduced it to the world, which was like telling a very witty joke or some marvelously resonant parable for the first time. People could really see what we were talking about, especially after they played it. They'd say, "Ah, yes. Exactly. I get it. This is so cool!"

But then, we and the game were attacked by people who never played it but assumed that the presence of paintball guns somehow supported violence. Of course, in football and hockey, where they show highlights of people knocking each other's heads off, this criticism is virtually nonexistent. We had to fight this bad reputation that we really didn't deserve. And the business became somewhat difficult for me. The commercialization of the game, which literally turned it into what I perceive to be little more than shooting each other in the woods, cost me my entire interest in it.

ADAM: It turned into a team game when you started to turn it into a business, basically.

CHARLES: Yeah. That's right. But initially, we wanted it to be both a team and an individual game. But the individual game just sort of died out, out of lack of interest.

ADAM: That's mystifying.

CHARLES: Yeah, I thought so. I mean, to me it's a much more interesting version of the game. And would continue to be, I think. Maybe nobody even knows about it anymore. I don't know. But to me it would still be a more interesting version even given the high powered guns and the maga-

zines that hold hundreds of paintballs. Given all of that it seems to me it would be more interesting than the team version.

ADAM: Well, you know, maybe it'll come back.

CHARLES: Maybe it will. That would be great.

Charles Gaines is an extraordinarily prolific and accomplished writer, published in magazines ranging from American Sportsman *and* Forbes F.Y.I. *to* Architectural Digest *and* Men's Journal. *He has also written various books, most recently,* Survival Games (1997). *He was also author of the international bestseller,* Pumping Iron (1974), *and Associate Producer of the film based on the book, starring Arnold Schwarzenegger. He and his wife of 37 years currently live in Nova Scotia.*

PAINTBALL EVOLUTION

ADAM COHEN: Steve, it's great to have a chance to sit down with someone who has been around the sport for as long as you have.

STEVE DAVIDSON: Thank you for having me.

ADAM: Let's jump right into the thick of things.

STEVE: Sure. Where would you like to begin?

ADAM: Everyone has their own take on the initial game. What do you make of it?

STEVE: Yeah, the story's kind of become the game's creation myth. A couple of guys had a debate about survival skills, and agreed on a way of settling it by playing a free-for-all version of capture the flag. The fact that a forester won without ever firing a shot is significant. It's a true story, and it's a simple one that tells you what the game is all about.

ADAM: The fact that being the last one standing isn't just about shooting loads of paint.

STEVE: Yes.

ADAM: Let's discuss how the game became widespread. That's what we're really interested in learning more about from you.

STEVE: Okay. Well, after that first game, these three guys, Hayes Noel, Charles Gaines, and Bob Gurnsey knew that this could become something more than a free-for-all recreational activity. They saw an entrepreneurial opportunity. They went to a couple of different companies and attempted to have a gun made specifically for playing the game. They eventually had "Splatmaster" manufactured and they went to the company that had made the original gun that they'd used, which was the "Nelspot Marker" made by Nelson Paint Company, to get the paint, which was oil-based. This was within months of that first game.

I did play a couple of games when the oil-based paint was still around, and boy are we all glad that was short-lived.

ADAM: Pretty disgusting, I take it?

STEVE: We're talking turpentine parties after every game, or just burning your clothes. But it was

STEVE DAVIDSON'S PAINTBALL BIOGRAPHY

When Steve Davidson began playing paintball in 1983, he fell in love with the game.

1983 Began playing paintball

1984 Formed Muthers of Destruction team

1986 IPPA representative for NJ & Coordinator of Team Registration program

First article printed in APG magazine—*10 Ways to Becoming a Better Team Captain*

1989 Columnist for Paintball Sports International, PaintCheck & Paintball News; Forms Werewolves competition team

1990 Introduces team rankings & seedings; ranking & seeding services for World Cup, Lively Masters, ASO series, Paintcheck 5 Player & other events; Forms World Paintball Federation

1991 Authors, *MAXING: A Guide to Winning in Tournament Play*

1992 Organizes National Professional Paintball League

1996 Secretary, NPPL

1997 Forms GTO tournament series

1999 Introduces United States Paintball League patented game format (visit getfitnow.com for more details!)

fun. I wouldn't change the way it was then, but I'm glad we're using water-soluble food dyes now.

Anyway, they started franchising the game across the country. Jerry Braun in upstate New York was one of the first franchises, as was Deborah Dion out in Pittsburgh.

Around that same time it didn't take more than maybe about nine months there were at least two other franchise corporations on the scene. One was based in Florida called the "Ultimate Game" and the other was Pursuit Marketing Incorporated (PMI), which remains one of the biggest and best

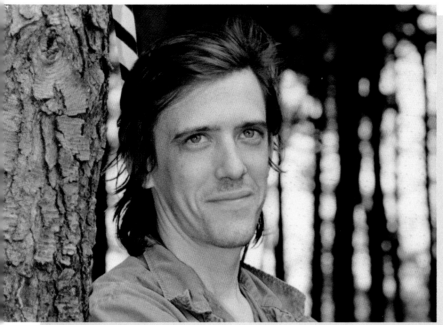

distributors in the industry today.

National Survival Game (NSG) had a turnkey type of an operation: "We will supply you with the paint, with the guns, with the goggles, the rules of play, the insurance, and show you how to set a game up."

You had to buy everything from them. Until some far-thinking individuals said, "I ought to be able to find something similar elsewhere for less." People approached Nelson directly, and they had no hard core exclusivity agreement with NSG. Before you knew it, Skirmish USA, Paul Fogal's company, entered the scene. Fogal had approached NSG, but they couldn't work things out. He basically said, "No way," to their rates and went and started searching for other suppliers. He hooked up with Jeff Perlmutter from PMI.

Ultimate Game didn't last. They got crushed in what I call the Franchise Wars. NSG eventually went away because they remained, I guess the word would be "hidebound." They had a vision of what they thought the game should be and how it should be played and what you should use and how it should be organized. They weren't really interested in adjusting themselves to changes in the industry.

ADAM: Are we still in 1981?

STEVE: We're still in 1981, but we're kind of talking about stuff that happened between then and 1983. Specific dates on these things, I can't give you.

ADAM: NSG goes south within the first three years?

STEVE: They were still around and doing well, but they didn't have an adaptive long-term strategy. All of these independent fields were popping up all over the place. Then, Perlmutter introduced the water-soluble paintball. That opened things up for a large number of people. Abolishing the need for turpentine parties was progress.

NSG also had a tournament series and you could only qualify for this tournament series by finishing first or maybe second-place at a regional tournament that was held at an affiliated NSG field. So, for the first couple of years, the only tournaments were being played by NSG teams or maybe local stuff, but not on a national basis.

In 1986, Fogal had his first major national tournament with Perlmutter, and Jerry Braun had the Air Pistol Open. The word "Open" is what's significant there because any team, whether they were coming from an NSG field or not, could enter this event. That was a major step toward opening up the game across the board.

ADAM: And technologically?

STEVE: Tech-wise, the mid-eighties were explosive. During 1981, 1982, and the first half of 1983, people were playing with paintball guns that were hand-cocked, single-shot, twelve gram deals. Nelson's Nelspot 007, NSG's Splatmaster, and Benjamin Sheridan's PGP were the three that you had available to you. They were all tilt-feed/gravity-feed types of things.

At the end of 1983, people started putting pumps on the Nelspots and PGPs. The plastic Spotmarker from NSG became basically a low-

The guns on the next few pages are identified by manufacturer, type and description, in this order.

cost, field rental piece of equipment and the "Tech Wars" started to pick up steam. Very shortly after the pump was first introduced, and this is still 1983/1984, Constant Air (CA) came out. Some ingenious people figured that there had to be a way to hook a larger canister of air up to their gun. They found a way to do it and, bang, they were immediately banned from tournament play. which slowed things down tremendously for a good couple of years.

ADAM: Were they welcome at Jerry's Opens, or not even those?

STEVE: No, absolutely not. People, including me, fought it viciously. To us, the whole game, the nature of the competition, was about to change radically. If we allowed those guns in tournament play, everything would be different. The simple necessity of having to change those twelve grams after twenty or thirty shots maximum, the necessity of having to carry that stuff, of not being able to stand there for fifteen minutes, made the game a certain, special kind of experience.

ADAM: So you weren't opposed to the CA technology *per se*. You just wanted the competition to be driven by tactics rather than guns.

STEVE: That was the issue. There were people out in California in particular who had gone the Constant Air route. Interest-

ingly enough, the Iron Men, who are one of the top teams now, were originally a CA team. They beat everybody, left right and center in California, but they didn't do any of the tournaments because they didn't want to give up their CA. They were the best team in the country at the time, but they couldn't prove it because they weren't willing to compete on the level that all the competition teams were.

Gravity Feeds came in right after the pump—again, the end of 1983, beginning of 1984—PVC pipe and a forty-five degree elbow. Then, around the middle of 1984 Gramps and Grizzly's started producing guns that came with those features standard.

ADAM: So the technology was driven by recreational play? It seems that way because the tournaments resisted these new tech features, but they were selling well to the rec players who were in the game for the fun of it.

STEVE: Sort of. It's interesting because you'd go to the tournament and you'd sit there and talk about all the nifty things that you could do to your gun, or that you were planning on doing to your gun, or that somebody else was thinking about doing to their gun.

We all recognized that there had to be some kind of a leveler at the tournaments. A bunch of people who were more into military simulation than they were

Carter; Buzzard; Top Level custom made tournament pump gun. Includes Smart Parts barrel. *Courtesy of Ralph Torrell*

Gotcha; Deuce; Double barrel stock gun with two-step trigger. *Courtesy of Ralph Torrell*

Palmer's Pursuit Shop; Nasty Typhoon; Customized double barrel semi with muzzle brake, double finger trigger, cosmetic trigger guard, bottleline with mounting brackets, and iodized blue. *Courtesy of Ralph Torrell*

Airgun Designs; Sydearm; *Courtesy of Ralph Torrell*

Nelson Paintball Company; Nelspot 007; 12 gram pump gun. *Courtesy of Rob Rubin*

Nelspot 007 with grip removed showing 12 gram CO_2 cartridge.

Sheridan; Piranha; Pump gun with 12 gram six pack from AirGun Designs, Inc. *Courtesy of Rob Rubin*

Detail of six pack.

paintball were trying to get things like smoke grenades and hand grenades and walkie-talkies and heavier weaponry introduced into tournament play. In response to this, Fogal was the one who put it the best: "We can count on the fact that every paintball player is going to have a gun, but if we start asking everybody to have to bring forty smoke grenades and radios and all this other kind of stuff, we're just going to price ourselves right out of the market. So we have to make a conscious effort to cut it off somewhere. Where should that cutoff be?"

Things went back and forth for a while. Jerry limited the barrels to ten inches; you couldn't have a barrel more than ten inches long.

ADAM: That doesn't make too much of a difference, does it?

STEVE: No, it doesn't make a difference. But we were trying everything. People were trying to sneak that kind of stuff in all the time.

There was a huge fuss over back check valves, these things that keep the pressure in the gun even when you remove the twelve gram or the bottle from it. It made it so you could remove your gas source and still have five or six or seven shots left in the gun. That was a big deal because we trained ourselves to listen for low air levels. You'd think to yourself: "He's about to change twelve grams, so we're going to rush him and take

him out." Well, if I'm that guy running low and I've got a back check valve, baby am I ever waiting for you to come at me. I'm going to make the biggest, most obvious twelve gram change that I possibly can. Some cocky guy's going to charge me, hopefully with all of his friends, and I'm going to take'm out. "Boink, boink, boink! See you all later. Thank you for listening!"

ADAM: Back checks sound very cool. Did they survive?

STEVE: No, those were banned. That little extra ability seemed to us like tinkering with the game, and we wanted to keep things very balanced and clear in terms of the mental and physical requirements.

ADAM: So the back check valve came along in 1984. 1984 seems like a big year for the game.

STEVE: It was a huge year for paintball technology. Absolutely. A lot of stuff was introduced in 1984. The back check valve came along with the CA.

Another big thing was a barrel extender. You take a piece of aluminum, stick it on the end of your barrel, and you have a longer barrel. Now, what that did for anybody? To this day, we still don't know. But somebody brought out the first barrel extender and they sold like hot cakes. So somebody else said, "Well, I'm going to come out with a field strip screw set for the gun," and people were begin-

Werewolves, 1989. Steve Davidson sits third from left, front row.
Courtesy of Steve Davidson

ning to realize that they could make serious money selling paintball equipment.

ADAM: Cleaning kits and harnesses emerge circa 1984?

STEVE: Everything, all kinds of stuff.

ADAM: Flak jackets and shin guards?

STEVE: You name it and it probably had its origins back somewhere between 1984 and 1985, right around in that period of time.

ADAM: Was there anyone keeping track of how many people were playing?

STEVE: No, it was really a very garage-type business. Somebody would order twenty guns from NSG and post business cards to resell the stuff at the local restaurant. Stuff like that.

Fogal was actually marketing himself. He went on to teach a lot of people how to play, how to do that. Jerry [Braun] also, and Deborah [Dion], too. Sat Cong Village out in California, Three Rivers Survival Game out in Pittsburgh, NSG, Skirmish USA, National Survival Game-New York, and then a little bit later on, Challenge Park in the Chicago area. Around Chicago you come upon the really big fields that pioneered how to market the game to people, how to set up the game for people, how to get folks to come in, what to

charge, how to organize, how to train referees—all those kinds of things. Those five fields are really the major contributors to all that kind of stuff.

ADAM: And virtually all of these fields were playing the basic Total Elimination and Capture the Flag types of games.

STEVE: Yes, exclusively. The first scenario game was, I think, 1985.

ADAM: Actually the first game sounds like a scenario game.

STEVE: I guess you could probably put it like that.

ADAM: But it soon thereafter became a team-based game.

STEVE: That that was probably the way NSG decided to package it. Somebody somewhere recognized that twelve individuals running around in the woods was not economically viable. So they probably figured, "We'll play 'Capture the Flag'." I'm sure that those were the words used by somebody somewhere.

ADAM: And the other major game would have been just total elimination.

STEVE: The total elimination games were pretty funny. You have to understand, the games were initially two hours long, on hundreds of acres in the woods. I played a couple of games where neither team saw anybody from the other team, and it lasted the full hour and a half. Of course, it was fun. You were crawling around in the dirt and leaves. You were scanning for opponents. But after a couple of games where you literally couldn't find the people you were supposed to be shooting at, it just seemed silly. And the field-owners were losing money, because they weren't selling paint.

Then again, the objectives were totally different then. Your goal was to get somebody to surrender to you, to psyche out the other team. Today, it's more about actually getting in their

Line SI; Bushmaster; Sliding stock. *Courtesy of Rob Rubin*

Line SI with stock extended.

Worr Games Products; '95 Autococker; ACI expansion chamber, hardline bottom line, copperhead sight, Lapco barrel. *Courtesy of Rob Rubin*

Pro-Team Products; Retro-Valve Micromag with double trigger in Red Nights, with Millenium Series nitrogen system (gas-through foregrip). *Courtesy of Steve Davidson*

face and pumping them full of paintballs. The technology supported that kind of play because you could only get so many rounds out of the gun in a minute.

I loved it. If you could convince somebody that you could shoot, or if you could get somebody to fire and blow their wad before you had fired, then you could get them to surrender. There was a lot of sneaking around, a lot of finding the perfect ambush site. It was beautiful when they couldn't see you, had no idea you were going to be there, and you just know that plenty of them are going to come walking past that one particular spot. Knowing was as much fun as springing the trap.

ADAM: But then, somewhere along the line, they started to make the fields smaller.

STEVE: It started when some genius, somewhere, recognized that the more paint they got their customers to shoot, the more money they would make.

ADAM: The field owners made this happen?

STEVE: I would assume so. It kind of went hand in hand. The field-owners want to sell paint. That's their job, to sell paint. The players like to pull the trigger. And boy, do they. If you go to any field and you take a look at how much money they're spending at the target range just goofing off. It's incredible. But they're having a great time, and that's the bottom line.

ADAM: As the game has become more about splattering opponents with paint, are people spending more on paint now than they used to?

STEVE: Interestingly enough, the average usage per player has not changed significantly, in terms of the amount of money they're spending on their paint. For instance, back in 1983, 1984, 1985, if you were spending twenty cents a ball and carrying a hundred rounds onto the field, you were spending X for a day's worth of play. Now, the price has come way down, so you're carrying a case, case and a half out onto the field, literally thousands of balls. You're still spending the same amount of money, but you're shooting more paint.

ADAM: The player's perception is that they're getting more bang for their buck.

STEVE: Right. On top of that, some unsung hero recognized that when the games lasted more than fifteen minutes, customers end up sitting around while two or three people are running around in the woods trying to find each other. So fields started to get smaller. Smaller fields require fewer referees. Faster games, field owners gave people the feeling that they had played more frequently. I don't think anybody could tell you exactly who brought that concept into being.

ADAM: Sounds like a smart business move.

STEVE: Yeah. I don't think a lot of people realize that the concept of smaller tournament fields came from England. They were the ones that introduced the postage stamp size and everybody said, "Ding, ding, ding, it's a lot easier for four referees to cover two hundred feet by a hundred feet, than it is forty acres in the woods.

ADAM: Let's talk about the tournaments.

STEVE: The first tournament was in 1983—an NSG National Survival Game Championship. I believe it was the Taxidrivers from Hell, a Canadian team, that won. I think NSG held a national tournament through 1990. NSG's structure of only allowing teams that came from the regional championships was cutting down on their attendance because there were fewer and fewer NSG fields. Fields realized they could thrive by going independent.

ADAM: So suddenly you have all these independent groups. How do they get together? How do they form a tournament? Spontaneously?

STEVE: Yes, pretty much. Jerry decided that he wanted

to do his Air Pistol Open and Fogal got together the same year with PMI and started the North American Championship. That lasted five years and then faded.

Lively came along in 1989 and showed everybody how to do a trade show. He's definitely great at that. There's always been this disparity. The people who put on these major events know how to do one thing really well—put on a great trade show and lots of parties, or run the game on the field so that it's fair and quick. But they've never put the two together. That's the nut that still has to be cracked.

So NSG faded out. Jerry had his two Air Pistol Opens. But that was it for him for a couple of years.

ADAM: And up to this point, it's virtually all been outdoors?

STEVE: All outdoors.

ADAM: Let's back up from tournament play for a second. When did recreational indoors paintball start?

Sheridan; KP2; Stock gun with horizontal side mounted ammo tube. *Courtesy of Ralph Torrell*

Palmer's Pursuit Shop; Hurricane (serial #47); Originally a pellet gun, converted in 1992 to a constant air semiautomatic. *Courtesy of Ralph Torrell*

Palmer's Pursuit Shop; Squall (3rd one ever made); Semiautomatic spring feed, quicksilver, insta-pierce. *Courtesy of Ralph Torrell*

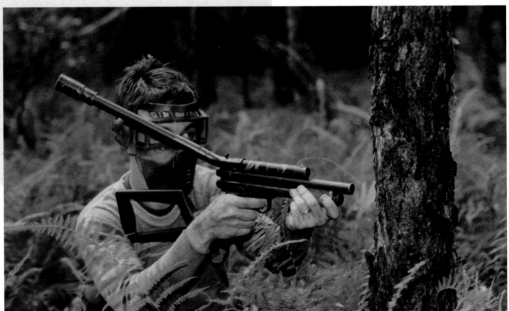

Member of the team, Lords of Discipline, at the 15-Man North American Championships at Skirmish, USA. That series ran from 1985–1990. *Courtesy of Cleo Fogal*

Crossman 3357 Spotmarker; 50 caliber paintball gun. *Courtesy of Ralph Torrell*

Crossman 3357 open to show removable cylinder.

Pro-Team Products; Car 68; Police and military training semi-automatic. Can also come with 35 mm grenade launcher attachment. *Courtesy of Pro-Team Products*

Car 68 with stock extended.

STEVE: The first person to open an indoor field was Caleb Strong up in Buffalo, New York. That was in November, 1984. That was pretty cool. I went up there with Paul Fogal to check it out, because he was thinking of opening up an indoor location in Philadelphia. They had this maze built, it was totally alien. Like no paintball we had ever seen before. Going through a door became an entirely new experience for me, let me tell you, because you had no idea what was happening on the other side. They played freaky music. There were places covered with black plastic so it was pitch black. You could not see anything in those areas. You were thinking somebody was in there. And if there was, they'd be able to see you well before you could see them. So I almost died a couple of times just because I was preoccupied with the dark sections. Then Paul and I would approach a door and we'd talk about who was going to go through it first. "Well, you're smaller, Steve." "Okay, Paul." [*Laughs*] That was just great fun.

ADAM: Let's get back to the tournaments.

STEVE: Okay. So Lively became the big thing on the tournament scene in 1989. We had Jerry with the Air Pistol Open, we had North American Championships and NSG still kind of all running simultaneously.

ADAM: Throughout the mid- to late-eighties.

STEVE: 1987, 1988, yes. Lively introduced his event in 1989. He got everybody in the industry to support it and that became the big thing. North American Championships went away quickly. Jerry was still there for another year or so and then he introduced the World Cup, which was supposed to be the first tournament that was going to have a hundred thousand dollar prize. Didn't quite make it, I think he gave away about eighty-two thousand dollars, which was still significant at the time. Nobody could compete with what Lively was able to do.

Eventually, Lively held five events a year, across the country in Tennessee, Texas, Chicago and San Francisco.

ADAM: No professional teams yet, right?

STEVE: Right. Everybody who played in tournaments was a professional team, literally. There were maybe five hundred people across the country who you could call professional tournament players, and everybody knew who everybody else was. We saw the same faces at every single tournament. The same rivalries were carried from one event to the next.

ADAM: Was there any emphasis on drawing people in to watch these things happen?

STEVE: No, none whatsoever. It was a very closed, tight-knit, insular community. We knew what we were doing and everybody else sucked. No offense, but you know how it goes. We were into our own cool thing.

I was big into science fiction before I got into paintball and I was putting on science fiction conventions and stuff like that. Paintball was built on the same kind of insulated special kind of a community. We were more than happy to see each other in the city and then next month in another city.

ADAM: So nobody was in a rush to promote this game to the masses?

STEVE: The field owners were into getting new people to come out and play, but the person who made the transition from a recreational player to a regular member of a team had to be tough-skinned and talented. You had to be very motivated and to get noticed and invited onto a team.

On the other hand, these teams throughout the '80s and early '90s were fifteen player teams. Organizing fifteen solid players who had the time to practice, the time to travel, and the money to afford everything... it wasn't easy. We wanted players who could think on the run, and there were so few. Every fifteen man team from those days could have used another two

or three or four players, but they just couldn't find bodies. It's amazing to me, looking back now, that I played with such a tremendous team.

ADAM: Today's tournaments mostly have 10-man and 5-man teams. What happened to the 15-man team?

STEVE: It's definitely history. A combination of factors just made it untenable. First of all, it wasn't easy to get 15 man teams together, so there really weren't that many of them. And as fewer of them were able to make the tournaments, the promoters started to raise their prices. The total effect of this was lower attendance at the tournaments. Around 1992, Jim Lively had the idea that making the teams smaller and reducing the entry fees slightly would get far more people to attend. Boy was he right. The team size requirement was reduced from 15 to 10. So if it cost $100 for a 15 member team, they dropped the price to $70 for a 10 player team. Attendance blasted off, so the promoters were making good money off of this move. But the game play suffered. It was far easier for teams to get into tournaments, but the level of competition really started to drop. Then the promoters wanted to move to 5 player teams. Well, it doesn't take much to realize where this was headed-the pro-

Tippmann Pneumatics; SMG 60; Bulldog version, first full automatic, requires 62 caliber paintballs, first paintball gun banned. *Courtesy of Cousins Paintball*

Components Concepts Inc. (CCI); Phantom; Stock class with 45 grip frame and vertical 12 gram adapter. *Courtesy of Cousins Paintball*

Kingman; Spyder S.E.; Double trigger with expansion chamber, locking external velocity adjuster, and 45 grip. *Courtesy of Cousins Paintball*

moters were getting richer and the players were getting worse.

NPPL was formed at the end of 1992. It was made up of 24 team captains. I was the coordinator for the first year, and I pretty much gave up playing so that everyone would view me as neutral. From the start, one of our central concerns was that diminishing team size requirements were diluting skills. Just about everybody could put a team together, and just about everybody did.

NPPL wanted to preserve the highest possible level of competition, to set competitive standards that average paintball enthusiasts couldn't meet unless they put significant time and energy into training as a team. We were really pushing for the division that eventually arose at tournaments between professional and amateur game play. The NPPL tournaments in 1993 made this distinction for the first time. People registered themselves as pro or amateur according to their own sense of their level of play. What was really

ingenious about this first year was that all of the teams competed against one another in the first round. The idea was that amateurs should experience the difference so that they could see what it takes to take their play to the next level. It was humbling for a lot of teams that thought they were good because they'd played several weekends together and done well against lame competition. For other teams it was eye-opening, because they were quite good, held their own, and saw possibilities for their team play that hadn't occurred to them. Based on their records in preliminary rounds, the top 8 pro teams went forward into exclusively professional play to determine the professional champions, and the top 8 amateur teams moved on to compete among themselves for the amateur title.

If an amateur team placed ahead of a pro team in the preliminary round, they had the choice of going pro, literally in the midst of the event! In fact, in that first year, Dallas 1993, a team did this and ended up taking 4th place!

In 1993 and 1994, there was a balance in the number of amateur and pro players. In 1995, however, there were almost 3 times as many amateur teams. Depending on their draw, some amateur teams had to play against pro teams whereas other amateur teams didn't. So this had awful consequences, and it still does today, because

ADAM: You sound like you want to get back into the fray. Any chance that we'll see you in any tournaments.

STEVE: Truth be told, there's simply nothing like playing with people whose minds you can practically read.

Given the chance to play at that level again, and I mean with a truly fantastic team that could compete for a title, [*grins*] I would have to go for it.

you get good amateur teams taken out of the running and ill feelings. They simply haven't reset the rules to reflect the reality that there are so many amateur teams.

Anyway, all of the tournaments pretty much adopted this pro/amateur distinction by the mid-1990s, or simply banned pro teams from certain tournaments.

ADAM: How do you feel about 15-man versus 5-man teams?

STEVE: 15 man teams are harder to put together, but you can do more with them. More is possible in terms of tactics. People don't account for the substantial role chance and dumb luck play in a 5-on-5 game. I mean really, you lose 1 guy and you've lost 20% of your force! On 15 player teams, you can adapt after losing 8 guys and go on to win the game. There's very little opportunity for true team play in today's 5-on-5 game. It was more rewarding and more competitive with 15-man teams. More about skills and training than it's become. That, at least, is my perspective on it.

The British had 12-on-12 for a while, but that became 10-on-10. It's strictly 10- and 5- man teams now.

Flag in hand, Steve Davidson sprints to victory.
Courtesy of Steve Davidson

The Paintball Necessities of Life

• Goggles • Guns • Hoppers • Compressed Air • Paintballs

GOGGLES

It's all fun and games until someone loses an eye

Without a doubt, protective eyewear is the most essential piece of paintball equipment you will ever purchase. A paintball travelling at 300 feet per second fired from 20 feet away can easily obliterate an eyeball, so safety must be your primary concern. As Rob Rubin is fond of saying to beginners before he takes them out for a game, "Your goggles must remain on at all times when you're on the field. If I see you even start to lift them, I'm going to tackle you, which may be unpleasant, but is infinitely better than losing an eye. Do yourselves a favor and follow this rule." Whether you are playing at a field or in your backyard, be sure to wear a paintball certified goggle system. Reliable goggle systems can be purchased for $30–$40, but the better ones cost $80–$90.

Most come with face armor and ear protection, which is required at every reputable field. The lens must be American Society for Testing and Materials (ASTM) tested, and approved for paintball. Other goggles are not acceptable, because they simply can't withstand the impact of a paintball.

Superior goggles come with features that maximize your field of vision, minimize glare, are well ventilated to prevent fogging, and have lenses that are easily and quickly replaced. They also use materials that increase the likelihood

There are many different kinds of goggles, and some are bound to fit you better than others, both physically and monetarily. We recommend trying on different kinds before making a purchasing decision.

Is that a gun in your pocket or...

Firepower

The second most important piece of equipment is your paintball gun, sometimes referred to as a marker because it literally marks other players. For the purposes of this book, guns are used only to shoot paintballs (and wouldn't it be a better world if that were the case). As you'll see, guns come in all shapes and sizes, but employ very similar firing mechanisms.

Main Body

The main body or frame of the gun is the handle, trigger, and the chamber, which contains the cocking mechanism and the bolt.

Some guns give you the option of attaching your own barrels and different sized hoppers and compressed air. The chamber or breech is where the ball awaits the rush of air that fires it when you pull the trigger. Near the chamber is something called a *ball detent*. This mechanism holds the paintball in place so it doesn't roll out. It also stops more than one ball from feeding into the chamber. The paint-

ball is fired out of the chamber and through the barrel. The barrel is a long tube that guides the paintball in a straight path as it leaves the gun. There are many styles available and they screw into the main body. Many say that brass barrels are the best because they have the least friction on the paintball (they are the cheapest). Others swear by heavier stainless steel barrels. Some only play with aluminum. A lot of designs have holes (called porting)drilled into them in different patterns.

Keep the ammo coming!

Hopper or Loader

Basically a hopper is a plastic inverted bottle that holds your paintballs and allows them to feed into the chamber. Most hoppers rely on a gravity feed approach. Some however, are motorized and ensure that another paintball will fall into place after one is shot. If rapid firing is key to your game, make sure you have one of these.

Hoppers come in all sorts of sizes, some hold only 40 balls, while others can hold up to 300. The range of sizes is as follows (60, 80, 100, 130, 150, 200, 230, 300). Of course, by the time you read this, larger sizes may be available. Smaller hoppers are lighter, but carry fewer balls, creating that possibility of being caught short at the worst possible moment. The larger the hopper, the more balls you can fire before having to reload. Of course, this also makes the gun itself heavier. Most experienced players gravitate toward the large hoppers.

Bringing on the air!

Air Power

The air tank is crucial. On most guns, it attaches horizontally off the back of the gun, and literally screws on. Some players prefer a vertical mount to keep liquid CO_2, which is an inevitable and potentially very annoying byproduct of firing, on the bottom of the tank away from the gun. The most common propellant used in paintball is CO_2. Almost all fields supply a tank with their rental guns. Other propellants include nitrogen and high pressure air (HPA). HPA is just regular air. The great thing about it is that it won't freeze or turn to liquid in the cold like CO_2 and nitrogen. HPA containers have very high pressures (as high as 4500 psi).

Most of the tanks are currently made of aluminum, which is preferred to steel because it is lighter. More expensive air tanks enable you to check the status of your air reserves. Some of the more elaborate models can even be worn on your back. This changes your experience of the game entirely; the gun no longer has weight, and you're not going to run out of air as quickly, but you're running around with air tanks strapped to your back, which some players find annoying.

STEVE DAVIDSON   BEING CAUGHT SHORT

"When I started playing in the early 1980s, fields were charging twenty to thirty cents a ball and fifty cents a twelve gram. You were considered a nut if you carried more than about fifty rounds onto the field. Well, I was a nut. I carried a hundred rounds. You see, I got caught short one time. But never again. I'm never going to be stuck out there without ammunition again."

Paintballs

By now it's probably clear that a big part of this game is about splattering paintballs on your opponents. Paintballs come in a variety of sizes: .50, .62 (which is often called, .60), .63, .68, and .72 caliber. .68 caliber paintballs are spherical and dominate the market. The paint substance is composed of washable, nonflammable, food grade dye. In the early days it was oil based, and players held *de facto* turpentine parties at the end of the day. Not so anymore. Today, regular laundry detergents will do the trick!

Accessories

In most cases, you play a couple of 15 minute paintball games using 1 air tank and topping off your hopper in between sessions. But there will come a time when you'll be playing a significantly longer game, and will need to replenish your supplies on the field. Or, a ball may break in your gun, and you'll need to clean it with a squeegee on the fly. In those moments, you'll be glad you brought the following accessories.

Harness—Usually something worn around the waist that holds extra supplies—extra air, extra paint, maybe even smoke bombs. Typically they are called 4-1 or 8-1 or 6-1. The "1" is usually a vertical receptacle for an air tank. The other numbers signifies spaces for horizontal guppies (tubes for holding paintballs).

Squeegee—An instrument you'll find enormous useful if a paintball explodes in your barrel. This is also useful for the maintenance and upkeep of your gun.

Enter a game with these add-ons and you'll never be caught short

Remote—An air supply separate from your gun carried on your harness. This tank is connected to your gun by a long, flexible hose. This is useful because it takes weight off your gun and makes it lighter and more maneuverable. It is a cheap addition. A good used one runs about $30–$40.

Now let's take a look at the game of paintball, from the perspective of a new player.

—AWC

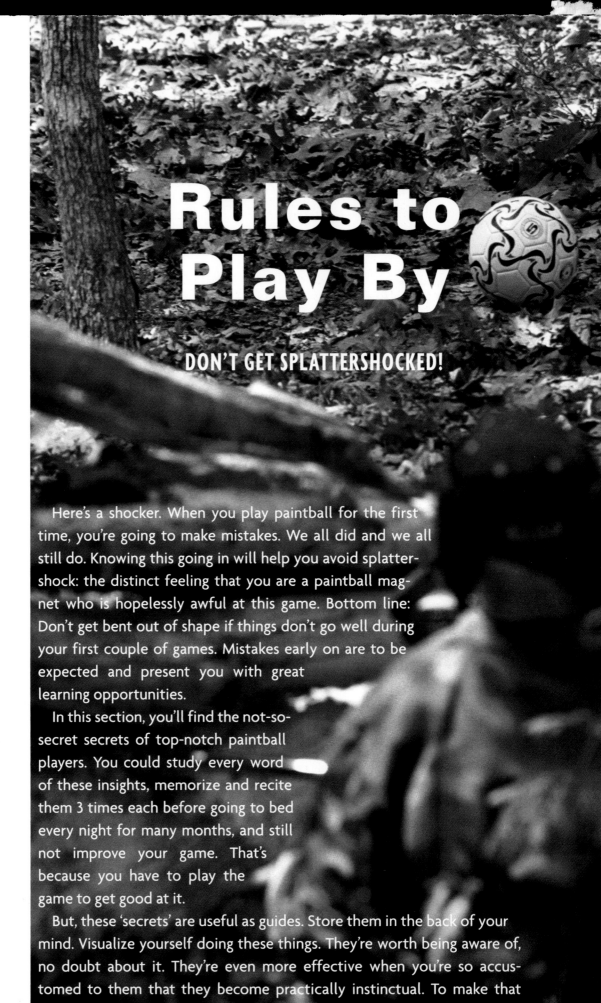

You're

not

a

paint

magnet,

you're

a

newbie!

Rules to Play By

DON'T GET SPLATTERSHOCKED!

Here's a shocker. When you play paintball for the first time, you're going to make mistakes. We all did and we all still do. Knowing this going in will help you avoid splatter-shock: the distinct feeling that you are a paintball magnet who is hopelessly awful at this game. Bottom line: Don't get bent out of shape if things don't go well during your first couple of games. Mistakes early on are to be expected and present you with great learning opportunities.

In this section, you'll find the not-so-secret secrets of top-notch paintball players. You could study every word of these insights, memorize and recite them 3 times each before going to bed every night for many months, and still not improve your game. That's because you have to play the game to get good at it.

But, these 'secrets' are useful as guides. Store them in the back of your mind. Visualize yourself doing these things. They're worth being aware of, no doubt about it. They're even more effective when you're so accustomed to them that they become practically instinctual. To make that happen, there's absolutely no substitute for playing experience.

The key to becoming a player whose name strikes fear in the hearts of your opponents and commands respect among the elite is quite simple. Play the game. And then play it again. And then play it some more. Play with and against people who are better than you are. Stand back from the game and see it as a whole. Experiment with being aggressive and defensive, with taking different positions. Be creative. Above all, play the game for the fun of it. That is, after all, the main point, and, it just so happens that having fun will make you demand more of yourself every time.

You have to spill much paint before the wisdom in the following tidbits will become second nature.

Being a great paintball player is a path, not a destination. Enjoy every second of your journey!

- **The very first rule is never EVER take off your goggles!** This can't be stressed enough. Taking off your mask can be very detrimental to your vision's health. A paintball travelling at 10 feet per second would easily pop your eye out of your head. **Don't ever take your facial protection off.** Even in designated areas, look around yourself to make sure there isn't some doofus waving an uncorked gun.

- Make sure you understand your gun and its limitations, whether it's a rental or your own.

- As soon as you get off the field of play, put a barrel plug in the end of your barrel and switch on the safety. This is essential paintball etiquette and is only meant to save you from experiencing or causing excruciating pain or injury to others. If you see somebody waving a gun around that doesn't have a plug in it, remind them to put one in immediately.

- **Paintballs do not hurt when they hit.** Well, sometimes they hurt a little bit, but usually they just sting for a moment. You won't really feel sore until the day. I have found that paintballs that hit you and don't break hurt a little more because they hit and bounce off. The time they are in contact with you is shorter and thus the force is greater (for all you wannabe nerds out there, the impulse equation from physics justifies this statement). When it does break, it is in contact with you longer and is cushioned by your skin, fat, etc.

- **Wear dark clothes; don't wear white.** White is just too bright, you will be too easy to spot and eliminate.

- **Wear some type of boots or comfortable hiking/running shoes.** Some people prefer football or soccer cleats. They are comfortable, light, quick, and provide excellent traction in grass and mud. A lot of paintball players are using cleats these days.

- **Always be honest.** If you get hit and see the splat on you, please raise your hand and exit the game. Redeem yourself in the next game; there's always a next game. People who try to wipe their paint off and think they can get away with it are simply lame. Ask yourself if being perceived as a loser is worth staying in the game. When everybody knows you're a cheater, you'll find it increasingly hard to find anyone who wants to play with you. ***If you cheat, you'll never truly win!***

- **Don't ever call an advanced paintball player a cheater.** They hate that and take their games really seriously. No matter what happens, don't do this. That is how seriously some people take their game. They are mostly very honest, down to earth people. But, sometimes they'll respond less than graciously. And you know what? It just isn't worth it. If an advanced player (or any player!) cheats on a regular basis, talk discreetly about it to the referee and your friends between games.

- **Don't be afraid to ask or learn.** Even with the amount of information technology available these days, broadband connections to the web sites like splatterzone.com or warpig.com are no substitute for asking questions on the field between games. There are certain basic things that more experienced players can clarify for the beginner (e.g., tactical stuff, tidbits of advice) that may make a difference in your play.

- **Always appoint a team captain and follow his orders no matter what.** The team captain does not have to be the most experienced or the wildest or the most intelligent person in your group. But there has to be one captain. Follow orders even if you think you have a better plan. Don't be a gloryhound. When a team commits to a plan, it's able to do things that individuals acting alone can't do. Obey your captain even if it does not conform to your method of play. If you think you have a great plan, ask to be captain for a game. You have nothing to lose.

- **Be alert and never focus too much on one thing.** Don't keep shooting at the same guy behind the same bunker over and over again. Move on and surprise him from the side or another angle.

- **Don't stay in the same spot too long.** If you are in a fort, don't keep shooting from the same side forever. It's not productive. Go to the other end; go to the second level. Move away from the bunker, walk out unprotected and hold people down. *Don't stay put!*

- **Never give up.** Whether you run out of air, paint or energy, just don't ever stop or quit. You are still useful. No one has to know that you are on your last leg.

- **Never call yourself dead if you are unsure.** If you question whether a shot hit you and splatted, call a paintcheck and the referee will find out if you've been eliminated. Don't just call yourself out because you felt a hit. Wait for the referee to confirm.

—AWC

That's just for starters!

Mistakes New Players Make

WHERE THE HECK AM I?

Beginners are so pumped up with adrenaline that they aren't able to focus on the game as a whole. They tend to lose track of their position in relation to their teammates and foes. Because they feel like they're all alone in the game, they tend to be overly concerned with protecting themselves. Rather than engaging their opponents aggressively, they crouch behind the thickest bush or in the deepest hole available. Effectively, they take themselves out of the action: they can't see anything, are unable to provide information or cover fire, and are basically squatting on the spot where they'll be eliminated. They may tell themselves that they're in a great ambush position. The problem is that most beginners who think this way end up getting themselves ambushed. Take a few deep breaths and look from side to side every once in a while. Stretching your neck out before playing is a helpful way of reminding yourself to look from side to side.

CHARGE!

Some beginners are so pumped up that they run headlong into the fray only to find themselves pinned down by copious hostile paint without support or a good escape option. Their initial eliminations can be fantastic to watch as they squirm under a barrage of paint, but they probably don't feel so great. So listen up! It's always a good idea to choose your first shelter before the game starts. A good shelter is one that will provide you with reasonable cover, while allowing you good opportunities to see the field, shoot, and advance. You must be within range of your opponents, but not so close that you can't use trees or barricades for cover. If the shelter you're behind is so small that you can't stick your head out, make sure you'll have a teammate behind you and call for him to keep your opponents busy while you reach a better position.

ARE YOU MY MOTHER?

It's going to sound simplistic, but you should really take a moment to meet the people on your team. You don't have to swear blood oaths, but it's definitely in your interests to talk to them a little and briefly study their appearance. The last thing you want to do is shoot your own teammates, and they'll be more likely to respond to your pleas for help if you call them by name.

HEY, THAT HURT...WHOA, THAT ONE REALLY...OUCH!!!

To watch the way they go out, you'd think newbies are masochists. When hit, they'll wait for the incoming paint to stop pouring before they stand up and walk away. This means they'll get out wearing two or three layers of bright colors. The best policy is to get out of the way of incoming paint and stand up right away. Remember, if you surrender and your opponents keep pumping you full of paint, referees will take *them* out of the game! So if you're shot, and know it, get up and out of the way quickly.

EYES WIDE SHUT!

Usually, if you see your opponent before he spots you, you've won. Of course, although this fact is probably self-evident to most beginners, they tend to be averse to sticking their heads out for a look-see at the action. So they never look around. Then, the newbies who do use their eyes tend to get tunnel vision, focusing so intensely on one single direction that they they close their ears to all noises, especially those coming from their sides. Don't be afraid to look around. You need as much information as you can get. Of course, your head will be a target, so look by the side of your barricade rather than above the top of it. If you decide to look above the top, don't do it for more than one or two seconds. It'll take that long for your opponents to spot you, take aim, shoot, and hit you.

FOR OUR MAIN COURSE, WE'LL BE SERVING A SITTING DUCK...

Newbies don't move enough. If you're not useful where you are, don't stay there.

The game is about moving, sighting, and shooting. It is dynamic. There may be situations in which you will be playing defense or setting up an ambush, and staying put is appropriate for a set amount of time. But for the most part, responding to the game as it evolves requires you to stay in motion. If the rest of your team breaks through the enemy's defenses, it means they would have done better with you among them; additionally, there

are no opponents left to protect your station against. If the rest of your team is beaten, they may have done better with you among them, and when your opponents arrive at your base, boy will you feel alone! Another example: Look at a newbie under fire. He's trying to make himself as flat as possible. As flat and useless as a flat tire. When you're in a position where you are easily pinned down, with no close help at hand, there are only three things you should think of doing:

1. Get away as fast as possible
2. Shoot back
3. Yell for help and indicate your opponent's location. If they're shooting at you, it means they've spotted you, so don't be afraid to give your position away.

Finally, when you are spotted (when you shoot at someone, you almost always are), be prepared to move to a new location so your opponent won't know where you are or from where your next shot will come.

HELP ME ... HELP YOU

Beginners very seldom communicate well. A beginner keeps his problems to himself (he doesn't ask for help when needed) and doesn't brag about his knowledge (he doesn't tell you about the opponents he's spotted).

The only good reason to be quiet is to remain stealthy. Once you're spotted, there's no reason not to yell, scream, and shout if you have something useful to say. You'll get the help you need, and give your teammates the information they need to kick in.

I LOVE THE SMELL OF PAINTBALLS IN THE MORNING...

Usually, beginners are very accurate and seldom miss a player who's 10 feet away, especially if he is on the same team. They imagine that their gun has the power to nail targets over a hundred yards away. They also shoot too soon, and at everything that moves. Of course, all this does is give away their position and waste paint. If you haven't been spotted, your first shot must take your target out. Wait until the flight path is clear, or until the opponent sees you. Be patient, especially when you're on defense. The price of paint being what it is, they think that a ball that doesn't end on an opponent's camouflage is lost, so they never provide cover or intimidating fire. Sometimes, you have to shoot at opponents you can't see.

- **To help a teammate out of a dire situation!**
- **To make an opponent nervous behind his tree!**
- **To keep his head down while one of your teammates is closing in on him.**
- **To make noise to distract opponents' attention.**

—AWC

Durty Games

THERE'S MORE THAN ONE WAY TO...

Hi there. Durty Dan here. These games were designed with established fields in mind. That is, the area is all set up, marked out, has flag stations and the like. When writing the rules, I tried not to insult your intelligence by mentioning painfully obvious facts. I figured I didn't have to tell you that the games start and end with a whistle or horn. You will also notice that a lot of rules from the basic Capture the Flag game are repeated in each game, I've done this so you don't have to keep referring back to the original game. Each game stands on its own.

Field owners will find these games an interesting addition to the games they may already run on their field. You may need to adapt the rules to your own particular needs, but remember that safety is always your number one concern.

I purposely did not include games like speedball. (These games and other games requiring structures will already exist where the structures exist on the field.) Not every field will have a speedball course, a village or a fort. The reason for not including these types of games is an attempt on my part to make these games universal. With a little preparation you should be able to play these games on any field in the world.

Speaking of fields, do not confuse "established" fields, with "commercial" fields. Established fields have a playing area already set up to play at least Capture the Flag. Whether it's a "legitimate/commercial" field or a "bootleg/outlaw" field is beside the point.

I have been to some "legitimate/commercial" fields where I was afraid to take off my goggles at any time, unless I was in my car with the windows rolled up. I have also heard of a "bootleg/outlaw" field who sent a guy home for having a hot gun!

Unless otherwise stated, these five rules apply to all the games in this chapter. These are referred to as...

GENERAL RULES

1. All players must begin the game at their flag station (or assigned starting point) and cannot leave that area until the game begins.

2. Players who are hit are out of the game.

3. Players who are eliminated may not, by word or gesture, indicate any intentions or locations of the opposing team members.

4. If a player is eliminated while he is carrying the flag, he must drop the flag where he was hit, or hang it on the nearest available object (not another player).

5. When a player is carrying the flag, it must remain visible at all times and be carried in the hand, over the arm, or around the neck.

—DD

Known as the "World's Most Famous Recreational Player," Durty Dan started his writing career in 1992 when Randy Kamiya (then Editor for *Action Pursuit Games Magazine*) published his first article in the February issue. Since then he has written for *Action Pursuit Games*, *Paintball Sports International* (in his column Rec-Ball), *Paintball Industry Magazine* (no longer in publication), *Paintball News*, *Paintball RAGazine* (no longer in publication), and *Paintball Magazine*.
He has been playing since 1984 and has just recently celebrated his 15th anniversary of playing paintball. Since 1992, he has had an amazing two hundred and fifty articles published, and is in the process of writing a paintball book.

CAPTURE THE FLAG

Requirements

Two flag stations

Two even teams

Two flags, hung in opponents' flag stations.

Duration

30 minutes

Rules

All players must begin the game at their flag station (or assigned starting point) and cannot leave that area until the game begins.

Players who are hit are out of the game.

If a player is eliminated while he is carrying the flag, he must drop the flag where he was hit, or hang it on the nearest available object. (Never another player).

Players who are eliminated may not indicate any intentions or locations of the opposing team members.

When a player is carrying the flag, it must remain visible at all times and must be carried in the hand, over the arm, or around the neck.

Objective

Capture the opposing team's flag and return it to your base!

CHARGE OF THE LIGHT BRIGADE

Requirements
Two flag stations.
Two even teams.
Two flags hung in opponents' stations.

Duration
20 minutes.

Rules
All General Rules apply.

Objective
Hang your flag in the opposition's flag station.

SHOOT THE CAPTAIN

Requirements
Two flag stations.

Two even teams.

The teams are brought to their respective flag stations.

The Captain is tied to one end of a 20 foot rope, the other end of which is tied to an immobile object like a tree or fence post.

To spice up the action, tether the Captain's gun rather than him.

Another variation is to limit all offensive players to 20 paintballs and give the Captains unlimited amounts of paint.

Duration
30 minutes

Rules
The Captain cannot undo his tether.

If playing the tethered paintgun variation, the Captain can abandon his paintgun, but cannot use another paintgun.

If you use the limited paint option, players cannot share paintballs.

General Rules 1,2, and 3 apply.

Objective
Eliminate the opposing team's captain.

DUEL

Requirements
Two players are the duelists with the same type of pistol.
A third person to play the Warder.
A clear area.

Duration
As long as it takes, usually no more than 12 seconds.

Rules
Two players stand back to back.
The Warder is standing about ten feet to the side.
Both players are armed with pistols. The pistols each have one paintball in them ready to fire.
The paintguns can have no other paintballs in them. This is a one shot deal.
The warder then says, "This, Gentlemen, is an affair of honor. You will take ten paces on my command, then turn and fire. If either of you turn before the count of ten, it will be my unfortunate duty to shoot you down." (Or something to this effect.)
The duelists then pace off in time to the Warder's cadence. At the count of ten they turn and fire.
The paintball has to break for the elimination to count.
Players cannot side step or lie down, but they may kneel if they wish.
No other rules apply.

Objective
The person who is not eliminated wins.

ATTACK AND DEFEND

Requirements
Two teams of equal strength:One team, the Attackers; the other, the Defenders.

Choose a defensible area to serve as a flag station.

Defenders should be restricted to the confines of the flag station.

Set boundaries that limit the movement of the defenders out of the flag station.

Duration
10 minutes.

Rules
Defenders cannot leave the flag station area, or the areas of the flag station they are charged with defending.

The Attackers can attack from any place on the field.

General Rules 1, 2, 3 apply.

Objective
Attackers: Pull the flag off its support (a string, branch, cone, etc.)

Defenders: Stop the Attackers from pulling the flag.

ANNIHILATOR

Requirements
Set up multiple five man teams.

The maximum limit is four teams for every acre of playing area.

Place teams in the area so that they are not in line of sight of each other.

To make score-keeping easier, the teams may be accompanied by a referee and each team may should their own distinct color of paint.

Duration
30–45 minutes

Rules
Teams will stay in their starting stations until the start of the game signal.

Teams get points for each elimination they inflict on other teams.

There are no points for surviving members of the team.

General Rules 1, 2, 3 apply.

Objective
Survive and be the team with the highest score at the end of the game.

BLACKJACK

Requirements
Two flag stations
Two even teams
Two flags, hung in opponents' flag stations.
Each player is only allowed 21 paintballs.

Duration
30 minutes

Rules
Players are not allowed to share paintballs.
Players who shoot all of their paintballs must
   leave the game immediately.
All General Rules apply.

Objective
Capture the opposing team's flag and return it to
   your base!

BUNNY HUNT

Requirements
A "Bunny" (one person) and Hunters (everybody
   else).
One player volunteers to be the Bunny. To give the
   Bunny some kind of advantage, choose one of
   these options.
OPTION 1-Give the Bunny a semiautomatic
   paintgun plus a garbage can lid or other device
   to use as a shield.
OPTION 2-Give the Bunny as much paint as he's
   comfortable with, and restrict the Hunters to 20
   paintballs each.

Duration
20 minutes.

Rules
If the Bunny chooses OPTION 1, hits on the shield
   do not count as an elimination.
The Bunny has a 5 minute head start into the
   playing area.
A signal will be given so that the Bunny knows
   when the game is started.
All hunters must start at the same time and from
   the same place.
When using the limited paint option, if a hunter
   runs out of paint, he is out of the game.
General Rules 1, 2, and 3 apply.

Objective
If you're the Bunny, SURVIVAL IS THE GOAL!
If you're a Hunter, eliminate the BUNNY!

RECON

Requirements

Multiple Five-Man Teams.

Checkpoints (one for every team on the field) are spaced throughout the field. Each is clearly marked with a flag or similar ornament.

Each checkpoint also has a gun hanging from a string. Each checkpoint has a different colored gun.

Each player has a card attached to his wrist (a playing card will do!) by a string, rubber band, or elastic band.

Each team starts near a checkpoint.

Duration

20 minutes.

Rules

Players must mark their card with the guns provided at the checkpoint.

Every team member must attempt to mark his card, although this is not mandatory.

Players who are eliminated are not allowed to count the points they collected with their final team score.

General Rules 1, 2, and 3 apply.

Scoring

- 1 point for each different-colored mark on a card.
- 5 bonus points if all team cards are marked by at least two checkpoints.
- 5 bonus points for each additional checkpoint where all team cards are marked.
- 2 bonus points for every team member with card marks from every checkpoint.

Objective

The team with the highest score wins.

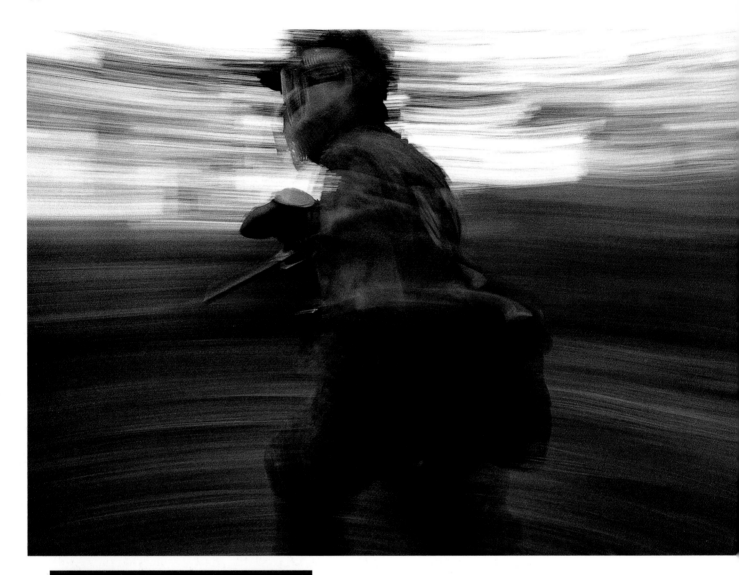

GETTYSBURG

Requirements
No bulk loaders, loading tubes or any solid apparatus used to hold or feed paintballs.
Two flag stations.
Two evenly numbered teams.
Two flags, hung in their respective flag stations.

Duration
30 minutes.

Rules
Players can carry as many paintballs as they wish.
Paintballs must be loose or in a plastic bag.
They cannot be in tubes, hoppers, or any kind of bulk loading system.
Players can only load paintballs by hand, one at a time into their paintguns and cannot load another paintball until they shoot the one in the paintgun.
General Rules apply.

Objective
Capture the opposing team's flag and return it to your base.

DOWN BUT NOT OUT

Basic Requirements
Two flag stations.
Two even teams.
Two flags, hung in their respective flag stations.
One white sock per player to be provided.

Duration
30 minutes.

Rules

1. When a player is hit, he calls himself out and lays or sits on the ground (using common sense). The player then places a sock over the barrel of his paintgun to indicate that he has been hit. He cannot move from this location until tagged. This is referred to as Waiting.

2. If a waiting player is tagged by a teammate he is back in the game. (The player, of course, removes the sock.)

3. Players who are waiting cannot shoot or disclose the positions or intentions of opposing players.

4. If a waiting player is tagged by an opposing player, he is out of the game.

5. If a waiting player feels that no one will find him, or he is tired of waiting, he can take himself out of the game. In this case the player cannot be tagged back into the game.

6. There is no limit to how many times a player can be tagged back into the game.

7. Players waiting to be tagged cannot shoot or be shot at.

8. All General Rules 1, 3, 4, and 5 apply.

Objective
Capture the opposing team's flag and return it to your base.

PAINTBURNER

Requirements

Create, depending on group size, as many three man teams as you can.

Odd players out will wait in the Designated Holding Area for enough eliminated players to return and will make up the next in-going team.

Teams start the game in different areas of the field.

Duration

30 Minutes.

Rules

1. Once a player is hit, he proceeds to the Designated Holding Area.

2. Once there are three players in the Designated Holding Area, they rejoin the game as a new team.

3. A referee will escort a newly formed team out into the field, away from the action and any other teams, if possible and signal their entry with a short whistle blast.

4. Players cannot shoot or be shot at while being escorted by the referee.

5. Only General Rules 1, 2, and 3 apply.

Objective

Fun! In which case, everybody wins!

REINFORCEMENTS

Requirements
Two flag stations.

Two even teams.

Two flags, hung in their respective flag stations.

Flag stations double as Reinforcement Rally points.

Duration
30 minutes.

Rules

1. Eliminated players go back to their flag station.

2. One player wears a special armband. This is the only player that can go back to the flag station to get reinforcements.

3. If the player wearing the armband is eliminated, he proceeds back to the flag station. He then collects those players who wish to rejoin the game and he himself rejoins the game. In this case the eliminated players have not choice but to be reinforcements. They cannot stay behind and defend the flag station.

4. Players can elect to stay behind and defend the flag station, with the exception of REINFORCEMENTS Rule 3. When they return to the flag station they are automatically active defenders.

5. Players returning to the flag station must physically tag the flag to become active defenders. If the flag is not at the flag stations the players are considered out of the game as they enter the flag station.

6. Players who are hit are out of the game but the player is only out until he reaches his flag station. Players eliminated at the flag station are out of the game.

7. Only General Rules 1, 3, 4 and 5 apply.

Objective
Capture the opposing team's flag and return it to your base.

KICK THE BUCKET

Requirements
Two flag stations.

Two even teams.

Instead of flags, a bucket is placed on the ground under where the flag usually hangs. This bucket must be made of a light plastic (remember, someone is going to kick this thing).

Duration
15 minutes.

Rules

1. The bucket cannot be moved by the team which owns it.

2. If a player is hit before he kicks the bucket, the kick (if completed) does not count as a win, the referee then resets the bucket as quickly as possible.

3. Only General Rules 1, 2, and 3 apply.

Objective
Kick the opposing team's bucket over.

TROPHY HUNTER

Requirements

Players act individually to gather trophies on the field. No teams.

Each player wears three armbands on one arm (these are referred to as trophies).

Players are interspersed in the playing field.

A signal will sound every five minutes (referred to as the five minute signal) and will be different than the start and end of game signal.

(The period between these signals will be referred to as the waiting period.)

Duration

30 Minutes.

Rules

1. Players who are hit must drop to the ground (using common sense) and remain motionless and quiet until the next five minute signal.

2. Another player (not necessarily the one who hit him) has the waiting period to collect one trophy. Once the trophy is taken no more trophies can be taken from the player during that Waiting Period.

3. When the five minute signal sounds the player is immediately in the game.

4. Only general rules 1, 2, and 3 apply.

Objective

The player with the most trophies wins.

HOSTAGE RESCUE

Requirements
Two teams:
1. Rescuers
2. Terrorists

Terrorists pick one Rescuer to act as the Hostage.

Two hostage holding areas are designated. The location of one of the hostage holding areas is disclosed to the Rescuers. Terrorists do not know which location was disclosed.

Establish an area the Rescuers will have to take the Hostage in order to win the game.

This is known as sanctuary.

Terrorists know where sanctuary is.

Duration
30 minutes.

Rules
1. Terrorists are given a five minute head start to take the hostage to one of the hostage holding areas.

2. A start of game signal is given to let terrorists know when the game has begun.

3. Terrorists cannot move the hostage out of the hostage holding area.

4. The Hostage cannot attempt escape.

5. If the Hostage is hit, the team that hit him looses.

6. The Hostage must have at least one Rescuer with him when he reaches sanctuary for the Rescuers to win.

7. If the Hostage finds himself alone for some reason, after being rescued, he must stay where he is and wait for the Rescuers to find him again. He may call out for help if he wishes.

8. Only General Rules 1, 2, and 3 apply.

Objectives
Terrorists: Stop the Rescuers from bringing Hostage to sanctuary.

Rescuers: Bring Hostage to sanctuary.

TAG

Rules

1. No teams-this is a free-for-all!
2. Select a person to be "It."
3. Disperse players in the playing area.
4. The player who is "It" starts the game by sounding the start game signal.
5. The player who is "It" must wear an armband,which must be clearly visible.
6. When a player is hit by "It" he must stand where he is. The player then receives the armband from "It" becomes the new "It."
7. The player who is "It" and the player who is receiving the armband cannot shoot or be shot at.
8. The new "It" puts the armband on and cannot shoot or be shot at until the player calls out "ready."
9. The new "It" cannot shoot at the old "It," and vice versa.
10. When "It" has been eliminated, the game is over.
11. Only General Rules 1, 2, and 3 apply.

Objective

Everybody wins by just having fun.

TRAITOR

Requirements
Two Teams

Two flag stations required but only as starting points.

A deck of cards is taken two kings and two jacks are removed, then a number of normal (nonface) cards are taken from the deck.

The number is the total amount of players MINUS 4. (It's minus four because two people will be drawing jack and two will be drawing kings.)

Then two piles are made, a king and a jack goes into each pile and then the remainder of the cards that were drawn will be separated evenly between the two piles.

The two piles are shuffled separately and one team will draw from one pile and the other team will draw from the other.

Duration
30–45 minutes.

Rules
1. Only those players who drew the kings are to reveal their cards. The players who drew the kings are the leaders for each team.

2. The players who drew the jacks are the TRAITORS. They do not reveal their identity.

3. Leaders will wear two armbands on EACH arm to designate themselves as leaders.

4. Traitors may turn on their teams at any time they see fit, once the game starts.

5. Only General Rules 1, 2, and 3 apply.

Objective
Eliminate the other team's leader.
(If the TRAITOR eliminates the leader the opposite team wins. e.g. Red team TRAITOR nukes Red team Leader, Blue team wins.

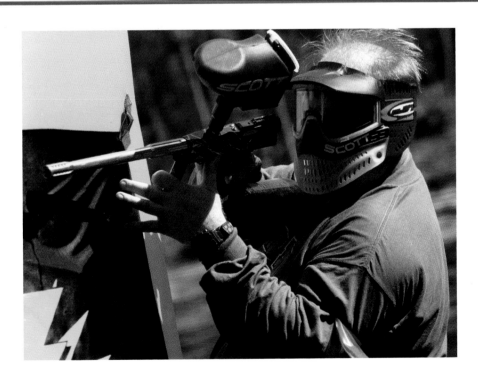

HITTING HOME ON THE RANGE

I often harp on about marksmanship and accuracy. I advocate shooting hundreds of balls at the range. But, for most people, this is not very entertaining.

Just because I love you guys and gals so much, I've invented seven fun games for you to play on the range. All games can involve any number of players, taking turns, unless otherwise noted. Also, the games are more or less designed to allow a mix of technology, semis can go up against pump and stock classes.

So now, not only will you be having fun, you'll also be learning a valuable skill. (Whether you want to, or not!)

HIDE 'N' SEEK

Requirements
No teams-everyone for themselves.

Rules
1. Select one player to be "It."
2. Establish a "home" area and within It, an object players have to tag to be "home free."
3. Establish two different signals, one as the start/end game signal and one as "home" signal.
4. All players gather at one entrance to the playing field.
5. The player who is "It" begins a slow count to one hundred, during this count the players race into the playing area and hide.
6. At the end of the count the player who is "It" sounds the start game signal and enters the playing field.
7. Players must try to make it back to "home" before getting caught by"It."
8. The player who is "It" does not have to hit the players to eliminated them. He simply calls to them and points them out ("It" has to actually see them at the time) and the player must go back to "home."
9. Players who are hit by other players or the player who is "It" are out of the game and must return to "home."
10. Each player returning home, no matter what the reason, must sound the player "home" signal.
11. The game is ended when the player who is "It" is hit.
12. Only General Rules 1 and 3 apply.

Objective
Long Version—The player, when he or she was "It" who caught the most players. (Players hit by "It" are not included in this number.)
Short Version—(One game) the player who eliminates "It."

How to Settle a Tie
Replay the game from beginning between tied players. Repeat if necessary. With Reach for the Top, replay the last round, players must get 10 for 10. For One Player Dual replay one round for the best time.

RAPID FIRE

Requirements
More than one shooter.
5-10 targets

Rules
Select a number of targets (between 5 and 10)
Shooters fire at the targets as fast as they can, but are restricted to shooting at a target only once.
An official measures the time with a stop watch.
Penalties: add one second to the time for every miss.
To win: Shortest time.

RANDOM RAPID FIRE

Requirements
Ten targets, each has its own number

The official calls out the numbers in random order (the order is determined for each player by a random drawing of ten numbered cards, prior to the player's arrival on the range.)

Shooter can only shoot at the target whose number was called.

Official calls the number (after the first target is called) as the player shoots the previous target.

Penalties
Add one second for every miss

Add two seconds for shooting at the wrong target (hit or miss)

Objective
Shortest time

SNAP SHOT

Requirements
Players and targets, as many of each as you want.

Rules
1. The paintgun cannot be put to shoulder or brought to eye level.
2. Several targets at several different ranges, number and position are up to the players.
3. Players are restricted to as many paintballs as there are targets, and can only shoot at each target once.

Scoring
Add 1 point for each hit; and

Subtract 1 point for each miss.

Objective
Person with the highest score wins.

LONG SHOT

Requirements
One target—a small can placed on an object at least 3 feet off the ground.

The can must placed so that it will fall over when hit.

Rules
Players shoot at can until they hit it and knock it to the ground.

Official counts the number of shots it took them to knock the can over (including the shot that knocked it over.)

Objective
Hit the can in the least number of shots.

REACH FOR THE TOP

Requirements
10 targets
-3 at short range (15–20 feet)
-4 at medium range (35–50 feet)
-3 at long range (80–100 feet)

Rules
1. Three rounds of shooting
2. To pass the round

First round—minimum 6 out of 10

Second round—minimum 7 out of 10

Third round—10 out of 10 (at this point the player has completed the game).

3. If the minimum is not met, the player cannot proceed to the next round and is eliminated for competition. Players can score higher than the minimum.

4. Players are limited to 10 paintballs per round.

5. Players can only shoot at target once per round.

Scoring
One point per hit.

Objective
Have the highest score.

FOLLOW ME

Requirements
Two shooters.

Rules
The two players flip a coin to see who will be the first shooter.
The first shooter calls a target and shoots at it.
If the first shooter hits the target: the second shooter must hit the target as well;

If the second shooter misses the target, the first shooter gets one point; and the first shooter calls a target and shoots again.
If the first shooter misses the target: the roles are reversed. (e.g., Billy is the first shooter, Joey is the second shooter. Billy misses, Joey takes the first shot until he misses)

Objective
The first shooter to reach 20 points.wins.

ONE PLAYER DUEL

Requirements
One player and one target

Rules
1. Player stands with his/her back to the target.
2. On command from official, the player begins to pace off, according to official's count.
3. Player turns and fires when official says "Fire".
4. Player is only allowed one shot.
5. Official starts timer at the start signal and stops if target is hit.
6. If the target is not hit, the round is not counted.
7. Players have three chances (rounds)

8. The players must be at the following distances, order is random, as chosen by the official (one distance for each round). Official draws only three distances out of the five.

   -10 paces;

   -5 paces;

   -3 paces;

   -8 paces; and

   -12 paces.

9. Players take the best time out of the three rounds. If the player missed in all three rounds, the player is disqualified.

Objective
Hit all targets in fewest turns.

Photo courtesy of Jerry Braun

The BIG GAME

"When it comes to paintball, I live for the Big Game!"

For some players, the tournament is the highest level of play available. For others, like me, the pinnacle of paintball is **the big game.** An army of players, cheap paint prices, freaky people in hilarious costumes, big-name celebrities, massive confrontations, a sense of comraderie—the big game is where you'll find all of these things and more.

SO WHAT IS THIS BIG GAME THING?

In my neck of the woods when ten people show up to play, we say it's a good sized crowd. If forty people come, we praise the paintball deities for smiling upon us. I've heard some players talk about 200 players just arriving on a single day; if I ever experience anything like that, I'd be temporarily paralyzed with happiness.

But the Big Game blows all of these experiences out of the water.

Technically, the 'Big Game' is one that has a large number of players on the field at any given moment. Regionally, a game with 70 players at an unknown field is certainly awesome, but it pales in comparison to games with well over 500 players. These are the numbers you'll find at the Skirmish World Record Games.

Scenario Game or Big Game?

You may have heard of 'Scenario' games. It's true that those games attract large numbers of players, but they aren't what I mean by big games.

Scenario games either reenact an event of real combat, or invent a plausible chain of events for players to act out in a sort of large-scale, live-action, role-playing game. Role-playing games are not new. The concept has been around in paper formats before 1975 with such staples as Advanced Dungeons & Dragons (TSR). Players are even given a new identity to assume during the course of the game. It's pure fantasy play, and it definitely appeals to many paintball players, but it doesn't have anything to do with the Big Game.

Big Games are still paintball games, only on a larger scale. They have flag objectives and eliminations. Of course, players can assume any identity they wish to, but they are not playing out a 'story' as they would in a scenario game. No matter what or whom they look like, the game they're playing is still "Capture the Flag" or "Total Elimination."

Well run scenario games have point values for achieving special missions. Such as holding a 'bridge,' capturing a specific target, achieving specific operations and so on. This is meant to bring the scenario somewhat close to the actual event that occurred (or, at the very least, to what the organizers want to accomplish). Teams get points for achieving specific objectives, and a winner is tabulated at the end of the game.

The distinctions between scenario games and some big games may blur. Some big games have 'objective flag stations' to be held for points. And some are worth more than others. It helps to be 'in the know'.

Scenario games and Big games do share a bit in common, and, with a little tweaking, you can use the following information in both contexts.

Recon!

The first step is to find a big game. Where should you look? They're advertised in many mainstream publications, and by word of mouth. Ask the guys who run the fields you frequent; they should know (they're probably as eager to go as you are). You may wish to find somewhere close to home, although traveling can be half the fun if you're with friends!

It's very important to *know what you're getting yourself into before you play a big game.* Once you've discovered one, call for information. You want as much time as possible to plan properly for this kind of event. I recommend at least a month, but three months is better. You want to know the cost of the event and what it covers (e.g., does it include CO_2 and nitrogen refills?), how much paint will cost (or, even better, if you can bring your own?), will food be provided or available. You get the idea.

If you're not familiar with the area, ask about where you can stay in the area (e.g., local hotels, motels, or campgrounds). Most big game flyers will include most of this information, but it's still a good idea to verify everything , just in case something has changed.

Another good idea is to ask about the field. Knowing a bit about the terrain can be a good thing. My feet were sore for weeks after playing on the rocks of Pennsylvania. I could have protected them better if I'd learned about the field in advance.

The newest venue for information about big games is on the internet. You may already know about 'rec.sport.paintball' and 'alt.sport.paintball.' Through these two usenet newsgroups you can gain access to what I call the 'paintball hive-mind.' If you have a question about a specific field or a place that you've never played before, you can probably get an answer in a few days from someone who has been there. Some events have web pages about them as well.

The more informed you are, the better time you will have.

GEAR, GARB, AND GOODIES

What Do I Bring to the Big Game?

Bring what you bring to any paintball game! Yourself, goggles, harnesses, gun, gloves, squeegee, and all that stuff you probably play with all the other times you play. If you wear contact lenses, bring your eyedrops. Always bring multiple pairs of underwear and socks and backup sneakers or boots. Just make sure you've packed everything you need. When you're a few states away from home, realizing you forgot your goggles is pretty demoralizing.

Then there are the things you'd never think of bringing, but they don't hurt.

Bring extra money. Whoever thinks you can bring too much money is silly. Some big games have a vendors tent with more goodies to bring home with you. Not to mention how quickly eating out drains your cash no matter how affordable. Bring a tent, or some kind of portable shade; parking lots never have trees in them! Lawn chairs are great (trust me, car bumpers get uncomfortable after a few minutes!), and a cooler filled with ice, water, and Gatorade will make you the envy of many dehydrated participants. Packing a small first aid kit is invaluable as well. You get the idea.

Preparation is the key to playing the big games.

Arrival

As with any major event, showing up early has it's advantages. Better parking is worth it, believe me! If the event starts at 9 AM, you want to try and get there by 7:30 AM. I've had to walk a half a mile to the staging area with all my gear in tow. Avoid this if you can.

Once there you want to sign in right away. The sooner you do, the easier it is to get all your gear together, chronograph in (all guns must fire under 300 fps!), and just get comfortable. It's also pure joy to sit back and watch the people arrive in a panic as they try to prepare for mass orientation in under 10 minutes.

I'm Here, Now What?

First, relax. It's just another game of capture the flag. It's just that this time you've got company. You may have as many as 500 people on your team-way more people than you're accustomed to. But that's still not a problem.

Just like a normal walk-on day, you go through an orientation speech. Pay attention to it! You may have played a billion times before, but it's important that you listen to this orientation!) They will go over the rules of the game, as well as special rule variations specific to the big game. And it's important to be at least acquainted with those rules.

Paintball Sam's in Racine, Wisconsin runs a few big games every year. One of the rule modifications there always involves medics. If you are hit below the knee or below the elbow you are 'wounded.' You can be 'healed' by a designated 'medic' player three times before you are eliminated from that particular game.

For some time, the rule stated that a hit below

Welcome to the Game of Paintball

the knee, elbow, and above the chin line counted as a 'wound.' The year they switched to head shots counting as eliminations was confusing to a lot of the players who weren't paying attention to the orientation speech and frustrating to those of us who lit them up.

Listen to the rules at the beginning of the game!

Motor Easy

One of the things I cherish about the big game format is how laid back players are, in general. Sure, you get your hyper players out there who make down-the-middle rushes. But, for the most part, everyone is in a casual frame of mind. Sometimes players hang up the camouflage for a day. Among the things to expect people will be wearing, I've seen jeans and t-shirts, tuxedos, three-piece business suits, a Fred Flintstone outfit, a Moose hat (I mean antlers and all!), Viking helmets and costumes, even a Waldo sweater (as in "Where's Waldo?"). Me? I wear a deer costume. It's a midwestern thing.

Meanwhile, other players dust off their stock guns to play amongst the other semi-autos. (In the midwest, it's rare to see one on the field at all. Big Games bring them out of hiding.) When there are a few hundred opponents, you know you're going to meet at least a few of them. So some players generally take it easy on firepower for the day.

Before I forget, let me mention that you should leave your temper at home. A big game is not for proving how many people you can eliminate. Angry, overly intense players ruin this kind of experience for everyone else. Your priority at this game is to relax, have fun, meet people, and make friends! This is another major difference between the Big Game and Scenario Games, which tend to be intense because people are making believe that a great deal is at stake (e.g., the future of human civilization, the outcome of WWII).

Tactics aren't as important in the Big Game as they are in normal play. Having a few tricks up your collective sleeves isn't a bad idea, but any more organization than that and you're going to end up in pretty lame arguments with people who have thought way too long and hard about the game to be enjoying it.

As you'd expect, most players will play offense. This is natural. People generally feel safer when they're flanked by hundreds of players. On the offensive side, there's a lot you can do.

As much as I hate to say it, grandiose military tactics can work on big game fields. This is due to the size of the field, and the game's typically longer time frame. Checking with the rules is important here. Do you have enough time for wide flanking maneuvers? Do you have time to make an ambush happen? These are things you need to know to avoid expending tons of energy only to discover that the game is over before you've engaged anyone.

The Big O

Grab as many people as you can for your flanking moves. Sometimes it's a good idea to make a 'sacrifice' maneuver to spring ambushes, or to determine numbers. Also, keep in mind the overall objective. Fifty people chasing five guys for an hour is a waste of time that you could be using to build momentum.

Players have a tendency to group in a circle formation, and you should use this to your advantage. The front-most players should be watching forward, the rear-most players should be watching the back (literally facing backwards and walking backwards!), and players on the sides should be covering your group's flanks. You have to think as a very large pack of wolves on the prowl. You have to trust everyone else in the pack to do their part. **Trust works if everyone is equally committed to it.**

Having a 'team' mentality helps, but knowing

how to get your fellow teammates to share it is important as well. You can do this by rallying everyone in earshot to move forward, or go through the bunkers. Or by adding yourself to the push so you can gain some more feet of real estate.

Shouting has its time and place. Once you and another person pushes forward whoopin' and hollerin', people will be more apt to follow you. This is a 'herding' effect that I touch on in detail a bit later on. By the same token, there's something to be said for people who hang back and observe the whoopin' and hollerin' advance, especially if it's ambushed. Then it's their turn to shout out the position of the other team, direct people to regroup and engage, pursue, or retreat.

Transmitting information from one side of the playing field to the other is vital. Send more than one person as a messenger. The faster you can tell the "center" crowd that the "left" crowd is punching through the left side, the more people you can slam through it, and the more likely it is that you'll win the game. If you hear something about a push, or that the opponents are making a move, pass it along as fast as possible, and make sure you get a few more to pass it as well.

Information is power. Spread the word.

Individual Offense

Big games get chaotic. So, despite their size, what you do as an individual can make a difference. The first thing you should realize is that, outside of your friends, you are surrounded by individuals.

Paintball is a team sport, and remains so even if both teams consist of 300 people a side. Stuff happens, however. Your entire team gets shot, or they all abandon a situation and you find yourself alone. What can you do? Switch gears.

Lone Hunter Mode

Now you are the lone hunter. You are individually outnumbered, but that's not really important. As an individual, you have strengths against big numbers of opponents.

Sink into your camouflage and start to crawl around. It's nerve-wracking to let a team of guys walk past you, but let them go. Sneak up on your opponents and take out a few of them from behind. Then, run for the hills. You may be able to draw them away from your teammates or your flag, weakening their offense. Or, you can go for the other team's flag! You may be able to fake them out, saying you're on their team (if the rules allow it).

As a loner, you'll experience the game at a higher level of alertness. You have to watch your own back. Your movements must be quick, subtle, and quiet. You will only fire your gun if you have a clear shot.

Even if you get eliminated, you can still do a lot for your team. If you think in ratios, if you eliminate 5 players, and tie up 20 more in the process, that's 25 guys on you that aren't on your team's flag station. And if you can tie them up for a length of time, you'll really be doing a favor to your team.

Or, perhaps you'll become a spy. As a spy, your challenge is to gather intelligence behind enemy lines about their allocation of resources, sheer numbers of people in certain places and the direction their moving in, and then to get it back to your forces in time for it to be useful. The cool thing is, you can always switch into 'Lone Hunter' mode if it looks like there isn't enough time to get your information back to your people. Let out a shout that gives away an enemy position (this works better if you have a friends in your main group who will know what you mean when you holler!), take a few of them out, and start running. Of course, doing this kind of thing is dependent on the length of the game.

Which brings me to defense.

"Are we leaving any defenders?"

I actually heard this on a big-game field once.

A Big Game defense is fully dependent on the

Photo courtesy of Jerry Braun

scenario objective. A game of "Capture the Flag" will have more defense than, say, capture and hold a point bunker. I'll talk about both types.

First, let's look at Capture the Flag defense. A good defense can hold off an opposing offense. But what is the best defense?

A common 'big game' mistake is to make the offense the defense by not letting anyone through the cracks. This isn't a good idea, because then only a few players can slip through to capture your flag. Leaving a few people behind, or at least near the back of the field is always a good idea.

A good defense is layered. Meaning that you have players 200, 100, and 50 yards out, then the final flag station. (This can be modified, but you get the idea.)

However, the defense should be aware that if they can not stop and rout the offense by 70 yards out, the game is pretty much over (Again, this distance changes from field to field, but if they can longball you *en-masse*, you're history.) I call this the 'Final Approach' zone. In this zone, the offense gets motivated to win, and your defense has nowhere to go.

Bottom-line
If you run out of real estate,
you're a sitting duck.

Other big games have specific point bunkers. These work differently. Your team gets points by holding such bunkers for allotted periods of time (20 minutes), or on specific time marks (every half hour) Defending this type of bunker is different.

For starters, you probably have to defend against 360 degrees of terrain. So having a lot of defenders is a good idea if you have the power. You are probably going to want to organize the same kind of layered defense as I had mentioned earlier, for many of the same reasons. Your 'final approach' distance will be shorter, but it may be worse. Always try to leave an avenue of escape if you can. That way you can always do an end run and flank behind the other team. If they totally surround you, it's over.

Still, if the other team surrounds you or reaches the "Final Approach," your chances are not totally gone. You can get reinforcements from some angle if the game allows for reinsertions or if your team-mates find you. Hold your position as long as you can. If you get eliminated after the points are allotted, you've done your job for your team.

Either way, stopping a rampaging offense is no easy task. You do it through sheer will, determination, and discipline. Shooting a lot of paint doesn't hurt either, but it's not necessary. As a defensive group, you don't want to all concentrate on one 'zone'. You want to take a line of approach, and cover it. Communicate with your teammates, and have overlapping lanes of fire. The idea is to stop their forward movement and rout them.

By halting their approaching push, they have nowhere to drive but backwards. This breaks their attack momentum, and they lose the 'will' to keep driving at you. It's hard to recover from a rout. The hard part is figuring out when to change gears from defense to offense, or even if you need to go at them. That becomes a 'feel' thing, best determined by experience and what's happening on the field.

When the offense gets into the "Final Approach" zone, they tend to get a little blood-thirsty. Meaning that they start to 'smell' the flag, taste the victory. If you get caught as a defender in this situation, you will get pounded unless you can rout them.

If you do get tagged, the best thing to do is scream, "I'm out! I'm hit!" repeatedly and just vacate the hot zone as fast as you can. Keep your paintgun high (Don't worry about your barrel plug, you'll have time to put it in when you're out of the hot zone), Then, put your barrel plug in. It'll save you from getting more welts than you deserve.

The Human Herd

When a few hundred people are milling about, they usually act like a mob. If you have mediocre leadership skills you can guide them. Heck, even if you have none it's really easy. You just may need to shout (or a megaphone will substitute nicely.)

There's always times when you see from your side that another side of the field needs reinforcements. That's when, classically, you start shouting "SHIFT RIGHT! SHIFT RIGHT!" When the shift begins, just guide players to the appropriate area.

Unfortunately, there's usually at least 20 people trying to do this. All you can really do from the rear ranks is become a 'caller'. This is the player who announces to the pack where opponents are. "THREE BEHIND THE SPOOL! TWO BEHIND THAT TREE! TEN ON THE LEFT TAPE!" The caller is the first player to go hoarse, by the way. The caller can also do the same thing from the front line as well.

SOUNDING SCARIER THAN YOU ARE

Once one player starts to scream like a maniac, other players will join in and follow him. I'm not sure why it works, but it does. (I think it's a psychology thing, I'm not sure.) You don't have to scream. But sometimes that really does the trick!

A good example of this happened in Racine Wisconsin's Big Game a long time ago. While sneaking around on the tapeline, I heard someone playing a bugle, it was the classic "Charge" tune. Soon followed by the loudest screaming match I've ever heard, and what sounded like a stampede. Thankfully, the player was on my team. We used that momentum to carry us to the flag and victory.

"Rebel Yells" "Kamikaze Screams" "Whoops & Hollers"

Primal screams do two things. They provide an adrenaline rush to your teammates who will rush into positions without fear. Moreover, it scares the living daylights out of your opponents. This intimidation is infectious on both sides, and can get a lot of results quickly. It burns your team out quickly, however, so use it only when things stagnate or when you need to make the push.

Part two of the process is getting your teammates to go with you. Some people have the charisma to do it, some don't. Sometimes all you need to do is get into a great position and coax your players to join you. Other times you need to make an impression.

Making a bold—read: *stupid*—charge to take a bunker will do this. People will be impressed you made it and either join you or shake their heads in disbelief. Either way, you'll have their attention. Use the opportunity to yell to them to move up. Keep reassuring your teammates that you're going to win, you've got the opponents on the run, and so on.

The idea here is to get your players to move up as one group rather than piecemeal. See, the more people moving forward, the better your odds are in getting things to go your way. So a lot of people moving together is a good thing. And convincing a bunch of walk-on players to all do this is part diplomacy, part intimidation, part luck.

But when they all go at once, you've got something good happening, and then it's up to you and the two or three other guys who are interested in taking the lead to maintain it!

Radio Communications

The ability to communicate is always important in paintball, especially in the big game format. Knowing what is happening on the other end of your skirmish line becomes more difficult when you can't see the length of it.

Many big games allow the use of radios as long as you do not cross-talk onto the referee channels. Radios put a whole new dimension on the game.

Remember, you're not going to be alone, so some common courtesy is a good thing. Use a 'push to talk' radio system if you can. I've experienced hard breathing sounds and shooting pain in my right ear. That's not fun, by any stretch of the imagination.

Keep your radio chatter as short as possible if you're in a firefight. Too much information can be confusing and useless to your other teammates. Assume that nobody cares what your teammates think of your paintgun or the referees. Save that for after the game.

Be courteous to your fellow players, and let them have some air-time as well. If you need to talk that much, switch stations.

Radios also have a dual-edged purpose as well. Whatever you broadcast can (and usually will) be intercepted by your opponents, and be used against you. I've personally used this phenomenon myself to try to convince opposing players to surrender the flag. (I bribed them with a six-pack of soda! They respectfully declined.) Another use is to run a campaign of false information on the assumption that you'll keep your opponents off-guard if they think you're moving in one direction, but then end up doing the opposite.

Several models of radios are available, I prefer a hands-free model with a remote push-to-talk button. This way, I can control what I broadcast. I place the button in my off hand, and run the wire down the sleeve and under my pullover. This way I don't have to reach over to broadcast anything, and the electronics are protected under my pullover.

For scenario games some players go as far as to use portable CB radios. I've also heard of a few people who used a cellular phone when the situation got desperate. I think that's a bit extreme myself, but go for it if it works for you (and it's allowed by the rules).

Photo courtesy of Jerry Braun

GO GET'EM!

With these small bits of information, you're set to go.

All in all, the 'big game' is tremendously fun, no matter where you go to do it. The key to this kind of event is forethought. To quote a song by Rush "An ounce of perception, a pound of obscure." Being prepared is the best way to enjoy the 'big game' and to avoid unpleasant 'surprises' along the way. And remember: Never say 'follow me' and trip into the creek. You'll have a lot of soggy compatriots.

—RR

THESE LADIES ARE 2DIE4

Meet *Karen Barber and Sarah Stevenson, two of the top professional paintball players in the world.*

ANDREW FLACH: We were just at Skyball (Toronto, 1999), and your team, 2 Die 4, was there, and The Iron Maidens were there. As far as I know, those are the only two all-women teams playing at a semi-professional tournament level.

There are some co-ed teams, but the vast majority of the paintball teams that regularly compete are all male teams. Tell me about your experience as women in such a male dominated sport? Are you treated with equal consideration? Are you considered an equal competitor?

SARAH STEVENSON: It's getting there. The first time that I played with Maidens, the guys had the attitude, "Oh, we're just playing a bunch of girls. Big deal! We'll smoke 'em." And they were pretty much right. They did, but not because we were women.

We stayed with it. We plugged away, trained ourselves, and now we're kind of a wild card. They don't know what to do with us. They don't know how to predict what we're going to do. Most teams are very predictable. You can read the field and know generally where they're going to go. As you saw at Skyball 1999, our team pulled off things that the other players never expected.

It's been nice to see that we register on the men's respect meter. All it took was a year and a half, hard work, practice, and execution, and now the other teams can't take us for granted. Attitudes changed pretty quickly once we started to win.

ANDREW: So the two of you first played together on The Iron Maidens?

From Left: Karen Barber and Sarah Stevenson

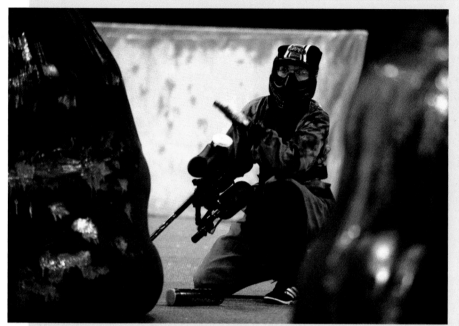

all that testosterone. I did become accustomed to that style of play. The guys I played with are all like brothers to me. They always took care of me and made sure I was okay.

The men didn't treat me any differently, which I respected, and they knew that's what I wanted. I always worried that they were just keeping me around because my husband was on the team. We had this talk many a time, and that wasn't the case.

In fact, for a couple of years, my husband stayed with the All Americans and I went to the All Americans 2. I decided to see what it was like to step down a level and play the amateur league. We eventually went pro because we kept working at it.

KAREN BARBER: We met each other at World Cup '96.

SARAH: We had known each other before, and then I went and talked with the team and the team captain, Tracy Roberts. Tracy was just absolutely crazy about Karen and for good reason. Tracy had been in the sport for a long time and knew about Karen and had watched her career as a paintball player evolve. We discussed things and decided to let Karen and a few other All Americans play with us at a tournament in San Antonio.

We contacted Karen and a couple of the other All Americans and they agreed to come down and play with us. This was a big coup. Our team was legitimized overnight.

ANDREW: When did you start playing with The Iron Maidens.

SARAH: Around the middle of 1995.

ANDREW: Having played on co-ed teams, and having played on all-women teams, have you noticed any difference in the way the team works.

SARAH: Completely. Yeah, you're looking at two polar ends.

KAREN: The men are definitely more competitive and more aggressive than the women. Probably

I definitely think that women, individually and as a team, are more level headed, more patient. And some of them are better shots. Women are few and far between in this sport, but if you find the right ones and put them together, I believe women's teams would be very dangerous.

SARAH: I agree with Karen. Women are a notch

more level-headed than men on the field. They have their mind set on where they want to go as a team, and they're a little more deliberate and less erratic than their male counterparts.

The men's teams that I've played on—probably the most serious being a team called Texas Shock Force—were tremendous. But they couldn't quite set their egos aside and play the game as an entire team with one unifying goal. They couldn't knit it together.

Whereas, when 2 Die 4 went to Skyball, I had no problems with egos on the team. No particular team member felt a need to be the star of the show. And I went up and told one of my players: "You're going to sit this game. I'm going to put so and so in." "Sure, no problem," was the response.

In my experience, men hear this kind of statement as, "You're just not good enough for this game, so I'm going to put somebody else in." So they can tend to get a little disenchanted, to put it mildly.

KAREN: Women tend to reason it out and deal with things. That's been very refreshing with this group. I haven't had to deal with any of that. Our team members are very supportive. Like a family.

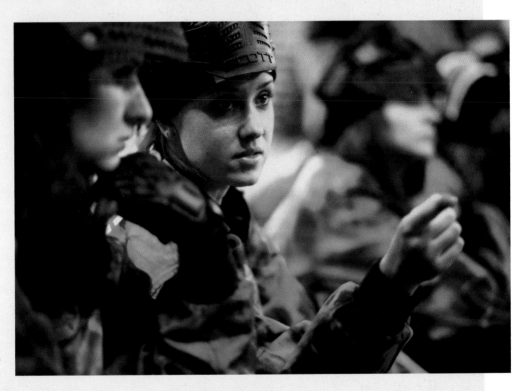

ANDREW: What is your goal with 2 Die 4? As captain, where are you taking the team?

SARAH: Pro status. I've always wanted to go further, I've always wanted to go higher, but I don't want to get onto a team that's already pro, I want to build a team that can do well in any competition.

ANDREW: So you got on the telephone and called Karen at some point. Karen, what did you think when the idea was broached?

KAREN: At first I didn't grasp the seriousness of her proposal. I knew she had asked me to play and that she was going to organize this team. And I said, "Okay, yeah. That'll be fine." And then I realized that all the girls involved were very serious and very talented. I saw right away that we had a good group of people that could probably go further.

ANDREW: Do you think we'll see separate women's paintball leagues, the way they have segregated basketball?

KAREN: Not for a long time, if ever. We're far from having enough players.

SARAH: I don't think the women would really want that. I like the competitive level we have now in a co-ed environment. We compete effectively as it is.

ANDREW: Paintball is a sport where skill, technique, and decision making take precedence. Just

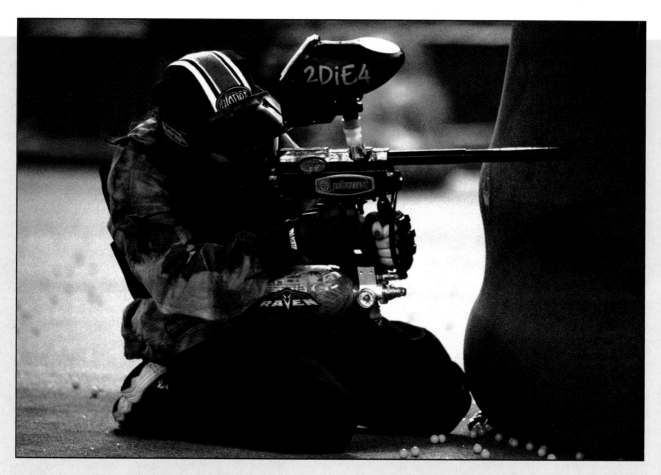

the fact that you have testosterone coursing through your body, doesn't mean you will win more games, does it?

KAREN: Well, I've always thought the All Americans are where they are today because they're the most competitive group of people I've ever met in my life. For instance, we'll be waiting at the airport because a plane is delayed. They find something to do and make a game out of it until each person wins. Everyone has to win.

I've never met women like that before, that competitive. I think that's one thing that the men have that we don't. Innate competitiveness. Maybe professional women volleyball or softball players have it, but most women simply aren't like that.

ANDREW: How about in terms of strength issues. Would you say that paintball is a fairly accessible game for both men and women?

KAREN: Yes.

ANDREW: In terms of competition?

KAREN: Hmm. I don't know about that. In one way the sport's changing now, at least in the NPPL. You need to be fast and aggressive. Running quickly is becoming important. Unfortunately, speed is one thing I lack.

ANDREW: I'm sure if you had a couple of fast running players, sprinters, on the team...

SARAH: And a lot of teams do...

ANDREW: ...that might even things out, don't you think?

KAREN: Yes. You need key bunkers and they are always the front ones that you have to hit. You need to get people into those quickly. We used to play with three or four "backup" players. Now there's only one or two. The rest of the team is forward. You have to be aggressive, because the only way to get the other team out is to keep moving or just go "bunker" them. That's the trend in competitions today.

ANDREW: What words of encouragement would

you have for women interested in playing paint-ball?

SARAH: Stick with it. Don't let the things guys say get in your head. Somebody's always going to give you a hard time. I've found that in a lot of sit-uations—being a Mom, I'm able to see this—men at the fields will test a woman the same way a kid would test a Mom. They see how far they can push her and see what they can do, maybe to get her to leave.

These guys think: "Paintball is our world, stay out of it." And, maybe four years ago, that would have been the case, for the most part. And so they would test and they'd push and they'd do the "Hey baby, hey honey," thing. That's gotten better, but they still will push on the women to see if they really want to stick around. Maybe they're a little intimidated by the presence of women, since there's a ton of baggage attached to being eliminated by a girl. I say stick it out.

ANDREW: Is paintball as a sport arriving at time when it can develop as its own unique co-ed activity? Is it poised for that?

KAREN: I think it's always going to be co-ed. I don't think there will ever be enough women inter-ested in playing the sport continually. Women get married, or pregnant. And, today, if you ask a girl, "Would you rather run around in the woods, where you may break a nail or get paint in your hair, or go swimming or play volleyball?" ...

ANDREW: She'd choose the other sports?

KAREN: I think she would, without ever having tried paintball. You find very few women who absolutely love it and are willing to make a seri-ous commitment to playing the game regularly.

Some women are also very intimidated by the fact that it hurts when you get hit. They don't like pain. I think women, even though they give birth, don't enjoy that kind of pain.

SARAH: And I just want to say—it's a different

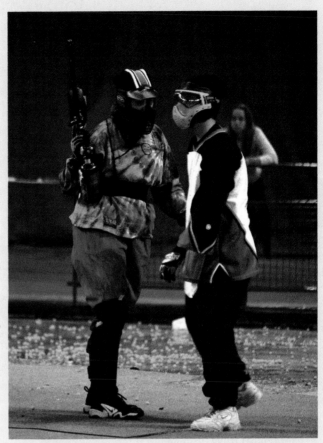

Member of 2 Die 4 discusses a call with a referee at Skyball in Toronto, 1999.

breed of women that wants to do this.

ANDREW: So women are concerned about get-ting hit by a paintball?

KAREN: Oh, yeah. I mean, when I used to work in an office and wore a dress and nylons, people would see the bruises left from paintballs and say, "You are absolutely a mess."

SARAH: It's always a good idea to wear protec-tion—cups for the men, padded bras for the women. They're available. Use them. You're a lit-tle silly if you don't.

ANDREW: It's been great meeting with you. Are there are any last thoughts you'd like to share with our readers.

SARAH: We appreciate the support that we do get from people. At Skyball, men and women came up to me, shook my hand, and said, "Your team is a good example of how teams should be at these events."

And that means a great deal to us. We don't want half compliments. Don't say, "Well, I've got to go back home with my tail between my legs because a girl shot me." Don't give me that. Give me, "You play well. You're a good player." Not as a woman. Just as a player. Period.

If more men in this game would adopt that way of thinking, that would be tremendous. In paintball, the men have all kinds of support. They have oodles of support. Verbal support from the crowds. Financial support in the form of sponsorships from the manufacturers. We're starting to get the sponsorship and we are starting to get the verbal support, too. We greatly appreciate that.

All we ask is to be treated like equals on the playing field. Give us your game, and we'll give you ours. May the best players win. It's as simple as that.

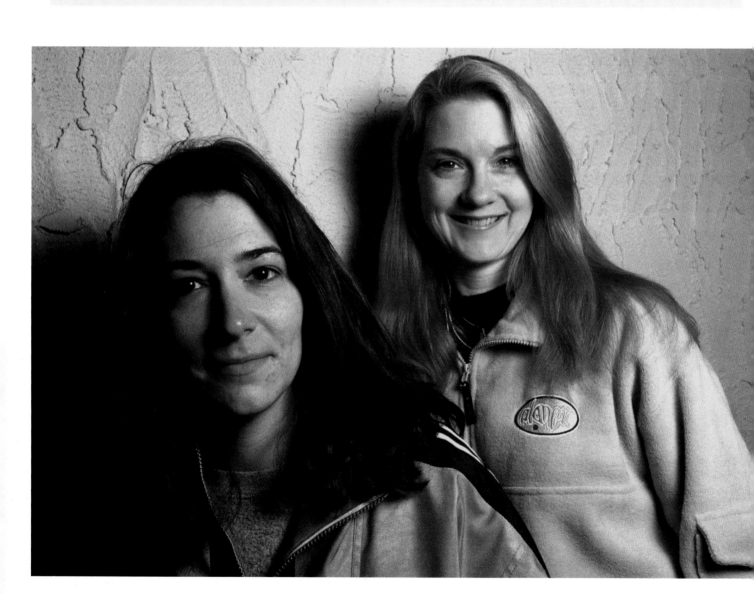

INDOOR PAINTBALL BY THE OCEANSIDE

Jay Tavitian

An Interview with Jay Tavitian, Manager, Oceanside Indoor Paintball, Long Island, NY.

Jay at Oceanside

Indoor paintball can be a wild experience; it's fast and furious, dark and dangerous, and has more bunkers than you can imagine. If you want to experience the wide range of paintball play, you must check out the indoor game!

For this interview we met with Jay Tavitian, Manager of Oceanside Indoor Paintball, at his 10,000 square foot facility on Long Island, New York.

ANDREW FLACH: Jay, what's the fundamental difference between the indoor and outdoor paintball experience?

JAY TAVITIAN: The difference between the two fields is like the difference between night and day. Outdoor fields present a slower game. They tend to be more strategic and tactical, whereas the indoor game is played at a much faster pace. Tactics have their place in the indoor games, but everything's done at a very quick pace. I mean, you take your eyes off the field for one second and someone's come right up on the side of you already. With the outdoor field you can close your eyes for a few minutes, and you probably won't miss much.

Also, you get a lot more distance on outdoor fields. The guns are set up differently. The velocities are higher out there.

ANDREW: What's the velocity of a paintball indoors versus outdoors?

JAY: It's 220 feet per second indoor. The outdoor field's are usually 290. When you're outdoors, you need more distance. I'll put it in perspective: if you get a player that's playing here constantly and they're real good at the indoor field, they go to the outdoor field they get a reality check out there.

They try to move fast and they wind up getting shot up because there's a lot more open space out there. If you get an outdoor player in the indoor field, they'll sit back and relax. And they'll get shot up.

ANDREW: Indoor is just a different flavor of the game. Some people like chocolate ice cream, other people like strawberry ice cream.

JAY: Exactly.

ANDREW: Hard core indoor players probably have little or no interest in going out in the woods and shooting guns. Other guys who are fanatical about the outdoor game just aren't into the indoors style. They want the big field.

JAY: I originally played on outdoors fields, and then I made the transition to an indoor field. So I know both sides. What you're saying is true. But then there are people who just love both.

For some people, when winter comes, that's it for playing. They can't play the outdoor field because it's too cold, and they don't want to freeze, so they put the equipment away until spring time. Other players think "it's getting too cold to play outside, so it's time to go indoors for a while." So they start coming down to the indoor field on the weekends just to keep themselves in shape and ready to go when spring returns.

ANDREW: It's really just a matter of the individual player finding what it is that they like to do.

The indoor game has it's own sort of unique flavor because you're covering less ground between bunkers. Then again, you've got to constantly move because the other team is covering ground quickly, too. So there's a different speed to the game, it's almost more like speedball?

JAY: Basically, yes. You can call it a hundred percent speedball.

ANDREW: How do you find playing without a flag? Does it make for a different kind of a game just from the mind set of the player?

JAY: Yes. We used to use a center flag. We just took the flag out. The game is basically total elimination, and because you're in close quarters here, we felt a flag would just be overkill.

Which isn't to say that we didn't try having a flag. But you have to understand that people's primary objective in a small space like this is not to get hit. So with the flag they were thinking: "If I keep going for the flag, I'm getting hit." Then everybody sits back and the flag just sits there and no one touches it. So we just took it out and went to an elimination game.

ANDREW: Do you have other variations of the elimination game you play?

JAY: We change corners, we switch sides. This totally changes the field. Everything's opposite, backwards, and upside down. When we do this, even our regulars stand around with their guns in their hands just shaking their heads. They have no clue about where to go or what to do, and they love it. All you've got to do is just start from different corners and it just totally throws the whole game off.

Another thing we do is take "the house" out of bounds. The house is a key objective on our field. You can control the game from that position. We declare it out of bounds and we square the field off. You take the house away from everybody and they say "okay, now where do I go?"

ANDREW: Explain your version of the elimination game.

JAY: Let's say you have 20 people. It's 10 on 10 with a ten minute maximum game. The object of the game is to eliminate the other team before time runs out.

ANDREW: Indoor fields are ideal for urban and suburban settings where there's not a lot of land to play in. You can play year round in fair or foul weather. I played at another indoor field. They turned all the lights off except for a black light. Do you play in the dark?

JAY: No. The problem with playing in a darkened environment is safety. Not only the safety of the players, but the safety of the referees. It gets dark enough in here, but you can always still see what's going on. We don't need to turn off the lights to make it fun or challenging.

Besides, the worst thing you can do to a person is take their eyesight away from them. Once you blind them, they lift the mask. If the lights are off they lift the mask thinking "I'll see better without the mask." Now the referee can't see the player lifting the mask, and a person takes a shot in the eye. Then you're out of business or in serious trouble.

Safety is our number one priority. We just don't take chances when it comes to safety.

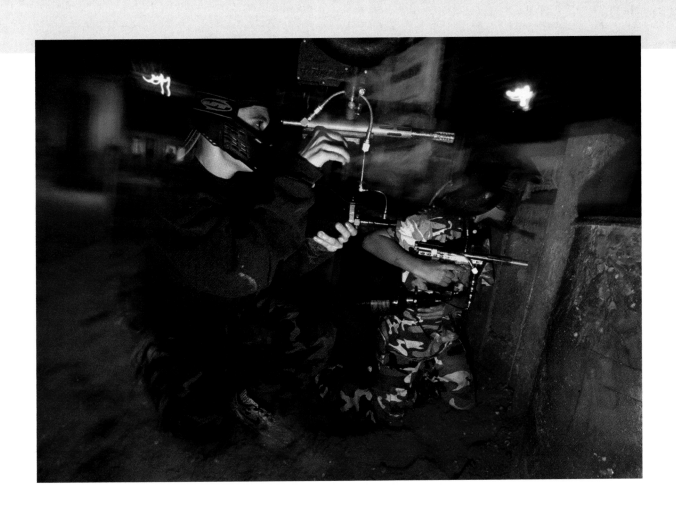

FIELDS OF DREAMS

Paul Fogal

Achieving the ultimate recreational paintball experience drives Paul Fogal, Founder of Skirmish USA, located in Jim Thorpe, PA.

When it comes to recreational paintball, Skirmish USA is one of the best run facilities out there. It offers plenty of fields to choose from encompassing wide variety of playing experiences and environments-from deep woods to wide open spaces. Over 700 acres and 44 fields are devoted to the recreational paintball experience. Every other year, the World Record Game attracts over a thousand players from all over the world.

If you want to know what makes for a great paintball experience, there's one man to ask, Paul Fogal. He has set the standards for recreational play.

ANDREW FLACH: What are your standards for a successful day of paintball?

PAUL: You should have an exciting time running around with your friends in the woods, and no complaints about the service at the field. If you and your friends leave with a smile on your face, we've done our job.

In a way, it's a people movement business. We try and move you efficiently, so you're out there playing as soon as possible and can play the number of games you want. Then we try to change the games and the terrain around so you've got to think a little bit about what you're doing. You shouldn't be running to the same tree all day. You'll play one time and you're on one side of the field and then the other side of the field and sometimes you go to another field or sometimes you might play three games on a field if you really like it.

We try to give the players the field experience they want. One field might have more open terrain and another might be real thick. One might be dry, another wet. Then we have the Village Fields and the Scenario Fields where there are buildings, structures, and unique bunkers.

ANDREW: A field like The Alamo?

PAUL: Yes, there's a couple like The Alamo. People like to play those fields at the end of the day. They're bigger and they're paint-eaters. Near the end of the day, when players want to run out of paint, we hear them say "The hell with this hunting thing. Let's just shoot it out."

ANDREW: From what I observed from just a brief experience interacting with your staff, it strikes me that there are several keys to your success. And I think these are things all people should expect when they go to a paintball field. Number one is the emphasis on safety. Safety is paramount.

PAUL: The most critical safety issue is that you have to keep your goggles on your face at all times on the field of play. There are some people who don't understand that and you have to keep pushing them and reminding them. Some people just blank out and start to lift their goggles after a game is over. You just can't do that, and we never let people forget it.

Beyond keeping their eyeballs in their heads, we like our players to feel like they're spending most of their time doing what they came to do. Players are there to get their money's worth. They expect to be moved efficiently through the entire process—get their release forms filled out, get their gun and equipment rentals in hand quickly, buy paint, get to the field. Players should be able to start playing very quickly and play as many games as possible during the course of the day. Sufficient logistics are of primary importance.

To accomplish this, we need a professional staff—motivated, helpful people, who know how to treat customers properly and handle situations

in an appropriate manner. People who enjoy delivering on customer service.

ANDREW: You're doing something right in terms of the way you're conducting your business. People speak very highly of their experience here. Word of mouth is priceless. People tell other people, "I had a great time at Skirmish. They were really nice people, I felt really comfortable, and their fields are awesome." These are all things that add up to a successful operation.

PAUL: You have to run your field in a professional, businesslike manner. That has been a problem in paintball, but it's improving. For years there were a lot of fields that weren't being run well, but as the sport matures, only the fields that have their act together will survive. Most of the poorly run fields are dropping by the wayside. Not long ago, an insurance guy told me he figured that about forty percent of the fields still didn't have any insurance. That's just ridiculous. Wake up, field-owners. You could lose everything and hurt paintball's reputation in the process!

ANDREW: It seems that to engineer a fun day of paintball, a certain plan is required. Are you guys following a program, whereby teams that start on field "A" will move on to field "B", whereas teams that start on field "Y" go on to field "Z"?

PAUL: No, it's not that scientific. There are large, open fields and small, wooded fields, and fields thick with 15-foot-high rhododendron bushes. We have a general manager, Karen, who evaluates the groups and she puts them on the field where she thinks it's appropriate for that group to start. For example, if it's forty people she puts you on a field that would handle forty people size-wise.

During the course of the day, the judges talk to the players, who are usually pretty forthcoming about what they want. They'll request fields, and we try to accommodate them.

There's one person whose job it is to keep track of who's playing where and they radio in about which fields are open. That person will look at the group and see how many people there are, see what fields they've played, which field is open. You just try and vary it a little bit. You're kind of throwing them a curve, keeping things exciting and new.

I really think the secret to our success is that the fields are a little bit bigger and there's a little bit more anticipation before the shooting starts than in most places. Most places really pack you in.

ON FIELD DESIGN

ANDREW: Who's job is it to design the field?

PAUL: Dewey Green and I are the chief designers. It's a constant tinkering and feedback process. Various judges and players also make suggestions regarding their preferences and desires. Once or twice a year, a group of us will get together over beer and pizza. We brainstorm new field designs and game formats.

THE ROLE OF THE JUDGE

ANDREW: It seems important to have someone on the field who is a representative of the paintball field's operator-the judge. What is a judge?

PAUL: On a recreational level, a judge is a combination of referee and guide. He or she helps the group with their equipment, leads them through the day, and then will make some calls on the field. By the very nature of the fact that you're playing on a number of acres in the woods, the referees cannot make all the calls. There always has to be an honor factor.

The best judges are people with extroverted

personalities, who kind of enjoy the woods. A lot of the judges are there because they like to run around in the woods. I often hear them say things like, "I sit behind the computer terminal all week, so it's fun to get out here and get some exercise."

ON CLOTHING

ANDREW: How should I prepare myself for a day of play? What would you recommend as the proper clothing?

PAUL: Just wear old clothes. If you have a set of fatigues, wear them. Dark colors are a good idea—black, brown, green. Clothes that you will not mind getting wet, dirty, muddy, or splattered with paint.

Your basic rental gear.

As an option, most fields offer some sort of camouflage overalls, or "cammies," for rent. You just step into them; they fit over your clothes. At the end of the day, you turn them in and let someone else worry about cleaning them.

Shoes are probably the most important consideration. Go for something light with ankle support and avoid heavy boots.

ANDREW: What about food and water?

PAUL: A good field will provide that stuff for you. Of course, you can bring your own. A good field will have adequate food service and drink. You've got to stay hydrated to avoid cramps and overheating.

WHAT KIND OF GAMES ARE PLAYED

ANDREW: What are the different games you play at Skirmish?

PAUL: There are an infinite variety of games you can play. Center Hang is when you put one flag in the middle of the field and both teams try to get it and take it through to the other team's side of the field. It's like scoring a touchdown. That's a pretty popular game.

The top one is certainly Capture the Flag. The second most popular game is probably Center Hang. Number three would be Offense/Defense or Attack and Defend. One team defends their position and the other team just attacks it and they usually have to go in and get the flag or pull it down, or take it out beyond a boundary.

Frankly, the twenty-four hour scenario games are my favorite. They are as interesting as the people who come to play them. We're talking serious paintball hobbyists. In a twenty-four hour scenario game, you've got what seems like unlimited time. So you're not worried about it. And the field of play is huge.

You can go out on a mission and it might take you two hours to try and attain a certain objective. The guy that's directing it, the scenario director, he's just playing with you. He basically sends you out on this mission and then calls up the other coordinators on their radios and he gives them codes that tell them where you're going so that you can be ambushed.

Now, you as a player understand that he's doing this, so you know you have to be careful. Your opponents are going there for the same reason and maybe they've had a half an hour head start on you. Even though you know what's going on, there's still a great deal of suspense.

Sometimes a squad will go out and count how many tents are set up in the enemy's base camp. The players have to try and get that information and bring it back. You earn points if you complete that mission.

Another mission may involve a downed pilot in Sector Five on your map. One of the judges goes out and lays there and makes believe he's the downed pilot. Sometimes they've got to take a stretcher out there, put him on it, and bring him back on it. Very intense stuff.

Whatever the mission, scenario games are highly complex and some people are really into this role playing. Guys come out here with night vision goggles, radios, set up "booby traps" and ambushes. We even have homemade tanks.

We do run three or four scenario games a year, but we only do two twenty-four hour games. The other ones last about eight hours—we call them "mini-scenarios."

ANDREW: How does outdoor paintball differ from indoor paintball?

PAUL: When you play outdoors, the fields are larger and it takes time before "engaging" your opponents. From your position, you can see them coming and you can watch and you can hide and you don't have to move.

Whenever I've played indoors, there's no ambush factors really. You can hide against this wall, but your opponent is still right there . You cannot set an ambush and watch him moving towards you, waiting for the right moment to open fire. Everything happens at a much further distance in the woods, so it's not quite as scary. Indoors can be pretty scary. People are shooting at close range, surprising you from around corners and obstacles.

ANDREW: That's how I experienced it. Indoors does have a frantic intensity. This one place I went to played the Mission Impossible theme before the game. Everybody gets revved up. Add that to the craziness that you're already experiencing. It was wild.

At the very end of the game, I had run out of paint, but I was still able to get these guys out because I was adrenalized. I just shouted, "You guys are out. Drop your guns right now." They didn't even question it. I love that energy rush. What is it about the game of paintball that you enjoy?

PAUL: I play paintball because I like the game itself. My son and I went out and played the other day. He's starting to play very well, so now I can play with him on an equal basis. It was fun for me- not just because he's my son, but because I'm engaged in this competitive experience that is so exciting.

Paintball is a great equalizer. Psychological make- up, not social status, really attracts certain people to the game. I played on a team that included a couple of guys that were engineers, a fellow who was working for AT&T, another who was a mason's helper, one was unemployed, another guy drove a forklift in a factory, yet another was a movie stuntman. All different walks of life come to have fun in the woods.

For me, male camaraderie and bonding are a large part of my enjoyment of the sport. I liken it to the way primitive hunters must have felt at the end of the day:

"We just had a successful hunt. We just killed a woolly mammoth." The sense of having survived is unique.

MISTAKES TO LEARN BY

"DOH! I'M OUT AGAIN!"

Every player who is new to the game makes the same basic mistakes. That's part of learning the game and a necessary step to becoming a skilled paintballer.

Reading about what not to do won't prevent you from making mistakes. Playing paintball is the only way to learn what you can and cannot do. To be more precise, playing paintball well is the inevitable result of learning not to force yourself to do things that simply can't be done.

Moving, shooting, and communicating are critical to successful play. Failure to use these skills consistently and creatively will almost always result in an early elimination.

GETTING FROM HERE TO THERE

You can't get an angle on your target if you don't move. You can't grab a flag if you don't move. Learning to move, especially while someone is shooting at you, is perhaps the hardest paintball skill to master.

You're going to get hit when you play. Even the best tournament player on the face of the planet has been hit thousands of times. Most of those hits occurred while they were moving. That's because they've learned that failing to move will get you eliminated every single time, while moving may offer you some chance of staying in the game.

The purpose of moving is to 'get an angle' on your opponents. If you or one of your teammates can see the side or rear of an opponent, you've gotten the angle, and usually an easy elimination.

SHOOTING

Face it. In order to take someone out of the game, you need to hit them with a paintball. In order to do this, it is necessary to pull the trigger of your gun.

Far too many players get taken out of the game because they fail to realize what a versatile tool their paintball gun can be. Not only can it be used to shoot an opponent, it can also be used to keep an opponent from shooting at you.

Your paintball gun can be used in a wide variety of offensive and defensive ways—from the 'one shot, one kill' of the sniper to the diversionary shooting of air while reloading. After your brain, your gun is your main tool on the field. Use it.

This doesn't mean that you should start the game pulling the trigger. It does mean that before you play it would be a good idea to step over to the target range and get used to the feel and operation of your gun. Shoot a few targets. See how accurate you are; how fast you can shoot, how far you can shoot. And, once you know what you can do with your paintball gun, remember to use it when on the field.

COMMUNICATING

In order to be able to move, to find targets, or maybe even just to find out how to get back to the flag station, you'll need to communicate with the other players on your team.

During your first few games this may be very difficult, especially if you are playing with a group of relative strangers. Nevertheless, talking can help you stay in the game longer, and may even help you get more eliminations.

The purpose of communicating is to coordinate your moves on the field with your teammates. At first it could be something as simple as asking a fellow player if they can see any opponents ahead of them. Or perhaps even if they know where the other team is!

The important thing to remember is that your unknown teammate will be very happy to have someone to talk to, and please remember that answering a teammate is just as important as asking your own questions.

As your knowledge of the game increases, communicating will become a very effective tool which you can use to flank opposing players, determine the number of remaining opponents, coordinate charges or 'pushes' and transmit some very sophisticated information about what is happening on the field.

MORE "LEARNING OPPORTUNITIES"

Once you get past the basics, you'll find yourself running into a whole host of other little lessons and tricks. Learning them will smooth out your game and keep you in the action longer. Although these aren't nearly as important as the three basic skills, learning them will increase your enjoyment of the game.

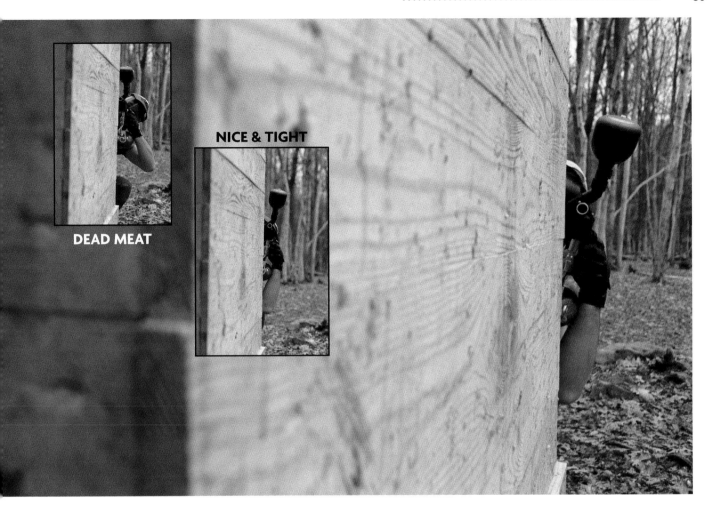

DEAD MEAT

NICE & TIGHT

LOOKING

In order to stay in the game, new players need to avoid tunnel vision, or the tendency to fixate on one object, one opponent or one activity, to the exclusion of all else.

To avoid tunnel vision, practice shifting your attention among all of the activities in the game in a regular order. Look to your left, look ahead of you, look to your right, check your gun's condition, the paint in your loader, check your rear and your front, and then repeat the procedure.

Eventually you will learn to split your attention properly. You will also learn what you need to pay attention to and what you can ignore. Your main goal during your first few games should be to get a pattern down and then remember to use it.

"WHY IS MY GUN SHOOTING SIDEWAYS?"

This is a simple, yet forgettable, skill. Before you go on the field, make sure that your gun is clean, your goggles are clear, "your tank has enough gas," and you're carrying enough paint for the game.

SELF-ELIMINATION

Too many players lose game-time, and valuable experience, by thinking that because they've run out of paint or air, or their gun goes down, the game is over for them.

You can leave the field if you want to, but why would you want to. Stay and concentrate on learning. Find ways to stay in the game longer. Learn to hide. Learn to crawl. Learn to bluff the other team.

Get as much playing time as you can, regardless of the condition of your equipment.

FAILURE TO REDUCE THE TARGET

Making yourself small is an important skill. The smaller you are, the harder you are to see and to eliminate. In order to 'tuck in' effectively, you have to be aware of exactly where your arms, legs, head, gun, and other equipment are at all times.

This is one of those skills that simply takes time to acquire. However, you can speed up the process by paying attention to where you get hit after the game and by looking at how you take and use cover during the game.

Once in cover, pull your elbows into your body. Tuck your legs in. Get your head down. When you come out of cover to view the field, only expose one eye. While you are shooting, keep your gun barrel as close to the edge of your cover as possible.

Don't use a classic shooter's hold on your gun. Twist the arm of your trigger hand down under the gun. Place the arm of your support hand under the gun as well. When done correctly, both of your elbows should be almost touching on or in front of your chest.

TELEGRAPHING YOUR MOVES

When you break cover, and if you really want to play you're going to have to, you don't want to meet up with a paintball just hanging in the air waiting for you.

Take the precaution of varying where, when, and how you break cover. If your head constantly pops up over the top of a bunker, in the exact same place every time, someone on the field is going to target that spot and keep on shooting at it until you are gone.

To avoid telegraphing, never pop out in the same place two times in a row. Change everything: pop out low on the left, high on the right, from close in on your cover to backed away from your cover. There are thousands of ways you can break cover, and you should be trying to use every one of them.

FAILURE TO USE ANGLES

If you are using cover properly, the last player on the field who is a threat to you is the one directly in front of you. Once you're down behind that bunker or tucked in behind a tree, you can't shoot at the players to your front, and they can't hit you.

This basic situation means that you must shoot to the sides, or at an angle from your cover. Forget about the players in front of you and look for the ones off to the left and the right. Look deep across the field if you are towards the center, or look out to the opposite boundary if you are near the tape. You'll be surprised at how many targets you can find.

LACK OF AGGRESSION

Being aggressive does not necessarily mean running straight down the field hollering your head off. And yet, you might be surprised to learn that this actually works once in a while.

Aggression is a finely balanced thing; too much and you end up in an over-exposed position with the inevitable result. Not enough and you end up making your moves too little, too late.

Pushing the envelope will help you learn just how far you can go. Next time you play, try to get to a piece of cover that is just a little closer to your opponents. And then the next, and the next. Try to get behind them. Try running further down the field at the opening of the game. Push it, and then keep on pushing it. If you see an opportunity to win the game, rally your teammates around you, and make it happen.

A MULTI-DIMENSIONAL GAME

Paintball is not just a stand-up game. It's a kneeling game. A crouching game. A lying game. A crawling game. A timing game.

Being in a particular location on the field at the beginning of the game may be very safe. Towards the end of the game, the same spot might be the last place you would want to be.

If you can't move up the field by running, try crawling. If you are lying behind cover and can't make the shot, try it from a sitting position. If you want to move to another position, wait until no one is looking at you.

Use the entire field, all of the time.

—SD

PART 2

GUNS

The Science of Paintball

PAINTBALL 101

Required reading for hard core paintball enthusiasts!

At its inception, paintball borrowed its technology and science from other sources out of sheer necessity. There was no such thing as a 'paintball gun', a paintball designed to be shot at 300 feet per second, paintball specific goggles, or any other piece of specialized equipment, simply because the game did not yet exist. But there was precedent for the development and production of these things, so paintball really hit the ground running.

During paintball's formative years, enterprising individuals and companies developed products using a trial-and-error, cut-and-paste, tinkering-in-the-garage approach. In scientific circles this is known as an 'empirical' method. You come up with an idea, build something based on the idea, identify its flaws and errors by using it, make corrections, add refinements, and continue on to a finished product.

Science, in the form of highly educated and degreed individuals working out complex formulas on blackboards, was not necessary. That work had already been done. The art of creating paintball products and equipment was simple and straightforward. If you could understand how a paintball gun worked, if you could cut PVC tubing with a hacksaw, work a mill or a lathe, or sew a few pieces of material together, you were in business.

Things have changed dramatically over the past decade and, while it is not yet possible to earn a degree in paintball science (something which is not all that far from happening), *a firm grounding in such things as physics, ballistics, pneumatics and hydraulics, chemistry, materials science and related disciplines, will come in very handy when attempting to work with today's paintball technologies.* And paintball players may even find all of this interesting, too!

One of the most interesting aspects of paintball is the wide range of sciences, both hard and soft, that it touches upon. The fact that equipment designers use the laws of physics is no surprise, but the use of the 'soft' science of ergonomics (fitting tools to the human body) might be. The use of ballistics is another obvious match for paintball. Psychology's relationship to paintball, on the other hand, is less intuitive; nevertheless several well-respected psychologists have studied paintball in relation to risk-taking behavior, stress, and a variety of other aspects of human behavior.

Just as scientific disciplines underly the paintball industry's growth, unique technologies that have emerged from paintball have found applications beyond the game. At present, gas regulators developed for paintball guns are used by a major manufacturer of computer chips (for clean room regulation), a tire manufacturer is investigating the use of pressure gauges designed for paintball (for use with self-inflating tires for military vehicles) and aerospace technicians are investigating paintball gun electropneumatic systems as possible maneuver control systems for small spacecraft.

Paintballs in Space!

This is only a brief sampling of how far and wide paintball science has already spread.

For those who do want to delve into the science of paintball, a basic understanding of physical laws, calculus, physics, ballistics, aerodynamics, pneumatics, fluid dynamics and electronics will give you a good start.

HOW PAINTBALL WORKS

Integrating scientific disciplines in the name of paintball fun!

The art of designing a paintball gun (or a gun barrel, goggles, or propellant system), is an interdisciplinary one. You can't work with electronics to the exclusion of ballistics; paintball technology requires an understanding of how these and other scientific disciplines interact.

You also have to appreciate the fact that no one knows everything yet. There are still some very interesting puzzles to be solved.

Newtonian Basics

To understand the science of paintball, you need to start with Isaac Newton. Newton discovered the law of gravity (he's the guy the apple fell on) and several related laws of motion and energy that affect everybody and everything.

Newton's laws can be found in any basic physics text. A summary is provided here.

- Two objects with mass attract each other; the force of attraction is proportional to their mass and depends upon how far apart they are. This is gravity.

- An stationary object will remain stationary unless something acts upon it. Likewise, an object in motion will remain in motion unless something acts on it. These are laws of motion.

- Energy is never lost, although, it may take different forms. Now you know the conservation of energy principle.

How do these laws affect paintball? It should be obvious to anyone that a paintball fired from a gun is not going to keep on going forever. Gravity will eventually pull it to the ground. You need something to get a stationary paintball started; how expanding gases propel a paintball down the barrel of a gun is partially a result of the effects of the laws of motion and conservation of energy.

These are fundamental laws of the natural universe. Only by taking them into account, can you truly understand how and why a paintball gun works the way that it does, or why a paintball behaves as it does after being fired.

Fluid Dynamics

An understanding of fluid dynamics also comes in handy; this is the study of how fluids (in this case, gasses) operate in varying conditions, as well as how to manipulate them. This particular science is one that is still not completely understood, not even by NASA. However, the laws of fluid dynamics tell us certain essential things, such as the fact that the faster a fluid is moving, the lower the pressure will be (and consequently the temperature). These laws explain to some degree what happens when a stream of moving gas interacts with a stationary mass of gas, or why a golf ball with dimples travels farther than one without dimples—or, for that matter, why a paintball with dimples does not travel as far as a paintball without them.

Fluid dynamics can be used to understand and manipulate the way in which the gas propels the paintball, how it flows down the barrel, how to get faster or greater flow of gas through a regulator and related uses.

Ballistics

Ballistics is the science (and art) of the motion of projectiles. How and why do a rock shot from a catapult, a bullet from a gun, a man from a cannon or a paintball from a paintball gun behave the way they do? Ballistics attempts to answer these and other questions. It is also used to predict what might happen to a projectile given a particular set of circumstances (e.g., the shape and density of the projectile, its mass, the speed at which it is fired, the air density, gravity, the angle of the shot).

Some specialized equations, formulas, factors, and laws have been developed specifically for the understanding of ballistics. Among these are:

- The *ballistic coefficient*—a constant relating to the mass and shape of the projectile

- The *form factor*—another number which mathematically represents the shape or surface area of the projectile.

Because (1) the ballistic coefficient is essential to any equation which seeks to explain how a paintball in flight will act, (2) the form factor is critical to establishing a ballistic coefficient, and (3) developing an accurate form factor for the paintball has proven elusive (given its large size, small mass and inconsistencies of its surface features), the ballistic properties of the paintball have yet to be accurately modeled or understood.

So how does all of this relate to paintball?

Is a paintball a solid mass, at least for the purposes of resolving an equation? Does the fluid (paint) inside the shell move? If it moves, does it move enough to affect anything? Does the shell rotate around the fluid when the ball is in flight or does the fluid move?

Fluid dynamics quickly gives way to aerodynamics—the study of the forces acting upon an object which is moving through a gas. The most common application of aerodynamics is the airplane. The forces that aerodynamics studies are the same ones which make an airplane fly. A law of fluid dynamics, Bernoulli's Law, states that the faster a fluid (or gas) moves, the lower its pressure will be. An airplane's wing takes advantage of this *force* by causing the air which travels over the top to go faster than the air passing under the wing: since the pressure above the wing is lower, the air below the wing wants to move in that direction, creating lift and allowing airplanes to fly.

If a paintball were perfectly spherical in shape (which it isn't) the airflow around, over and under the paintball would be the same. Does the addi-

tional friction caused by the seam of the paintball create any lift? Does it cause the paintball to rotate so that it presents the surface area with the least resistance to the air? Would a spinning paintball behave differently from a stationary one? Would the direction of spin affect its flight?

These questions are being asked today by paintball researchers and designers. A huge debate currently centers on what effect (if any) *forward* and *back* spin has and if the 'Magnus Effect' is operating. The Magnus Effect says that a spinning object will have regions of higher and lower pressure around it, which will create lift. Theoretically, if a paintball is backspinning the air moving over the top of the ball is moving faster than the air below the ball, creating lift, while frontspin causes the air below the ball to move faster, which might actually cause the ball to drop towards the ground faster than if it weren't spinning. Musket balls are a pretty good analogy for paintballs (they even have seams from molding); perhaps the mass of the musketball has more influence.

> If you could see the ball as it flew from your barrel, the ball would either be spinning towards you—backspin, or away from you—frontspin.

Might controlling this spin allow paintballs to travel further? Will a ball that is spinning rapidly be more stable than one which isn't? Bullets are spun by their barrels, so that they are spinning around their long axis. This gives them stability in flight. Do the same forces act in the same way on paintballs. Most of the evidence seems to say, "No," because paintballs are not spun anywhere near fast enough to gain any benefit from this effect. Furthermore, testing seems to indicate its spin will probably have negative effects on performance.

PRINCIPLES OF GAS PROPULSION

Chemistry and Paintball

Chemistry should not be overlooked either. Imagine the precision needed to create a gelatin shell that is elastic enough to withstand being accelerated to speeds in excess of 300 feet per second in a few milliseconds, yet also remains brittle enough to break against a relatively soft and yielding surface after it has given up most of its momentum.

However, there are several things which are much better understood than the flight characteristics of paintballs. The 'Gas Laws', for instance, were formulated in the 1700s and remain fairly predictable to this day. Among other things, the gas laws state:

- A gas will expand to equilibrium. In other words, gas in a closed volume will be at the same pressure everywhere in that volume.

- Gas pressure increases proportionally to temperature. This means that pressure in a given volume increases when it is heated and decreases when it is chilled.

- Gas pressure also increases proportionally with a decrease in volume. This means that if you compress gas in a volume to half its original size, the pressure of the gas in the volume will double. If you increase the available volume by doubling it, the pressure will decrease to half of its original pressure.

Taking advantage of the action of gasses according to these laws is what allows a paintball gun to fire a paintball. Gas (carbon dioxide, nitrogen, or air) is compressed into a tank, such that the pressure of the gas inside the tank is many hundreds of times greater than the surrounding air. This gas stored under pressure is an energy source, better known as 'potential' energy.

Potential energy is energy which is waiting to be used. Energy which is being used is referred to as Kinetic energy.

When you open the valve of the tank, the gas contained inside wants to achieve equilibrium with the surrounding volume, which in this case happens to be the Earth's atmosphere; 14.7 pounds per square inch is the generally accepted air pressure at sea level.

When we use compressed gasses in a paintball gun, we are turning potential energy into kinetic energy, or transferring the energy we get from the gas to the paintball. This occurs by briefly opening the valve to the propellant tank, which allows some high pressure gas to escape into the barrel of the gun. This gas enters a volume in the barrel which is behind a loaded paintball. The energy in the expanding gas is sufficient to overcome the balls' inertia (its tendency to remain motionless and its tight fit against the wall of the barrel), which pushes the ball down the barrel. Energy continues to be imparted to the paintball so long as the gas behind the ball, seeking equilibrium, continues to expand.

Understanding the gas laws allows us to 'regulate' (i.e., finely control the duration and volume of a gas flow) gasses, to use gas as both a mechanism for firing the paintball and re-cocking a semi-automatic gun, and for a variety of other applications.

Electronics, and even computer science, have recently been rearing their heads in paintball as well. The latest technological buzzword in the sport is *electropneumatic*. This is simply another name for using electronics in place of mechanical systems in some semi-automatic paintball guns. Initial attempts at marrying the space age to the steam era have proven quite successful. There is no doubt that many more advances will come in this area.

There are many other scientific disciplines pushing the paintball we know and love today toward an even more amazing tomorrow. So many, in fact, that it is impossible to cover them all adequately. It is amazing though how rapidly the science of paintball has progressed from a garage-tinkering hobby to the cutting edge of various scientific endeavors.

—SD

JOHN RICE **ON SAFETY**

Paintball has developed extraordinarily fast over a very short period of time. We've come a long way from the traditional little pistol that used to fire one shot and then required a reload. And everyone used to wear a completely unsafe goggle system. Nowadays you're going up eighteen shots plus, and the goggles are designed to withstand the impact of balls traveling 200 miles per hour in rapid succession. It's a whole new standard of safety for a whole new kind of game. As an industry, we've agreed to hold back on firing rates. My technology could take us up to thirty shots per second, but is the player ready for that? Is the safety equipment ready for that intensity? No matter what, safety needs to set the limit for the implementation of new technologies. On that, we should all agree.

Principles of Worr

Bud Orr

"My dad always said, 'If some guy built it, then you can fix it.'"

In 1953, Bud Orr learned about engine conversions from his father. In 1960, he worked for the U.S. Air Force as a jet fighter mechanic. In 1969, he started working for the Navy overhauling ships (literally, entire ships!). He took up scuba diving, and soon began learning about air flow, gas pressure, and soon began redesigning regulators and compressors. Then, in the mid-1980s, Bud fell in love with paintball. Much of what makes paintball what it is today is directly attributable to innovations pioneered by Bud Orr, founder of Worr Games Products.

ADAM COHEN: So how did you discover paintball?

BUD ORR: Well, one day I came back from vacation and my family wanted to go play paintball. My son wouldn't go unless I went. So, we all went, and basically, I think I rented a PGP at the time and I got shot up pretty bad. And, of course, I loved it.

ADAM: This is back in 1985?

BUD: Yes. And from that point on, we went ahead and went back the next weekend and I thought I could do better because I had thought about the game. The same thing happened, but I figured out why they were shooting at me. Every time I released a CO_2 to change it, they'd run up on me. They were listening carefully and knew when my gun was dead.

So, I went home that week and developed a little device that enabled me to vent CO_2. The following weekend I had more success. I'd vent it, they'd run up, and I'd shoot them. Then, I started modifying guns because I didn't have enough CO_2's. So, I made a manifold so I could actually bolt more CO_2's on it. I was into scuba diving at the time and designed some stuff for the scuba diving industry, so I had access to these little quick release devices. I used them to make it so that you didn't have to expend CO_2 until you pulled a lever.

So, I made a manifold, I bolted two of those on there, and I went out and played all day with two 2.5 ounce CO_2 cylinders.

ADAM: Up to this point, you were doing this primarily because you just loved the game?

BUD: That's right. I just loved it. It was an adrenaline rush. Up to that point... well, I've been a racer all my life. I'm real competitive as far as racing is concerned—drag car racing, sports car racing, boat racing, motorcycles, you name it, I've done it.

The adrenaline rush was just about like it was in racing, only it lasted longer. Just the thrill of the hunt and of being hunted. There's nothing like it, not to this day. Two hours of pure adrenaline rush.

I just started improving the guns. We went to stick feed and then I went over to Sat Cong village and I was a gunsmith there. And in late '86, I was shooting Annihilators. I was actually buying and selling them, and I couldn't really get them from the guy that was making them. He sort of laughed at my ideas for improving the gun. So I went home that week, designed in my head what I wanted to build, and prepared to put it together myself.

Autococker, in all its glory!

I'd been thinking about it for a long time because of all the problems that people had, and different types of play and different atmospheres of play.

ADAM: What were the central problems you wanted to solve?

BUD: I thought it was important to have a feed system on the gun, as well as a constant air system attached directly to the gun. I thought the gun should be closed so that you couldn't get sand in it. Stuff like that. I wanted to build a pretty accurate gun. I didn't like the idea that you couldn't change barrels.

I really didn't like the idea that you had a hose going to the gun from a remote CO_2 system. But, before that, I started to use what they call Ansel bottles; they're for CO_2 cylinders that are made out of steel. I'd mount those on the Sheridan rifles. A guy could play all day on a single bottle of CO_2.

Then I started refilling the cylinders at that point, and I designed an apparatus that we could transverse fill. I don't know that anybody came up with that before I did. Basically, I actually had the first commercial transverse filling.

And from that point on, I was building guns with all kinds of bottles hanging on them. Then I went home one night and I was watching "Miami Vice." Before I watched it, I went out and had a body and frame made in about two hours. After the show, I spend most of the rest of that night building the gun, which became the Sniper.

The next morning I finished it. I went to the Sat Cong village at Battondoon and shot the guy who had laughed at me in the butt. [Laughs]

ADAM: When was this, now?

BUD: That was late 1986.

ADAM: Wow. So in essence your first year of involvement with paintball was just one innovation after another.

BUD: Oh yeah, I never quit. It was just one thing after another for a couple of years. It was neat. The technology was so young; there weren't very many innovative products available. A few people had some really cool stuff, but I wanted it to be more. I pushed the technology a few logical steps further. That's what the Sniper was. It was the first actual paintball gun, the first that was manufactured explicitly for paintball. As opposed to being modified for paintball.

Most of the guys took pellet guns from Sheridan, and they took paint markers... 007's that were made for marking cows... and I think there were a couple of other guns out on the market at that point. Players would take the top barrel off and put a barrel on it and use it for paintball.

I built that first gun. It was the first paintball gun with a direct feed; the first gun out with a closed bolt system that you could field strip. You could actually adjust the velocity without having to tear the gun apart to clip springs.

It was also the first gun to offer a removable barrel. It was one of the leaders in the pumps and stocks, where you had a stock come with it standard.

ADAM: So, within your first year of playing the game, you had started up a company for manufacturing and selling these guns.

BUD: Yeah, I founded Worr Games Products in 1987. It was Thanksgiving of 1987 when I actually incorporated the company, bought my first trailer, and started a business.

Then a year later, in 1988, my Dad was sick. I put in for a leave of absence, so I could spend some time with him. And then he passed away before I even got the time off. That was a bad break. So, I just took the leave the absence.

Now I had worked for the United States government for 22 years, overhauling navy ships in private shipyards. Got kind of tired of that. My wife made pretty good money, so we sat down and figured out that we could live off her paycheck if we needed to. So I just started manufacturing guns in 1988.

I had four months. Four months to make it or break it, you know? And it took off from that point. My daughter, a friend of mine, and my wife and I committed to it.

ADAM: So, you never turned back.

BUD: Our growth was amazing. It was just one innovation after another until 1991. Our company came up with the first speed limit. And we invented the first barrel plug, the first constant air gun, the first screw-in barrel. We had the first ammo box. Actually, we were neck and neck with another company, but when we started making them, we were the only one in the market addressing this need. Russell Maynard, who was the editor of APG at the time, and I made the 45 round ammo box happen.

We spent hours making this ammo box, so it would feed well. We figured it out and it was a huge hit. We sold over 500,000 ammo boxes. From there, we went on to speed ball.

ADAM: How did you come up with the idea for the barrel plug?

BUD: Out of necessity. Guys would come up to the window of our retail store, which we ran for about 5 years. My wife would take a gun from a guy and it would go off and just miss her. She's nice looking, blonde, blue-eyed, and I just didn't want to

see her get hit in the face with a paintball. So we actually came up with a barrel plug.

ADAM: So you invented it to protect your wife?

BUD: [*Laughs*] Yeah, but we knew it would be good for the market.

The original barrel plug was designed so that if you were shooting at 350 feet per second or under with a nine-inch barrel, the ball would not make it to the end of the barrel because of the air pressure. It would just cushion and stop the ball.

And then, in 1988, I was flying back to see a gentleman named Ray Gong. This man was spearheading a drive to legalize paintball in New Jersey. In 1988, if you owned a paintball gun in New Jersey and got caught with it, you'd go to jail. [*EdNote: At the time, paintball was legal in 48 states. Only New Jersey and Massachusetts made it illegal. Currently, paintball is legal in all 50 states.*]

So, Ray Gong, myself, Jessica Sparks, and Russell Maynard went to the Supreme Court in the State of New Jersey, and it took us two sessions to get an old law overturned so it was actually legal to play paintball in New Jersey.

ADAM: Cool.

BUD: Yeah, it was a battle, but we won. Anyway, I was flying back to meet with Ray, and I met some women and children whose fingers broke when they were hit with paintballs. Like I said, there wasn't a chronograph at the time. Very few people used chronos. The way they adjusted a gun's velocity was pretty crude. If the gun shot bark off a pine tree, it was shooting too hot. So, you turned it down and cut the spring until you shot and the bark didn't come off. That was supposed to be a safe level. Of course, people were still getting their fingers broken, which was intolerable.

I went to an orthopedic surgeon and asked him what were the average pressure level and types of pressures that fingers could withstand in terms of the impact of a paintball. He told me that the average would be about 12 pounds of energy.

I calculated the weight of the paintball and all that stuff and came up with 300 feet per second. Not that the gun shot very well at that speed. It was simply a rational safety factor; guns wouldn't break bones at that level. So, I was the one to come up with 300 feet per second, which is the paintball velocity at virtually every outdoor field. They turn it down even more for indoor fields, to about 270 feet per second or lower.

ADAM: From that point forward, the key challenge was developing guns that fire reliably and accurately at that speed.

BUD: You bet it was. And we even accounted for variations that might make the gun fire hotter all on its own. You know, people make mistakes, like setting their gun out in the sun. My gun, if it gets up over 1100 pounds of pressure in a chamber area, would fire at about 320 feet per second. But after 1100 pounds, the gun simply won't fire.

The weight of the hammer and the chamber pressure, the spring pressure, and the speed of the hammer are all designed to prevent the valve chamber from opening until the pressure reaches the level that fires at 300 feet per second.

We didn't have regulators at that point. Around 1990, Tom Kay, inventor of the AutoMag, and I solved that problem. Tom Kay and I are extremely good friends. We actually met in '87 or '88, and I flew back to meet him, and we were going to do some projects together. I had the ammo project and he and I were both independently plugging away on the semiautomatic at the time. When I walked into his facility and sat down and talked to him, I was shocked. Right there on his desk was almost an identical copy of what I was working on.

He and I thought the same way. As a matter fact, the only difference was in the hammer. He used rubber bands to adjust the pressure, as far as pulling the hammer back into place, whereas I used an old beat up spring. That was it.

And, so we made a deal. I'd go off on ammo box, he went off on the semi. Eventually, I actually made my semi and sold it to PMI.

None of us had a lot of money back then. I helped him out and he helped me out. Tom still comes out once a year and we go over old times. There's nothing that we hide from each other. We're fierce competitors on the open market, but we're still really good friends. And I think we'll remain that way the rest of our lives.

ADAM: Tell us about the origins of the Autococker.

BUD: Well, in the early 1990s, semiautomatics were coming and, to be perfectly frank with you, I really didn't like that. Back then, I was trying to push on people what I liked about paintball. I thought the idea of semiautomatics would subtract from the development of paintball as a highly competitive, skills-oriented game.

Paintball was originally designed to highlight individual skills. The point was never what a player had in his hand. It's great that Hayes [Noel] came up with the paintball gun, but even he thought of the gun as a means, not an end. The game was originally about survival, and that's the way I always looked at it. The way the game forces you to improvise is so unique. I've actually thrown paint balls at people and got them out because I was out of CO_2. That's the thrill of it. Not firing tons of paint. Anyone can pull a trigger, but knowing how to do it so that you prevail is the real thrill.

ADAM: Suddenly it looked to you like the technology was going to upstage the skills.

BUD: Yes. And it has. The game I loved is hard to find. Whenever you can sit back and just hose paint at somebody, it takes away from the sport.

So, at that point, I didn't want to be a semi-guy. But Tom had brought out the automatic and, from a business perspective, I was just forced into it.

I had a bunch of ideas. I ran across a gentleman named Jamell, out of Sacramento. We put our ideas together and came up with the Autococker.

Jamell got out of paintball and I continued on with the Autococker. We're talking 1990, because I sponsored the Ironmen team that year. It was one of the first teams I ever sponsored, and they used the Autococker.

Up to two years ago, some of the guys on the Ironmen team still played with pump guns. There are actually point men who play with a pump gun. Some of them hated the semis, couldn't get used to them. And we're talking about amazing point men, guys who are doing a ton of shooting in every game.

The Autococker is actually a pneumatic system that I bolted on to a pump. If you take the pneumatic cocking system off, you have a top of the line pump on the market. The closed bolt system, which is a design of the Autococker, seems to have good range and consistency. Too many gun manufacturers fall short of that, even today.

Then we came up with regulators and regulating systems. That's the first one. Unique Sporting Goods brought out a design for an on-off valve

that goes into cylinders. And it would be a nightmare to make any of those valves in quantity, so we came up with another design, and that's the on-off valve that's on the market right now. That's probably one of the last, really influential projects that we were responsible for.

ADAM: So, how would you describe the state of the Autococker today?

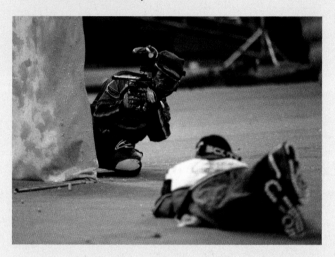

BUD: Great. If you look back at the history of paintball, this gun's back in all the magazines. It came out in the second or third issue of APG, and it's been in there ever since. It's outlasted all other guns on the market. I don't know of any gun right now—with the exception of the PGP—that was on the market 10 years ago.

ADAM: Have there been any modifications to it? Significant modifications in that time?

BUD: Every day. And all of the modifications that we've made on the Autococker will fit on the original gun. So, no matter what year's model you own, even if you bought one of the first ones, ten of which had no serial numbers, all of my modifications to date will fit on that gun.

That's what makes the Autococker like a 1911 Colt .45. It's a standard that ages quite well. And many people make a living off of making accessories for the Autococker. Modifications on it are unlimited. Every time I think I've seen them all, along comes something new.

ADAM: Is there anything you can share with us about the future of Worr Games paintball guns?

BUD: Sure. We're heading into electronics. We're already working on them. We're actually working on retro-fit kits for the Autococker so that it can become an electrically operated pneumatic system. Like everything else in this world, the gun is going to be computer-operated.

ADAM: Like the Angel.

BUD: Yes. If you really look at the Angel, it's basically an open bolt 'cocker, because they use a three-way. As a matter fact, the valve system in the Angel is identical to mine, just scaled down a little bit, which we talked about. I mean, they didn't copy it; what they've done is pretty great. They made it work.

ADAM: Do you still play the game, Bud?

BUD: Oh, yeah!

ADAM: And when you do, what are some of the accessories that you use with your Autococker? Are there any you can't go without at this point?

BUD: Not really. When I go out to play, I usually pull a new Autococker off the shelf, one that's ready to ship.

That's how I know whether my stuff is good enough for the public. If I see somebody who would like what I have, and I know he can't afford it, I usually give it to him when I'm done for the day. I haven't done that lately because most of the people out there that play nowadays can afford to buy my stuff, I guess.

It costs a lot of money to play nowadays, and that's annoying. When I first started, it would cost me $25 bucks a day, because when I started, paintballs were anywhere from 12 to 15 cents a piece, and we were shooting enamel paint.

So, when we went out and got hit with enamel paint, we had to have turpentine with us to get it off our skin. And the safety equipment that we used back then? We wore sunglasses.

ADAM: Anybody lose an eye?

BUD: [*Laughs*] How we didn't blast our eyes out of our heads, I don't know.

ADAM: What do you think about the state of the game?

BUD: The survival part of it is just a great mind trip. I hunted animals for quite a few years, and I was pretty good. I never got skunked in all the years I hunted. I went to areas where they said there were no deer or antelope, and brought out my animal.

So, I classified myself as a pretty good hunter. And I often wondered what it would feel like... you know, I was in the military, so I've been hunted, but that's quite different. The sides were rarely equal, and if you got caught, you might die. Paintball provides an altogether different feeling.

When you're the hunter as well as the one being hunted, and it's not your actual life so much as your pride as a survivor that's on the line, it's just a great experiment. The experience is a test of survival skills and instincts. A bunch of people put themselves in this context where only one can emerge a victor. I haven't been able to duplicate it in any of the things I've ever done in my life. And I've taken my life in my own hands in many ways.

I've jumped out of planes, scuba-dived, participated in every type of extreme sport except bungee jumping. Paintball is just a greater thrill than any of those things.

ADAM: Do you believe that the game today is very different from the game you're describing.

BUD: Today's game can get a little weird. Referees blow a whistle to start the game, and people who don't even see anybody start shooting paint. It's literally impossible that they could hit anybody, but that's irrelevant to them. They are there to shoot.

Right now, there's no adrenaline rush for me unless I play with some of the veterans of the game. They don't shoot unless they have a clear shot and the time is right. These people who just start shooting at anything, who think the ability to shoot, not to hunt, makes them good, they're the ones who've taken over the contemporary game.

ADAM: You ever talk to kids about your way of playing?

BUD: Actually, yes. I was with some kids in New Jersey, and I taught them how to hunt. They took a whole new look at paintball; they felt the adrenaline rush I get from the game. They were turned on by the idea of a guy stepping over them who doesn't even know they're there.

ADAM: Is there any effort currently underway to promote paintball as a survival game?

BUD: I would love to change it back. You know, I love kids, kids are the backbone of our lives. And if I had my druthers, I'd like to take kids out and spend about five or six hours teaching them survival skills in the woods. Then you test those skills by putting them up against another group of kids that are equally trained and go play paintball the way it used to be played.

And if they want to use a full automatic, they would get only 200 rounds. I used to go out with 20 rounds on me, and take out four or five people.

The game was quieter, but no less active. It was more intense.

We used to crawl on our hands and belly over rocks. I'd be crawling... I could crawl right underneath someone... and before they even knew I was there, I got'em all! And I'm a big guy. That's the thrill!

Other times, I'd walk in on a group of people that thought I was on their side, which you accomplish by keeping your armband away from their eyes, so they can't see it. I'd take out 10 of them before getting hosed, but it was worth it.

ADAM: Are there plans to resuscitate this style of play on a widespread basis?

BUD: Yeah. I talked to Hayes Noel about it. Yes, I would say there are plans. Somewhere along the line, when I slow down a little bit from what I'm doing now, I'd like to be involved in that.

There are people that I know who do play this way now. They're renegade players. They take 30 people out in the forest with two cases of paint and play paintball the way it was meant to be played.

ADAM: This is "outlaw" paintball?

BUD: Yeah, 'outlaw,' 'renegade,' it's all the same thing. It's just about a bunch of people who are sick of going to a field where everybody just wants to hose everybody else. Sometimes it gets pretty bad. On some fields, you shoot a guy 15 times in the goggles and he says he's not hit. Some people can't deal with the most basic rule: if you're hit, you're out. Hold up your hand and walk off the field.

I've gone to seminars, talked to people and some of the older groups that used to play paintball, and they would love to see the old game mainstreamed. Some of us set up some games with pump guns that are played on an individual basis. We've offered a $10,000 purse for first, second, and third place.

There's 10 people playing, and you're against all of them. That's the way to play paintball.

ADAM: That's definitely old-school paintball.

BUD: Yup. That puts a whole new aspect on it. We used to play one on one. We used to play "hare and hound" at Easter time. They'd send a 'hare' running, and then release a 'hound' every 15 seconds. They were all against each other, but the goal was to eliminate the hare. So they're hunting someone who can shoot back at them, and they have to look over their shoulders, because every hunter has incentive to take out the other hunters as well. It was awesome. And I think they still do it like that in some places. But those are just scenarios.

We'd take Easter Day, get 30, 40, 50 people out there, and run two or three games, with everyone fending for himself. There's just not a rush like that. It's unreal.

ADAM: You and Hayes Noel are birds of a feather on this view of the game.

BUD: That guy is incredible.

ADAM: Have you played with him?

BUD: Never played with him, but have you ever met him? That guy is just absolutely top of the line. He's just a really neat, fun, individual. I don't know of anybody that could say anything bad about him. He's put me where I am, and I appreciate that. He just started paintball. I'm one of the people that followed in his footsteps when he backed out of it.

ADAM: If he hadn't played that first survival game...

BUD: ...I wouldn't be in business today.

You know, I had often thought about what he thought about, but I didn't know what to use. I was going to use blow guns or darts or slingshots. I always wanted to see if I could survive in the woods, with people chasing me around.

ADAM: Looks like you got your wish.

BUD: Sure did.

ADAM: I really appreciate your sharing your insights with us.

BUD: No problem.

AUTOCOCKER

ANGEL

Red lines indicate the action of the bolt.
Blue lines trace the path of the gases.

GUTS

SHOCKER

AUTOMAG

How the Angel Got Its Name and Everything Else You've Always Wanted to Ask This Man

John Rice graduated college with a degree in metallurgy and spent 12 years at TI research laboratories in Cambridge, England, and another 5 years at GE/GEC joint ventures based in England. He specialized in materi-

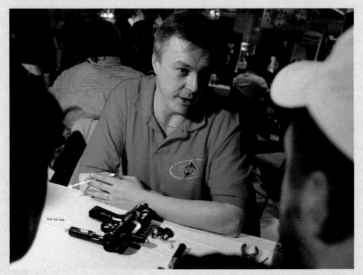

als technology, high vacuum and surface coating technologies for Joint European Toruss at Harwell Atomic Research. He joined WDP in 1994, working in their new product developments division, and signed on full time as Technical Director in 1995. At 35 years-old, John has been married for 13 years and has a 9 year-old child. His first gun was a Bushmaster, his favorite pump gun is the Sterling, and his first semi-automatic was the Automag.

John Rice and his gun, The Angel, are legendary in the paintball industry. One of the most coveted guns around, the Angel is the first electropneumatic gun to arrive on the scene.

BY KRISTEN "LADY ATTITUDE" KLEIST

3-PLAYER: THE BREAKOUT

Stay alive! That's one important rule for a three-player event. True, this is ideal in any tournament, but in three-player one body is 33 per cent of your team. Losing one player is the equivalent to the loss of your arms. It is hard to be aggressive with no arms. In fact, with just one player down, most teams are on defense until they can make the odds equal. A key to keeping all three players in the game is to have game plans that are proactive, with good teamwork. What, then, can your team do to prepare and be proactive? Let's examine the breakout.

The breakout is the beginning few seconds from the start of a game (Game On!) until the players are in their first bunkers. This can be the pivotal point in any game. So, let's start right here. Having a game plan is your first order of business.

The most typical plan of attack in a three-player game is the V formation (see example 1). Named for obvious reasons, this is the most deployed attack. You have one player run center and one player down each tape. Usually the center player gets further downfield than the two tape line players. Of course, all fields are different but you can generally pull this type of formation off.

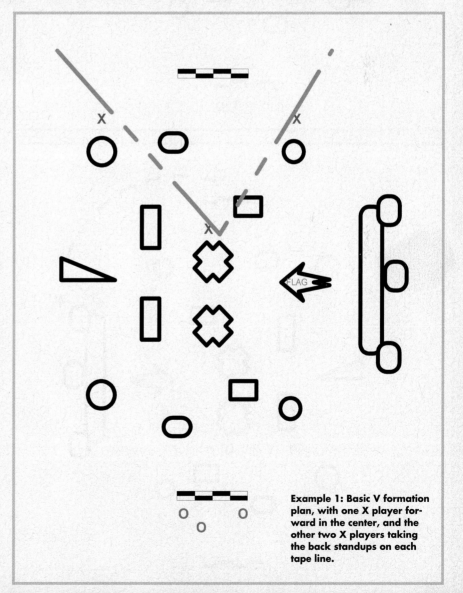

Example 1: Basic V formation plan, with one X player forward in the center, and the other two X players taking the back standups on each tape line.

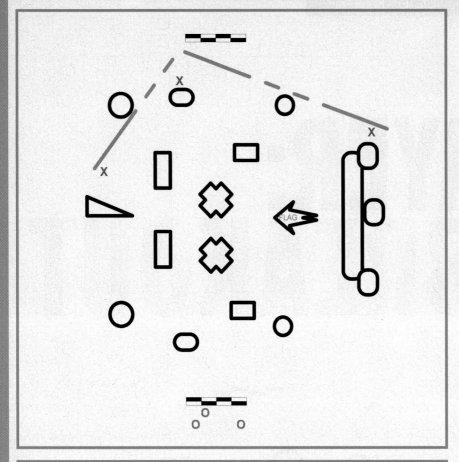

Let's look at this same attack with two front players and one back (see example 2). The second example is still a basic V formation. This formation is generally good because it allows good field coverage. You can control your lanes and lock down the field.

When formulating your breakout plan, consider the fact that you ideally would like to take out as many of their players as you can. If you can take out just one of their players on the break, you can capitalize on their lack of firepower and diminished field coverage.

But again, let's look back at our examples. You will notice that there are only a few "good" bunkers a team might use. If you can predict where a team is likely to go, you can have one, two, or even all three of you shoot that player's lane (shooting a lane is the act of shooting paint into the running path of a player). As you predict your opposition's moves and pick that shooting lane, be aware that this shooting lane also exists for your team. And by choosing a path around it you can hopefully increase your chance of survival.

You now know where you are going, how you're are going to get there, and the actions you will take along the way. The last final breakout issue is what to do once you have gotten to your initial bunker. This is still part of the breakout. If you were successful in eliminating one or two of the opposition, what will you do? What if your teammates were eliminated? Run these scenarios through your head before the start of the game.

Just for examples, let's go through one of them here.

GAME ON! You run to your bunker on the far left tape (snake side). You

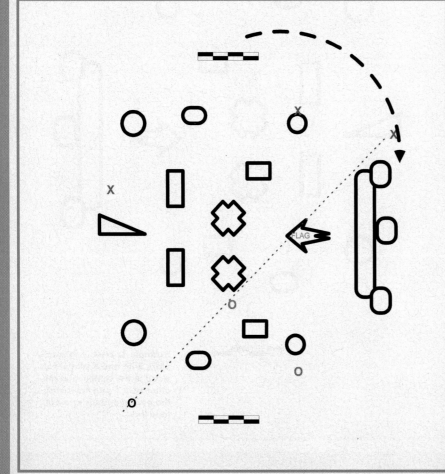

Example 3: Leaving from the top (far flag station), one X player makes it to the head of the long snake bunker, and takes out the O player at the far back crossfield. O got one player into an X bunker not quite at midfield and the other O player pulls in short at the back. One X player takes a lot of ground in making the triangle bunker at midfield, and the other X player is in a back bunker but has good eyes on the flag. O is down one and it is looking real good for the X team.

IN FACT, WITH JUST ONE PLAYER DOWN, MOST TEAMS ARE ON DEFENSE UNTIL THEY CAN MAKE THE ODDS EQUAL. A KEY TO KEEPING ALL THREE PLAYERS IN THE GAME IS TO HAVE GAME PLANS THAT ARE PROACTIVE, WITH GOOD TEAMWORK.

delay a few fractions of a second to lay down a stream of paint and manage to take out the opposition on your right tape. You make your bunker and yell out the code for the elimination you got (Blue One! for example). You hear both your teammates confirm (Blue One! Blue One!). You also hear that there is a player in the X and another in the left can. You know you can move down the snake and your team knows that they can move with you. This is a good breakout (see example 3).

Overall, the best advice I can give a team that is entering a three-player event is to really know your teammates, and have a game plan that you have put some thought into. Take your teammates' skills along with your own, and use them to formulate your strategy. Always start with the breakout and go from there.

Best of luck and may the paint never break in your barrel. ✳

Kristen "Lady Attitude" Kleist writes from southern California. www.oldschoolchallenge.com.

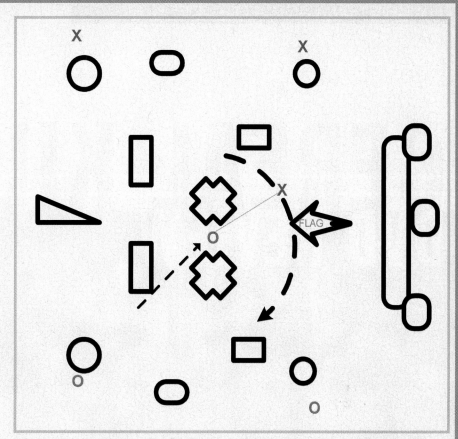

Example 4: X leaves two players back, one on a side, and O does the same. Neither team can protect their forward player all that well. The forward X player made an aggressive move toward the flag to make an elimination even though he had to leave protective cover.

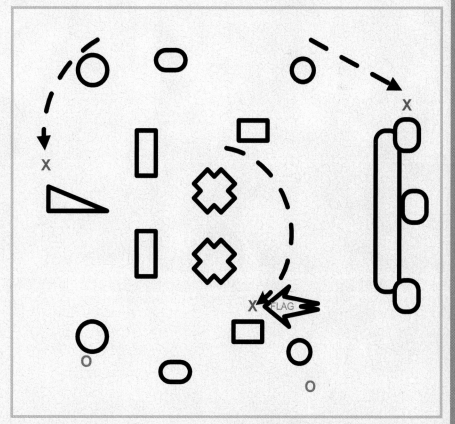

Now it is 3 X against 2 O, and center X can go right on taking real estate while his back men move up.

CEREAL KILLERZ
DVD REVIEW

ANDREW FLACH: Where did the idea for the Angel originate?

JOHN RICE: There are certain stars in paintball, players who are very skilled and fast on the trigger. Joe Public wants to be a star. So, I think, how can I make "Joe" a star? The first question in my mind was "how easy is it for 'Joe' to pull a trigger?"

I thought that if I could make it possible for anyone to pull a trigger real fast, as fast as someone who's super fit, it's going to appeal to that player because achieving something awesome will feel "easy."

Now, if you have something that's mechanical and there's a certain timing sequence to maximize the rate of fire, you have to be quite skilled in coordination to achieve the desired result. That's a disadvantage to some players, whereas it might be an advantage to others. So I wanted a leveler, I wanted everybody to have their 15 minutes of fame. That's where electronics come in.

ANDREW: Did you wake up one morning and say 'Eureka'?

JOHN: No, it wasn't as easy as that. If you could have seen the prototype you'd know what I mean. It was spread over about a 5 foot table—bits of valve over here, some electronics over there. Have you ever heard the term "Heath Robinson?"

ANDREW: Heath Robinson is a term? No, I haven't.

JOHN: "Heath Robinson" is English terminology. He was a famous artist who used to draw crazy machines to solve simple problems. Like America's Rube Goldberg. Our first products were like that.

ANDREW: In other words, it did its thing, but you couldn't fit it into a gun.

JOHN: Exactly. But we were thinking about how we were going to make this work. Some of the technology simply wasn't available at the time. That was a major hurdle. I was quite fortunate that, with my background in the industry, I could apply certain industrial technologies to paintball. My former research and engineering experience exposed me to a wide range of possibilities.

New types of materials and different ways of doing things. I realized early on that what I wanted to achieve with a paintball gun could only be achieved with electronics.

I had to take a lot of what the individual did out of their control. I just wanted them to point the gun and pull the trigger, I didn't want them to have to apply any further skill to that process. Basically, that's what the electronics do.

The Angel was born out of my desire, my frustration, my blood, sweat, and tears. And also out of the faith of people like Gerard Green. He believed that we could come up with a product that would work.

We targeted a niche market; the Angel is aimed squarely at the top pro player. It's made in England, and, as I'm sure you've heard, it's very expensive. That's the first thing people say: "It's expensive. Why should I pay that much money?" The answer is that making things in England is expensive. Our labor costs are very high. Machine costs and raw materials are more expensive. These facts, in conjunction with our commitment to R&D and next generation products, plus the level of customer support we offer, lead to an expensive product, but one with a great deal of value built into it. The consumer is receiving the most technically advanced paintball gun in existence.

Europe nowadays cannot rely on a mass market. I don't know if you're aware of how the European market works, but mass marketing in Europe is dead. We can't compete with Poland or Taiwan. So, we specialize. In Europe, everything's moving towards specialization.

ANDREW: Craftsmanship is a way of adding value.

JOHN: Exactly. So we set up the Angel, developed it, launched it, aimed at a very small niche, low production numbers, at the top end player. Due to it's success, it's actually cascaded down, which has surprised us. We're amazed at how many Angels we've sold. And we're actually seeing young kids buying them. 12-year-olds are hassling their parents to buy them. And yes, we'll build a rapport with the parents, offer them support. But that's amazed us.

Our product was not targeted at them. And you know, when you see a young lad come up to you, 12 years old, and he's holding his Angel up, it does knock you for six a bit. [*Laughs*]

One thing we recognized very quickly was that our product was moving across the pond, and to support customers we had to come to America on a regular basis. Because if you're asking someone to part with a lot of money and they say, "I've got a problem, where do I go?", you better be able to answer them.

ANDREW: So, what year marked the origin of the Angel?

JOHN: The first working prototypes that you could actually hold in your hand and play with appeared in 1995. That's when you could actually say "this gun looks like an Angel."

ANDREW: Who named it?

JOHN: Dave Poxon, our Marketing Director. Have you ever heard of a rock group called Saxon? It's a heavy metal group, early 80s, and he used to be its manager. He was into marketing, and he knew which way the music industry was going. He said "Angel is going to be a big word on the music scene," and he chose it as the name of our gun, too. Sure enough, records come out with "angel" themes and lyrics, and it became this new happening thing. That's his skill.

That's how the Angel name came about. It was called the Angel V6. We chose V6 because it sounds gutsy, earthy. In America they like V6. It was V6 because it's 6 volt, no other reason. Amazingly, we dropped the V6, but people over here still say, "Oh, I've got a V6."

Also, the Angel had another appeal. It's a little mysterious. A little sinister. A little dangerous. You could turn a dark side to it. That's where the Dark Angel was born.

ANDREW: Double entendre.

JOHN: That's it. And it worked very well for us. So that's how the Angel got its name.

Another interesting bit of Angel trivia is the fact that on the packaging, the gun depicted is a left-handed model. The reason it is photographed this way is because I'm left-handed. It wasn't until very late into the design and production of the Angel that we spotted the oversight.

Andrew: So the early production models, the design models...

JOHN: ... are all left handed.

ANDREW: What is it that makes the Angel a unique paintball gun for the player?

JOHN: First of all, the shape works well. It's very sleek, very modern looking. That's come out of European styling more than American styling. In America, space is so free. Everything in the U.S.A. is big. Look at your appliances, look at your cars, look at your houses. You've got space, and you like to fill it. The Americans also like to bolt things on and add things because of this perception that there is no space restriction. In Europe, everything's got to be small. We made everything small deliberately.

People buy instant prestige when they buy an Angel. They're buying something that is European, that is new, that is unique.

Andrew: Tell us about the Angel's technical features.

JOHN: With the Angel, you can have a very short trigger pull. In fact, the first prototype triggers were so soft you could literally blow on them and they would go bang. People shot themselves a good deal. [*Laughs*]

So the trigger is very easy to use, everybody can pick up an Angel and achieve a very high rate of fire. They don't need the skill to do it.

Manufacturer: Warped Sports Type: Dark Angel Description: Customized and modified Angel with double trigger. *Courtesy of Rocky Cagnoni.*

ANDREW: Now, when you pull the trigger you're activating a circuit?

JOHN: You're basically starting a sequence of events.

ANDREW: What is the sequence?

JOHN: The sequence of events is basically as follows. When I pull the trigger, I start an elaborate clock which now needs to drive electro-pneumatic valves and solenoid valves. And what we've actually got is a Japanese valve. We call it a "fourteen way valve."

It's called that because it has fourteen gas galleries. It's a very reliable valve. The Japanese have done an excellent job in miniaturizing it for me. What that then drives is a traditional mechanism, and although there are several unique features that we've patented in that mechanism, it's still using gas to fire a paintball.

Gas comes into the fourteen way valve and it drives a servo. A servo is how to get some movement using less force, like your brake servo on a car. If you didn't have a servo, you'd be pressing on that brake with all your strength to get an effect. The servo translates a mild force into a heavier force.

For example, if I have a very small piston, I could lift a 300 ton weight with my thumb. I'd only move it very slightly, but I could do it, because I could apply force over a very small area, the way a car jack works. It's mechanical advantage. That's what a servo does. A servo actually drives what we call the spool.

The spool changes gas direction, which drives a hammer forward, and that hammer will strike a valve. Just how long that valve is open for is controlled electronically. Controlling it electronically is extraordinarily efficient. This is all happening in sixteen milliseconds. Sixteen thousandths of a second! This eliminates the "chopping of paint."

ANDREW: And chopping paint is?

JOHN: It's where your bolt or your mechanism comes forward, and it literally chops the paintball in half, before it's properly positioned for firing. You can make guns shoot incredibly fast, but you haven't got a hope in hell of shooting paint. Because if a gun's shooting faster than you can feed it paintballs, it turns into an emulsion gun.

ANDREW: You're blasting out broken paintballs.

JOHN: So with the Angel what you can do is actually adjust the timing. Now, because I can control the timing of the firing mechanism through electronics, I can achieve a very high rate of fire. The Angel has the fastest rate of fire of any paintball gun available.

ANDREW: Which is?

JOHN: Currently we've kept it at 13 shots a second, but 18 shots per second capability is built into every Angel. And yes, it will shoot at that rate for those who have discovered it.

ANDREW: Semi-auto or full auto?

JOHN: Either. There's a set of dip switches on a chip inside the gun that changes the mode of firing. You have semi-auto, full auto, three shot burst, and a "zipper burst."

ANDREW: What is a zipper burst?

JOHN: Zipper burst was developed in reaction to what they called the "Turbo Trigger." Essentially, it's an eight round burst. It's purpose was to show the

Wire synchronizes electronic loader with firing rate of the gun.

farcical nature of some of the current definitions of a trigger action. But that's another story altogether.

ANDREW: Would you have specific loader systems that are recommended for use with this or do people widely use whatever they desire?

JOHN: The most popular system is made by Viewloader. It's a motorized system. However, the paintball industry is on the verge of the next big step, which is force feed.

The limiting factor with any of the current loader systems is gravity. Once you take gravity out of it, rate of fire can go sky high. Way above 30, even hundreds of paintballs a second. It's virtually unlimited, in theory.

THE AIR SYSTEM

ANDREW: The Angel is a compressed air gun, right?

JOHN: Correct. Carbon dioxide is a very harsh gas, and the trouble is it's stored in its liquid state. As it turns into gas, its temperature drops. The colder it gets, the less it wants to give off gas. I call CO_2 a "dirty" gas because it's slow to fill up, it freezes, it's not very temperature stable, and it's very abrasive. The ice crystals that form in it are actually physically abrasive to gun parts.

For running a paintball field, CO_2 is attractive. It's cheap, it's simple, because all you're buying are cylinders of CO_2, you don't have to have a high pressure air regulation system.

With the classic 12 ounce cylinder, you can get 2000 shots off under perfect conditions. Such are the thermodynamics of CO_2. That means you fire one shot, you allow the gas pressure and the temperature to recover, and then fire your next shot. Paintball guns aren't used that way, of course. Paintball guns are shooting faster and faster.

ANDREW: So, in other words, the CO_2 has a lag time between shots caused by the nature of the gas.

JOHN: Yes.

ANDREW: Because each shot costs pressure, and it takes time to get back up to pressure.

JOHN: Up to pressure and temperature. So you can take a CO_2 gun and fire it. The number of shots you get out is phenomenal initially, but things go downhill from there.

ANDREW: So compressed air was your vision from the start.

JOHN: Yes. That was the only choice, in my view. I wanted air, nitrogen. I did not want CO_2.

ANDREW: Now, I heard you use a term earlier, low pressure regulator? The LPR. That sounds like a scuba diving term.

JOHN: Because the Angel is pneumatically driven, I need a lower pressure to drive my pneumatics. My servo valve will not survive high pressure, so I needed a lower pressure to do that.

ANDREW: So you need something to stage it down.

JOHN: Correct. The LPR.

THE INFINITY BARREL

ANDREW: What kind of barrel systems do you use? Do you develop your own?

JOHN: We make our own barrels, which we call the Infinity Series. Barrels are such a personal choice. I could sit here and say Infinity barrels are the best barrel in the world and believe it. But in the end, it's very personal.

ANDREW: What are the unique features of the Infinity barrel?

JOHN: It's a step bore. Have you heard of step boring barrels?

ANDREW: No, tell me what that means.

JOHN: Step boring a barrel is an old system in the manufacture of real firearms for many years. Basically it's a barrel with two bores, each with a separate diameter. The smaller bore provides the acceleration and the wider bore provides guidance. The holes in the side provide a silencing effect.

Now, previously everybody's accomplished this step bore manufacturing process in a two part design. Our two bores are achieved with one tool. Traditionally, step boring required people to hone a bore of one diameter in the first tube, and another diameter in a second tube. Then the two tubes would have to be mechanically joined.

We actually achieve two bores with the same equipment. If you look down the barrel, you can actually see the two bores. Hold it at a distance, and you'll see something like a ring. That's where the two bore diameters meet. No seam is visible.

We don't hone. Some people hone barrels out, we don't. We use a technology that was developed in Germany, using special types of tools and special high pressure coolants. It gives us an edge that no one else has. I believed it was the best way to go. I don't have any misalignment problems involved with joining two points together.

THE LED DISPLAY AND THE FUTURE OF ELECTROPNEUMATIC GUNS

ANDREW: I notice there's a LED on the back of the Angel? What information does that give the player?

JOHN: Looks good, doesn't it?

ANDREW: Yeah.

JOHN: A cosmetic thing. Seriously, though, it's a safety feature. Somebody can see it from a distance and know the gun is on and capable of firing. It's a visual indication, too. When you pull the trigger, the LED changes color. The gun makes a bang sound, but it allows you to see that information.

ANDREW: Have you ever thought of putting a counter on the Angel?

JOHN: No comment. But, if you're asking me where paintball's going, I'll tell you where I think it's going. Electronics are here to stay. You're going to be hooking them up to your computers, you're going to have digital displays. You're going to have RS232 ports, infrared links. You're going to have user interfaces, you're going to have head up displays. That's where the sport's going.

ANDREW: High tech all the way.

JOHN: Technology is being applied to everything. People are timid about electronics initially. When we first launched the Angel, people said "Oh, it's going to be unreliable," or, "It's not going to work." There was a lot of negative speech about electronics. Electronics are used in every walk of life. Anything you do counts on electronics. That's a trend that's only going to get bigger. And soon, any competitive paintball gun will be electronic as well.

ANDREW: What's the next step for WDP? How long is this version of the Angel going to be around?

JOHN: No comment. [Smiling]

ANDREW: Why are you smiling?

JOHN: I could tell you, but then I'd have to kill you.

ANDREW: [Laughs]

JOHN: Just wait and see.

F/A THE DAY AWAY

Single-Action. Auto-Trigger. Pump-Action. Double-Action. Semiautomatic. Full-Automatic.

Paintball guns have evolved radically over the past eighteen years, driven by players' fervent desire for ever increasing rates of fire. This has become a source of contention, concern, and debate among members of the paintball community.

Back in 1981 and 1982, when this great game was just getting started, there were really only two gun choices: the side-cocking Nelspot, remembered by its users for the calluses it left on their fingers, and the rear-cocking Sheridan PGP. Both guns had to be recocked between shots using a rather complicated procedure. For the Sheridan, you had to turn the bolt a quarter turn, pull it back until it clicked, tilt the gun back, so the ball could roll into the chamber, tilt the gun forward, push the bolt back in, and then turn it back a quarter turn. For the Nelspot, you had to raise the cocking lever, pull it back, tilt the gun forward, tilt it back, push the lever forward, and then lock it in place.

It's hard to remember the procedures in correct order, let alone retain the mindset necessary to shoot someone two or three times using it! It's no wonder that players were considered to be paint hogs when they carried more than 50 or 60 rounds per game.

Rate of fire was not something that concerned those who played the game in its infancy. Waiting an hour for a single elimination was common. Forcing opponents to surrender was considered the highlight of the game. But then, what more can you hope for when you can only fire about three rounds per minute?

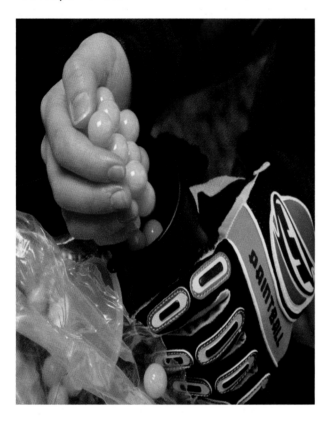

Missed shots, chopped balls, empty firing chambers, and general frustration led many players to concoct their own solutions to the problem, beginning with the pump. A relatively simply modification, the pump did away with the need to pull and turn the bolt. Shortly after, someone came up with the idea of the 'gravity feed,' which meant that it was no longer necessary to roll the ball into the chamber. Both ideas were combined and the paintball technological revolution was underway.

The new ideas caught on quickly; less complicated guns meant more people could play the game. More paint being fired meant that game site owners were making bigger profits. Start-up manu-

facturers now had hundreds of potential products and a new audience waiting for them.

Players quickly became obsessed with how many balls they could fire per second. One player remembered his/her course in basic firearms, shaved a gun sear, and created the auto-trigger, a device that eliminated the need to pull the trigger when firing. Your average player, someone who owned their own gun and played regularly, could now pump out four to five rounds per second. Legendary players were clocked at seven rounds per second!

The quest for a user-friendly gun now turned into a mania for increasing rates of fire. Before anyone could figure out how to make a semi-automatic, at least two companies marketed a double-action, the first pumpless paintball gun.

Unfortunately, the mechanics of a double-action (releasing the sear and resetting the bolt in one pull of the trigger) created a slower rate of fire, relegating these guns to the backwater of paintball technology. However, the first generation of semi-automatics was not long in coming.

First introduced around 1990, most new semi-automatics were technological disasters. They were prone to breakdowns and leaks, in addition to being poorly designed and sensitive to weather conditions. Manufacturers were rushing to supply a new demand.

The first protest against this increasing rate of fire made itself heard around this time. Probably due more to the bad performance of the new guns than to anything else, many tournament teams refused to use semiautomatics and lobbied tournament promoters to ban their use also.

This protest was short-lived with the arrival of the second generation of semiautomatics. They were more reliable, less complicated, and backed by some of the most respected companies in the industry. Seeing a trend in the making, many event producers offered 'open class' competition where any gun was welcome. High profile teams began endorsing them and semiautomatics quickly became the guns of choice.

Gun designers and experienced players had learned something over the intervening years; paintballs are only accurate within a very limited range. Beyond that range, luck plays a huge role. The only way to increase the chance of a hit is through volume and persistence. Once players realized this, the quest for increasing rates of fire swept all other priorities aside. The need for a fully automatic paintball gun had arrived.

The late 1990s ushered in the second introduction of the fully automatic. In 1985, Tippmann Pneumatics introduced the SMG-60 (later converted to the SMG-68), which could fire up to twenty balls with a single pull of the trigger. It met with mixed reviews from the players; some feared it and felt that it represented a safety hazard, particularly at close range, leading it to be banned from many playing fields and events. Other players had nothing but contempt for its users, after having learned that once the clip was emptied the user was vulnerable as the SMG could take well over a minute to reload. The gun itself was a good performer, accurate and very robust, but just a little ahead of its time.

Other companies, like Palmer's Pursuit Shop and Pro-Team Products, introduced novelty full-automatics around the same time. These were extremely expensive show guns that were designed more to demonstrate technical prowess than to create a marketable product.

It took over a decade for development to come full circle with the introduction of the electro-pneumatic paintball marker. Once you start running a gun with a microchip just about anything is possible.

In 1995, Tippmann Pneumatics introduced the F/A, a spring actuated full-automatic. It's only real drawback was that after reloading, the user had to crank the spring by hand. Later that same year, Smart Parts introduced the Shocker, an electro-pneumatic paintball gun with three modes of fire: single shot, three round burst, and full automatic. At the same time, Airgun Designs unveiled the Reactive-Trigger Automag (RT) and WDP from England introduced the Angel, another electropneumatic equipped with multiple modes of fire. Shortly after the introduction of these new guns, the rate of fire debate began and has been going strong ever since.

Smart Parts engineered an after-market upgrade for their gun called the 'Turbo Board,' which was able to anticipate the user's highest firing rate and then reproduce that rate, even if the user was pulling the trigger at a slower rate.

Although not truly fully automatic, the RT was dragged into the same category of 'super-semi' because of its ability to fire at very high rates with little intervention by the user. The Angel was also classed as a 'super-semi' because it had the ability to replicate the performance of the Shocker and RT.

The electropneumatic paintball guns are amazing performers. In fully automatic mode, they can put out a total blanket of fire. Two or more of these guns used by experience players can virtually shut down an entire field of opponents.

Yet while at first enthusiastic about the ability to shoot more paint—half the fun in paintball is pulling the trigger—players have begun to complain about getting hit. Field owners have become concerned over their insurance liability and the loss of customers due to the perception that, "playing at

Getting ready for a game

Guns

that field will get you lit up." Goggle manufacturers are asked if their lenses and frames can withstand, "multiple impacts in a short period of time." Paintball technology has, in a way, become a victim of its own success. The gun manufacturers give the players exactly what they are looking for, but maybe not exactly what is needed for the game to thrive.

Is it safe to subject players to a situation in which they can be hit by up to sixteen rounds per second? Does paintball need to limit its technological growth? Is there such a thing as a reasonable limit for high rates of fire?

Some members of the paintball community advocate a self-imposed rate of fire limit of thirteen and half rounds per second (the current high without electronic assistance). Some also recommend such artificial fixes as a three round limit, which means that players must stop and check on their opponents' condition after firing three rounds. Others are making suggestions for new rules such as an engagement range limit, the separation of players into classes based on their guns, or limiting the amount of paint that an individual can carry.

These solutions are impractical, so it is doubtful that any of them will find widespread acceptance. Players will continually seek to enhance their technological edge. The bottom line is that if they can't do it on the commercial paintball fields, they'll do it on private fields. Players, regardless of their stripe or 'the truth', love to boast that their rate of fire is better and faster than everyone else's. Silly? Yes. A reality not likely to change anytime soon? You bet.

A three round shot limit is completely impractical; new players can barely remember how to pull the trigger, let alone stop themselves after three counts to inquire about the status of the person who is shooting paint at them. All it takes is one player to decide that he/she will fire four shots before checking. Furthermore, there is absolutely no way that a referee can keep track of how many rounds different players have fired at any given time.

Any rule that does not take into account the natural way that players participate is bound to fail. Players do not carry signs saying, "I surrender," which automatically deploy whenever an opponent gets within a certain distance. New players, who are the most likely to order the guns with the highest firing rate, and then complain strenuously about getting hit too much, resort to instinctive responses during the game (e.g., holding the trigger down and firing as fast as they can at anything and everything that moves, or just hiding when they get hit and getting bunkered for their choice). Such responses do not follow rules.

Fields can try to organize games based on technology, but the reality is that few fields ever have enough players in each category or class to make this economically viable. You can't ask paying customers to play with two or three other people based on the type of gun they purchased. After a few days without much competition, they'll find somewhere else to go.

As time progresses, the industry will come to realize the truth about the recreational sport's business: paintball companies are firmly in the business of giving the customer what they want. It is a field's business to provide a fun and safe experience, without the customer having to be confused by artificial rules and restrictions whose use and enforcement are dependent upon them. If pain and multiple hits are customer concerns, products which reduce the impact should be introduced, or a lower velocity limit should be imposed.

The irony of this situation is that lots of paint being fired translates into industry success. Because of that incentive, the rate of fire will be difficult to limit. If it's possible to create a paintball gun that can shoot one thousand rounds per second, someone is going to build it, someone is going to buy it, and someone is going to get shot by it. The demand underlying this trend pretty much obliterates all other considerations, unless safety issues are not properly addressed.

The only real question concerns how the industry is going to respond responsibly and effectively to emerging technologies. Will the new super guns be embraced by commercial fields, where their use can be controlled and supervised, or will they thrive in the riskier, uncontrollable private field arena?

No matter how the industry responds, paintball players need to consider that the game is really not about the paintball gun. Yes, obviously, the gun is a key tool, and there's nothing wrong with wanting the latest and greatest semiautomatic. But using any paintball gun prudently is a responsibility that ultimately falls to the players of this game. If you love the game, hopefully you'll take that responsibility seriously and insist that your fellow players do so as well.

—SD

EDITOR'S NOTE: As of August 8th, 1999, several of the major gun manufacturers agreed to establish a voluntary moratorium on the manufacture of full-automatic paintball guns, and further agreed to limit the upper rate of fire of all semiautomatic paintball guns to a maximum of 13 rounds per second.

ABSOLUTELY SHOCKING

Left: Adam Gardner, Right: Bill Gardner

GETTING TO KNOW THE SHOCKER

ANDREW FLACH: What's the story about the Shocker?

ADAM GARDNER: Many of our ideas come out of the fact that we play at the highest level all the time and we're constantly looking for the edge. The edge in racing can be quite small, but at the highest levels, a small competitive advantage makes the difference.

I'm head of the product development team, and what we are always looking for are ways to improve the gun so that my game is improved. If my game can be improved, then everybody else's game can be improved.

In building the Shocker, we've integrated the best

concepts: minimum ball breakage, long range accuracy, aesthetics. These are the things serious paintball players want. Add to that, it's the first electropneumatic paintball gun. Other people will argue that, but the bottom-line is, we have the patent on it.

ANDREW: Can you explain what that term means? Electropneumatic.

ADAM G: Guns all involve timing. Timing means that the bolts have to operate in such a way that a ball is dropped, a bolt moves forward, and a gun fires. Pretty simple process that really doesn't change from gun to gun, except in terms of performance.

We brought in electronics because they are precise. Mechanical timing can't be held to the same standards in terms of timing. We combine two solenoid valves together with digital electronics. Solenoid valves are electrically fired valves. The result is extremely good control over the timing of the way the gun fires. This adds tremendous performance consistency and the possibility of new features.

On the mechanical side, we wanted the lowest pressure, longest range, most accurate gun we could find. And with low pressure comes minimal ball breakage, because there's not as much energy exerted against each ball.

Then there's accuracy. The gun is unique in that there's no anti-doubler. Most guns have anti-doubler devices—these are devices balls settle into and rock against. Without an anti-doubler, what happens is, if you hold the bolt open in the back, two balls can roll in. The anti-doubler prevents the second ball from rolling in. But under rapid fire, you still have to push the ball past it. Not on the first shot, but on the following shots.

The Shocker uses only timing to hold the ball. We never push it past anything. So, there's no little ball bearing, or spring. Nothing is pushing sideways on the ball as it's firing.

Beyond the super low pressure and everything else, we're also not interfering with the ball shot to shot. The accuracy level we've been able to achieve with this gun is beyond anything we've ever seen.

Again, the reason for all of this is that I want to go out and win my paintball games at the highest levels of competition. I'm not saying, we're not here to make money because we are, of course. But I think that we're in this business because we love the game, and that ensures that we'll pro-mote new technologies that make a difference in game play, not merely in profit margins.

ANDREW: Was there one concept you started with when developing the Shocker?

BILL GARDNER: Low pressure. I determined early on that low pressure was absolutely necessary. Low pressure was the primary concept. And then, electropneumatics. The concept was to combine low pressure and electropneumatics.

As I saw it, that was the way to make better guns. Bringing those concepts together opens up more opportunities for developments in paintball gun technology. More components can be used at low pressure than at high pressure. Things don't wear out at lower pressure. Your gun will last longer, and parts will last longer, too.

ANDREW: How long did it take to develop this idea?

BILL: Two years, at least, and lots of money, effort, and designs that weren't right. These designs look simple only after they're done right.

ANDREW: What are the Shocker's features?

BILL: It likes to shoot consistently and it doesn't break paint. It's got three fire modes: three-shot burst, single shot, and fully automatic. It's one of the only guns you can fire consistently fully automatic without breaking paint.

There's also another very controversial feature that it has, which is called a Turbo Board.

ANDREW: What's a Turbo Board and what does it do?

BILL: The average player can only pull their finger at a specific speed. And everyone wants to shoot fast. You've got a lot of people who are dexterous and can shoot very fast. So we developed a technology called Turbo. It's a trigger enhancement. You still have to move the trigger full speed, and you still have to fire, but it allows you to achieve better consistency than you could without it. It's not so much fire rate, but consistency.

And when the Shocker first came out, the fire rate was 11.2 shots per second, which is fast. Anyone could pull the trigger and fire at that rate. It's not a fully automatic gun, it's a semiautomatic gun.

ANDREW: Where does that fall into the rules?

BILL: For a year, we've been fighting with the various rule-makers to determine what's legal and what isn't. And what they've come down to now is they say, "You can use your Turbo Boards if you want to, but we're going to limit your fire rate to 9 shots per second."

ADAM G: So that's fine with us. That's what I use anyway. And yet, there are other guns that use very light touching methods that can shoot 13 shots a second. So, it becomes a matter of semantics. In other words, if I'm shooting 11.2 shots a second with turbo, and you're shooting 13 with a light trigger, what's the difference?

We can do things that make it a really unique gun. What we've done with this technology is make the first three shots normal fire, so you can aim them. After the third pull, you kick in the enhanced mode and you can sustain a faster rate of fire.

ANDREW; In terms of the electronic circuitry, one of the things that came up when we spoke to the guys out at Skirmish was that the older guns are easy to maintain. With all the new circuitry in here, is the Shocker something that you can foresee a recreational player having?

BILL: 85%–95% of our sales are recreational. We had mothers phoning up here for that gun, and we sold out and sent them to one of 30 dealers that we hoped had guns in stock. These are strictly recreational players, 13–16 year-old kids.

ADAM G: People want exhilaration. Especially the new generation. Kids love fast firing guns. They love things that fire fast and move fast and shoot fast.

ANDREW: I'm thinking more about just the sophistication of the technology. In other words, like circuit boards.

ADAM G: See, electronics scare people. People who don't understand electronics assume difficulties and problems come with electronics. The bottom line with electronics is that they're dependable.

I'm not going to say to you that this is as dependable as a pump gun, because I'm sure it's not. It's much more complex than that. We're moving the bolt 11.2 times a second. We have a lot of things going on. In the end, we're a service oriented company.

If you have problems with your gun, we aim to get it back to you within a week. Sometimes we can't meet that, but we usually do. We train our dealers. Everybody can come in and take our training session. And the sport has professionals, like golf pros, who run shops all over this country.

Then there are user-support groups. Go to the Shocker web page and you'll get a feel for the community of users surrounding our product. The site just evolved on its own. It's got pictures of every way to fix the Shocker, constant discussion about the way it works, full blown color pictures.

ANDREW: I'm very impressed with the gun. Having just seen and test fired it, I'm thinking this is pretty cool. Seven hundred bucks is not small change, but I'm tempted.

BILL: There's something you've got to understand here. Unlike any other gun out there on the market, you get a top of the range barrel with it.

Plus, you get one of the best regulator systems with the gun, and the gun does not rely on anything else for velocity.

I think what you're getting at is, why would the average recreational player pay $600–$700 for a gun?

ANDREW: No, that's easy to see. People get caught up in the things they love, and you're catering to their desire to own some of the finest equipment available for their hobby. I mean, the Shocker is fun times 20.

BILL: You figured that out in five minutes?

ANDREW: My only question is, if I drop it or it gets dirty or muddy, can it stand the abuse? Will

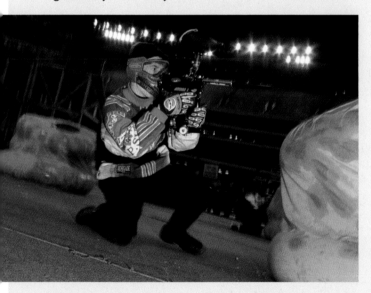

these cutting edge, finely tuned components stand up to intense, real world use.

ADAM G: We played last year with these guns in Vegas. Vegas is the worst scenario—desert conditions, desert winds.

We're usually sick for two weeks afterwards because you can't talk from the dust getting in you. But these guns can handle it. The guns have a special coating so you can almost submerge them. We don't recommend that. The point is, they can take the punishment.

ANDREW: Out at Skirmish, there are places where you can easily drop this into a creek.

ADAM G: It's a good question in general for players. There's certainly different levels of maintenance. The bottom line is any of your top guns require higher levels of care than your other guns do.

And you have two types of people. You've got the people who are willing to do it, and you've got the people who aren't. The people who aren't, they send it somewhere and incur the expense of having someone else deal with it.

The people who are willing to maintain their guns, they do the cleaning themselves. Frankly, it's not hard. People who would never imagine themselves working on a paintball gun manage to do it pretty well. But, no matter who you are, we recommend buying the gun from people who support their product.

You'll avoid frustration if you have a place staffed by knowledgeable people who can help you out.

All guns need a certain level of service, and the electropneumatic guns are no worse than anything else. But they are newer, and that means not as many people know how to work on them right now.

Within two years, probably every good field and dealer in the country will understand how to work on the Shocker. Some of the older guns have been around for so long that we all know how to work on them here, because we worked on them for years.

ANDREW: So if I spend this much money on such a sophisticated piece of equipment like the Shocker, can I really play hard with it?

ADAM G: The answer is yes.

ANDREW: Is there anything else you wanted to add about the Shocker in terms of unique features, concepts, a funny story? Anything?

ADAM G: Well, the only thing I want to add is what you just said a few minutes ago. This always happens with the shocker—the fun factor. You grab that gun and shoot it... and then you keep shooting. It's hitting the same target in the same spot, and that experience is ultimate. The gun is easy for us to sell. "Here, just shoot it."

Anytime you do something well, whether you play football or play piano well, whatever it is that you excel at, there's going to be a group that loves you and a group that hates you.

We're the people who do things well. As you go around the country, you're going to find a whole group that hates us. We go out and beat the heck out of a lot of the top teams in the world and they're all connected to the dealers and the distributors and the stores. They definitely don't like us.

We're beating them in paintball, we're beating them in the market, we're beating them everywhere. So, you'll have a very mixed reaction. But what I can tell you is that if you put that gun in the hands of anyone who can afford it, and they get an opportunity to use it, they're going to have more fun in that day of play than they ever had before.

In our opinion, they're going to have more fun because we have built the Shocker around the idea of consistent velocity and consistent controls. It's fun and safe in one package.

ANDREW: Do you find people shoot the Shocker with a remote air system more than an on-gun system?

ADAM G: All of the pros used to use remote. And then staying in bunkers and everything like that became more important. Tightness became more important. The ability to shift hands with the gun and speed and things like that became more important.

So, all the pros stopped shooting remote, and when that happened, so did everyone else. It's a funneling effect that influences everybody in the industry. Kids start saying, "Well, you know, that guy on team X doesn't use remote. Look how he bunkered that guy."

So, what you'll see is that you'll have this very influential group of professional players, and they lead the sport in one direction. And then you'll have all your manufacturers down here, and they just look at them as expensive people that they have to pay to use the products. Of course, they want everything for free. And that's all true.

Again, what's unique in our case is that we're in both places at the same time. We know that what we need is something people will want, and we take that pretty seriously.

What was the original question? I'm sorry.

ANDREW: It was a good answer.

Shocker Cleaning & Basic Maintenance

This section is provided to show one player's cleaning procedure for an electropneumatic gun, following a day of recreational play at an outdoor field. Please consult the instruction manual that the manufacturer provides for guidelines specific to your gun.

After a day of play at the field, a rainy day at that, Sarah Stevenson shows us how she cleans her Shocker. Keep in mind—this is an unrehearsed cleaning session. Anything can happen!

SUPPLIES NEEDED:
Cloth towel; rubbing alcohol; squeegee; Phillips screwdriver; Allen wrenches; awl; dental pick; cotton swabs; lubricant (Dow 33 silicone grease); paper towels; rags.

Never use oil or Teflon tape!

1. Take the hopper off and set it aside. Remove the powerfeed plug from the loader elbow and set it aside. Remove the 60 cubic inch tank by unscrewing it from the regulator.
The tank valve can be run under warm water to remove paint and dirt.

2. Remove the barrel by unscrewing it.

3. Turn the gun over, get a good grip on it, and remove the air hose. It is held in place with a pressure fitting and is removed by pushing in on the hose while holding on to the fitting. It should pop right out. This hose supplies the air from the MaxFlow fitting to the gun.

4. Use an Allen wrench to remove the Max-Flow cradle, which is held in place with two Allen bolts. Use a little elbow grease if needed.

5. You will notice there are two suction connections with o-rings.

6. Remove the Max-Flow regulator.

7. Now we begin removing the bolt assembly. In a counterclockwise motion, twist the knob on the back of the gun that retains the bolt cylinder.

8. Remove the bolt assembly by pulling it out. This is the bolt that pushes the ball out of the gun. Lay it aside for later cleaning.

9. Use a chamois squeegee to clean the barrel housing.

10. Use alcohol impregnated cotton swabs to thoroughly clean the barrel housing area. Any dirt or debris left behind can cause the gun to malfunction.

11. Clean the feeder tube assembly with your chamois squeegee.

12. Clean the Powerfeed plug by wiping it down with a rag.

13. Clean the barrel with the squeegee.

14. Here's a very real reminder about why you should not work on your gun with the air supply attached. During this cleaning, we found two balls still in the system!

15. Now let's turn our attention to the regulator. First, wipe off the excess dirt.

16. Follow that with a more detailed cleaning using cotton swabs and alcohol. Note that dirt is everywhere, including threads, openings, and crevices. Care should be taken to remove it all.

17. Carefully remove grains of dirt from the suction assembly by using an awl. Also use the awl to remove dirt from the cradle.

18. Using the Phillips screwdriver, remove the grip. Since this is an early model, we need to access the battery compartment to disconnect the batteries. Newer Shocker models feature an on/off switch.

19. Disconnect the batteries by pulling apart the connection. Do not grip the wires when disconnecting the battery. Only grip the connectors!

20. Replace the battery in the housing, leaving the wires disconnected. (Remember to reconnect the battery next time you want to play!)

21. Remove the air assist elbow. The air assist applies gentle air pressure to keep the paintballs moving down the elbow into the breech.

22. Wipe down the gun from top to bottom,

23. Clean the air assist elbow with your squeegee.

24. With cotton swabs and alcohol, clean the threads and seating area where the air tank attaches to the Max-Flow system.

25. Wipe down the bolt. Remove all old lube and dirt.

26. Use a dental pick to clean the holes in the bolt. Get the old lube out before applying new lubricant.

27. The opening at the end of the bolt can get jammed full of paint and broken balls every time you push your squeegee down the barrel to clear a jam. Make sure you clean it out well.

28. Apply a small amount of Dow Corning 33 Silicone Grease to your finger tips and then spread the lubricant throughout the bolt assembly. Movement of the bolt should be free and smooth.

ALMOST THERE...

29. Take care to lubricate all areas where parts of the gun come together—especially o-rings and metal-to-metal contact areas. The lubrication will help make the Shocker easier to disassemble next time.

30. The disassembled Shocker with maintenance and cleaning equipment.

—SS

Choosing a Barrel

In order to avoid any confusion when it comes to purchasing a barrel for your gun, we'll get this said right up front:

Buying a barrel is a highly personal, non-scientific activity that you could spend a lifetime mastering.

By this we mean that there is no tried-and-true method for purchasing the 'perfect barrel.' Most paintball players are absolutely convinced that they already have the perfect barrel—namely, the one screwed into their gun when they buy it. If this were true, if each gun came packaged with the perfect barrel, then there would be no need to purchase an aftermarket one. That brings us to the critical question:

Is there a need to purchase an aftermarket barrel? The answer is yes... and no.

Most guns are purchased with a 'stock' barrel. Originally, the 'stock' barrel was all you could get. Most gun manufacturers made and continue to make fine barrels. However, once removable barrels arrived on the scene, which not only promised superior performance but were definitely far easier to clean, somebody was bound to make an aftermarket barrel that actually was 'better.' Major growth of demand for aftermarket barrels soon followed. As a result, most gun manufacturers have stopped making expensive stock barrels and instead provide a basic one for you to use until you can go out and purchase a 'perfect' one. Today, there are at least twenty (if not 40) different barrel brands.

But it doesn't stop there. Each brand of barrel has to have a different model for each different gun on the market. Add to this the fact that there is no industry standard when it comes to the manner in which a barrel is attached to a gun, and you have a huge number of barrels available across a wide range of prices. Most are threaded (like a screw), but there are several models which use a 'twist-lock', and several which use a pressure fit.

Barrel Length Counts

Most everyone agrees that you need at least 8 inches of barrel to make the most effective use of the gas and to give the ball some accuracy over decent ranges. After that there is virtually no agreement. Barrels come in lengths ranging from 8 to 18 inches. The length of a barrel also affects the issues of gas volume and pressure: guns with very low operating pressures will require a longer barrel.

Barrels are also made out of several different materials. Aluminum, brass and stainless steel are the most common, but you also can find carbon-fiber barrels and mixed-material barrels. Different inner-coatings also have been added (teflon, for instance), as have various forms of rifling. Barrels can come with 'muzzle breaks,' spiral rifling, gas porting, and a whole museum's worth of external patterns, sculpturing, and colors.

The barrel's inner diameter also varies. This might not seem to make sense. After all, a paintball is .68 caliber, right? Well, in fact, that's not entirely true. The *ideal* paintball is perfectly round and exactly .68 inches in diameter, no matter where you measure it. A real paintball is anywhere from .65 to .70 inches in diameter, sometimes oblong in shape, with a seam around it. In other words, it's far from a true sphere. Paintballs are commonly referred to as small-bore (.65 to .67) and

big bore (.68 to .70). Because of this, the inner diameter (or ID) of a barrel can vary from as small as .685 to .692. Admittedly, this is a relatively small difference—but when it comes to performance, it's a critical one.

Every paintball barrel manufacturer out there will say that the most important factor in choosing a good barrel is picking the right paint. After that, they'll say that the 'fit' between your barrel and the paint you are shooting is the next most important thing. They're right.

Of course, there are the ambient or 'local' conditions, things such as temperature, humidity and air pressure, that also affect performance: the barrel you use today with such amazing results may

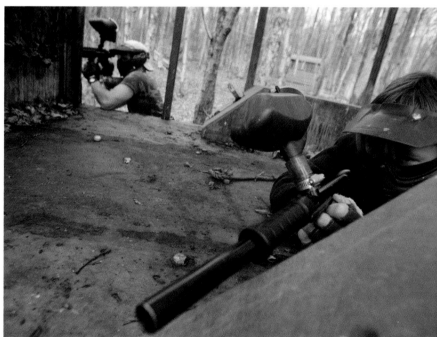

belong in the bottom of your gear bag tomorrow, even if you are shooting the same gun, with the same paint at the same velocities as the previous day. The differences in performance may be due entirely to the changing play conditions, and they aren't necessarily your barrel's fault.

No one who plays paintball for any length of time always shoots exactly the same paint each and every game. Paint varies from brand to brand

(and from batch to batch). In order to counter this, most serious rec players have adopted the strategy of collecting a variety of barrels, in different lengths, with different IDs, made out of different materials, so that no matter what paint they are shooting, they will always have a barrel that makes a good match.

The general rules of thumb when buying a barrel relate to the ID, the length, the material it is made from, the presence or absence of rifling, porting and breaking, and the barrel's aesthetics.

Fortunately, you can be a little more discriminating (although you will probably end up with your own barrel bag eventually). When it comes to ID, most companies tend to make one to three different 'bores' (the tube inside the barrel is the bore). These bores generally correspond to a 'tight', a 'medium,' and a 'loose' fit. Tight bores are for small bore paint, loose bores are for big-bore paints and medium bores are for everything in between. Brands that only offer one or two bore sizes usually make a tight and a medium, since most paint tends to be small these days.

Try and settle on a particular brand of paint to use most of the time. This might be a brand offered by a local retailer, the brand of paint sold at your local field, or the paint recommended by local experts. Find out what 'size' this paint is (call the supplier if you have to). Your general-purpose barrel should have an ID which matches this brand of paint, since this is what you will be shooting most frequently.

Material really has only one determining factor, and that is its weight. The lightest barrels are generally 'composites' (carbon fiber) and aluminum, although some companies are doing amazing things with stainless steel. Brass is next in weight, followed by most stainless steel barrels. (Don't forget that the length of a barrel also contributes to its weight.) The smoothness of a barrel's bore is an important factor. The smoother it is, the less friction will be experienced by the ball as it travels through the barrel. All of the materials mentioned have roughly the same smoothness factor, so this is not a huge consideration. Sometimes smoother surfaces actually create greater drag. This is exactly why choosing a barrel is an art, rather than a science.

When it comes to porting, breaking and rifling, it's probably anybody's guess as to which implementation creates the best range or accuracy. Rifling is a technique borrowed from firearms technology. A helix of ridges and grooves is cut down the length of the inner surface of the barrel. These are used to grab the soft body of a bullet and cause it to spin. This gives the bullet greater stability in flight. Unfortunately, paintballs are not solid, aerodynamically shaped objects, and conventional rifling can't be used because it would rip and shatter the paintball. Nevertheless, barrel makers have come up with at least three paintball versions of the same thing, none of which work by 'spinning' the ball, but which can aid it in other ways. Polygonal Progressive Rifling (Armson) barrels have twenty-eight blunt-edged lands (the ridges of rifling) which curve down the inner surface of the barrel. These provide a greater surface area for the ball to seal against and help stabilize the ball as it leaves the barrel. Spiral Porting (Smart Parts) uses a patented external version of rifling. Two lines of 'ports' (holes drilled through the body of the barrel) are created down the length of the barrel in a spiral. This relieves pressure behind and in front of the ball and allows the ball to make a smooth transition to the air. Straight Rifling (J&J) uses four straight lands cut down the length of the bore to provide greater stability and better control of the ball as it moves through the barrel.

Most barrels, however, are 'smoothbore' barrels; they have no rifling of any kind. By the way, players have had tremendous success with all bore styles.

Guns

Muzzle Breaks are another adaptation from 'real guns.' They are typically used to suppress noise, reduce pressure at the muzzle (when the gun is fired), and suppress the 'flash' coming from a barrel. In paintball guns, it is generally believed that a muzzle break will aid the ball when it makes the transition from the barrel to still air. Muzzle breaks can be found on a wide variety of barrels.

Porting is generally used for its sound-suppressing qualities. Small holes (of varying number and size) are drilled down the length, or a portion of the length, of a barrel. These are not cut in a spiral (like the external rifling), but in straight lines. Sometimes slots are used instead of round holes.

And now we come to length. Determining the ideal length for a barrel is the biggest source of controversy when it comes to barrels. Some people swear by long barrels, some by short ones. Some are convinced that thirteen inches is what you need, while others think that sixteen inches is the mandatory minimum. The truth is that only a gun's manufacturer (or someone who works closely with a particular model) knows what the 'best' barrel length for that gun is. In general, you need the length of a barrel for two things.

- First, it needs to be long enough so that an optimal amount of gas will get the ball up to the desired velocity.

- Second, it should be long enough to give the ball some accuracy in its flight. However, if a barrel is too long, it will slow the ball back down again.

Unfortunately, these factors vary from gun to gun. The most efficient barrel, in terms of gas use, is one that is exactly long enough, and no longer. This may not be the same length as is required for the desired degree of accuracy, so choosing a length becomes the art of balancing these two goals within a range that is good for that particular gun.

Usually, an inch or two in either direction won't make a tremendous difference: if your gun 'needs' a twelve inch barrel, you'll still get good performance out of a ten inch barrel or a fourteen inch one.

The basic rule of thumb regarding length seems to be that if you are planning on playing up-front and personal (close to the other team), you want a shorter barrel so that you can 'tuck in'; and it will give you the kind of accuracy you are looking for with short to medium ranges. If you are planning on longballing (shooting long distance), you'll want a longer barrel to increase your sight radius and achieve greater accuracy. Remember to keep in mind that these are relative lengths, based on the kind of gun you are shooting.

A barrel's look is nearly as important as everything that has gone before. If your barrel looks cool, then you look cool, and it hardly matters whether you're hitting anything or not! WOOO-HOOO! (Just kidding.)

Most barrel manufacturers have developed distinctive styles for the outer surface of their barrels. Grooves, cuts, slashes, stippling, bumps and ridges have all been cut into barrels. Then there's color; you can get a barrel in just about any color you can imagine. Other manufacturers have begun to add graphics to their barrels and feature things like flames and skulls. Your typical macho-stuff can be found in virtually infinite variety from the tasteful to the tasteless. Chances are, whatever look you want, you'll be able to find a barrel to match it.

When you finally do go to purchase a barrel, remember to take along the information you've gathered about the kind of gun you are using and the paint you'll be shooting, remember that no barrel lasts forever. Think of your first barrel purchase as the beginning of a long and rewarding learning process, and save up your money so that you can afford to buy the next best thing.

A LOOK DOWN THE BARREL

A Brief Overview of Choosing an Aftermarket Barrel That's Right For You!

ANDREW FLACH: What does the barrel have to do with the game? Why should I consider an aftermarket barrel?

BILL GARDNER: Keep in mind that the gun manufacturers have a lot of competition, and they put very little money and effort into their barrels. Most stock barrels are not much more than a piece of aluminum with a hole in it.

And the manufacturers know that the players are going to want to go buy an after-market barrel anyway. So, it's probably the number one accessory out there for paint guns and the one where you'll see a big difference.

There are some accessories you can buy that will improve performance a little, and there are some that will do a lot. The barrel makes a big difference in performance.

ADAM GARDNER: There are basically two types of players. There's the person who really doesn't care, technically, about how the barrel works. They see that it shoots further and more accurately, and that's what they want. Results. Others are more technically inclined and want to know the theory behind the barrel and why it shoots better.

BILL: First, I have to sell you on a theory. Originally, everyone thought that a ball coming out of a barrel at 300 feet per second would travel exactly the same distance, with the same characteristics as any other ball coming out of any barrel.

The thing that they're forgetting about is aero-dynamics. You know, not everyone realizes that balls change shape as they're flying through the air. They're gelatin, so they distort. Beyond that, even fewer people know how to make barrels that enable a paintball to travel further and more accurately. There's a lot of science behind this.

What that means is, if you have a barrel that's too tight for your gun, gases will hit the ball too hard and distort it, squeezing it and changing its shape dramatically. This decreases its aerodynamic power.

When a paintball gets slammed with the gases, it gets crushed, and then as it flies through the air, it's expanding and contracting with the initial energy that hit it. The softer you hit that ball, the less you distort the shape, and the more aerody-namic it remains during its flight.

Now, that's what we call low pressure. At Smart Parts, we aim for a low pressure approach, delivering a high volume of gas at a low pressure, thereby creating less of a distortion on the ball.

So, first, that brings you to the gun. You have to

go to the guns before you go to the barrel. There are two basic types of guns-there's the blow forward gun, meaning the bolt is open and the ball sits in there and when you fire it, the bolt closes, hitting the ball and firing the gun.

And then, there's a closed bolt gun. In a closed bolt gun, the ball's in the breech with the bolt closed behind it.

So, the difference is the bolt's position when you fire. And the other difference is that the open bolt guns for paint ball need to have a ball retainer, to keep the ball from prematurely lodging itself in the barrel.

And since the paintball is held in place by the ball retainer, we recommend a barrel where the ball will roll right out of the gun, if the ball retainer weren't holding it in place. And the accuracy and consistency will be there, if the barrel is just slightly larger than the ball.

Now, in closed bolt guns, you don't want that. You want a situation where, if the ball sits in the barrel, you can very lightly blow it out with a light puff of air.

ANDREW: And it should not roll out?

BILL G: It should not roll out. If it does, when you go to shoot somebody, you'll lose the first ball and you'll have to fire twice.

ANDREW: What about rifling?

BILL G: As far as rifling goes, we patented the rifling on our barrels. It's probably what made our business successful. We do spin the ball.

The Smart Parts barrel puts a very light spin on the ball. It's not disruptive. And what it does is, if you have a bell curve or distribution and you fire other than Smart Parts barrels, you'll find that when they reach the end of their energy curve, when they're way out there, they can fall in any direction. They can drop left, they can drop right, they can drop randomly—it's a random pattern.

But the Smart Parts barrel, you'll find that the end of its trajectory, it will generally always fall in

one direction. That gives you a little bit more control over that flight path. A competitive edge.

ANDREW: How about choosing barrel length?

BILL G: Well, related to the gun, again, and this is going to be a slightly different concept. Beyond open bolt versus closed bolt, you have high pressure guns and low pressure guns.

A high pressure gun is a small chamber with a lot of pressure. When you fire the gun, it imparts the energy very quickly on the ball. So, I like to call it large baseball bat versus small one. You want to hit 300 feet per second with a whiffle ball bat, you're going to swing the thing really hard.

If you want to hit 300 fps with a nice, big wooden bat, you know you don't have to swing as hard. So, the high pressure/small chamber guns

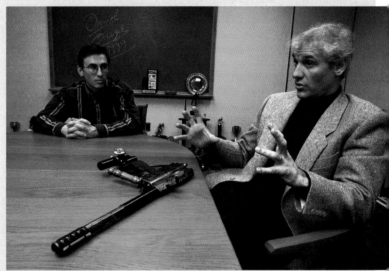

don't need as long a barrel to get the velocity up to two or three hundred feet per second.

The bottom-line is that low pressure enables you to use more of the barrel length. You'll find, though, that the average barrels will be 12–16 inches. That's what everybody's comfortable with. A lot of recreational players use an 18-plus inch barrel. It's fine for fun, but as far as maneuvering in your bunkers, you're knocking into things all the time and it's very difficult to change directions.

Regarding the choice of the barrel and the barrel

length: the guns favoring lower pressure can use a short barrel, but will appreciate the extra expansion area of a longer barrel to move the ball steadily rather than abruptly up to top speed. Less distortion equals more accuracy. It's all a matter of keeping that ball aerodynamic.

So, if you've got a gun that's hitting so hard you're breaking paint, then what you can do is turn your velocity down and increase your barrel length.

For example, during the summer, you may shoot all day long and not break a ball. But when the temperature's cool, the balls get a little bit more brittle, you find yourself shearing paint. One of the things you can do to alleviate that problem is to go to the long barrel. Now, your velocity's gone up, but you can turn down the pressure.

On the tournament level, barrel length becomes an issue of ergonomics. "Can I move quickly in my bunkers?" For front line players, they don't need quite as much accuracy as back line players, who'll tend to use a longer barrel.

But in terms of the recreational player, it's also a matter of "which barrel makes my gun work in the most conditions." Too short a barrel will definitely lead to accuracy problems.

ANDREW: What about unusual barrels, for special playing situations?

BILL G: We make a huge variety of barrels. People love gun barrels that look good. You know, cosmetics is important in this sport, almost as much as it is in skiing or snowboarding. I guess if you break it down and you ask yourself, "What gun do I have? Is it high or low pressure? Is it closed or open-bolt?" Those are the critical, first questions.

Then you say, "Okay, what type of bunkers do I play? Do I want a short barrel where I can maneuver very quickly, or do I want a longer barrel with a little bit more accuracy?" And then you start to ask, "What conditions? Am I playing in the winter, the summer? Am I breaking paint? Is my paint in good condition?" These types of questions usually lead people to buy a series of barrels for their gun that fit the various conditions they encounter as a player.

And then the other big question involves the cosmetics. "If I look good, I feel good, and if I feel good, watch out!" So, you say to yourself, "Well, do I like purple splash?"

So, certainly looks matter in your choice of barrel.

It Ain't Just Paint

Have you ever eaten a bowl of jello? Maybe it had whipped cream on top, or fruit buried in it. Did you ever watch it wiggle and shake? It's not possible that there is anyone in the world who hasn't at least *seen* jello.

Well, if you haven't then you must be the only person on the face of this planet who hasn't seen the substance paintball shells are made of.

It's called gelatin and it was invented circa 1900 as a 'neutral' food that could be added to just about everything and flavored to taste like just about anything. For a brief period, it was a popular delicacy, reserved for kings and queens and aristocrats.

Today, of course, gelatin no longer holds such a lofty position—definitely not in its capacity as the shell of the humble paintball. It's no longer a privilege to eat gelatin—although doing so won't harm you. Gelatin has been run through some pretty high-tech processes that make it just strong enough to be shot from a gun, yet brittle enough to break when hitting cammo'ed paintballers more than 100 feet away. Nonetheless, gelatin is quite digestible. (As any newbie will attest!)

Gelatin is created by 'rendering' the soft tissues, hooves, bones, and other unmentionables left over after a pig or cow has been prepared for market. During manufacture, sorbitol (a preservative), some glycerine, and starch (to give the shell 'body') are added to the mix. At the end of this process you get long, thin, sticky sheets of gelatin.

Using a process originally developed for the pharmaceutical industry, these sheets are then used to mold the shell of the paintball. As the sheets of gelatin are fed through an encapsulating machine, they pass through a reservoir of fill or paint. The two halves of the ball seal together and the entire paintball is left to dry.

The inside of the paintball is what really counts, though. Because gelatin wants to absorb water (just drop one in a glass of water and watch it swell), the 'paint' inside can't be water-based. In fact, during paintball's formative years, the paintball fill was oil-based.

Over the years a 'water-soluble' paintball was developed that replaced the petroleum-based oils with mineral, vegetable, and fish based oils. The most commonly used natural oil is polyethylene glycol. To this are added starch, which serves as a thickener, and water. Artificial, non-toxic dyes are used to provide color.

Everything that goes into a paintball is edible, non-toxic and completely biodegradable.

If it weren't for the taste, you'd be tempted to eat them.

—SD

RON OLKO, TECH REP FOR AIR AMERICA, SPEAKS WITH STEW SMITH AT THE 1998 WORLD CUP ABOUT HIS COMPANY'S AIR SYSTEM:

STEWART SMITH: To start, what are you cleaning the regulator with and what are your lubricating it with?

RON OLKO: Just wipe it off with a rag or paper towel.

STEW: No solvent?

RON: The only solvent that you'd want to use at all is maybe a little bit of rubbing alcohol. Rubbing alcohol works really well because it doesn't promote rust. It cleans up the paint and it evaporates. You don't want to use too much alcohol on the regulator though, because it can ruin the o-rings. But generally, you just wipe it off. You very rarely need any type of cleaning fluids.

You get all the paint off, any broken shells that may be in there, and then you lubricate it. Really, one of the best lubricants to use is automatic transmission fluid. It's readily available, and it's not corrosive on the o-rings. You want to avoid most real firearm solvents. Those are terrible, because they're meant to break out carbon deposits in guns, and there are no carbon deposits in here. What ends up happening, if you put that on a paintball gun, is it attacks the o-rings, causing them to swell and break down. When the o-rings get damaged, you get leaks, and they're a problem. You want to avoid that.

You also do not want to lubricate with any type of aerosol, WD-40, or something like that. That's very bad. WD-40 is so thin, the o-rings will absorb it and swell up and cause the gun to jam.

BASIC FIELD STRIP

RON: As far as basic service and trouble-shooting goes, if there's a problem, check out the

whole valving. It's either dirty pins, springs getting compressed over time, or dirt where it shouldn't be.

STEW: What are some indicators that those items are dirty or something's wrong with them?

RON: You'll have erratic output. High or low pressure swings. You have two gauges on the system. You have your bottle pressure, your high pressure gauge. This tells you your unregulated pressure. Then you have a low-pressure gauge that shows you when there's a load on the system, what your output pressure is. As you pull the trigger, and cycle the weapon, you'll see the needle deflect or bounce. If there's a slow recovery from that deflection, that means there is a problem. If you see the needle swing past your set pressure, and it keeps climbing, that's another indicator that the valve pin is not seated properly. The system is not regulating the pressure correctly. Any kind of leak, however small, will affect your pressure. When I take the regulator apart, I'll show you the piston. There's an o-ring on it that can get dirty or worn or harden over time and cause a breakdown. It's a little thing that can make a big difference, and it's easily consumer replaceable. We've made this a very simple and user-friendly system.

STEW: Looks like it's no more complicated than regular scuba gear. It might be a little more difficult.

RON: No, actually, for the average paintball player, this is probably easier to maintain and troubleshoot than a scuba system. It's best, though, especially in situations like this tournament, to leave repair to technical representatives, which is why we're always out here. We come out early. We stay late. Make sure players get quality service, make sure things get done right. A lot of consumers outside the tournament circuit don't have direct access to tech support, and don't have the knowledge base. So, you'll see them putting black rubber o-rings in there which may last for one cycling of the gun and then blow apart, or they wrap teflon tape around internal portions of the regulator. They're thinking, "Hey, it stopped leaking, so it must work, right? Wrong. That's why a step-by-step process like this is really important. Our air system is very easy to maintain. We try to educate our customers. They get an operator's manual that outlines these same procedures, how to troubleshoot.

STEW: For the basic servicing of the Air America system here, what tools do you need to have?

RON: The main tools you need to do any consumer level maintenance would be a set of hex keys, a main set of 16ths, 5/32nds, a pick or o-ring tool, and a 7/16ths open-end wrench. That'll perform 99% of the maintenance. Q-tip swabs and some rubbing alcohol to clean out dirt and debris, and a lubricating oil or grease.

STEW: Any one in particular for lubrication that you recommend?

RON: What shouldn't you use? A lot of players use vaseline, or auto grease on the piston. Any kind of grease other than this silicone lube I'm using collects dirt. Lightweight motor oil will work fine, as well as gun oil. Any of these can be used to perform routine maintenance and lubrication. In addition to the piston, we also put oil on the mainspring, also called the spring pack. It's a series of stacked concave disks that doesn't look much like a spring, but the concave disks working against each other provides a spring

action. If you don't keep it lubricated, and the disks become corroded, it increases friction and the spring becomes less effective or erratic, and pressure adjustment becomes difficult. So we put a light coat of oil on that spring, which I'll show you when we take it apart, and a light coat of oil on the piston o-ring.

STEW: So you can use petroleum products to lubricate it?

RON: We'd rather the consumer use a urethane-friendly lubricant, a non-penetrating type of lubricant. Over time, the o-ring will become hard or swell and tear if they use distillate-type lubricants. This silicone compound we just started using is an industry standard o-ring lubricant. We find that it works very well. But it's not readily available to all of our consumers. So I recommend a light lubricating oil, friendly for urethane products.

AIR VS. CO$_2$

STEW: So why air and not carbon dioxide?

RON: Carbon dioxide is a compressed liquid gas. It's more unstable than air and very susceptible to temperature changes. Since it's a liquid, we have a problem. Even with an anti-siphon tube, when a player tilts his bottle down, he is going to get some liquid up into the hose that can cause the gun to freeze up. At a minimum, you'll get hot shots in excess of 300 feet per second, which can be potentially hazardous. With the anti-siphon bottles of today, the technology has advanced to the point where it is safer, but there are still problems. There are always temperature fluctuations. Not to say that CO$_2$ is a bad way to do things, you just have to be aware of how it works. The majority of the entry level paintball guns and field owners still use compressed CO$_2$ because it's more affordable at this point. Due to the materials and labor that are involved, our compressed air systems are a lot more expensive than buying

••

mass-manufactured 12-ounce or 20-ounce CO_2 bottles, which you can pick up for 40 or 50 bucks, depending on the size of the bottle.

STEW: Does it help with cyclical rates of fire? Remember we were talking about using the Shockers and the Angels. They wouldn't use carbon dioxide, would they?

RON: A low-pressure gun needs more volume. Volume is a big deal. One player in a 10-man competition, two 5-man teams going at it, can go through up to 2500 rounds in one game.

The guns vary. Take an Autococker, for example. There are so many after-market products that change the flow dynamics and the volume characteristics that are available for that gun. The average shot count for an Autococker with a 4500 psi system may be 1600–1800 shots per fill. Variations in barrels and different types of actuating mechanisms will affect performance. Different manufac-

turers recommend different volumes. So, we say the average is probably about 1800 shots for this system here. But when you get into a Shocker, with its high-rate of fire and particular volumetric efficiency, it's not going to work for a player who wants to shoot 1800–2,000 rounds. That type of gun typically eats more air than others.

STEW: What do they use to get the volume they want?

RON: They use CO_2. We can use this same type of bottle with a CO_2 valve. The threads are standard. So they can get more with the CO_2 in this same sized bottle than you would with compressed air. There's a trade-off, because now you're carrying around 30 ounces of CO_2 in a heavy bottle. We looked at that added weight, at the risk level involved with carrying that around, and went with compressed air.

DISASSEMBLY AND BASIC MAINTENANCE OF THE REGULATOR

1. The first step in disassembling the regulator is to remove the locked tournament cap that holds the regulator adjustment nut in place.

1A

1B

STEW: Can you describe the relationship between the regulator adjustment nut and the tournament cap?

RON: By turning the regulator nut with a hex key, the outgoing pressure is increased by turning it in a clockwise motion and decreased by going counter-clockwise. The tournament cap is locked down, so when the system is not under pressure, the regulator nut does not move. It's called a tournament cap because without it, you would be able to adjust the regulator pressure during the game and increase the speed. This would allow you to get further down the field, but you'd be shooting at other players with a hot gun, so it became a standard rule within the NPPL to have a locking tournament cap on your air system. With the locking cap, you won't be able to increase your pressure on the field and then leave it with a lower pressure.

STEW: How does being able to adjust the pressure affect the gun's performance?

RON: Each gun operates at a different pressure which affects performance. By adjusting the pressure, you're modifying it for that type of gun. Automatic style requires 600–900 psi to operate, depending on what type of valve work has been done to the gun. Standard Autocockers require anywhere from 375–500 psi to operate. This allows you to adjust the air system to whatever inbound pressure your gun requires.

STEW: And then the tournament cap locks that setting?

RON: The tournament cap locks that setting down, so when the air system is de-gassed, there's pressure on the adjustment nut. At that point, when you have to empty your tank, or it is loose in your gear bag, the nut won't float around and change the pressure setting.

2. The second step is to remove the regulator adjustment nut. As we remove it, the mainspring (the spring pack) comes out with it.

3. Remove the mainspring from the regulator nut. Remove the piston from the piston bore.

Stew: Can regular players do all of this? Ron: Yes.

4. Inspect the mainspring for tightness in the disks, corrosion, and check the lubrication.

5. Check the o-ring on the piston for any obvious nicks, cuts, scratches, discoloration, water saturation, or swelling. Replace the o-ring if necessary.

6. Take the piston housing off and inspect the regulator seat for any clues to problems you may have been experiencing. This is where we get into the regulator a little further than we would during regular maintenance. Troubleshooting a problem like broad swings in output flow, which may indicate a failed valve system, requires us to perform this inspection.

7. Inspect the white seating material (the little, white, plastic washer). Look for dirt, or the center hole appearing oblong instead of round, which would indicate that the pin is travelling in a direction that it shouldn't be. Then remove the regulator seating material from the piston housing with a pick.

8. Using a clean rag or preferably a cotton swab with a little bit of rubbing alcohol on it, clean all the mating surfaces of debris and oil. Pay close attention to the area that the regulator seat fits into.

9. Remove the regulating valve pin and the cone spring from the gas distribution body. Inspect them for any damage. Over-adjusting the regulator nut can bend the valve pin shaft. Make sure that the pin is straight and not marked up, and check that the cone spring isn't compressed or stretched due to improper installation. Watch for the natural compression that occurs with time and use.

10. Now, with a clean cotton swab or rag, clean the internal surfaces of the gas body, removing any debris, oil, or moisture.

11. This is as far as we go. After making sure that all of the surfaces are clean, we're going to work backwards and reassemble the regulator. The regulator seat (white washer) that we removed is made of hard urethane and can be used only once. It's a compression fitting. The two halves of the regulator, the gas distribution body and the piston housing, have sealing beads that make an indentation on the seat. Once you separate the two parts, the regulator seat needs to be replaced with a new one. Place the disk in the recessed area of the piston housing.

13. Replace the cone spring by fitting the tapered end on the short back-retaining shaft of the valve pin.

12. Now replace the valve pin by inserting the long shaft of the pin down through the regulator seat.

14. Firmly re-seat the piston housing on top of the gas distribution body. Fit the wider end of the cone spring into the recessed retaining pocket for the valve pin. Reinsert the four retaining screws. Take an Allen wrench and tighten the screws down gradually in a diagonal pattern. Tighten the opposite corners to evenly compress the seating material between the two halves. Tighten so that there's no gap between the piston housing and the gas distribution body, nice and snug, not over-torqued, but not just hand tight.

15. Lubricate the piston with a light coat of oil or silicone grease, and re-insert it flat-faced down, open end up, into the piston housing.

16. Insert a lightly lubricated mainspring into the piston.

17. Thread on the regular adjustment nut over the mainspring. At this point, we fill the bottle with nitrogen or compressed air, testing the regulator for any leaks.

Now

you're

ready to

get back

in the

game!

18. Thread the tournament cap onto the regulator adjustment nut. Set your outgoing pressure using an Allen wrench, and lock down your tournament cap. Tighten its retaining screws.

LIKE A ROCK

Dennis Tippmann, Jr.

STEWART SMITH: Tippmann is the first name we heard of when we started out to make this book. How long have you been in the paintball business?

DENNIS TIPPMANN, JR: I've been doing this since 1986. So, it's been 13 years now. I don't know of any bigger companies in this industry that are older than we are.

STEW: As an established leader in the paintball industry, how do you explain your success?

DENNIS: We keep improving the quality and the price point of our products. The mass market volume sales we do enable us to do this, and our commitment to improving upon our guns in ways that are cost-effective for us and our customers keeps us ahead of the game.

STEW: Your guns are definitely affordable.

DENNIS: We make valuable guns that simply perform reliably and consistently over time. They're easy to maintain and we support our products very aggressively.

STEW: Your guns are also unique in that you diecast them in aluminum.

DENNIS: That's right. It definitely saves us money because we can avoid the more expensive class of machining.

STEW: Do you find the diecasting durable?

DENNIS: Oh, yes. Basically, it's the same material. Diecast aluminum is very tough.

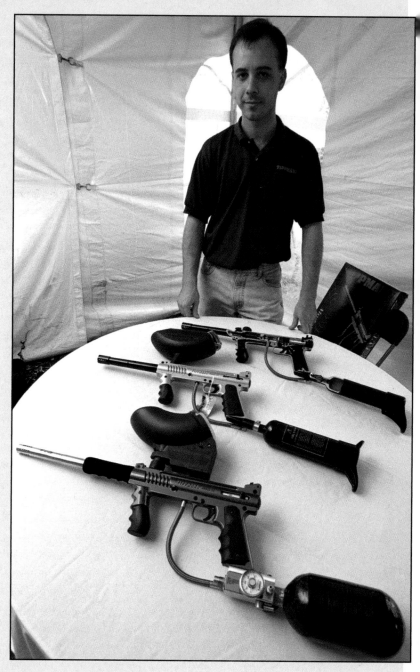

STEW: How do you explain the popularity of your guns with field owners?

DENNIS: Rental places need our expertise. They need good, reliable, affordable guns, and they want the best CO_2 system guns they can buy. One thing we've always been good at is making great CO_2 guns. The rental guys need parts and service, too. That's another thing we do well. We get parts to them quickly. We offer one-year warranty on all our equipment. Because renters are more abusive and the gun gets used everyday, our support of fields is critical to their success.

They need a gun that's extremely durable, and a company to back it up. That's why they use our equipment.

STEW: Tell us about your Tippmann Model 98.

DENNIS: Sure. Our guns have always been solid, but we want to start introducing some of the high end advances to the mass market. Model 98 brings an advanced trigger system to the masses. Real high end guns go out of their way to build really good trigger systems, so that's where we've started. We've made the trigger really light on this gun, and it shoots very fast.

STEW: It's a reactive trigger?

DENNIS: Yeah, we call it the hyper-shot trigger. A light trigger with great response pressure. You see, on some guns with light triggers, the trigger doesn't swing back after you fire. We don't have that problem. The Model 98's return pressure gives you "lightness" speed and control.

STEW: So can you take the stock 98 out of the box, and add on bit by bit until you're up to a tournament level?

DENNIS: Yes. Absolutely. In fact, there are companies right now that are buying these receivers off us raw and doing stuff like this to them because we diecast that receiver. We don't have much money invested in the receiver anymore. So they're buying the receivers and making a number of little jazzy modifications to them. Double triggers and stuff like that.

As we're doing a lower-priced gun, we have the volumes real high. We can afford to diecast it. And then they can take that same diecasting, go and modify it, whatever they want.

STEW: Are you in any retail stores?

DENNIS: Wal-Marts and K-marts are what we're looking at right now. The guns are actually in Dicks, which is a sporting goods store, and some Sports Authority stores carry them.

STEW: What is an expansion chamber?

Dennis Tippmann, Jr. points out the CBX valve in this cutaway of a Model 98.

DENNIS: This is the first upgrade you would perform on a Tippmann Model 98. A lot of players put a barrel on right away and expansion chamber kit next.

Because CO_2 pressures go up and down, sometimes you'll get liquid CO_2 in your gun. Liquid CO_2 can be hard on a gun. You point your gun down, the liquid enters your gun and it responds by shooting really hard and erratic. The expansion chamber helps eliminate this effect. It makes it harder for liquid CO_2 to form and get into the valve of the gun. So it's just a way of making CO_2 work a little bit better.

STEW: Tell us about how your gun works.

DENNIS: When you pull the trigger on the gun, you release the bolt, and the rear bolt is connected to the front bolt. That'll shuttle a ball into the barrel. Now when the rear bolt gets clear forward, it hits the valve. When the valve is opened, pressure goes two directions. A very little bit goes to recock the gun, maybe 10%. The rest of it goes around the valve and shoots your ball. A little bit of pressure comes to the rear bolt, and recocks the gun. Normally, you wouldn't even be able to let off the trigger by the time the gun's recocked. The sear hits the back of the trigger, and then you let out the trigger and it reengages the top of the trigger for the next shot. There's a latch to hold the ball in place so it doesn't roll out your barrel until the trigger is pulled.

STEW: This latch is a piece of rubber?

DENNIS: Yeah. So, it's really a pretty simple system.

This is what they call a blow-back system. The bolt's blown back. There's two other systems. The blow-forward system, like your automatics, and the closed bolt system, which is like a pump gun with an automatic pump. What they mean by closed-bolt is that the bolt's forward, ready to fire. When you pull a trigger on a closed-bolt system, the bolt's closed. That means the bolt has already shut the chamber off. When you set the gun off, the ball's already in the barrel.

So the closed-bolt is like a pump gun, with an automatic pumper on it, like your Autocockers.

STEW: Autocockers are closed bolt?

DENNIS: Yeah. Automags are blow-forward, and mine are blow-back. Tippmann actually invented the blow-back system. We've got the patents on it.

STEW: The most efficient use of air would be the blow-back system?

DENNIS: They all run pretty neck and neck. I think the Model 98 is extremely efficient. But right now, I'd say probably the most efficient system besides this gun would be your closed-bolt system, which is found in Autocockers. They're extremely efficient because of the way they use the exact amount of air needed to cock the gun, and the exact amount of air needed to shoot the gun. Since the systems are all compartmentalized, it's easier for them to achieve high levels of efficiency. It took us a lot of tuning to get to that level. So Bud Orr's guns have been efficient for a long time.

And the next level we'd step up to is the CBX valve. It's our high performance valving system, and we're sure players will notice its advantages, particularly its reliability.

STEW: And this is something that you developed?

DENNIS: Yes. I do all the drawings. I make the prototypes. My father and I sit down and go over the designs before they're made. Some of the other guys actually cut some of the prototype parts. Some of our prototypes are cut out of solid aluminum. I'll draw a 3D model of the gun on my computer, which then actually talks to a milling machine. It writes a tool path that'll cut that shape out of a block of aluminum. So those prototypes are made out of solid aluminum. And that same software can be used to make a mold.

STEW: You have a family business. That's wonderful.

DENNIS: Yes, as far as design and conception. Yes, it really is.

STEW: Thank you for sharing your time and insights.

DENNIS: It was a pleasure.

Cleaning of a Tippmann Model 98

KEEP IT CLEAN

This is an ad hoc cleaning, the kind most recreational players will do after a solid day of play. Keep in mind that proper care and maintenance of your paintball gun will provide you with many years of reliable and safe fun. Of course, some people will leave their gear in a bag and worry about it tomorrow... but why should you?

You've made an investment in your gun and part of that investment is your time. Take the time to clean your gun after a day at the field.

I performed the following gun cleaning on a Tippmann Model 98 with a Lapco barrel.

1. Remove the air tank first by turning slowly to release the pressure. Shoot the gun a few times to degas the entire air system. Note: shoot into a garbage can or cardboard box. Never into the air or at someone. And not with the barrel plug still in the gun.

2. Repeat this process, turning the air tank, and degassing the gun, until the bolt flops forward. This is an indication that it's okay to remove the air tank fully. The reason to take this care and not twist the air tank off fully in one go is to protect your o-rings.

3. Using an Allen wrench, remove the loader from the feed neck by loosening the retaining bolt. Unique to the Tippmann feedneck is a set of "teeth" that grip the throat of the feeder. Don't try to yank the loader out. Loosen the retaining bolt (be careful not to lose the nut), and remove the loader when it pulls freely.

4. To clean the loader, stick your pinky in the feed neck, and check for paint. If it comes out dirty, wash the loader in the sink with some warm water.

5. Remove the barrel. Notice the "fat" threads, which are due to the unique die casting techniques used in manufacturing the Tippmann 98. It takes just a few twists to remove the barrel. You'll clean it in a few moments.

6. Swing away the feed tube by depressing the front sight. This exposes the face of the bolt.

7. Examine the bolt area for paint residue and wipe it clean with a cloth.

8. Apply some oil to the bolt through the exposed breech. Pull the cocking knob back and dry fire it a few times. This distributes lubricant to most exposed bolt areas.

9. Pull the bolt back and apply oil to the back portion of the bolt. Dry fire the gun several times to distribute the lubricant.

10. Apply oil to the o-ring on the bolt. One drop on each side. Again, dry fire to lubricate.

11. Paint accumulates in the holes of the Lapco barrel. To clean the barrel, find a sink and rinse out the gunk.

12. Pour a little cleaning agent into the barrel, rotating the barrel in your hand as you apply the solution. Here, I used Armson cleaning solution.

13. Using a cable squeegee, scrub the inside of the barrel. Run the cable end of the squeegee through the firing end of the barrel and pull; this will draw the soft end of the squeegee through the barrel. Repeat the squeegee process a few times.

14. Rinse the barrel again in the sink to remove the cleaning agent.

You're done. Ready for another shot at paintball glory? Reassemble the gun, reversing the process described here. Take your time and do it right!

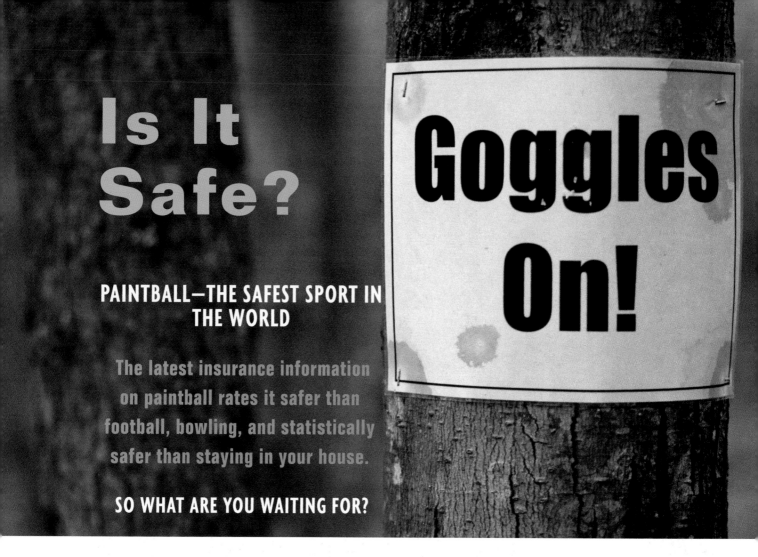

Is It Safe?

PAINTBALL—THE SAFEST SPORT IN THE WORLD

The latest insurance information on paintball rates it safer than football, bowling, and statistically safer than staying in your house.

SO WHAT ARE YOU WAITING FOR?

Paintball is an exceptionally safe sport. The reason paintball is so safe is that the safety precautions have been evolving as fast as the game has been evolving. Safety equipment is vital to paintball, and should never be ignored no matter where you play.

AGOG ABOUT GOGGLES

Paintball goggles are highly specialized for the sport and must pass strict ASTM standards for paintball lenses. For example, paintball goggles must be able to absorb the impact of a paintball moving at over 400 feet per second (that's over 270 mph!) fired from less than one meter away. Many new players assume they can wear ski goggles, tank goggles, shop glasses, sunglasses, or shooting glasses. This assumption is completely erroneous, and therefore extremely dangerous! Paintball goggles are designed to absorb impacts that would shatter other goggles or dislodge them from the wearer's eyes. Your eyes are the only bodyparts that you rely on and regularly expose during the game that can be catastrophically injured by a paintball; whenever you're around paintball guns, don't trust anything other than paintball goggles to protect your eyes.

Paintball goggles are also designed with the game in mind. They have a wider peripheral vision than other styles of goggles. Many styles can be worn over glasses. There are "thermal" systems available to help prevent goggles from fogging up. You can even get fans to blow in fresh air to help prevent fogging. Goggles also have attached face shields and ear armor, which you are required to wear at most fields. There are several styles and colors to choose from.

You must wear your goggles at all times when you're on the playing field or on the target range. Even when you're eliminated, you don't want to remove your goggles until you're in the staging area and off the fields.

Plug It Up

After goggles, barrel plugs are the most critical safety equipment you'll need to be in the habit of using. A barrel plug is a device you stick onto or into the open end of the paintgun's barrel when you are off the field. This device prevents a paintball from coming out the end of the paintgun's barrel. *When used with the mechanical trigger safety switched on, the barrel plug makes it safe to remove your goggles in a "goggles off" area.* Just having the safety on is not as "safe" as it appears. Using a barrel plug is a visual way to show your paintgun won't hurt anyone, and if anyone forgets to put one in their gun, you should tell them to plug it up immediately.

Every player must use paintball goggles and a barrel plug for their paintgun. More than any others, these two pieces of safety equipment make paintball safe for players.

There is one more vital piece of safety equipment that every good field uses regularly, and will make available for your use when you bring your own equipment. A "Chronograph" measures the speed of a paintball as it comes out of the barrel of a paintgun. In the early nineties, the IPPA (International Paintball Players Association, now disbanded) helped create a standard of 300 feet per second (300 fps) as the safest maximum speed for paintballs coming out of the barrel. This has held ever since. For indoor paintball, the top limit is usually lowered to 270 fps or less, depending on the field size. Higher velocities are unnecessary with smaller fields. If you have your own equipment, you will need to adjust it to get under the field speed limit.

Know where your gun's safety is and always use it. But don't stop there. Insert your barrel plug to ensure maximum accident prevention.

Safety—Above and Beyond

There is more safety equipment you can use as well, but it is not mandatory. (Read: common sense indicates that using additional equipment goes above and beyond the essential safety requirements.) This is effectively the point at which you can exercise your personal preference to accessorize for further safety. Some items make good sense to use. Men should wear a cup. Women should wear fem-guards to protect "soft spots." If you have bad ankles, wear shoes with ankle support or wear a brace if necessary.

If you have bad joints, or you don't like the idea of crawling on rocks and twigs, you can wear knee and elbow pads. Many styles are available, and many are paintball specific. If you slide a lot you may want knee/shin guards. If you crawl a lot, then elbow pads would be a good idea. It's all about wearing what you are comfortable moving around in. Wearing loose clothing will also help absorb some of the impact of a paintball. You don't want to go overboard, however. If your clothes are too baggy, you'll have a hard time moving around.

Other products are available for personal safety, such as neck protectors, hard or soft armored vests, gloves, head wraps and protective caps. Some people think you can't be too safe; others feel like they sacrifice agility and actually become more vulnerable to getting hit when they wear these extras. You'll have to make up your own mind about these items.

But, if I ever catch you not wearing your goggles on a paintball field, I'll tackle you.

—RR

NOTE: We included this article on safety in the GUNS section because paintball guns should not be discussed independent of safety gear. Read on to learn more about the assorted paintball gear you need to play this game.

PART 3
GEAR

To Thine Own Paintball Goals Be True

How to Make Sure You Have What You Need To Enjoy This Beautiful Game

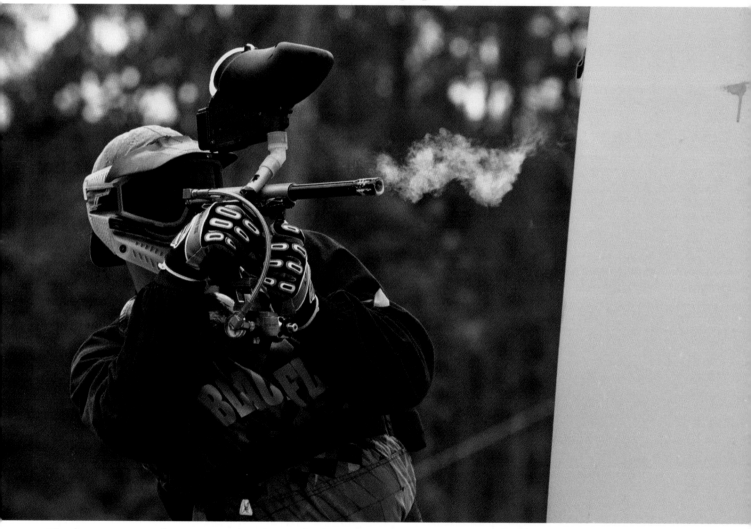

The best way to choose your equipment is to analyze what kind of player you are, figure out where you're going to use the equipment, research the quality versus pricing issues, and then, *and only then*, spend your hard earned dollars accordingly.

Equipping yourself to play paintball is easy these days. Almost too easy. You basically have three choices: use what the advertisers say you should use, purchase the most expensive thing on the shelf, or get what your local dealer happens to have in stock today and "really likes." In reality, many players use one or another of these purchasing methods to equip themselves or their teams. That's sad, because it rarely leads to an optimal purchase.

Caveat Emptor!

The only way to make sure that you have the equipment that's right for you is to become an informed consumer and think for yourself. One of the ironies of living in the information age is that we now have access to unprecedented quantities of data, which makes isolating quality information relatively harder.

The information in this section is meant to help you gain a complete understanding of the air systems that you'll want to use with your gun. You'll learn that making this selection is directly related to the kind of paintball player you want to be.

While this is not exactly a buyer's guide to paintball paraphernalia, my goal is to furnish you with a sense of direction when you start considering your key paintball purchases.

PRESSURE SYSTEMS

There are two basic kinds of paintball pressure systems or 'propellant sources' available for use with paintball guns. These are generally referred to as CO_2 (carbon dioxide) tanks and high-pressure or nitrogen systems.

Carbon Dioxide—Feeds Plants and Propels Paintballs

Carbon dioxide was the original propellant of choice for paintball. Small pressure bottles, holding 12-grams of gas (hence the name 'twelve-gram') were available for use with BB and pellet guns and were adopted for use with paintball guns. Several years later the idea of using larger pressure vessels, containing as much as 40 ounces of gas, was introduced. These systems allowed a user to shoot sev-

Old-school wristband 12-gram carriers.

eral hundred to several thousand paintballs without having to replace propellant sources and acquired the name 'constant air.'

Contrary to what some people believe, carbon dioxide is not a toxic chemical. It exists in fair quantities in the Earth's atmosphere and you exhale some every time you breathe. Nor does using a carbon dioxide system contribute to the green house effect: all of the CO_2 used in paintball systems is originally taken out of the atmosphere.

CO_2 has some physical properties that make it a good propellant; at the pressures and temperatures normally at play in a paintball gun, the gas can exist as a solid, a liquid, or a gas. This property allows a large amount of gas to be stored, even when using relatively low pressures. (CO_2 systems are generally considered to have working pressures of 800–1200 psi.) It is also a relatively dense or 'energetic' gas, which means that you get a lot of oomph out of just a small amount.

On the other hand, **one major drawback of using CO_2 is the fact that it can exist as a liquid, gas, or solid, literally at the same time, inside**

your pressure tank. This means that when the valve is opened, you sometimes get liquid CO_2, sometimes you get gaseous CO_2, and sometimes you get a mixture of both into the gun. This can cause wildly fluctuating velocities and ruin shooting accuracy. Additionally, some guns will become frozen and experience a drop off in velocity when rapid-firing occurs; each successive shot chills the gun further, sometimes causing it to malfunction or cease operating entirely. Finally, CO_2 systems are susceptible to negative effects from local temperatures; specifically, the colder the outside temperature, the less energetic CO_2 is. In such a situation, you're losing bang for your buck.

Constant air systems come in a variety of tank sizes and in several different configurations for attaching to your gun. Tanks can be purchased ranging in size from 3.5 ounces (the amount of gas the tank holds), 7 ounces, 10 ounces, 12 ounces, 15 ounces, 20 ounces and 40 ounces. Gun hook-ups are generally named after the manner in which they attach to the gun; consider the following.

A *back-bottle* system screws into an adapter mounted at the rear end of the gun.

A *bottom-line* set-up uses an adapter fitted under the grip.

A *vertical bottle* screws into a fitting underneath the barrel at the front of the gun.

A *California-style* bottle attaches the gun to a stock and uses an air hose to connect the tank to the gun.

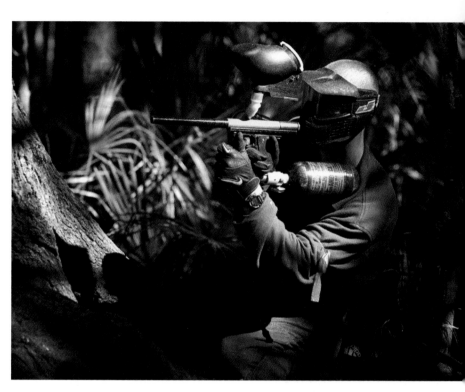

High-Pressure Air (HPA) and Nitrogen, Alternative Paintball Power Sources

High-pressure air and nitrogen systems utilize normal atmospheric air (a combination of nitrogen, oxygen, carbon dioxide and some trace elements) or pure nitrogen. Once again, this is not a toxic gas. In fact, nitrogen is the gas that makes the sky look blue.

Unlike carbon dioxide, air (or nitrogen) exists only as a gas at the pressures we use it for in paintball. This has the potential benefit of decreasing the shot-to-shot variation in pressure, thereby producing more accurate shots.

On the other hand, neither of these gases is as *energetic* as CO_2; the number of shots you get is less than you would get from a similar amount of CO_2. Therefore, to make their use practical, the pressure these gases are stored under has to be significant, far higher than that used to store CO_2.

Today, two basic nitrogen system models are used: The standard 3000 psi system and the 'tournament level' 4500 psi system. The benefit of going with the higher pressure is that you can store half-again as many shots in the same volume. Unfortunately, as of this writing, the paintball industry has only just begun to adopt HPA systems. The ability to fill 3000 psi tanks is not universally available and the ability to fill 4500 psi tanks is relatively scarce (except at tournaments and other major events).

HPA and nitrogen systems are referred to as 'regulated' systems. Why? Well, the pressure stored in the tank is much higher than the pressure used by the gun when firing a shot, so a device (the regulator) must be used to reduce the tank pressure to the gun's working pressure.

Several different makes and models are available, each of which uses different regulation systems and different methods for attaching to the gun. The most typical arrangement is a *cradle system*, which mounts the tank underneath the grip, and is connected to the gun via a high-pressure

Check out all those guppies. Smart players don't get caught short on paint.

line, or a *remote system*. Players carry the tank in a pouch mounted on their backs or at waist level, and a pressure hose connects the tank to the gun.

When choosing a propellant system for your paintball gun, the first question you need to answer is...

DO I NEED
A HIGH PRESSURE SYSTEM?

If the information on high-pressure systems confused you, and you're really not sure what it all means, the answer should probably be, at the very least, "not yet." Plenty of players have a perfectly wonderful time never using high-pressure.

The bottom-line is that you shouldn't pay for advantages that are negligible in the games you're playing. There are reasons why manufacturers offer high-performance options, and those reasons rarely overlap with the average player's priorities.

On the other hand, if you are a fiend for performance, or live in an area where you play in the cold (below 50° F) most of the time, then you can benefit from using a high-pressure system.

If you choose to go with CO_2, make sure that the model of gun you are using will operate efficiently on this propellant. Some guns are made specifically to use liquid CO_2, and therefore you will need to provide this kind of propellant. You will also need to determine the size of tank you should purchase: heavy shooters ought to carry a larger tank (15–20 ounces), while players who shoot less can get by on a smaller one. Especially for cold play days, remember that it's best to have several tanks on hand which can be filled and stored at room temperature for later use.

BRING ON THE PRESSURE

If you've made the decision to obtain a high pressure system, you need to answer two more questions.

Do the Fields and Events Where You Play Provide High Pressure Fills?

The answer to this is probably yes (although not necessarily for 4500 psi systems: these systems can be used with 3000 psi fills, you'll just get fewer shots per fill). More and more fields, and just about every big game and tournament, either already provide high pressure fills or will be in the 21st century.

The next question, and this isn't the first time we've brought it up, is...

What Kind of Player Are You?

For our purposes, players break down into three basic groups in terms of the environments in which they play the game. There's the tournament player, the "serious" recreational player, and the casual player. I'll deal with tournament players first.

Tournament Players

The "position" you play on the field virtually dictates the kind of gear you should be carrying. Yes, there's room for variation, but the pro is counting on team action and is playing a specific role in the team's use of tactics, so not every team member has to be equipped to the teeth.

Here, again, tournament players can be divided into three player types: *front, utility and cover.* Even if you are not a tournament player, you should consider the following descriptions of playing styles and see how you match up.

Front players are the ones who break out of the station with the intention of achieving a forward field position. They've got to move fast and need to have versatile skills. They never know what contorted position they're going to have to fit themselves into to make shots and stave off elimination.

Cover players provide direction, coordination, and cover fire for the front players. Cover players need to be able to shoot volume.

Utility players are players who are able to fill both roles, but their game plan is not to concentrate on either one particularly. They need to be able to move, they need to be able to shoot, and they're usually changing positions quickly. Some teams call these players "wingmen" or "support" players.

Front Players

Since speed, weight, and size are at a premium for the front player, I recommend that these players use a small bottle, on-gun system. They're usually going to be "tucking in" throughout the game, drawing fire rather than shooting, so a small system will provide enough air for the several hundred shots they may need to take. The configuration for mounting the bottle on the gun ought to allow front players to use it as a stock, since aimed shots are critical for them. This player definitely benefits from a compact mounting configuration.

Cover Players

Cover players, especially the *hosers* out there, ought to be carrying a large bottle remote system. This player needs the capacity, since chances are his job is to shoot *beaucoup* paint. Keeping the bottle off the gun gives the player more mobility, especially when firing longball style; besides, most large bottles are, in all practicality, just too heavy to mount on the gun.

Utility Players

Utility players need both the mobility for speed and the capacity for shooting. A large bottle is recommended, but this type of player ought to think seriously about mounting it on the gun, because he just might end up *filling in* at a forward bunker. The large bottle makes the gun a little more awkward when you're moving, so I recommend experimenting in a few games with a remote and an on-gun configuration to see which works better.

Serious Recreational Players

The serious *rec* player comes in several types as well. There's the "for-fun-team" type, who ought to read the above tournament player section for our recommendations.

Then there's the regular "no-team" player, the player with a few friends who is a regular at the local field.

Here, the choice of bottle is actually a combination of the type of role this player likes to perform and the type of field that this player usually frequents. If the field is a long distance from the nearest fill facility (or if the field has no fill facilities), then the larger bottle is called for because it gives the player more games without having to reload.

On the other hand, if fills are readily available (and relatively inexpensive), then you'll want to get the kind of system that best compliments your playing style.

While it's true that some folks do shoot a lot of paint in rec games, most of the time the games are of short duration, so more often than not a smaller system will do.

Scenario game players will most probably want to go with a large bottle remote system. These players are usually out on the field for several hours at a time. The large bottle will support this, and its remote configuration lets them keep it out of the way.

Casual Players

Most casual players rent their equipment, but for those who don't, a small, on-gun system is probably the best choice. More often than not, they don't need the volume capacity of a large tank, and usually they're also looking to stretch their paintball dollars.

When you're just starting out in paintball, it really makes no sense to make any purchases. Play at different fields and use different guns and air configurations.

Indoor games and speedball games almost always dictate a small, on-gun system. The games are over fast and space is at a premium in both formats, as is speed. Because of these facts, a casual player's rental equipment is only marginally less effective than a rec player's owned equipment (though, of course, this is going to vary from field to field).

> *Again, it really comes down to the player's skill and good fortune.*

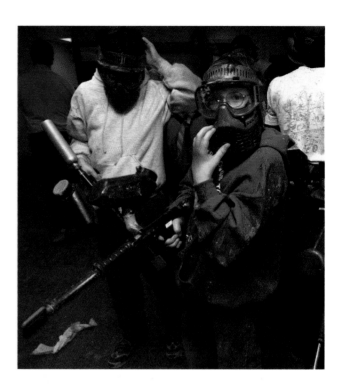

ULTIMATE CHOICES

If you are serious about paintball and play with some degree of regularity, you'll probably find yourself in need of several different configurations, and will most likely end up obtaining both a remote and an on-gun set-up, as well as a large and a small capacity bottle. This might sound like a sales pitch, but in reality, matching your system to your playing needs does help your game. Without both types of bottles and both types of mounting rigs, your options are limited.

SAFETY

High pressure *sounds* more dangerous than the carbon dioxide-powered, lower pressure systems. In fact, many of the high pressure systems out there have been tested to meet military specifications and are designed in such a way that a catastrophic failure of the system will *not* result in rockets or shrapnel. In this respect, it's possible to say that high pressure systems are actually safer than carbon dioxide systems.

However, with high pressure systems, you are dealing with pressures three to four times greater than those in carbon dioxide systems. So one safety requirement is clear...

DON'T FUTZ AROUND IN THE BASEMENT WITH A HIGH PRESSURE SYSTEM!

- With a high pressure system, as with any pressure system, you must always depressurize the system when storing it.

- If you are using a remote with your system, make sure that your hose is always under control.

- Finally, do your homework. Before you buy one, find out if the system you want to purchase meets the U.S. Department of Transportation (DOT) burst and hydrostatic test requirements. A legitimate system must be able to contain pressures four times its working pressure.

HIGH PRESSURE SOURCES

Eight companies currently manufacture and sell high pressure systems in the paintball market. First into the market were Air America, Air Power, Gov-nair (UK), Paintball Mania Supplies, Smart Parts, Pro-Team Products, and Pursuit Marketing Incorporated, all of whom offer high pressure systems in various configurations, for both on-gun and remote set-up.

Beyond the position you play and the various features of individual systems, high-pressure tanks come in two varieties—preset regulators and adjustable regulators. The difference is that the output pressure of pre-set regulators can't be adjusted by the user, while adjustable regulator systems can be.

Most guns and most players—except for those playing at the tournament level, or those who are performance gurus—can do just fine on preset systems. Some systems from PMI (Crossfire) and Paintball Mania Supply (Micro-reg system) are preset systems and can be obtained for a lower investment than adjustable ones.

Pro-Team products recently introduced a low-price adjustable system (Millennium Series) and adjustable regulator systems are also available from Govnair (MAX Attack), Air America (Armageddon, Apocalypse, and Raptor systems), Smart Parts (Max-Flow), and Paintball Mania Supply (Mini-reg).

—SD

BACK PLAYER

The back player usually carries the heaviest load. This player is responsible for most of the cover fire for his teammates. He usually is the eyes of the team and is responsible for relaying the opposing teams' movements. The back player will usually control his team's movement on the field. As an example, in 5 man paintball if the back player is aware that 2 players have been eliminated from one side of the field he may move his front men on that side further up the field. This player usually spends the entire game yelling codes and raining paint. For this reason, his equipment should be chosen for maximum distance and firepower. His pack should carry a large amount of paint. (Keep in mind that if you carry a half case of paint but can only shoot 800 rounds your extra paint will be useless!) Not all game situations require huge amounts of paint. Use common sense. If you are playing a 5 minute game on a speedball field, 1200 rounds of paint is overkill. Your teams game plan may also influence the amount of paint you carry. Some teams sit back and wait for something to happen while others go out and make things happen. If your team averages a very short game, carry less paint. If they sit in bunkers until the last 30 seconds you may need to carry more paint. Again, keep in mind that if you are going to carry it, you should have enough air to shoot it. The back player will find it helpful to be able to shoot left and right handed. In most cases the largest bunkers are at the back of the field. That does not mean that this player has the luxury of hanging the entire left side of his body out while trying to shoot right handed out of the left side of the bunker. It may also be helpful to have the ability to shoot with more than one finger. If you have to give cover fire for an extended period of time your index finger may appreciate a brief rest. The job that the back player does is not the most appealing job on the field to most players. That fact makes this a hard but important position to fill.

The Key for Mark Smith's Illustrations

1. Baggy Uniform—should be loose for flexibility and to deflect paint
2. Baggy Pants—the looser the pants...
3. Cleats—should be comfortable
4. Stripes on Cleats—any color on feet may draw attention to you, especially when crawling, color them black
5. Elbow Pads—under uniform (optional), lightweight and comfortable
6. Knee Pads—should be soft and comfortable, covering knees and shins, should not restrict movement
7. Hat—soft fabric helps with hard hits and may deflect paint
8. Rubber Visor—keeps sun out may deflect paint
9. Ear Protection—prevents ear damage
10. Rubber Lower Mask—when selecting a mask make sure the lower half is rubber and not hard plastic
11. Thermal Lens—helps prevent fogging during play
12. Squeegee—for quick barrel cleaning, comes in several lengths, should match barrel length, can be placed in knee pads, placed on a string around the neck or various other locations for quick access
13. Battle Swab—for cleaning hopper necks and barrels
14. Back Pack—should be sized appropriately for the position being played, should be comfortable, avoid a pack that places all those hard loaders down an exposed side of the body but make sure that you can get the loaders out
15. Velcro Waist Strap—avoid plastic or metal, hard surfaces break paint
16. Suspenders—use to help balance a heavy load of paint, should have soft connectors
17. Gloves—protect and hands and may deflect paint
18. Viewloader—choose one that is appropriate for your gun type and the amount of paint you want to have available, remember that this will greatly affect the weight of your gun
19. Battery Operated Feeder—keeps paint flowing efficiently into the gun
20. Timer—absolute necessity, keeps you aware of when the game is over or the one minute warning is up
21. Codes on Lid—the lid of your Viewloader is a good place to apply a sticker with codes that are difficult to remember
22. Codes on Inside of Lid—good place for a backup set of codes
23. Viewloader Lid Left Open—allows you to load while continuously firing at a target during a crucial time of the game
24. Bottle on Gun or Remote Line—front or mid players should stay away from remote lines, they become tangled and slow running, some back players choose a remote line to reduce weight of the gun
25. Drop Forward—moves bottle forward and makes gun shorter
26. Adjustable Drop Forward—allows bottle to be moved forward or backward to make gun shorter or longer
27. Air Intake Cover—keeps dirt out of your bottle
28. Bottle Pivot Adjustment—allows bottle to be twisted to one side or the other, may make gun smaller
29. Shroud—covers 3 way valves on an Autococker, saves on cleaning
30. Barrel—should be rifled, should be chosen with length determined by the position you play, example: a front player usually does not have to shoot the distance of the field and benefits from small size in a tight bunker
31. Lightweight Barrel—reduces weight of gun
32. Handgrip—steadies gun for a more accurate shot
33. Extra Loaders Taped Together—can be carried to a bunker, allows you to carry extra paint without adding weight to your back
34. Cup—crucial in importance, second only to a mask. Unfortunately many players neglect this, they are the ones that are carried off the field
35. Armband—given by the judge before the game, make sure that it is comfortable and does not restrict movement

Gear

key on page 177

MID PLAYER

The mid player tends to be a fill-in man. He will usually start the game in front of the back player and behind the tape runner. This player needs to be very versatile. In any given game he may start as a "back player," move in to his middle position, and then jump in front of the tape runner becoming the point man. He is crucial in relaying codes from the back player to the tape runner and vice versa. This player's primary job is to keep the tape runner alive and in the game. It is important to keep in mind that the tape runner is often under heavy fire and unable to look or shoot. This is where the mid player steps in. He may give cover to allow the tape runner to get up or he may merely talk to the tape runner to keep him comfortable. For example, it is very comforting for the tape runner to know that someone is watching over him. The mid player may constantly repeat: I've got your front or everything is okay. By the same token, if the mid player is forced to turn his attention elsewhere, he needs to let his teammates know this, also. The mid player's gun is usually smaller than that of the back player. Keep in mind that flexibility is very important to this player. If the back player or the tape runner is eliminated, he may be called upon to assume those roles.

Gear

key on page 177

TAPE RUNNER

The tape runner should carry the lightest load and be your fastest runner. This player usually takes the most aggressive position on the field. This positioning usually makes him a big target. He is the guy that the back player on the opposing team is dumping all that paint on. He will usually shoot the least amount of paint and should, therefore, carry less than the mid or back player. This is the player that is most often called upon to go bunker someone or sacrifice himself. His primary job is to get into his bunker, make himself small, and find a way to shoot effectively. At the start of the game he should be conscious of where his gun is in relation to which direction he is running. As an example, if he is running to the left, and he carries his gun in his right hand, he is giving the opposing team a nice, hard target. If, however, he carries his gun in his left hand his body helps cover it. This can be made more or less effective depending on how you swing the gun. The closer you keep the gun to your body the more effective this will be. Do not fool yourself into thinking that you are going to run and shoot. It will slow you down, and it would be extremely unusual for you to hit anything. The tape runner should have the smallest and lightest gun. He will be trying to live and be effective in the smallest bunkers. For this reason, he should be very conscious of what he carries. Only truly necessary items are worth taking in.

Gear

AFFORDABLE
Invaluable
Paintball
Paraphernalia

GET THE BIGGEST BANG FOR YOUR BUCK

Here's a list of simple, low-cost necessities you can purchase that will add to your enjoyment of the recreational paintball experience. Most items can be purchased at general merchandise stores, like Wal-Mart or K-Mart, at sporting goods stores, or at military surplus outlets.

1. A decent pair of ankle supporting shoes. High top style cleats are the best.

2. A pair of gloves. Can even be gardening type gloves. Less than $1.00 a pair. Cut the fingertips off. Bicycle gloves are great, too.

3. Knee Pads. The only way to slide.

4. Elbow Pads. Crawl without pain.

5. A good watch with a timer function or a kitchen timer. To keep track of time elapsed during games. Glue it to your loader's lid.

6. Fleece shotgun swab. A 12 gauge for barrel-cleaning.

7. M16 Ammo Pouches and belt.

8. Wool cap, to protect your head from close range hits.

9. Camouflage BDU pants and top. These come cheap if you buy them used.

10. MRE's (Meals Ready to Eat) In case you get hungry during those long games.

11. Toilet paper. It's a messy game, after all.

12. Military helmet storage bag, for your goggles.

13. Insect repellent with DEET. Avoid Lyme disease and keep away the bugs.

—SD

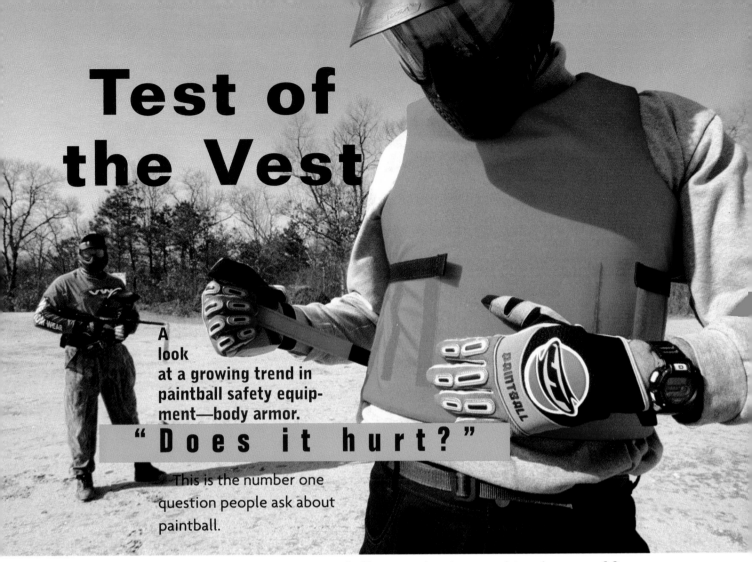

Test of the Vest

A look at a growing trend in paintball safety equipment—body armor.

"Does it hurt?"

This is the number one question people ask about paintball.

With the increase in paintball gun technology pushing the rate of fire ever higher, there is a definite need to provide players with safety equipment that can handle these new conditions. And as more people get into the game, why hurt 'em?

Rose and Dan Drewek have a deep love of paintball that goes beyond playing. Their dream is to have a profound impact on the industry by promoting safety. In 1993, they opened an outdoor paintball field in Canada. In 1996, they opened a retail store to better serve their customers and promote the sport. In 1998, they opened an indoor field.

Rose and Dan have been involved in paintball for 13 years. Dan has always been a tournament player, and has developed a number of local tournament teams. Dan currently plays for the Focus International factory team on the amateur circuit.

"I once had a child cry from the sting of a paintball at his own birthday party," explains Rose Drewek.

"I began to wonder if there were a way to run things so that people didn't have to be afraid of being hit by paintballs."

With this in mind, Paintball Encounters teamed up with Extreme Adventures, a Canadian manufacturing company, to develop a safety vest. They wanted to maintain authenticity and realism for players. They designed the vest to be the most universal piece of equipment available, next to a goggle system, and called it "The No Flak Jack."

Designed for both players and referees alike—in fact it was selected to be the safety vest worn by the referees at Skyball '99—the No Flak Jack is constructed of heavy Cordura material and is padded with closed cell foam. Two models are available: a recreational vest, which features a removable neck guard and an optional crotch protector (see *A Case for A Cup* and you'll know why this is a good idea), and a field rental version vest, which offers similar protection with a stripped-down design.

We decided to put the utility of a safety vest to the test as part of our field trials for this book. We wanted to see first hand whether the No Flak Jack lived up to the promises of its inventors.

A SIMPLE TEST

Our test was simple: four shots to the back and four to the front from ten feet away. Rob was shooting his Viper. Needless to say, I was reassured by Rob that he'd hit the target every time. This was good news, since I was wearing the vest.

Wham! Wham! Wham! Wham! to my back they came. The third shot landed on top of the second, right in the middle of my right shoulder blade. The impact was felt—in fact, the third shot did sting.

I turned around 180° and Rob repeated his

marksmanship skill four more times to my chest. Wham! Wham! The second shot threw paint onto my goggles. Wham! The last shot was a bounce, no break. Pain factor? None.

Removing the vest, there were no obvious welts, just a little redness. Twenty-four hours later where normally bruises would have appeared, there were none.

No marks. No welts. No soreness. Pretty Cool!

Since that day, I have worn the No Flak Jack under my coveralls on the field. I have been wearing the field rental model, because I like the design. Being a big guy, the straps tend to be a bit short, but nonetheless the vest does the trick.

Our conclusion: wearing a vest is an excellent safety precaution, especially as more and more kids are getting into the game. A close shot to the kidneys can indeed cause injury, so why risk it? If I had kids, and they played paintball, I'd make certain they wore a safety vest in addition to their goggle protection. It's a small investment (under $100), and well worth every penny to live to fight another day!

—AF

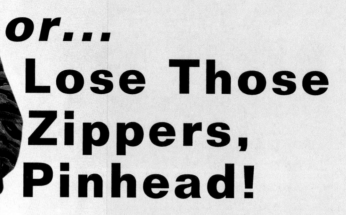

or... Lose Those Zippers, Pinhead!

AN INTERVIEW WITH GRAHAM EASTON AND ADAM GARDNER

ANDREW FLACH: Head to toe, what does the well-dressed player wear? Obviously, you're going to wear a pair of goggles. Would you wear a hat underneath your goggles?

ADAM GARDNER: I recommend it. As far as I'm concerned—the NPPL says you can pretty much put a pillow on your head, if you want to.

The point is that head protection is certainly something that I think is a good idea, and I think a garment of some sort on the head is a good idea, whether it's specially designed or not. I wear just a woolen winter hat. It doesn't hurt as much when you get hit in the head.

When it comes to clothing, we dress in layers. First, a long sleeved shirt. If you wear a T-shirt on the playing field, you're going to get a lot more bruising than if you wear a long-sleeved shirt. I strongly recommend a turtleneck because a turtleneck protects the front of the neck to some degree, and it certainly is a lot better to get hit in the neck if you're wearing a turtleneck than it is if you are not.

GRAHAM EASTON: And on top of that a loose fitting pull-over sweatshirt. One that's baggy and not tight to the skin. This will improve the odds that paint will not break when it hits you.

You don't want something that's super tight to the body because then the clothing tends to transmit the energy of the paintball to your skin. If your clothing hangs a little bit looser, it will absorb more energy before the paintball hits you.

Wear a top that doesn't have buttons, either on the sleeves or on front.

Buttons break paint. Elastic necks and cuffs are ideal. When you're crawling or moving through brush, you don't want your sleeve riding up your arm. Elastic will keep it where it should be. You can move, but you're not tight, you're not restricted. That's how you want to play.

The same holds true for your pants. No belts, no fly, no zippers. I would suggest something like stretch pants underneath the uniform as well-biking pants or long underwear. The undergarment should be tight, but then your second (outer) layer should be loose and baggy. You want to wear something that's soft and smooth and doesn't have a lot of zippers and buttons that are going to break paint.

ANDREW: Of course, you need something to carry paint. What do you recommend?

ADAM G: You'll find that the players have different budgets and different amounts of paint that they intend to shoot. A lot of your back line, bigger guys carry just as many rounds as they can carry. And then small kids and front-line players carry different amounts of paint in harnesses designed to accommodate them. One of the challenges is finding a harness that is comfortable to wear and that doesn't twist around to the front side of your body during a game.

GRAHAM: A good harness is one that will provide support to the lower back, as well.

ANDREW: What do you suggest you wear on your feet?

ADAM G: You have to be able to run to play paintball. If you go out there wearing your typical steel-shank army boot you won't be able to run. The best choice is a supportive high-top cleat.

Something to consider is the surface you'll be playing on. When you go into an indoor field, you are better off with a high-top tennis shoe. If you wear your cleats and you're playing on a cement floor, you'll start skidding.

One of the other things I can recommend highly: neoprene socks. It looks like part of a diving suit that's worn over the foot. In paintball, in various conditions, your feet get wet and cold, depending on where you are in the country. And even if they don't get cold, the neoprene sock prevents your ankles from twisting. It almost works as an extra ligament. We haven't had an accident in five years.

The negative side is they smell.

GRAHAM: When you lace your boot up, the neoprene sock almost conforms around the boot. So, it's very, very tight, very comfortable. And as the day goes on, you can just feel the support. I don't get swollen ankles anymore.

On your shins and knees, wear a nice pair of pads to protect yourself in case you slide or in case you accidentally fall. Obviously, everybody knows how painful it is to hit your shins or get a bruise on your knee, so why risk it? Protect your legs.

ADAM G: In paintball, you're always sliding. It's like football or baseball. When you run in, your gun's up, you're shooting and you hit you knees and you tend to slide in. And there are lots of things on the ground that really hurt when you slide into bunkers. So knee/shin pads are important.

ANDREW: Do you wear something like that to protect your elbows?

GRAHAM: I wear an elbow pad because I'm on the ground a lot. Indoor players tend to wear plenty of padding because they are playing on harder surfaces and the bunkers are of man-made materials. Outdoor players tend not to wear elbow protection. Unfortunately, they can be uncomfortable. It's a decision people make for themselves.

At least, wear gloves. Either full-fingered or fingerless gloves. They really help.

ANDREW: What about something like a Camelback or any of those water bottle things? Do you see a lot of that being used?

ADAM G: You mean carry a water bottle while you're playing? Paintball generally doesn't last that long in terms of an individual game to concern yourself with hydration during the game. Except during longer, scenario-type games.

It's important to drink plenty of water before games and between games. Some people don't and they get dehydrated. Being dehydrated can zap your energy, no matter what you're doing, but especially when you're exerting yourself.

It's very rare that you're going to play for hours without a break. When you have the opportunity to drink between games, do it. Speaking of hydration, a lot of people in the warmer climates feel that the less clothes you wear, the less dehydrated you'll get. It's actually the opposite.

If you wear a thin layer of clothes, the moisture on your skin is evaporating constantly. One of the most important things you need in deserts is a full winter jacket. You know those Middle Eastern robes that look so light? They just flow in the wind? Well, they're made of thick wool. They actually help preserve your body's moisture within the folds. The same principle is at work if you're dressed appropriately for paintball.

The hottest temperature at a tournament we ever played was 122 degrees in L.A. Heat is a problem with paintball. When it's this hot, cover yourself up, cool down, and drink plenty of water. Simple stuff, but it's easy to neglect.

ANDREW: Sounds like a day pack is needed to get your stuff to the field.

ADAM G: Paintball players are not carrying just a little bit. They are carrying a ton of junk. You've got a harness, you've got a few loaders of balls, you've got a case of paint or half a case of paint, you have

a gun, maybe a back-up gun. You have shoes, socks. They're packing a suitcase, not a day pack. Paintball is equipment-intensive, like golf.

ANDREW: So, another piece of gear is a decent gear bag.

ADAM: Sure. One thing kids do is use those wheeled coolers, the kind you find at the local K-Mart or Wal-Mart. They make a very good, inexpensive way of getting your equipment around because when you go to a paintball field you have to haul this stuff to where you're playing.

THE BEST WAY TO HIDE YOUR FACE

ADAM G: Goggleflauge was invented by George Davidson of the All Americans. In it's simplest form it's a great way to disguise your goggles. But it's more than that.

In paintball, one key to success is spotting your opponents and taking them out with a clean shot before they have a chance to do the same to you.

Why not take a little extra precaution and hide your face more carefully? After all, your round head provides an excellent target for the enemy. Your glinting goggle lenses call to him to put a nice shot between your eyes.

Why present a clear target? You've got your cammies on, right? Add on some Goggleflauge and you'll stay in the game that much longer.

If you use your Goggleflauge properly, you can slowly work your head up to a crack in the bunker you're hiding in and look right at your opponents without them even seeing you. A major advantage, I think you'd agree.

Another advantage of Goggleflauge is that it softens the blow. It may cause a ball or two to bounce off (and you know they don't count unless they break), but more importantly, if you get hit in the face at point blank range and you're wearing your Goggleflauge, you'll be a much happier player.

You know how your goggles have little holes in the plastic face guard? When a ball hits there it breaks into little pieces which fly at about 150–300 feet per second if you're hit within 5 feet. And when those innocent little pieces hit your skin... there's an ouch factor.

With your Goggleflauge, you may still feel it a bit, but it won't hurt as bad. That's a promise from the manufacturer.

If you've been eating paintballs by the bowlful, it's time to invest in some Goggleflauge, don't you think?

THE CASE FOR A CUP

Andrew Flach Recounts a Personal Moment
of Humility & Discomfort

To wear a cup or not wear a cup, that is the question. Of all the answers I've sought in the process of putting together this book, it is the most mercurial of them all. Some people swear by cups, others swear against them, saying they're too uncomfortable and restricting. Many players who never wear them can recall situations where they wished they had.

The first time I ever played paintball was at an indoor field called Dark Armies in Indianapolis, Indiana. As we went through the check-in procedures and briefing, we were informed that protective cups were available for purchase at $7 each. I skipped the additional investment and threw my extra bucks into more paint and a gun upgrade, naturally.

Wouldn't you know, in the early moments of my very first game, as I leaned stealthily out of a doorway... Wham! Wham! Wham! Three "precise" shots right in the crotch. Kinda took my breath away. "I'm hit. I'm hit," I cried, hoping to end the flow of balls to my already sore area. The shooter stopped, and I hopped out-of-bounds.

The lesson: paintballs can hurt.
My advice: wear a cup.

Lock & Load

Paintball loaders serve one purpose: to feed more paint into a marker more efficiently. The first "Loaders" were tubes that were a permanent part of a paintball gun. To load a paintball you had to rock the gun to roll a paintball into the open breech, and then cock the gun. "Rock-N-Cock" loading systems like this are still evident in Stock Class paintball guns like the PGP, Phantom SC, and P-68SC. Many players added a "speedloader" to these guns to add another tube, and another 10 paintballs.

The widespread desire to carry more paint in a gun led to a simple "Stick Feeder." It was essentially a PVC tube attached to a PVC elbow that was designed to come off the back of an on-gun feed tube. A sock holder prevented the balls from rolling out of the top. It was usually designed to hold another 10-15 paintballs. Anything longer was too much of a target. Later, when direct feed guns were introduced, many players still used a stick feeder for quite some time.

The Idema Combat Systems vest, filled with with tube loaders. Introduced 1988 — Discontinued 1991.

Many people made "Home-brew" loaders from all sorts of objects. The most popular was an old oil can cleaned out, the top made into a lid, and placed onto the neck of a paintball gun. "D.A.M. cans" were a mass-produced version of the oil-can loaders. This design eventually lead to the mass-produced "Worr Games Ammo Box." This box held 45 paintballs, and had an opening for tubed paint (as in 10 round tubed paint). The WGP ammo box had the advantage of being smaller and more streamlined than the oil-can style of loaders. It was an instant hit.

Larger loaders were introduced very quickly. The first was the "Whaler," which resembled a large sausage tube with "Magic Fish Lips" (no, I'm not making this up!) to aid in faster loading. The need for a better loader was answered by Viewloader, a company that introduced a modular 90-round hopper simply called "Viewloader." It had a clear flip lid, which was easy to look into and to load on the fly.

Viewloader also made 45-round hoppers with which one could fill this new loader. Other companies used this same principle to create a plethora of 100–150 capacity loaders. This was the norm, with a few larger loaders becoming available.

The only problem with all this was the paint. Many paintball guns wouldn't create enough of a 'kick' to move the paint around, and jams were common. Imagine having to shoot five times, shake your gun, shoot another 5 times, shake your gun, and doing this all day. Players wanted a solution, and Viewloader delivered one.

Viewloader created the first patented agitating loader, the VL-2000. It works by placing an electronic eye in the feed neck that tells a motherboard to rotate a paddle to move the paintballs around in the loader. They originally designed it on their 200 round loader, but with time and research it's become streamlined and efficient. Many players agree that the 200 round loader is the best for size, weight, and capacity.

The latest in high-technology is based on the VL-2000, called the "VL-2001." It's an electronic loader that you plug into the gun itself. The motor rotates and agitates the balls at a predetermined trigger pull. Electropneumatic paintguns like the Angel or the Shocker use this kind of loader, as the guns themselves are electronics-based.

Other loaders are still available. For example Indian Springs makes a 125 paintball hopper that's well suited for pump guns, if you're into vintage old-school play. Many other companies and loaders exist as well. Keep your eyes open for the next best thing—force-feed. But for the time being you have many excellent loaders to choose from.

-RR

Brief History of the Loader

A. 15 round stick feeder

B. Worr Games Product Ammo Box

C. Indian Springs 120 round loader

D. View Loader Revolution, Brass Eagle, with VL timer

Squeegees in a Nutshell

The Fine Art of Squeegee

WHERE TO START

There are two basic styles of squeegees on the market. Picking one is a matter of objective necessity and personal preference. Both clean out your barrel very effectively, but you may like one more than the other.

The first style is a "Stick" squeegee. "Stick" squeegees are long plastic tubes with a rubber disc at one end, and a spring-style action at the other end. To use this effectively, you push down on one end to push the rubber disk out. You need to flatten the disk out, and push it down the barrel.

When you release the top spring, the disk comes flat against the plastic tube, filling the barrel. When you pull out the squeegee, it pulls broken paint and shell out with it. Many styles have a cloth on the opposite end, with which you can clean any residual paint out of your barrel.

The other style is a "Pull Through" or "Cable" squeegee. The cable style has several disks on a cord, and sometimes a fluffy "Swab" on the end. To use one, you need to remove the barrel from the paintball gun. You place the end without the disks in one end of the barrel, feeding it to the other side. You then pull on that end to bring the disks through the barrel, cleaning out the paint in your barrel. The "Swab" removes anything that may be left in the barrel, making one clean sweep.

Both styles have advantages and disadvantages.

- Stick squeegees are easy to use and you'll be done in a jiffy, but they may not clean the barrel as effectively as a pull through.

- A pull through can't be used on some styles of paintball guns with "Fixed" (non-removable) barrels.

B

- Pull through squeegees can be folded, and fit into your pocket.

- Stick squeegees are bulky.

After squeegeeing your gun, you should clean off the disks. Placing a stick squeegee in the back of your knee and wiping it clean is a fast way to do this.

A. Straight Shot
B. Jerk
C. Battle Swab®
D. Power Squeegee
E. Barrel swab

-RR

If you borrow someone else's squeegee, it's good form to clean it off before you return it.

"PAINT IN THE HOLE"

DENNIS TIPPMANN, JR.: Paintball grenades are made of surgical tubing, which is like rubber tubing. Basically, we pump up this heavy-walled rubber tubing like you would a water balloon. It takes about 100 pounds pressure to pump these things up. Once they're pumped up, we put two balls in the end. The two balls are positioned right up by the neck that's holding all the paint back. Now the remaining chunks of tubes are sticking out there. We've pulled it and we put a cap on, and we put a pin in that keeps the balls in place. During a game, you pull the pin on the grenade (some guys pull the cap off, it really doesn't matter) and throw it. As soon as it hits the ground, the cap just pops off. The impact pops the two balls out and they just spray in any and every direction. They spray all over the place, and you'll get fully painted if one lands near you.

If someone threw one in the middle of a 100 square foot room, there would be speckles and quarter-sized splotches along all of the walls. So, yes, this can be a pretty powerful part of your paintball arsenal.

Sights & Scopes

All you have to do is line up opponents in your crosshairs and pull the trigger! It's that easy, right?

not quite...

THE HARD CORE TRUTH ABOUT SIGHTS & SCOPES

Many players use sights or scopes on their paintball guns to help improve "accuracy." I've seen some very impressive 20x-scopes placed on all sorts of paintguns. But do they really help your *accuracy*? Well, yes and no.

A paintball is not a bullet. Therefore, the accuracy of a paintball cannot be guaranteed. A paintball is filled with liquid, so all sorts of variables affect what happens to it once it's shot out the end of a barrel. The wind can catch it and blow it round. Extreme high velocity can make it unstable. Even the paint can influence your accuracy. Other things that affect the path of a paintball include:

- The gun and barrel brands and how they match-up.

- If your paint is dry or dimpled or wet.

- If your barrel has broken paint in it.

- The phase of the moon. (Just kidding, but you get the point. Many things affect your paintball's path!)

Adco Hot Shot, Adco vision 2000

Where a paintball is going to go is often an unknown. So, the scope usually out-performs the paint. This isn't to say that a scope or sight is useless. I've had a lot of success using them on my personal paintguns. You just need to understand a few guidelines for the use of these accessories so that you can optimize your experience of them.

HOW TO USE SIGHTS & SCOPES TO IMPROVE YOUR GAME

My opinion is that scopes have limited usefulness. Why? Magnification interferes with your aim. Your magnified perspective will usually be further ahead than the ball will travel. That said, I grant that sights and scopes are useful for looking downfield in the larger "big game" formats of paintball. In other words, use the magnification to look a couple hundred yards ahead to see if your competition is moving around out there, where they're headed, things like this. Of course, opportunities to do this are few and far between for most people. In most cases, you want a sight with no magnification that simply puts a "dot" in space.

Once you've gotten your sight, you want to "Dial it in." What is *dialing*? In an ideal scenario, realize that a sight can only tell you where the barrel is pointed, not where your paint will eventually go. A little experimentation will tell you where paint is likely to go when you're aiming at something within a certain range. If you can hit a pie-plate at 75 feet, you can calibrate or 'dial' your sight so that it will reflect where the paint usually goes at that dis-

Smart Parts HI VIZ

tance. This takes some time and patience. I like to dial in at 75–100 feet, as most of my shooting happens within that range.

In regular "toe-to-toe" play, you usually don't use sights. I find myself just shooting and following where the last ball went, or using the barrel itself as a large point sight. For long angle shots, or for ambush situations, sights work very well. My personal technique may not work for everyone, but it's worth trying.

Place the dot on your opponent's chest area. If a ball drifts in most any direction, it will still probably hit them. I like to keep both eyes open for a stereoscopic view, but some prefer to close one eye to concentrate on the shot. Either way works well. Then, simply pull the trigger in the same way that you would any other time. Don't change that detail, because if you do it won't "feel" right and you probably won't hit the person. Paintguns have no recoil, so slow trigger pulls aren't necessary. In some cases, it may not give you the best shot. Some players put a short "string" of 3 balls on a target, but sometimes that's not necessary.

Using a sight or a scope may or may not improve your game. Your best bet is to invest in an inexpensive sight to try it out. If it helps your game or you just really enjoy using it, you'll find no shortage of variety in terms of available scopes and sights.

—RR

Armson/Pro-Team Products
Pro-Drop Red Dot

PART 4

DRILLS

Warm Up Play Hot

Prepare Your Body to Optimize Your Game Play

After interviewing some of the top paintball players and paintball field owners in the world, it was apparent that many of the injuries that occur during a paintball game could be easily avoided by a moderate level of fitness and flexibility. In fact, the two biggest injuries are ankle sprains and muscle pulls (hamstrings and lower back). The ankle injuries can be decreased by wearing proper shoes such as high top cleats and a few basic calf exercises and stretches. The hamstrings and the lower back can also be strengthened by a easy routine of stretching and exercising. This chapter is devoted not only to preventing the most common injuries in paintball, but to assisting adventurous paintball players in becoming more flexible, faster, stronger, and healthier. Follow this step-by-step stretching program during the week and you will be able to splat your opponents with ease during the weekend paintball games.

Stewart Smith graduated from the United States Naval Academy in 1991. He then spent four years on SEAL teams, after which he was put in charge of the physical training and selection of future BUD/S candidates. Stewart currently runs the getfitnow.com family fitness center in Severna Park, Maryland.

WARMING-UP

Warming up prior to stretching, exercise, and playing paintball is absolutely crucial to injury prevention. You will find that your muscles are more flexible and react to stretching far better after a brief 5–10 minute warm-up. Do this by walking, jogging slowly, riding a bike, or doing 50 jumping jacks.

The objective is to get your heart pumping above its normal rate, which will increase the blood flow to the muscles that you are about to stretch and use. Stretching is not only the best way to avoid injuries, but also the best way to prepare yourself to get tight and small behind a bunker, and then explode in a sprint on the attack. Regardless of your age, paintball is a vigorous and challenging sport that will test your stamina. To take your game to the next level, give your body the attention it needs, and follow these simple guidelines.

YO!

We'll be covering only stretches in this book, so we encourage you to check out our workout resources for the active sports enthusiast by visiting the GetFitNow.com web site. As most of our workout books are derived from the finest fitness regimens in the world, those of our United States Armed Forces, we are certain that you will find them extremely helpful in training to become the ultimate paintball warrior!

S T R E T C H E S

UPPER AND LOWER BODY

Arm (Shoulder)

Drop your shoulder and pull your arm across your chest. With the opposite arm, gently pull your arm across your chest and hold for 15 seconds. Repeat with the other arm.

This stretches the back of the shoulder and muscles that attach the shoulder blade to the upper part of the back. This is the very root of most tension headaches. Keeping these muscles flexible will help prevent injuries caused by running and falling to the ground when you are seeking cover from incoming paintballs.

The Most Advanced Piece of Machinery in Paintball? Your Body.

Arm Circles

Rotate your arms slowly in big circles forward and then reverse. This will help prepare your shoulders for pushups, dips, and dumbbell work.

Triceps into Lateral Stretch

Place both arms over and behind your head. Grab your right elbow with your left hand and pull your elbow toward your opposite shoulder. Lean with the pull. Repeat with the other arm.

This stretch prepares you for the dumbbell triceps exercises, pushups, and dips, but also helps stretch the back muscles. This is a very important stretch for upper body exercises!

Chest

Stand with your arms extended and parallel to the floor. Slowly pull your elbows back as far as you can. Hold for 15 seconds. Do not thrust your arms backwards. This is a slow and deliberate stretch designed to prepare your chest for pushups, dips, and other shoulder/chest exercises.

Shoulder Rotations

Rotate your shoulders slowly up and down, keeping your arms relaxed by your side. Your shoulders should rotate in small circles and move up and down in slow distinct movements.

Stomach Stretch

Lie on your stomach. Push yourself up to your elbows. Slowly lift your head and shoulders and look up at the sky or ceiling. Hold for 15 seconds and repeat two times.

Hip Rotations

Place your hands on your hips and slowly rotate your hips in big circles clockwise and counter-clockwise for about 15 seconds in each direction.

**In a game where a miss is as good as a mile,
an extra show of agility,
degree of flexibility, or burst of speed can make the difference
between Triumph and Defeat!**

Thigh Stretch On Ground

Lie on your left side. Pull your right foot to your butt by grabbing your ankle and hold it with your right hand. Keep your knees close together and hold for 10–15 seconds. Repeat with the other leg.

Calf Stretch / Achilles Tendon Stretch

Stand with one foot 2–3 feet in front of the other. With both feet pointing in the same direction you are facing, put most of your body weight on the leg that is behind you, stretching the calf muscle.

Now, bend the rear knee slightly. You should now feel the stretch in your heel. This stretch helps prevent achilles tendonitis, a severe injury that will sideline most paintball players for at least 4–6 weeks.

Hamstring Stretch

From the standing or sitting position, bend forward at the waist and touch your toes. Keep your back straight and slightly bend your knees. You should feel this stretching the back of your thighs near the connection of the leg and butt. Now, slowly straighten your legs, feeling the stretch travel down your leg and behind your knees. You have just stretched the entire hamstring. Hold both the straight leg and bent leg stretch for 15 seconds each.

Most people pull their hamstring at the top part of the leg (where it connects to the buttocks). By simply bending your knees while stretching, you will decrease your chances of suffering the most common injury to paintball players.

Groin/Inner Thigh Side Stretch

Stand with your legs spread and lean to the left. Keep the right leg straight while pointing the toes up. Repeat on the other side. This will help prevent groin strains, another common injury to paintball players who play speedball and games with a similar fast-paced tempo.

Hurdler Stretch

Sit on the floor with your legs straight in front of you. Bend your right knee and place the bottom of your foot on the inside of your opposite thigh. With your back straight, lean forward in order to stretch the back of your legs and lower back. Hold the stretch for 15 seconds, switch legs, and repeat.

Ilio Tibial Stretch

Sit on the ground with your legs crossed in front of you. Keeping your legs crossed, bring the top leg to your chest and bend it at the knee so that your foot is placed outside of your thigh. Hold for 15 seconds and repeat with the other leg.

You should perform this stretch before and after running. This will help prevent very common over-use injuries in the hips and knees.

Knees-to-Chest

Lie flat on your back. Pull your knees to your stomach and hold for 20 seconds. You should perform this stretch before and after any abdominal exercise.

As you may know, the lower back is the most commonly injured area of the body. Many lower back problems stem from inactivity, lack of flexibility, and improper lifting of heavy objects. Stretching and exercising your lower back will help prevent injuries to this extremely sensitive area.

Butterfly

Sit on your buttocks with your knees bent and the soles of your feet together. Grab your ankles and place both of your elbows on your inner thighs. Slowly push down on your thighs.

AND NOW YOU'RE READY TO RUMBLE

Underestimating the stress you put on your body when playing this game is a surefire way to get injured or develop chronic aches and pains. If you do these stretches every day, and always perform them before playing paintball, you will be doing yourself a huge favor.

Stewart Smith's Paintball Workout is available on our web site, GetFitNow.com, for those of you interested in the achieving the highest possible performance.

PAUL FOGAL ON FITNESS
F i t n e s s   D o e s   M a t t e r

"I think one of the beauties of paintball is that just about anybody can play because you can play to your level of fitness. If you're scared or you're slow or you have a disability or something, you can play a static defense. You can guard the flag. You can be a central source of communication. You have options people who aren't in the best shape don't have in other sports. And if you happen to be in great shape and you're real aggressive, then you can go out on offense and you can run.

It certainly helps to be in some kind of shape, because then you really have your choice of how you want to play. And, of course, small, quick people definitely have an advantage. It's harder to hit a quick and small target. You don't have to be in particularly great shape to enjoy paintball, but the better shape you're in, the more options you have."

Stretch out and you'll feel better before, during, and after you play!

Tactical Drills for the Beginner

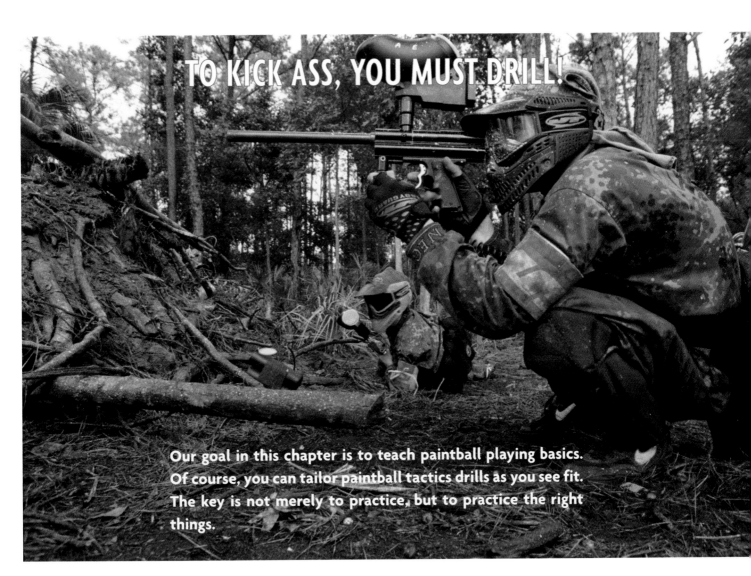

TO KICK ASS, YOU MUST DRILL!

Our goal in this chapter is to teach paintball playing basics. Of course, you can tailor paintball tactics drills as you see fit. The key is not merely to practice, but to practice the right things.

FIRST THINGS FIRST

Chronograph your paintgun to 285–290 feet per second (fps), the appropriate outdoor playing speed.

Each drill is a scenario. The object of each scenario is similar to what you will face on a normal playing day in both recreational and tournament play. Once you know the moves, you can repeat them with minimal effort. Think of them as "katas" of sorts.

Each drill should be performed from "both ends" if applicable. The idea is to combine all of the aspects of the game into your individual game. Even in a team setting, your individual moving, shooting, and communication skills will make or break a game.

SHOOTING DRILLS

You'll need the following supplies: Paper Plates (pie tins, frisbees, etc.), a stopwatch.

Obstacle course

Object—Run the course as fast as you can, hitting all the targets as you do so. This is a sample course, feel free to adjust it to your conditions and playing field. Just remember that the course should resemble a playing field as accurately as possible.

- On breakout, hit a 100 foot target

- From a bunker position, hit 75' and a 50' targets

- Run to new bunker, shoot a 75' offhanded shot (lefty for right-handers, righty for left-handers)

- Run to new position, shooting at a positioned plate as you pass it. (This is called bunkering or a 'takedown').

- From new bunker, take offhand 50', 75' shots, then regular hand 75', 50' shots.

- Take a 150' long shot from new position, then turn around for a 25' close shot.

- Stop watch at flag station bunker. Repeat the course until you improve your time and accuracy. Then change the course to give yourself a fresh challenge.

A SIMPLE RUN & SHOOT DRILL

Another simple Run & Shoot Drill is to set up a series of targets (in this case soda jugs hanging from a rope) and run past them, shooting as you go. Your motion, as well as the swinging of the jugs makes this a particularly challenging drill.

Of course, you do have options...

Two player option: Follow the same course with a player shooting at you as you run through it.

Team option: On the same course, one player moves while the second gives cover fire. When the target is hit, the second player leapfrogs to the next position.

Pressure option: Same course, teammate runs course behind you. If you do not hit your target before your teammate does, your teammate is allowed to shoot you to get you to move.

BACKFOOT TACTICS DRILL

Timed Offense/Defense

Needed—At least 2 players, position of defense (such as a flag station or a building), flag, stopwatch.

Setup—3 attackers to 2 defenders *or* 2 attackers to 1 defender

Scenario—For each defender, put 1 minute and 30 seconds on the clock.

Goals

- Defense must prevent a flag pull.
- Offense must grab the flag and get away clean in the time allotted.
- Offense may set up anywhere beyond 150 feet of the defensive flag.
- Defense may set up anywhere within 150 feet of the flag, the closer the better.

Lessons

Offense—Must be aggressive when the numbers are in their favor, and learn to push hard under time pressure.

Defense—Learn how to be patient and kill a clock when outnumbered. Survival is the key, and staying in the game under pressure is hard.

This drill can also be used to simulate defending an opponents' flag station while they are trying to bring your flag in for a win. For this, do 3 on 1. Your solo guy gets a minute to set up. The aggressors have 2 minutes to hang the flag.

WORKING WITH BUNKERS

All bunkers "work" (or *are worked*) in the same manner. Flat-sided ones are easier to demonstrate on. The drills I'm highlighting here apply for use of trees, brambles, or any similar protection.

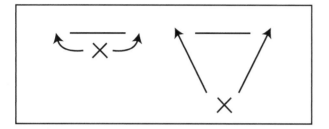

Take A Few Steps Back To Gain Perspective and Expand Your Field of Vision and Kill Zone

Get back if you can. You can cover more space with less effort.

Be Unpredictable

Move around in a position, because "Jack in the Boxes" get hit.

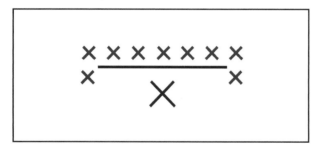

The little red markers represent all of the potential angles from which "X" can pop up and take shots at his opponents. Being unpredictable keeps your opponents waiting for your next move.

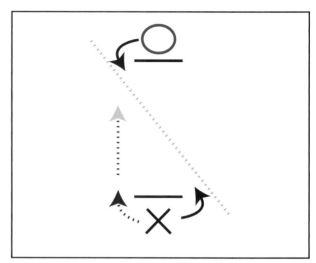

When "X" sees that "O" keeps emerging from the left side, he suspects his opponent is right-handed and relies too much on firing from the same place. They exchange fire along the pink line several times. Then, by shifting to the left side of his bunker and using his left hand, "X" surprises "O", and gets the elimination. "X" is right-handed, but he practices left-handed shooting to gain the advantage in scenarios like this one.

Downfall of the "Right Hand" Conspiracy

Actually, what we're talking about here has absolutely nothing to do with a conspiracy. It just happens to be the case that most people are right-handed and have a natural propensity to favor the right side of their bunker. From your perspective, that means most opponents will be emerging from the left side of their bunker. If you practice shooting with your off hand, you can make better use of your cover to eliminate your opponent.

This is pretty powerful knowledge, but you need to practice taking advantage of it!

Go the other way and take opponents out before they know what hit them.

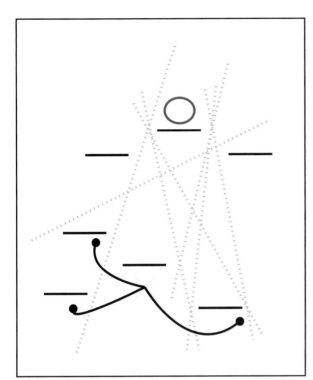

By moving behind different bunkers, even moving backwards, "X" is able to attain new angles of attack against "O." The dotted lines are shooting lanes that "X" can take advantage of if he's willing to take new positions.

Be Dynamic—Move From Bunker to Bunker To Gain New Angles of Attack

Use all the space you have available, even if it means falling back or shifting sideways. One person can take up a lot of space.

(A) "X" is in a tough spot. One moment, he's occupying two opponents. The next, he finds himself wide open to a flanking "O." While calling for support from teammates, "X" must act fast to maintain his position, using fire to literally "cover" his own position. This can't last for long!

(B) With support from a stealthy teammate who heard his coded plea for assistance, "X" is able to turn the opponents' perception of his weakness against them. As they move in for the kill, they are taken out by "X"'s flanking teammate. Now it's 2-on-1 in favor of our resourceful team "X" who quickly take new positions. *Never give up!*

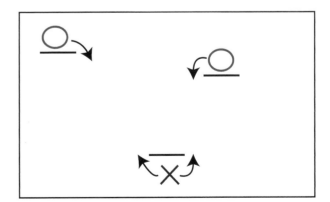

"X" is focused on the "O" right in front of him. This is exactly what Team "O" is counting on. A preoccupied "X" is easy to flank, as we can see from the first diagram. "X" is about to become "American History X."

A more mature "X" is moving in his bunker and looking for enemies on all sides. Here he has a good chance of keeping two opponents at bay, even taking them both out. Observe that if "X" has practiced using both left and right hands, he'll be more effective at keeping his opponents on their heels. Never stop moving behind your bunker. "X" should also communicate that he has two "O"'s in from of him and try to turn the tables on them with help from teammates! "X" may also want to try 'taking a few steps back' to facilitate handling this relatively precarious situation.

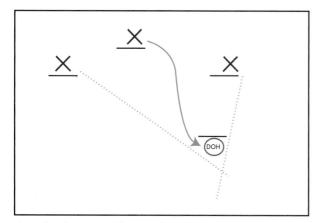

The Ultimate DOH! This is what happens to someone who doesn't communicate and doesn't play as part of a team. Or someone on a team that has been demolished!

If you're the only one left, and you find yourself completely overwhelmed, you still have options. As you can see, if "O" doesn't move, he's a goner. May as well try to take out as many of the opposition as he can!

**Avoid tunnel vision!
In a bunker, keep looking and shooting
both ways to keep your enemies at bay.**

**Look for natural holes in cover
(like barrels) and shoot through them.**

HERO TIME!

DELUSIONS OF INVINCIBILITY CAN BE USEFUL

Sometimes you need to act in a manner that others will perceive as incredibly daring and maybe even a little crazy. But in reality, a grand (or gutsy) move can blow open a game. Your opponents may fall into the trap of expecting you to be as cautious as they are. Suddenly, you're heading for an extremely aggressive position. They may get distracted by your audacity and pause before responding. If you pull it off, they'll feel demoralized and may be inclined to become preoccupied with your ominous position.

"I can't believe that guy just did that. What's he going to do next?"

These are just a few of the questions that you can implant in the minds of your foe with a bold move!

Another benefit of this is that it takes the heat off of your teammates, who should be able to take better positions while the other team is second-guessing itself. Of course, you should scream at your team to do this if they're not responding promptly.

**Aggression can be rewarded, as long as you are
in control and know what is going on.**

DRILLING FOR DOUBLES

Coordinating your game play with one other person makes you a double-threat both defensively and offensively. The following drills will enable you to practice basic coordination techniques that can lead to dramatic results in games. You'll take a couple of steps closer to an elevated understanding of paintball when you practice working in teams. Drilling 2-on-2 is a great way to work on coordinated offense and defense.

Low Man Approach With Cover
High man supplies cover by shooting over crawler. Crawler takes new position and shoots opponent.

Flank'em
One flanks left while other teammate shoots to keep opponent occupied and down. Flanker shoots opponent from new position.

Overbound
One moves, the other takes his place. This is called displacing. Keep moving up like the ends of a centipede.

Bait and Switch

Direct an opponent to one side of a bunker by shooting at one side consistently. It's human nature to move away from incoming fire, so this is likely to work. The opponent is likely to use the other side to "return fire."

Keep paint on the side your flanker is approaching to prevent your opponent from returning fire to that side and discovering your flanker. You are the bait. Your opponent will be flanked and eliminated in no time.

Overwhelming force

Having superior numbers does not guarantee victory. A patient and skilled opponent will pick your teammates off one by one if you're not careful and methodical about eliminating him. The idea is to get angles. The more sides of your opponent you shoot at, the less chance he has to hide behind cover to avoid you.

DO IT AGAIN!

Drills can be fun, but they are not ends in themselves. The point of doing drills is to improve your response to live game situations. **There's nothing as satisfying as bearing witness to your own improvement in paintball. The shortest path to that uplifting experience is a balance of frequent drilling and playing.**

—RR

COMMUNICATIONS AND CODES

Communication on the paintball field is vital to winning.

Lack of communication spells defeat for your team. If the other side has equal skills and is communicating better than you are, you'll be counting far too much on luck to win. Whatever methods you choose, pick a system that is easy to follow and remember. In the heat of the game, you can always rely on plain old English, but codes can be faster if used well, and they can confuse your opponents!

There are plenty of things to communicate on the field:

- The Status of Your Team-what are you going to do; what's your team's status
- The Status of Your Opponent's Team-what are they doing; what's their status
- The Status of the Overall Game-how much time is left; how many players are left
- Field Locations-where is everyone
- Junk Codes-designed to throw off the opponent, they are meaningless

Verbal Codes

These are faster to communicate than visual signals

Here are few examples of verbal codes (and their meanings) that have been developed by actual teams:

Fishing - I've got a gun jam
Sunshine Red - Everyone shoot right
Sunset Blue - Everyone shoot left
Going Shopping - I'm off to "bunker" someone
Mickey Says - Indicates how much time is left in the game. "Mickey Says Three" means there are 3 minutes remaining in the game.
Exxon - Reloading
Juice - The Flag
Visa - Attack (As in "Charge!".)

Field Locations can be identified by memorizing a simple grid describing rows and columns, or a clever code system. Draw a grid with an "x" and "y" axis dividing the field into 4 quadrants. Then, draw horizontal lines to delimit 6 "rows." Use colors to divide the field down the middle. "Red3", for instance, might describe a bunker in the 3rd row on the left side of the field. "Blue3 would indicate the same row of bunkers on the right side of the field.

A more complex system, but one which might be easier to remember, can be based on the map of the US, the hands of a clock, or the locations of stores in a shopping mall familiar to your team.

Make certain all players on your team know your code inside-out! You can tape a copy of the day's codes to the inside lid of your loader.

Codes can be based on a number of different schemes: car types, breakfast cereals, animals, cartoon characters...anything goes so long as it's easy to understand.

Here's a code based on airline travel:

Passport - The flag
Lost My Luggage - Gun Down
Found My Luggage - Gun Working Again
New York - The Right Tape
LA - The Left Tape
Flight Delayed - Reloading
Cancel the Ticket - Bunker someone
Disneyland - The Opponents Flag Station
The Gate - Your Team's Flag Station
In-Flight Movie - Your team has the advantage
Airline Food - You are in a bad position and could use some cover
Buckle Seatbelts - Everyone attack
Emergency Exit -The flag is in jeopardy

Obviously, codes can add a fun dimension to your game. Why not make up your own code and try it out with your friends!

Sarah's Drills 2Die4

Here are a few suggestions for drills from an expert at drilling, Sarah Stevenson of 2Die4!

Anyone can participate in paintball at any level regardless of size, sex, color, creed, beliefs, habits... basically, it's an open party. You don't even have to own your own gun or equipment! However, if you want to be any good at this game, you have to develop certain skills. The old adage about practice making perfect is as true in paintball as it is in any endeavor.

Paintball is a sport in which you cannot look at your opponent and assess them merely on a visual basis. This is primarily a marksmanship and reaction-type sport. So your opponent doesn't have to be the strongest nor the fastest adversary to beat you. How do you gain an edge in this game? You must be tuned in to the game, have a full knowledge of your equipment, and play within your own physical abilities.

The whole idea of drills is to help improve your reaction time and target shooting ability. The following drills work very well with a few basic supplies. You will need the following items at your disposal: empty milk jugs or coffee cans, rope, and a stop watch.

Target Shooting

1. Place 3 targets approximately 15 feet apart and at different heights (place on top of bunkers and hang from trees).

2. Walk approximately 25 feet away and face away from the targets.

3. Count down, 3-2-1, spin, drop to one knee and (shooting only three times at each target) shoot left, center, right.

How many shots did it take to hit the targets? Which one was easier to hit than the others? After you have done this a few times, change the placement of the targets and your distance (either closer or farther away) and repeat it for a while. This drill will help you with your speedball reaction time. When you have two players running at you and they are spaced apart, you won't hesitate to take them on and you'll have success.

Snap Shooting

1. Again, place a jug on top (or on the ground to one side) of the bunker.

2. Place yourself behind another bunker just opposite the target. Crouch on your knees and raise your gun to your shoulder, leaning close to the edge you wish to shoot from. Lean out very quickly, shoot no more than twice, and come back in to your bunker.

3. Repeat until you hit the target.

How many attempts did it take to hit the target? Now, start again, only this time lean out the *opposite* side from the one you did before. Practice right and left snap shooting. This is a *very* important drill. This exercise will save you more times than you can count. It applies in either woods play or indoor speedball.

One-on-One

1. Two players take the field at opposite ends, set your clocks for 3 minutes.

2. Face away from each other *completely* (gun and all)!

3. 3-2-1, GO! Turn and try and take out your opponent as quickly as you can!

The technique this drill practices helps players try and "rule-the-field." You must take control of the opposition as soon as you come out from your flag station. Start shooting at them, follow where they run to, and *do not let them come out from their bunker to shoot at you!* As you keep their head in their bunker, you attempt to move up the field (never taking your eyes off their position), keeping other bunkers between you and your adversary.

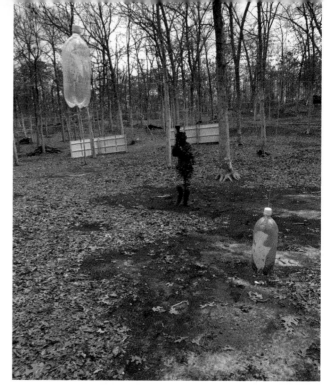

This does not mean that you must shoot at them all the time, but you must be prepared. Your gun should be raised at all times so you can shoot every time you see them move. Soon, you will be close enough to slow down your rate of fire, minimize movements, and watch for them to come out. Then, "WAP!" you got 'em!

After you practice this for a while, try a few two-on-one's, two-on-two's, three-on-one's, etc. This will help build you up to what it is like in a tournament level competition.

RUN & SHOOT

1. Set up a jug on top of a bunker or hang from a string to add motion and increase difficulty.

2. Walk approximately 15 yards away, face away from the target.

3. 3-2-1 countdown, turn and run, holding your gun in an upright position, and shoot at the jug.

At what point did you hit the target? How many shots did it take? Another twist to this is to put the jug in different positions—on the ground either to the right or left side of the bunker, "peeking" through a hole in the bunker, etc. Set up realistic scenarios and run through them until your accuracy and time improve.

Keep practicing and you'll earn the respect of your fellow players!

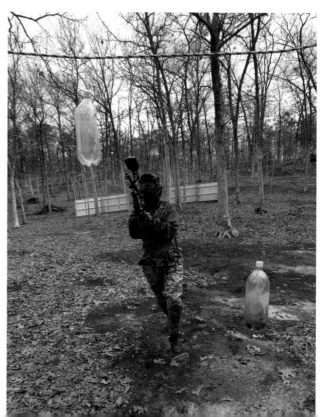

DRILLING FOR VICTORY

SNAP SHOOTING DRILL

If you have been placed into your bunker and cannot come out, snap shooting allows you to take one or two shots to get your opponent back into his bunker, giving you an opportunity to get out. It is important not to come out from the same spot twice in a row. You change the spots you come out from so opponents won't know where to expect you.

When practicing snap shooting drills, make sure you have someone there to point out areas you are leaving exposed (e.g., your hopper or elbows and knees).

GOOD FORM IS CRITICAL

Left, right, center, it doesn't matter where you come from as long as you never repeat the same pattern twice.

RUNNING MAN DRILL

The purpose of this drill is to learn how to shoot into the empty space that a target is going to enter just in time to hit it. This is called *leading*.

Use a live moving target—with that person's consent, of course—and stage it so he or she is running perpendicular to your position. Lead the person by putting a stream of paint into the direction they are moving, or over the bunker they are heading toward.

It is good to start at a distance of 100–150 feet. Shoot about 10–15 feet in front of your target, and have that daring soul run his or her fastest. There's no time factor in this exercise, but try to limit the number of rounds to about 20 per drill before starting over.

Drilled Running Man

By increasing the angle of your barrel, you will be able to increase the distance your paintballs will fly. At some point, of course, you shorten the distance the paintball will travel, but increase the slope of its descent.

LONG DISTANCE SHOOTING DRILL

When practicing long distance shooting drills, set up a target 200–210 feet in front of you. Limit the number of rounds in the hopper to time the drill and the number of shots you take. This drill teaches players how to control the arc of their ball so they can get the maximum range out of their shooting skill. Being a long distance shooter with accuracy is a fast track to legendary status in paintball lore.

At 200 feet, paintballs don't break that easily, as Steve points out. The longer the ball is in the air, the less energy it will have on impact.

Hopper Loading Drill

Learn to load your hopper without taking your eyes off the action. At first, perform this drill with an empty hopper and empty guppies. Get the motion down first before using paint (to avoid getting it dirty). With one hand holding your gun, perform your loading routine as follows:

A. Pop your loader's lid open.

B. Reach behind you and open your velcro harness.

C. Firmly grab a full guppy and bring it forward.

D. Pop the guppy's lid with your thumb.

E. Dump paint into your loader.

F. With the bottom of the now empty guppy, flip the loader's lid closed and snap the lid tight.

G. Toss the guppy aside and resume firing.

NOTE: This should be one smooth continuous motion. Practice until you get it right! Practice while you watch your favorite television shows and time yourself.

Blind Shooting Drill

There are times in a game where you are shooting without a clear view of your target. In these cases, you are "shooting blind." Blind shooting can be an effective shooting technique. The key is learning to identify a reference point that you can see from your firing position that relates directly to your opponent's position. This way you can stay safe in your bunker while you rain paint down on your opponent's head. He'll get dumped with paint and you can move on to your next unwitting target.

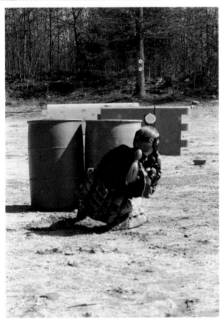

To practice, you and your buddy face off in opposite bunkers. From a quick peek, see if there is an object directly in line with their position. In this sequence you'll notice a tree directly behind your opponent's position in the background. Now, from the safe haven of your bunker, lay a stream of paint in the direction of the tree without overexposing yourself to return fire. Change the angle of your barrel to increase or decrease the range of your fire. By getting used to the feel of blind shooting in this manner, you'll increase your chances of survival, and become more of an offensive threat.

Out of paint?
Keep shooting anyway. The sound will keep your opponents' heads down while your teammates gain advantageous positions.

Out of air?
Throw paintballs. Heck, it'll keep them guessing and one just might break!

PART 5
TACTICS

A.C.T.

Rob Rubin's Customized Approach to Essential Paintball Tactics

"GETTING" PAINTBALL

When you first start playing paintball, you're literally bombarded with suggestions, advice, and ideas about the game. As is the case with most new players in any sport, it's easy to get overwhelmed just trying to keep up.

There's an easy way around "Information Overload."

You see, I've done a little work to fix this problem. And the good news for you is that paintball can be boiled down to a simple formula that's not only easy to remember, but even easier to carry out.

I call this "The Triad." It will carry you very far in your pursuit of paintball fun. You see, the game is only fun up to the point of elimination. Learning tactics is about learning how to stay in the game.

And the core of paintball tactics is the Triad.

Here it is.

A.C.T.-UNG Baby!

"Angles" "Communications" "Teamwork"

These are the three basics of paintball, "A.C.T." for short. That's all you need to know. This may sound simplistic, but even professional teams are always working on these three basic principles. Forget the gizmos, forget the gadgets, forget the tech-talk. These are the nuts and bolts of the game. If you want to be somewhere between competent and excellent at paintball, you must master "the Triad."

Why "The Triad"?

Much like a tripod, this particular trio of paintball skills works only as a whole. When you play them all, you get a whole game. It's easier to explain how they interconnect by looking at them in reverse order.

Do It For the Team

Teamwork can be as complex as 10 players moving as one mind, or as simple as finding a buddy and moving together up the tapeline. A second pair of eyes is invaluable, and a second shooter on a target can be the difference between wasting your time and eliminating your opponent.

Teamwork doesn't mean you're on top of one another, but it does mean you're working together for a common goal. One player is shooting at the opponent, the other player is advancing on him. That's great teamwork. One player is yelling positions, the other players are listening and moving accordingly. That's effective teamwork.

You can even have teamwork when you don't know anyone you're playing with!

In open fields or speedball games, I'll be the fool yelling his head off about where I saw players running to, or where they have people positioned. Why? Someone has to, and it may as well be me. Something as simple as "3 right, 4 left, 2 center" tells your team how they stack up against their foes. *Communication accomplishes teamwork.*

Communication = Effective Yelling

Sure, anyone can yell their lungs out. But it's effective yelling that makes the difference. Remember that teamwork thing? Here's the second part of it—communication.

Once you've buddied up, or you've decided to be a 'caller,' don't be shy. If you need some help, a simple "Help here!" gets the message across. You can get someone to move up to help you, or flank around to eliminate the opposing player who's shooting at you, and a lot of other things too.

New players often try to be 'stealthy,' and that works up to a point. One of my rules of thumb: "Once the other team shoots at you, don't bother trying to hide anymore." They've spotted you. It's useless to hide now. What you want to do immediately is get another player to help you out. Give them as much information as you can. For example:

"There are two guys in that bunker! Can you swing around and shoot them?" This brings us to the third leg—angles.

Angles

The term 'angles' covers moving, maneuvering, crawling, leaping, getting skinny behind a tree, and getting into a bunker so the other team can't occupy it.

Paintball is partially a game of real-estate, and getting angles is the way you use real-estate effectively. As an individual player, you want to take advantage of opponents who get 'tunnel vision' (players fixated on what's in front of them) by moving up on their flanks. A tree can only protect from so many directions at a given moment. The key is getting to an angle that renders your opponent's tree useless.

Your most frequent use of angles is to support your teammates. Most shoot-outs take place head on, meaning face to face. The idea behind 'angles' is to get to the side of your opponent while your teammate keeps your opponent's attention. After you make that key elimination, your teammate begins to move up while you support his advance similarly.

Pretty cool, isn't this?

You may already be starting to see the pattern.
You can't "do" one part of the Triad well without doing the other two simultaneously.

- If you don't communicate, your teammates won't know you need them to take a better angle on the player shooting at you.

- If your team won't move to better angles, your teamwork breaks down and you get eliminated quickly.

- If you don't work together at all, you'll find the day frustrating, because your team won't communicate and move together in any way.

A.C.T. is a simple formula, and it encompasses the essence of what you need to do to qualify as a great player. It's also adaptable to your later paintball games as well. The concept of "Angles" includes 'back doors' and 'key bunkers' and seeing holes in your opponent's line. Simple "communications" later become your team codes. And "Teamwork" becomes the backbone of your game.

Putting It All Together

Eventually you combine the elements of the Triad into complex "Swing" moves and "Sweep" maneuvers.

For example, the "Two Man Swing" uses all of "A.C.T." in rapid order. Your buddy starts by telling you the opponent's position (communication), you start shooting to keep your opponent's head down (teamwork) as your buddy moves up (angles), you continue to feed your buddy information about where the opponent is (communications/teamwork) as he slides into his new position (angles). Your buddy begins to shoot (teamwork) and tell you where the opponent is leaning out of (communications) as you move up (angles) to get the elimination.

All of this may occur within ten seconds.

For now, don't worry about achieving that level of play. It takes practice, a good memory, and adventurous spirit to get good at this game. All of that takes time.

For now, have a good time! Enjoy yourself! Try to remember to "A.C.T." Write it on the back of your hand if need be. Talk to your teammates about it, too. It's something that everyone and anyone can do with a little effort.

—RR

Once you have the Triad down, you'll be amazed how fast it can improve your game.

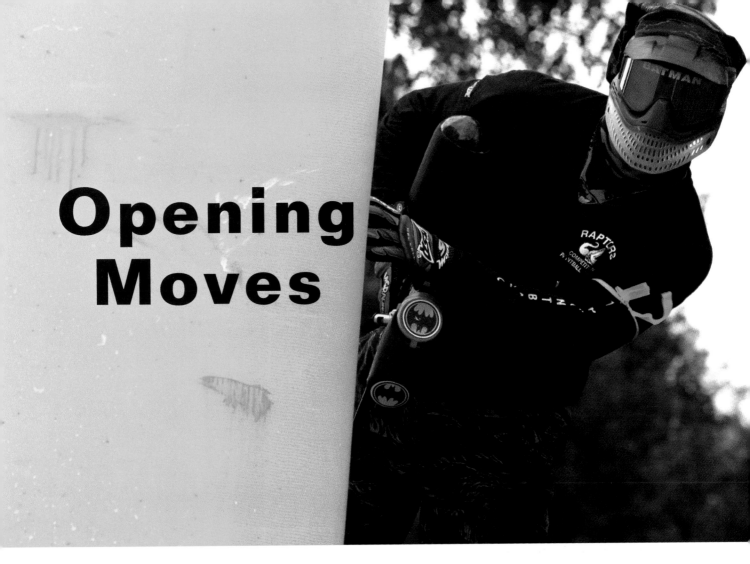

Opening Moves

Military strategy and tactics and paintball, for the most part, do not mix. Military jargon has been adopted by players out of convenience, but the principles of war do not really apply to the game. However, there is at least one aspect of paintball that mirrors almost exactly its military counter-part—the use of surprise.

Napoleon (among many other legendary military commanders) believed that the effect of surprise is the equivalent of having an army ten times its actual size.

Surprise is a critical aspect of tactics and it comes in two flavors—complete surprise and plain vanilla surprise.

Complete and total surprise is an elusive, ideal kind of thing, which does-n't really exist in paintball. At the very least, the other team knows the ter-rain, your objective, the size of your team, the length of the encounter, and when the contest will start. That's quite a bit of handy information. You can, however, achieve something close to complete 'paintball' surprise, but only at the very beginning of the game.

AT THE BREAK

It is only during the first few crucial seconds that the other team has no idea where you are going to go or what you are going to do. Once the game starts, after no more than about 30 seconds, the other team will at least know where a few of your players are. This is one reason why good teams and players spend more time figuring out their initial move than any other part of the game. The 'Break,' the moment at which a game begins, is your only chance to catch the other team with their pants down around their ankles.

After those first few seconds have passed, you can only hope to achieve vanilla surprises; these would be things like suddenly moving players from one side of the field to the other, a crawler getting into the midst of the other team's positions and spreading havoc, or a sudden push on a section of the field.

THE FIRST STEPS

The start, or opening move of a game, is an all or nothing affair, just like an opening move in chess. How you begin determines the entire outcome of the game: the countermoves your opponent makes and your counters to those countermoves, *ad infinitum*.

Two very important factors are set at the beginning: what terrain you choose and how you use your players, assuming you are the team captain. You can decide to take positions deep into the field (seizing portions of your opponent's half of the field); you can take terrain at the fifty (the mid-way point); or you can play the terrain 'short'—that is, take much less than your 'half' at the outset.

How you use your players depends partially (but not entirely) on the terrain itself, but more importantly it depends upon the tone of the game you wish to play. Playing an aggressive game generally means that you will commit most or all of your players from the beginning. Committing players means (1) you have given them a job to perform that will occupy all of their effort, and (2) it will be extremely difficult to position them. Playing a defensive game means that you will commit few to none of your players. And, of course, there is the very common tactic of taking those positions that must be taken and then waiting to see what happens, which is essentially a 'middle' strategy.

The three basic methods of playing the terrain and the three basic ways in which you use your players can be mixed and matched for an almost inexhaustible variety of game plans. Some real-world examples may serve to illustrate this.

- During an NPPL tournament game in Chicago, Bob Long sent one of his players to an aggressive location, well over the fifty, on his left tape—an aggressive, deep-field position. He then had that player tuck in, knowing that the other team would be forced to try to take him out. The final outcome was that the Ironmen's opponents lost four players in trying to eliminate the one player Bob had committed.

- At an NPPL in Boston, Renick Miller's Aftershock committed one player to a kamikaze charge down one tape, merely to attract the attention of the other team; this player was covered by two players on that side of the field who moved to about the fifty and then dug in. Meanwhile, the remainder of the team had been sent to the fifty across the middle and other side of the field in a 'waiting' posture. Once they saw the other team commit to attacking the sacrificed player, the Aftershock players in the middle pushed.

- At an NPPL World Cup in New York, the All Americans received the disadvantaged side of the field and were *forced* to play in a defensive posture from the beginning of the game; they committed no one to any specific action, but remained loose and mobile, stretched across the field just shy of the fifty, until opportunity came knocking. One bunker move led to another, and they handily won the game.

All of these plays were programmed from the outset of the game, based on the terrain, what the competitors wanted to achieve, and who their opponents were. These opening moves also were based on an honest evaluation of the limitations placed on each team, limitations created by the skill level of their players, by the nature of the terrain, or both.

Let's review the basic advantages and disadvantages of each of these strategies.

PLAYING THE FIELD

Aggressive—Deep Penetration

- Advantages—Surprises the other team, happens very quickly, adding confusion to the mix, and ends a game (one way or the other) quickly.

- Disadvantages—Concentrates a lot of your players in exposed positions; requires you to have 100% aggressive players; must be carried through no matter what, and ends a game (one way or the other) quickly.

Middle Ground—"Taking the Fifty"

- Advantages—As much terrain is taken as possible, without undue risk to players.

- Disadvantages—The other team knows (or should know) all the angles and how to play this area of the field better than just about any other area of the field.

Defensive—Playing the Field Short

- Advantages—Players can get set in position very quickly. Opponents are dealt with on terrain which is less familiar to them; typically opponents will not know shooting angles and will not have any pre-set positions to use.

- Disadvantages—Very little room for maneuver. No place to retreat. Usually restricts players to 'reacting' to opponents' moves.

In general, determining what 'mix' of playing styles to use depends upon what you and your teammates want to accomplish, and how much (or how little) the terrain of a given field will support those opening objectives. It would be foolish to overextend your players past the fifty, if there is nowhere for them to go once they get there.

The objective of an opening move is to prepare your team for the anticipated actions of your opponents and/or (and this is an important distinction) to place your players where they will be able to support your plan for the remainder of the game.

In order to practice these kinds of opening moves, you should constantly look for fields and games that will allow you to test different openings. For example, you can find the fast players on your team (or in your group) and, when playing on a field that has good cover over the fifty yard line, create a plan that pushes some of those players into that cover. Set the remainder of your players in positions that will support the forward players—some shooters who can pick off the opponents who will try to take your forward players out, some defenders on the other side of the field in strong 'hold' positions, a small reserve of players who can follow up on any push that your forward players may make.

On a field that offers good cover on your end of the field, practice setting up an ambush and playing the field short.

If you don't have any idea what a full-bore charge down one tape is like, pick a good field and give it a shot.

If you are playing tournament ball, remember that the number one rule for opening moves is to 'play the field,' not your opponents; it is far easier to analyze terrain before the game than it is to guess what your opponents will do.

-SD

Smart ideas work, bad ideas don't.

Back to Basics

Pete "Robbo" Robinson has been playing paintball now for 12 years. A native of the UK, for the past four years he has played most of his paintball in the States. He was asked by Bill and Adam Gardner of the All Americans to join them in 1994, and has won many titles with them. He then joined Aftershock and won two World Cup championships and a second NPPL Series title. Basically, he's in this game to be the best, and he makes a strong case for himself every time he plays.

As US editor of the hugely successful *Paintball Games International Magazine,* he has written well over 100 articles spanning ten years of playing professional paintball. He was also voted the World's Best Player in 1996. It's definitely time to tune in.

THE ONLY WAY TO PLAY PAINTBALL IS TO STAY IN THE GAME

In paintball, there are many people who have opinions about how the game should be played. You will hear and read about numerous theories and approaches, most of which are either unworkable or pretentious.

The game of paintball in its most basic form is the art of eliminating opponents without getting shot. *The definitive attribute of a good player, therefore, is his or her ability to stay in the game and eliminate opponents.* You will notice that I put *staying in the game* first. That has to take precedence over all else in the game of paintball. What is the point of being the best shot in the world when you're standing on the sidelines?

It may seem simplistic to say that to become a good player all you have to do is think about staying in the game, but it is neither simple nor easy to keep yourself in the game on a consistent basis.

At this point, let's clarify a few points. The techniques I will be discussing are wholly applicable to all levels of paintball. Whether you are a first time rec-baller, amateur, or pro matters not.

THE TECHNICAL AND THE TACTICAL

The tactical relates to those actions of the team decided upon before the game has started (i.e., whether you push one flank, or five players run down the middle). Anything involving predetermining players' actions on the field is tactical.

That said, however, I must say that the most important part of playing paintball, by far, is the technical component.

Good technical play defeats good tactics!

Techniques are actions a player undertakes to make sure he stays alive while endeavoring to eliminate the opposition. Basically, when you see a player behind a bunker snap shooting, ducking in and out, firing his gun from different spots at different times, you're watching someone employing techniques to enhance the effectiveness of his play.

ESSENTIALS OF TECHNICAL PLAY

Now, let's just run through some hypothetical situations. Imagine a player who sits behind a bunker and never shoots his gun. What is the likelihood he will be eliminated?

The only way this guy would be eliminated is if someone runs over and bunkers him. Stands to reason, right? Nobody else can shoot him because he never breaks cover to fire his gun.

From this we can readily infer that a bunker provides a safe haven. At the same time, it is of no use just to sit there without firing your gun. To win the game, the player has to break cover

and endeavor to eliminate opponents or, at the very least, provide suppressive fire.

Herein lies the central problem in paintball. As soon as you come out of cover, you are vulnerable. This fact forms the genesis of the whole philosophy of technical play.

The Principle of Paintball Technique
You must do all you can so that when you do shoot your gun, you give your opponents the least possible opportunity to eliminate you from the game.

No technique is fail-safe, but good technique can drastically reduce your rate of elimination.

Believe it or not, this is the secret of playing this game on the highest level. The ability to practice this philosophy separates the good players from the great players, great teams from championship teams.

Let me explain why.

If all ten players on a team were to practice the philosophy of play I advocate (i.e., to concentrate 100% on not being shot rather than allowing the secondary need of eliminating opposition to determine actions) then, by definition, the average life of the team as a whole would increase. Furthermore, if players spend more time in the game, that also means that, as a team, they are firing more paint than the opposition. That increases their chances

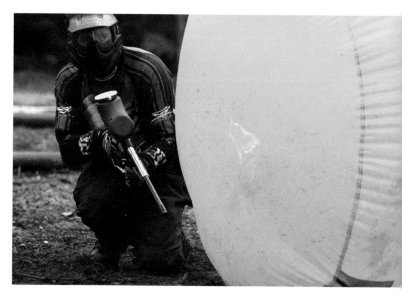

of eliminating the opposition and winning the game.

So you can see that by getting your team to concentrate on technical aspects of play, everything else seems to fall into place. Even if you're not on a team, it should be clear to you that honing your technique will enable you to survive longer when you're on a losing team, and may make victory possible when you're outnumbered.

A LOOK AT THE ACTUAL TECHNIQUES!

Now that we have established the importance of technical play, we have to look at what those techniques are, in terms of what to do and what not to do.

First off, we can reduce the game of paintball, in simple terms to ten one-on-ones. For the moment, I am using a ten man tournament team as an example, although what is to be discussed is wholly applicable to players at all levels.

If a target player is beading on me (i.e., lining his gun up on me and occasionally firing when I come out to fire at him), then there are a couple of things to remember.

First of all, never come out into an incoming stream of paint. Seems obvious, but you would be surprised just how many mugs do it. You have to wait until your opponent stops firing at you. Alternatively, you can move to the other side of the bunker, but this normally means you will be shooting back-handed, so I will ignore that option for the moment.

If you are right-handed, I take it for granted that you are shooting out of the right hand side of the bunker as you look at it. The reason is obvious; you show a minimum profile to your opponents if you shoot this way. That brings us to snap shooting.

Snap Shooting 101

Accepting that we never break cover into a stream of paint, we now have to create an opportunity to fire at our target. When your opponent stops firing, the best technique is to snap shoot your way into dominance. If your opponent is lined up and just waiting for you to come out, then this is what you should do.

Get in to your mind the approximate location of your opponent. You can do this quite easily by taking a quick look in the direction from which the sound of your opponent's gun is coming. You should already have a good sense of his location because you know he's generally going to be sitting behind a bunker just like yours.

Once you have established his location, then get yourself set to roll out of cover with an upper-body roll movement.

This takes a bit of practice, but generally I would sit with my legs in front of me, usually bent in front of my chest, in a position behind the bunker that just allows me to be safe. In other words, if I were to lean slightly outwards to the right, my opponent could eliminate me, but with a slight roll back in, he would not be able to see me, let alone tag me.

When you're set, roll out, fire two shots, and immediately roll back in. The reason for this rapid-movement, minimal-fire approach is simple. If your opponent has indeed lined up where you're likely to emerge, you have to take a shot at him and get behind cover before you get hit. That's not long at all; if you only shoot twice and roll back in, there is no way that your opponent can react in time to eliminate you. The window of opportunity you gave him is just too small, he will always be one step off the pace you are setting.

If you adhere to this technique, the only way you can get tagged is if your opponent fires randomly and gets lucky.

If you roll out of cover, and a paintball is already winging it's way over to you, you're a goner!

So there remain now two possibilities in this interaction.

1. You eliminate him by snap shooting
2. You have to modify your technique slightly

As you roll in and out of cover and fire your two-shot bursts, you are relying on a fair amount of luck to get your elimination. Nevertheless, many players are eliminated this way.

The reason you have to roll in and out of cover is because your opponent has the drop on you.

The key here is to turn the tables and get the drop on him!

At present, it looks as though he controls things by making you snap shoot, but what if we could push him back into cover leaving us to line up on him?

To put your opponent on the defensive, you must do two things when you come out to snap shoot. First, watch as you roll back into cover; you are looking for any movement of your opponent that suggests your two shots are so accurate that they forced him to get back behind his bunker. Secondly, listen carefully, because if you hear no shots coming back at you right away, it's likely that you forced him back, but failed to see it.

If you are looking for them, these two clues give you a chance to establish control of the situation. If you take advantage of them, you can line up on the guy who thought he had you right where he wanted you!

Suppress your opponent with protracted fire enabling one of your teammates to bunker him. At the very least, keep him out of the game with continuous shooting.

The big advantage in lining up an opponent is that you get a chance to 'read' all of his movements. After observing him for a while, you'll find that he becomes predictable. This predictability will eventually be his downfall. Be patient and persistent, and you'll know this fine feeling.

In everything having to do with paintball technique, the key is concentration. You must concentrate on staying tight to your cover and on timing your retaliatory fire.

This is the way to optimize your chances of eliminating your opponent and minimize your chances of getting shot.

We have now covered two of the most fundamental aspects of paintball technique. Whether you are an experienced pro or a first timer, staying tight and timing your shots will transform your game overnight.

-PR

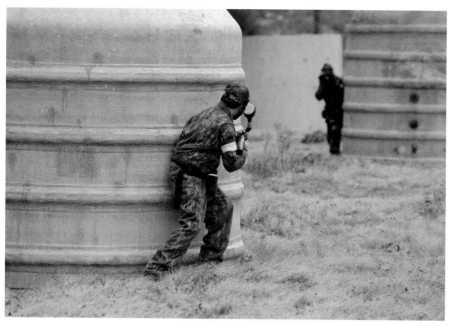

Mapping Your Game Plan

The Fake and Push

The fake and the push can be used on any field, but must be adjusted according to terrain. A critical component of this and any game plan is that your team should walk onto the field together. Each player must examine his own bunker and firing lanes. Both sides of the field must be walked. It is important to know what positions the opposing team may take. This will help you calculate the firing lanes and angles available from your bunker. This is the time to take note of bunkers that facilitate a pinch play. You and the other player on your team with the pinch shot must work together. Another important thing to keep in mind is that you may want to use the bunkers on the other side of the field as you advance. In this particular game plan the primary objectives are A5, B5, A3, and B3. A5 should be taken by the fastest tape runner. The back player, A1, has found a good shooting lane that cuts off the right side of the field. This lane cuts between bunkers and will be called Zone.

1. The objective for A1 is to eliminate player B3 at the break of the game. The objective for the players on the right side of the field is to eliminate player B5.

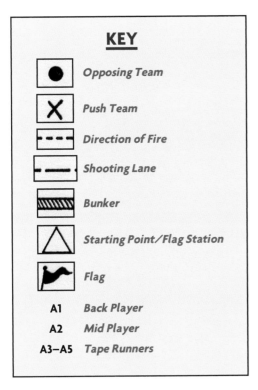

KEY

●	*Opposing Team*
✗	*Push Team*
- - -	*Direction of Fire*
—·—·—	*Shooting Lane*
▨	*Bunker*
△	*Starting Point/Flag Station*
⚑	*Flag*
A1	*Back Player*
A2	*Mid Player*
A3–A5	*Tape Runners*

2. Players B1 and B4 are not much of a factor in this game plan. As the back players signal, player A5 runs down the tape line. If player B5 is still in the game, A5 should eliminate him as he passes. A5 continues to run to the back corner of the field. This will cause the opposing team to turn in panic toward A5. It should be noted that if A5 had been eliminated prior to the signal, A4 would fill in. This is called a fake. A5 will most likely be hit performing this move. If he isn't, the opposing team has a huge problem. Timing is essential for this to work. Once A5 has begun his run, A2 and A3 should take advantage of the commotion and push the opposite side of the field. If the game plan has worked they should be able to eliminate some of the opposing team by shooting them in the back. Their primary objective would be to eliminate players B3, B2, and B1 in that order. A2 and A3 have now turned the remaining opposing players toward their side of the field. A4 should leave after A2 and A3. He should be advancing up the same side of the field as A5. His main objective is to eliminate player B4 and anyone else who remains. A1 follows A4 up the field. He should cross centerfield, picking up the flag as he advances. If the other players have done their job, all that is left for A1 to do is to hang the flag. This game plan incorporates four separate pushes. It is designed to keep the opposing team off balance. If it is executed well, the opposing team will be eliminated before they know what hit them. This is a very aggressive game plan. It is not simple to execute. If one player is too early (or late), the game plan may disintegrate leaving the opposing team with the upper hand.

Shooting Lanes

Shooting lanes should be chosen during field walking. The basic idea is to find a bunker on the opponent's side of the field that is key to their

game plan. Then find a way to eliminate the player who plans on getting into that bunker. The ideal shooting lane is a line of fire devoid of obstacles. The line of fire should drop the paint into the opposing player's running lane. In this example, player A1 shoots for Zone 1 dropping a line of paint into the path of B2 and B3. Mid player A2 stops half way to his bunker and fires into Zone 2, hoping to eliminate B3. This means that player B3 must cross zone 2 shooting lanes. This technique is used to increase the chances of eliminating a key player. Once B2 and B3 are in their bunkers (or eliminated), A1 and A2 need to take cover in their bunkers. Example 2 (shown in red) depicts 2 players firing in

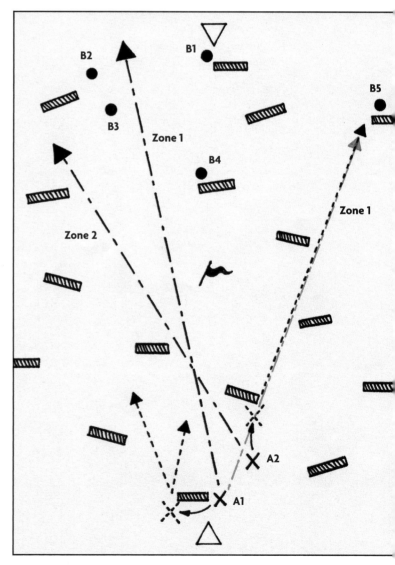

the same lane. This should only be done for an extremely key bunker. Player B5 must cross a firing lane with twice as much paint traversing it. This choice of firing lanes increases the chances of eliminating player B5. Hit or miss, A1 and A2 should get into their bunkers after B5 has passed the firing lane.

Keep in mind that shooting lanes are a great tool. They are not, however, foolproof. There is a certain amount of luck involved. This is a skill-based plan that should be practiced like any other. The back player using the lane needs to get a feel for the appropriate height to aim for. One trick to try is to aim at hip height at the entrance to the bunker. Even if the player comes in low he will usually not be below that point.

—MS

New Players' Guide to Cover

"Work your bunker." "Get angles from your bunker." "Slide out of your cover."

What does it all mean?

Cover is ... "Anything that protects or shields from harm, loss, or danger."

In paintball, anything between you and an opponent that will stop, disable or render useless a fired paintball is considered "cover."

There are two basic types:

1. "Hard" cover includes medium- to large-sized trees, rocks, and bunkers.

2. "Soft" cover, like grass, small trees, and shrubs.

Both types serve the same function, but you'll learn to use them differently.

Let's tackle hard cover first. Virtually all speedball fields are exclusively hard cover. Meaning there's a very solid object between you and the other guys. Big trees, rocks, and bunkers are solid cover from incoming paintballs. Some fields have berms, hills, and other terrain features that qualify as hard cover.

A berm is a ledge or space between the ditch and parapet in a fortification.

Anything solid you can place your body behind is hard cover. Seeing as most game situations involve *bunkers* (especially on speedball fields), I'll stick to using that term generically. Do a little mental dance and *bunker* becomes tree becomes rock becomes fort becomes wall becomes inflatable becomes corrugated piping becomes car becomes anything and everything solid. (Whew!)

I'll avoid the finer points of moving into a bunker. That's dependent on your speed and fitness level. Let's focus on what you do once you're in position. A common mistake is to get as close as you can to your bunker *no matter where you are on the field* and pop out for eliminations. It's not really a mistake, I guess. It made sense to me when I was new to the game, too. But, after studying videos, watching the experts play, talking to some of the best players I know, and reading stories about other players' approaches, it becomes obvious that this isn't necessarily what you always want to do.

Using Cover in Context

It remains true that the closer to the action you are, the closer to the inside of your bunker you want to be. If you're relatively far away from the action, you can afford to move farther back from

your bunker. It's called "sliding back" or "sliding out." This is useful because from farther behind a position, you can *control* more of the field laterally without overexposing yourself to your opponents. You can watch their movements from a good position and still use bunkers to maximize protection. If your opponents get closer, it's only a matter of moving up a few feet forward into your bunker to counter a move of 20 feet from your opponent. You also can avoid their shots entirely by leaning a few inches, rather than moving a few feet. This allows you to keep your gun in position to shoot back easily, and not have to reset your arm positioning. In the thick of a game, this can be the difference between winning and losing.

By sliding back, you also access more *angles*. "Angles" is a blanket term for shooting side to side from a position. Very rarely do you shoot at your 12 o-clock from a bunker. You're mostly shooting the 9 to 10:30 angle and 1:30 to 3 o-clock angles. Why? It's easier and faster to lean out the side rather than poke up above a bunker.

On a lean, your head and gun come out simultaneously. On a poke up, your gun and head are seen first, giving opponents a chance to take you out before you shoot.

Speaking of leaning out, most opponents lean out from your left. Why? As I mentioned back in the drills section, it's more natural for right-handed people to lean to their right, which puts them on their opponent's left-hand side. This means that you can anticipate most players' movements by aiming towards the left-hand side of bunkers. How? Tournament players preach playing switch handed. This is just a fancy way of saying, "You should learn how to use both hands." It's tough, but it helps. I lay on my side on the left side of a bunker and wait for their lean to my left and hammer down.

Imagine a line just over the top of your bunker, and just around the sides. This line starts from your

....

Teaching yourself to shoot effectively both right- and left-handed will help you work both sides of your bunkers and catch opponents off guard while keeping your exposure to incoming paint to a minimum.

opponent's barrel and continues past the sides and top of the bunker. Learning where that line will be when you attain a bunker position is the essence of understanding angles. And learning how you can extend this line will improve your game immensely. Watch your feet, your hands, head, your loaders, your harness—anything beyond that line puts you in jeopardy.

So how do you make these angles work for you?

Good question. The best way to do this is to develop a stable shooting stance that you like. This position should allow you to play in two directions at once, but also give you freedom to slide in when necessary. Some players get on their knees and play from there. Some players crouch down on their toes. And some go on one knee, the other one up. If you wear soft knee/shin guards, go with something like that to shield yourself from incoming

paint. Make sure you're comfortable in your stance. A Team Internet friend of mine has big thigh pains after a full day because of his technique. It works, however, so he still uses it.

With any stance you use, you want to try to *layer* your cover. For example, if you can line up several trees (or anything else that will protect you from opponents' paint), you can do something called "tree-walking" or simply "walking". Using terrain as in this manner will give you a freedom of movement that will make you uncannily effective. Like water, every time you move, your relationship to your terrain shifts. Take advantage of this zen approach, and your game play options will expand dramatically and unpredictably.

THE VIRTUES OF SOFT COVER

This conveniently brings me to soft cover. Soft cover is more about finesse and grace than brute force. Using soft cover requires a little more creative perception and quick-thinking than hard cover does.

Soft cover is anything that *may* prevent paintballs from reaching you, and is *likely* to if you are careful, but nonetheless isn't risk-free protection.

We're talking about stuff like twigs, leaves, grass, and small and thin trees.

In many cases, tall grass is just as good as a bunker. Grass will either break paint outright or deflect it in most cases. Unless someone rips a few hundred balls, nothing is going to make it through. Everyone has a story about the guy who hid behind a twig and never got shot. I know a few fields where I can get behind a shrub and nothing gets to me but splatter. This is beautiful cover; it allows you to watch the other guys and communicate what you see to your teammates who may not be able to see it.

Soft cover also includes some things you wouldn't expect. What should you use for camouflage? Get behind some grass or shrubs and lay still. If they don't see you, they can't shoot you.

Going back to our definition of cover, this seems to work. How about moving far enough back so they can't touch you with the longball? If you're fast, you can outrun a shooter between bunkers. Or you can pop your gun up and lay down a wall of paint at the other guy to make him duck. (Ever wonder why it's called "Cover Shooting"?) The three "Out's"—*Outrange*, *Outrun*, and *Outshoot*—are all good forms of cover, if you think of cover more broadly, as doing whatever it takes to avoid elimination.

All of this information takes a long time to master in practice. These are the basics. Take what you learn, build from experience, and enjoy!

-RR

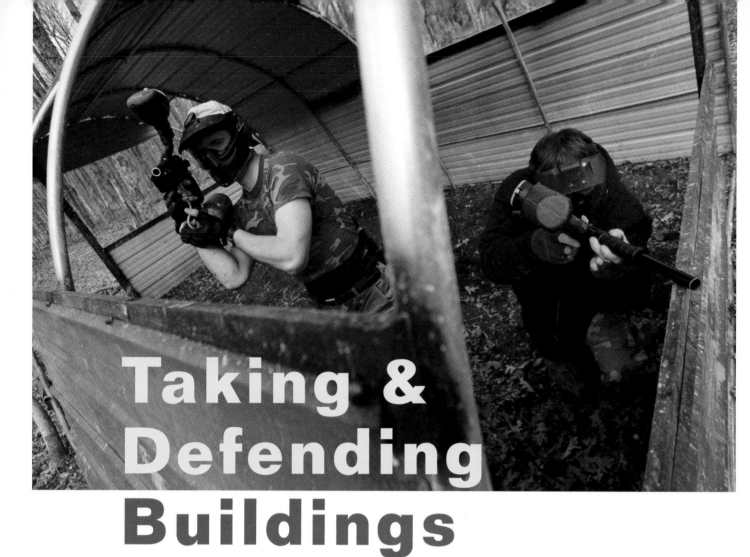

Taking &
Defending
Buildings

I've seen some beautiful buildings in the course of my paintball exploits. And I've seen some ugly ones. I've seen some that were crafted to look like UFO's and castles, others that looked like they were rescued from the garbage dump.

Everyone loves buildings, myself included. I just love attacking them, and you're about to discover why. When it comes to taking a building, I've got it down.

Most people see buildings as fortifications, and this is pretty accurate. In paintball, a building is a good solid piece of cover, which explains its popularity. On the surface, they look like great (read: *safe*) places to hang out. They have small holes to shoot through, combined with little or no exposure to incoming paint. Sounds like a dream come true, right? Newbies tend to see these structures that way, as well. But from outside of the walls, newcomers to this game get discouraged by buildings, and won't move on them. As a result, they get picked off with relative ease as they try to take buildings by force.

Most paintball buildings are usually about 2 meters in length and width. (That's about 7 feet for you Americans.) This makes them about 4 square meters of doom that I can exploit as an attacker!

Look at buildings as traps rather than as fortresses, and a world of attack possibilities will open up to you!

LIKE "THE DEATH STAR," BUILDINGS HAVE THEIR WEAKNESSES

Personally, when I'm approaching a building filled with paintball players, I know that I have an enormous advantage. First of all, buildings are not mobile. (If they are, they're called tanks.) This fact alone might scare you out of buildings for the rest of your paintball career. (You shouldn't let it, but more on that later.) Once inside a building (especially if there's more than one entrance), this is where you're going to stay. Sure, you can move around inside there, but you're still on the same piece of real estate.

Stuck in a building like a roach in a roach motel.

You can't flank in a building, unless it's an unusually long one. You can't really crawl. You can't do much in there other than defend perhaps 3 angles that the openings and the doorways will allow. Defenders tend to exploit this to a fault. They will defend those angles with their last paintball.

You can't win a game based on mobility by taking and defending a building!

As an attacker, exploit the isolation and siege mentality of a building defender. The fact that most of a building is impenetrable also means that its occupants have substantial blind spots. It also means that their ability to hear what you're doing on the outside is easily compromised, because in many cases the buildings are echo chambers; a few

shots against those walls while you're moving will make it hard for them to hear where you're going. Once you know the angles the building allows its inhabitants, you can use different angles they can't cover. If this sounds simple, that's because it is. You just need to be patient, perceptive, and decisive in your attack.

A building can be worked through or over if need be. For example, you can dedicate one shooter to a building and basically stop everyone in that building from poking their heads out. This tactic plays out in the following manner.

If three guys are inside a building structure, they have limited fields of view. They can't all poke out of the same window without missing something and/or becoming a huge target. Here's what you do. Place one player near the front of the building and have him shoot it up a little to make noise along the building's sides. I call this "knocking," because you're just making them nervous instead of trying to eliminate them.

The next move is a flanking maneuver exploiting the limited visibility of the building's occupants. If you can manage to put paint in the vicinity of or through the openings, you'll make the occupants sloppy and nervous. Before you know it, you'll have cleared the building, because they won't have seen or heard you come right up on top of them. Or, if all of their players are in the building, why bother to take it? If you can ignore the building, grab the flag while they're tied up with a well entrenched front shooter who has a great shot at their escape door.

Tactics for loners who must take a building

What if you're alone? Well, the principles are the same, but in this case I'll tie 'em up infinitely by shooting and maneuvering while they're ducking down from my shots. Either that or I'll just put paint into a hole until some poor dude pokes his head up to see what's happening. Poof—instant elimination!

WHAT BUILDINGS ARE USEFUL FOR

I've said some harsh things about paintball buildings. Clearly, buildings are the bane of those who misuse them.

On the other hand, buildings can be helpful to those who use them appropriately. For example, they should be used as cover. Despite everything I've just said, I'd like to remind the reader that buildings are more than just four walls.

When I'm using a building for cover I try to stay on the outside of it as long as I can. In this case, it's used like any bunker with the exception that the holes can line up to form a smaller hole for opponents to shoot through. I can shoot through easily, whereas my opponents can't.

I'll also back away from the building, and use it as a normal bunker that way. Buildings offer the

opportunity to become invisible to my opponents. I only use this as a last resort, however. Or I use it as part of my tactical plan. Either way, using a building must serve a concrete purpose for the team.

When you enter a building, you're making a commitment.

Sometimes you'll be making a whole game commitment, because you'll end up in an inescapable hot zone. Of course, if your objective is to make your opponents focus on you, this can work to your team's advantage. If you're not doing anything for your team, you're not doing your job. Too many defenders forget that, and they get eliminated or they simply don't get involved in the game.

After diving into a building, it's important to keep your ears open for teammates' communications and to make your shooting count for something. Like any bunker, you have to work it. Buildings need to be worked harder because you don't have all the openings a bunker provides. Tunnel vision is easier to slip into from inside a building; if the window faces forward, you tend to look forward. Work a building's entryways the same way you work its windows and its cracks. Stay on your toes, or you'll get trampled point blank.

You really need to have a lot of team support for your building players. You need mobile people on the outside of the building to prevent flankers from taking your position. You also can make yourself a 'distraction' so that your teammates shoot the guys fixated on eliminating you. If you lie in a building, they can't touch you. But they'll keep trying because they think they can, and your teammates will just keep getting eliminations.

In January 1998, I played at an outdoor speedball field in Florida that had a few buildings in the center. During one game, I made a very bold move and made the center building. I took a few shots from the outside and realized that my team needed a gun a few feet forward. So I went into the building.

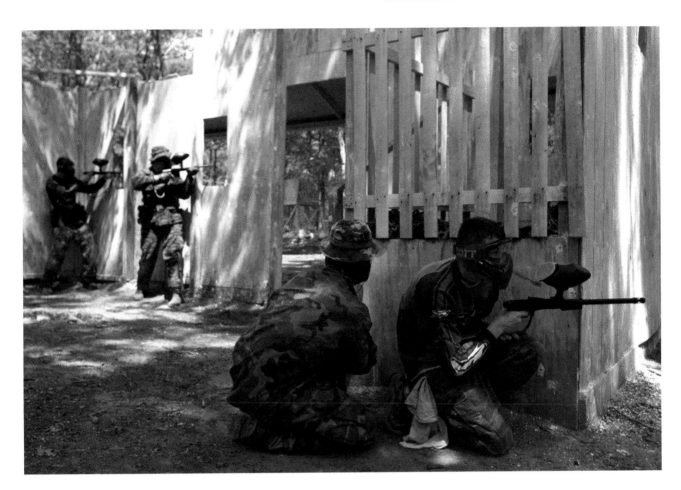

"What's on the right?" I yelled out. Some kid said there was a crawler parallel to me. I turned to look through the door, leveled the barrel, and put 20 shots into the shrubs, just hoping to get something to move, and I got an elimination. Immediately I looked left to see someone moving on the flank. I shot a few balls to stop him. No paint broke, but it stopped him.

The rest of the game flowed this way. A few shots left, a few right, a few more left, working the whole area hard. As the left was shooting at me, I'd work the right side. When the right would start on me, I would swing left.

What amazed me was how they wouldn't move up on me. Instead, they tried to longball my position and get a lucky shot on me. This was crazy; all I had to do to avoid shots in the building was shift a little one way or the other. Had they concentrated on my position and rushed me or worked on my

flanks before shooting me, I would have been a goner.

The building provided great protection, but without team support I would have been toasted. Against competition with better tactics, team support would have been absolutely essential to holding that position and turning it to our advantage. I was always trying to keep my flankers informed of our opponents' movements. Since that building was in the center of the field, I was able to act as a team caller, relaying information from side to side with great protection. If you're in a building and are not being useful, leave it before you get abandoned.

My team won the game after the other team wasted a good deal of paint on my position. I figured that the other team shot about 2000 paintballs at me in that game, but they just couldn't take me down because of their lack of coordinated teamwork and intelligent communication.

GETTING BUNKERED IN A BUILDING

The Element of Surprise

Inside a building, getting "bunkered" or "mugged" can be much worse. This is mainly due to the element of surprise. Here's a true story that illustrates what I mean. *Once upon a time, there was a big game in Racine, Wisconsin...*

Both flag stations were two-story castles, which are very impressive to the eye but brutally hard to defend. When the flag was about to come down, the attackers rushed the building, stuck their guns into the windows and opened up point blank. This was FUBAR for anyone in that building. Much bad welting resulted from this.

You see, your main danger, as both an attacker and defender of buildings, is that you're going to find yourself in a point blank scenario and get lit up within a second or two by players whose adrenaline levels are off the charts. Of course, this isn't actually dangerous. You're just going to get hit abruptly at close range and perhaps a few more times than you'd prefer. Later, you'll laugh about it. But, believe me, when it happens, you're going to rue the day buildings made their way into this game.

In a tournament, this activity can count as "Unsportsmanlike Conduct" or "Overshooting." In a recreational setting, you may be told to sit out a few games for overshooting.

My point? If you're going to rush a building, please be careful. Unlike a rounded bunker, you really won't see anything until the last second, and even then you could get bruised. Personally, I'd prefer to flank a building.

Overall, I try to avoid buildings. I can do more damage outside of them. But, sometimes, they're useful. They definitely make things more interesting for their attackers and defenders, and are part of the exhilarating paintball landscape.

—RR

CHUCK STONER, THE ULTIMATE SNIPER

ANDREW FLACH: What do you do as a sniper?

CHUCK STONER: As a sniper, I'm hunting. When I'm on the field I feel like I'm hunting people and what I try to do is set myself up in situations where people will approach me, enter my effective range, and not know where I am even after I've eliminated them. So whenever I'm on a playing field, I'll make the best possible use of the available vegetation and the terrain and the features on the playing field to make myself invisible.

ANDREW: How long can you possibly sit in one position for a game?

CHUCK: Of course, that depends on the game that's being played. In a scenario game, a 24 hour game, I can be on my own for the whole time.

ANDREW: But in one spot, physically?

CHUCK: It depends on how good the hunting is. If I'm entertained, feel effective, and my position isn't compromised, I can stay for a long time. That's just something that you learn as a hunter. You spend a whole day from sun-up to sundown in the woods, usually fairly stationary, especially if you're hunting deer or other big game.

Playing paintball is another hunting experience for me and it's kind of nice because I don't have to drag anything out. I don't have to field-dress anything I shoot.

ANDREW: In terms of picking a spot, what kinds of things would consider to be important?

CHUCK: I would say that there are half a dozen rules of thumb and one of them is that you're never more dangerous than when your opponent is unaware of your location. As soon as you begin to fire, if your gun is noisy, or if your movements are quick and jerky, you give away your position. Then, your fighting ability is compromised.

This pump gun that I'm playing with is very accurate. It has range that other guns don't and shoots very consistently to the same place, but if I'm competing against semi-automatic guns, once I give my position away then I can't function effectively.

People can't fight what they can't see. So, one of my other rules of thumb is that you should always set up fights on your own terms. That means that you're only going to win so many gunfights. I'm not actually on the field to be a gunfighter. I don't want to be a hero. I'm there to be dangerous. That's my function.

ANDREW: To create problems.

CHUCK: Yes. With that I mind, I always set my encounters up so that people fight me on my terms. I choose where to hide, I choose the shooting lane, I choose the terrain. That's how you can be most effective. Human eyes pick up erratic movement very quickly—rapid, jerky movements, swift movements. Our eyes are arranged that way. Consequently, when you move through the forest you should move very little and when you do move, you should move steadily and smoothly.

Even if you're going to be an effective sniper, it's not necessary to move painfully slow because there's just not as much at stake. You want to be able to get around the field and enjoy the game.

Most people are very untalented when it comes to training themselves to be a watcher in the woods. They tend to overlook a lot of things. It's that "you can't see the forest for the trees" thing. When you play the way I like to play you have to see everything. I developed this ability through years of hunting. You always look for bits and pieces of things rather than the whole item. If you go into the woods, and you're looking for a whole paintball player, you might get lucky and see that. Mostly, you're going to see hands and the corner of a goggle, or the tip of somebody's boot. You have to be able to interpret what you see and then incorporate that piece into the whole and identify your target. The same thing happens in the woods when you're hunting deer. You rarely see a whole deer. You see a tail, a leg, a hoof, an ear, an eye, a nose.

I like to play against players who wear colored lenses because I can easily see amber lenses and rainbow lenses. I can pick those out of the woods in a heartbeat.

ANDREW: What is a shooting lane?

CHUCK: A shooting lane is quite simply a path for your projectile to follow to the target. It's very important with paintball, because if you hit a twig at 280 feet per second, your paintball is going to splatter and never make the target. Just like you can effectively hide in a thicket of rhododendrons. You can be mostly in plain sight but people can't get paint into you. I don't enjoy playing that way because I clean my equipment up after every day of play and if I'm all spray painted with pink paint from head to toe, that kind of detracts from my enjoyment of the game.

As a matter of fact, I play not to be hit. I want to play the entire day and never take a hit, and I do that often, which is kind of unusual.

More than the shooting, I enjoy matching wits with the people that I play with. That's every bit as satisfying as shooting my gun. I try to understand my opponent right from the get-go. Usually, right after the first or second game, I can get a feel for the mentality of the team that I'm playing against, and I can identify individuals that I regard as dangerous and identify individuals that are a piece of cake.

ANDREW: So you're sort of like the wolf watching the sheep, right?

CHUCK: That's all part of setting up the situation. Remember what I said: "always fight somebody on your terms." It helps to know the fields. I only play here at Skirmish, so I have an advantage. I know the fields very well, so I can use all of the terrain. I can use the creeks. People don't realize it, but one of the most effective stalking techniques is to wear knee-high rubber boots and to move in a creek bed because the noise of the water conceals most of your movements.

ANDREW: Cool.

CHUCK: You're down a foot or two below the line of sight and you usually have creek banks on both sides. People just don't expect to see you wading down a creek that's got a foot or a foot and a half of water in it.

One of the things that's interesting about hiding, and I tell new players this all the time, is that you always find bunkers and trees and log piles and fox holes. Everybody thinks those are the ideal places to hide. I disagree. I want to hide where somebody is not going to look for me, and those places are intrinsically suspicious.

I strive for a shooting lane that provides me an effective, defensible, dangerous position to work from. That's what I try to do.

ANDREW: And a dangerous, defensible position to work from would be...

CHUCK: I need shooting lanes, I need to feel confident that I'm going to see everything, that I'm going to encounter targets. I need to position myself strategically where I can help my team because I'm not always out there to play for myself. I want to be somewhere useful. I want to encounter other players and I want to effectively engage them and paint them or send them in another direction.

ANDREW: What shooting stance do you prefer as a sniper? Would you use the prone shooting position?

CHUCK: Almost never! I never lay down on my belly. First of all, I've got a pump, and if you lay down in a prone position it makes it harder to work the pump. When you play, you should move very little or not at all. When you do move, move steadily with smooth movements. When things go south, and you decide that you have to move, be definitive. Move really fast! If you're laying down on your belly, you can't get the heck out of there if you need to. So I always play kneeling or standing.

Some players, especially those coming from military backgrounds, plop down on their belly as soon as they get into a fight. I just eat them up. Shooting from prone position may work in other situations, but when you're playing paintball, it's not completely effective.

ANDREW: I notice you play with a scope.

CHUCK: Yes I do play with a scope. While I'm picking my targets I keep the yellow lens cover down. If I take a hit in the lens of the scope then I've lost my targeting system. Just before I take my shot I pop up the lens cover and set my sights on the target, giving me a clear field of view.

It's a straight four power (4X) scope. When I originally put it on the gun, I had some problems with it because it made my targets appear so close that I tended to undershoot them. But I've just taught myself to play with it and now it's just part of my equipment and second-nature to me.

I can shoot like most people do: looking down the barrel and shooting. My pump gun doesn't have an auto-trigger so my rate of fire doesn't even begin to approach a semi's rate of fire. A Tracer or a Phantom with an auto-trigger can fire faster, but maybe not as accurately.

ANDREW: What shooting gear do you bring to the field with you?

CHUCK: I have my Bud Orr Sniper and I have

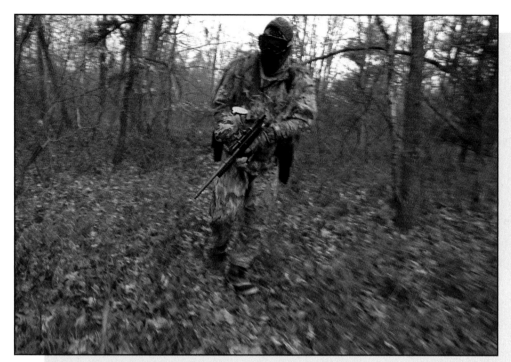

white background, such camouflages are very effective. I can almost disappear.

In the Fall, if it rains, the color of the leaves darkens. I have a camouflage pattern that's called Fall Foliage that is a very effective pattern in conditions like that. Like I said, I'm a hunter and an outdoorsman and a paintball player all in one. My investment in all this equipment makes sense.

I wear hand coverings and face coverings. For most people in the woods, those are the most noticeable parts of the body. And again, since human eyes are set up to see movement, concealing your face and hands is rather important.

ANDREW: Do you have any memorable experiences as a sniper you can share?

CHUCK: Here's a classic. I coached a player, Rob, a couple of years ago. He wanted to become a sniper. At one point in the game, he hid in the top of a blown down tree and four players on the opposing team walked right past him! He and I and some of our other players were working together to set up an ambush. Everybody has to contribute to make those work. Our contribution was to engage the approaching players and have them concentrate on us. Then Rob just raised up out of the blown down tree top (he was fifteen yards behind them) and they were all four lined up with their backs to him and he just went to work on them. It was beautiful. That's how I like to play. It was a most enjoyable success.

ANDREW: That's great. How about yourself? Ever been ambushed?

CHUCK: It happens to the best of us. I like to match wits with people, to out-think them. People are just like deer, very much creatures of habit. It's

my backup gun, a Phantom that I played with full-time several years ago. It's a good gun, shoots just as straight and just as far as the Sniper. I play with the Sniper because I like its heft.

I bring a couple of extra barrels and a couple of extra elbows. It's really important to have the right size elbows. A couple of squeegees, some gun oil, a gunsmith screwdriver for making adjustments on the guns. Spare parts, o-rings, various bits and pieces for the guns.

ANDREW: Tell me a little bit about your dress and camouflage. What kinds of things determine your choice of camo?

CHUCK: There are so many patterns out there. You have to have an artist's eye to be able to critically regard the terrain that you're going to play in, and then select the camouflage pattern that you think will be most effective. I have snow camo, I have camo for the summertime, and I have camo for every season in between.

In the wintertime when there's snow on the ground, I have some white coveralls with some branch lines on them that are actually meant to be tree camouflage. I found that up here in the woods, where there's tons of angular branch features with a not usual for someone to surprise me. But it's happened.

I was playing a couple of years ago with a friend and we snuck in on the back side of a flag station and went to work on the defenders and I thought I was doing really well. There was a six-inch puddle of water at my feet and all of a sudden this guy just reared up out of the puddle. He looked like a freaking' sea monster, slopping water and wet leaves dripping off of him.

I was astonished and stunned. I stood there with my mouth hanging open and got shot.

MAKE YOUR OWN GHILLIE SUIT

It's easy and fun to make your own ghillie suit. Here is a quick primer on do-it-yourself camouflage.

Items Needed

- A cotton landing net, the kind used for fishing

- Camouflage Webbing: Determined by the season and terrain. Choose several kinds as needed.

- Burlap Strips: Find some raw burlap material and pull it apart to get at the threads.

- Rit Fabric Dye: Choose earthy tones.

At least a day before, dye your burlap strips in various tones by following the directions on the package. Let dry.

Cut the landing net open so you have a rectangular piece as big as possible. Lay this on the ground.

Cut your camo-webbing into thirty-inch strips. (Webbing is preferable because offers a more natural appearance. Most foliage will transmit a diffused light and webbing does that, too. If your ghillie suit is made of fabric, when you're backlit

you will present a much darker, more distinctive silhouette. And an easy target!)

Fold the camo strips in half and then girth hitch them to the landing net. Don't just randomly attach them. Think about the patterns in the woods where you'll be using your suit and try to create an interesting, deceptive pattern.

Use the dyed burlap strips to fill in areas and add texture to the suit. Camouflage is an art, not a science. Use your imagination. Make several different kinds of ghillie suits to meet your needs.

Make separate pieces that can be used alone or together. You can make a back cover, a front cover, and a head cover. Attach these to your body with ties made of webbing. For your head cover, sew the landing net to a old cap, then apply camo netting and burlap strips.

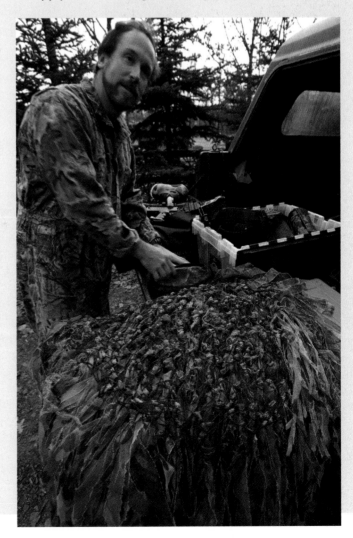

Paintball Snipers—From Myth to Reality

SOME MYTHS WERE MADE TO BE BROKEN

Occasionally on rec.sport.paintball ("the internet" for the paintball-playing crowd), some-one posts the question "How can I be a paintball sniper?" This guy gets a lot of ribbing, partly because of the anti-military movement in paintball, and partly because I don't think most players understand the usefulness of a hidden player in the modern game. There are myths about the paintball version of snipers, let alone the pop-culture version, that simply need to be exposed for what they are. Because of the

images we are spoon-fed by hyper-unrealistic movies and television shows, paint-ball players automatically believe that a sniper wears a bulky black suit, holds a gun longer than he is tall, and sits at the other end of a field putting paint onto a dime in the opponents' flag station. Sorry, no. Not in this game. At least, not any time soon.

Setting the record straight on paintball snipers.

First of all, real "snipers" need not apply. No matter how accurate your gun is (go ahead and spend a fortune on the best barrels, bolts, tanks, triggers, and sites), your pro-jectile is the weak link. Ever seen a paintball decide it wanted to make a hard left? I have.

Paintballs have a mind of their own. They're not accurate projectiles. Even in ideal circumstances, you really can't take someone out from as far away as an actual sniper with a special, high-powered rifle is expected to. You may or may not have figured this out yet, but basically, paintball is not, in the end, about the gun. The gun cannot outperform its ammunition. A roughly spherical gel-encased ball of colored vegetable fluids is not high-performance ammunition.

Instead of looking at someone as a "Sniper", look at them as a "Hunter." That's what they have to be in paintball. Sometimes you stalk, sometimes you hide, sometimes you shoot. You never line someone up from 200 yards away. So let's say you want to start playing like a hunter. How do you do it? It's easy, really.

If you move, you're not hiding.

Pick a camo that fits your terrain if you can. If not, make do with what you have. I've used realtree in a desert setting effectively before and it worked well. You also have to understand what your camouflage does for a living in order to use it.

Tiger Stripe fools the eye into 'sliding' past the camouflage. Realtree, Advantage and Treebark look like the background, and fool the eye into believing they're part of the background. Woodland, Dots, and others of this style appear mottled and try to 'blend in' like a smudged painting. It's much more complex than that, but you get the idea.

In the US region, when in doubt use Woodland. Very universal, very effective. The way I see it, the U.S. government spent a lot of money to make it work well, and they succeeded. Don't use specialty camouflage, French Lizard comes to mind, unless it's broad-based enough to fit in anywhere.

Probably more than you wanted to know, right? Well, if you take being a sniper seriously, this is pretty critical information. Take the time to pick the right camouflage!

The Sniper's Paintgun

I've never been a believer in new barrels, bolts, or anything like that. But you have to realize that I play normally with a fixed-barrel Piranha which is non-modifiable. So I'm biased.

Like many other people, I'm a believer in the target range. I've spent many cases of paint on the target range, and not just shooting for the heck of it. I'll try to hit all the targets on the range in order from front to back, then back to front. Then I'll put paint in the "0" in the number "50" on the sign. Then between the "1" and "2" on the "125 foot" sign. Once I have my effective range down in my mind, I can walk on the field with confidence. I know my range, and I know how accurate I am at that range. That takes years of experience, mind you, and it's not something you can learn from a book. You just have to go out and shoot paint at a target until you have the motion down.

SNIPING

Do Not Try to Be a Sniper... Be a Sniper!

So let's assume that you make it to the field in one piece, and you're ready to give it a go. Try some pre-game mental prep. Do this—hit the target range, plan your route, and review the team strategy.

You have to remember a few key rules here. Once you shoot a ball, the world will know where you are. This can be a good thing, as well as a bad thing. If someone spots you, they'll shoot a lot of paint at you. Either shoot back, dive for cover, or freeze. I'll address this in detail later, but for now, these are your good options. Take your time, relax, listen for opponents or teammates. Aural clues are easier than visual ones, especially when you're stalking.

Shooting is a skill that's a major factor in the game, the be-all-end-all of paintball. But, if you're trying to be sneaky, you generally want to make your first shot count. And the key to this is getting a good stance so your hand is steady.

I like having something I can shoulder up, usually my tank. But I've been using a lighter GTS stock lately, and they work very well with a remote line. It's just easier to hold a barrel steady when it's braced.

Taking aim is key. You want to hit something solid, like the opponent's gun or a harness buckle. Aiming for the chest area is good if you have the time to aim. If the paintball deviates a foot or so, you'll still hit the target.

Some say you should pull the trigger slowly, but I don't. Pull the trigger as you would normally. Don't change anything mechanical that you're used to. It's like changing the engine in your car to drive to a new job. Not really worth it. Just shoot in the same way you always do. If all goes well, you'll have an eliminated and confused player in no time. ("Where'd *that* come from!?!?")

Now, let's say that it all goes wrong.

Your barrel is wet and your ball skids left by a million feet.

Your target turns and spots you. Now what?

As I said before, you have options. Three basic choices include the following—(1) shoot back lots of paint, (2) dive for cover, or (3) freeze in place. I've done all three, and they all work depending on terrain, your opponent, and your positioning.

For example, if the terrain is thick and you're fairly far from your opponent, freezing in place will confuse him. He may not see you at all. Presuming you only shot one ball, he won't be able to get a good 'fix' on your position.

If it's more open and there's a lack of hard cover (trees, rocks...), let it rip. Keep the initiative in a situation like this. He's off guard, and you can make him react to you. Eventually, he will make a mistake and you'll get an elimination.

You can also dive for cover. But once you go to ground, the initiative is gone, you surrender it to the other team. Once you're on the ground get out of there, move back, move up, move *somewhere*. Just *move*! Get back to another position and try all over again. Or, fall back and watch your old position. The other team will probably run up onto it assuming you're still there.

The best way to learn how to do this is actually to do it yourself. Try being a sniper for a game or two; you may be surprised at what happens. It's another trick to put in your bag. Remember, being versatile is a large part of what will make your game more successful and keep it fresh and enjoyable over time.

—RR

DEFENSE

Not enough has been written about defense in paintball, and the reasons are apparent. Very few of us think of playing defense in paintball as either a glamorous or enjoyable experience. Indeed, most players' idea of defense is to hang back and shoot anything not friendly as it comes back to the flag station.

But this isn't defense, it's a siege mentality. Bona fide paintball defense is a multifaceted position that's all about controlled aggression. If you understand the dimensions of paintball defense, you will think twice before leaving it out of your game plan.

The idea of defense that true paintball jedi should employ involves channeling your desire to win into preventing the other team from winning.

What am I talking about? Soon, it will all make sense. Most paintball teams are very concerned with taking ground fast, slamming a tape, and being very aggressive in their actions. But a team has to balance that with some kind of defensive capability, and not in the classical "Old School" sense. Paintball is becoming a game of players with positional strengths. Once you accept that proposition, exploring the possibilities of defense becomes more interesting.

First off, let me define paintball-style defense. Defensive players are those on the team attempting to stop the opposition from scoring points. Eliminations, flag hangs, first pulls—all of these are points that can be prevented with a good defense, and not just in tournaments either. If you play for fun, you can play a solid defense and win with it.

What makes a good defender? The mindset of a defender is a combination of fierce pride and spartan commitment. "You're not getting my flag. You're not shooting my crawler. You're not getting that bunker. Not on my field!" Sounds a lot like an aggressor, yes? The difference is that as a defender, your "aggressive" goal requires actively preventing *them* from attaining *their* goals. Hence the phrase, ***Controlled Aggression***.

A fat wallet helps. Defense isn't cheap, you can shoot a ton of paint on "D."

So what's the purpose of defense? I've broken it down to four basic categories:

1. **Positional Defense**—Holding a single piece of real-estate with everything you have.

2. **Prevent Defense**—Also known as "Sitting". Playing solely to deny the opposing team from shooting your team or achieving their goals.

3. **Reserve Defense**—Staying in the back with the eventual goal of becoming an attacking player in a later stage of the game.

4. **Team Defense**—Playing the backfield to aid your forward players.

As a defensive player, you have to decide what style is best for your team and its goals and adapt on the fly. In a big game, it means holding the fort. In a hyperball tournament, you may prevent the other team from advancing and scoring points. In your rec-ball weekend, it could mean being the last line of defense because the corned beef sandwich you ate for lunch just isn't sitting right and running is more than you can handle. *Remember the team goal is important, and so is not barfing during a game.*

Paintball is, and always will be, a team sport.

Defense falls into two broader styles—"Passive" and "Aggressive." As the names suggest, the two styles reflect two different trains of thought, but one overall goal: denying points and positions to the opposing team. There's a general stereotype here for the two styles. "Rec-Ball" players are 'passive' defenders, whereas tournament players are 'active' defenders. Tournament teams leave no players back, but rec-players always do. Yes, it's a stereotype, but it's almost always true. As in everything else, there's a time to be passive, and other times when being aggressive is necessary. Learning the rhythm of the game is very important. It's key to know when you need to act, to feel the appropriateness of doing something. With this in mind, let's go into a little more detail on the four basic categories of defense.

Positional Defense is mainly a concern of passive defenders, mainly because it requires patience in the beginning and cunning when it hits the fan. Active defenders can use the principles of this to take and hold key bunkers and control zones from one spot on the field. Examples of this can be found mostly in big games where a flag station or a fort must be held. On tournament fields, situations arise wherein a defender holds the last few bunkers and tries to stop the offense.

Most positional defense originates in one location, and uses that location to fend off all aggressors. This is a very passive defense, and is very common in rec-play. From a position like this, you want to work around as in a typical bunker. But you have to keep your eyes open because you will more than likely be seeing more than one attacker and they have the maneuverability advantage and often greater numbers.

Aggressive Defense is about players having *zones of influence* that they can claim as their own. This is a very aggressive defense, because you as the defensive player are making the action happen and causing people to react to you. You're grabbing a section of field X by Y in size, staking a claim, and

putting up a sign that reads "No trespassers allowed." As a defender, it allows you to move around more and remain unpredictable. Slide forward to a position to stop them; scuttle to the other side of the bunker and shoot it up. While they're adjusting, move back a position and draw one into your barrel. Take him down and dive to another bunker. Scope out two bunkers you can dive between to make them wonder. If you can keep them guessing so they can't figure out where you are, they will hesitate to move up on you. My girlfriend calls this a "Field Mouse Defense" because it's what a field mouse does and, in her words, "What's more defensive than a field mouse?" Be elusive!

The Surprise Factor

You also want to have the element of surprise. You can accomplish this even if your enemy knows where you are. Consider the following scenario.

At the Ohio Bash, we had a position we had to hold for 5 more minutes so our team captain could touch the station for more points. I had a pump gun, and a few surprises. The team was laying paint heavily into the other team's attacking force. I put my body in front of our captain and began to pump paint to keep their heads down. I kept watching the time, knowing it wouldn't be long. With a minute before the call in, I grabbed a smoke grenade, popped the striker, and tossed it just over the lip of the hill.

It was a good throw, but the smoke wasn't thick enough for my liking. So I popped a red smoker with it and tossed it over the hill as well. "Hammer down!" I yelled. My teammates doubled their rate of fire, stopping our opponents' last minute push. Our captain touched the flag station, and we got our points and vacated the area. The opposing team wasn't expecting a smoke screen, and that stopped them long enough for our team to achieve our goal. This was Controlled Aggression exemplified.

Let it all hang out, but don't take unnecessary risks!

Prevent Defense

Related to positional defense, **prevent defense** uses similar means, but tends to be more useful in tournament settings. Simply put, you're preventing the other team from advancing instead of holding a position. For example, if the opposing team needs to eliminate five of your guys to advance, you fare better by sitting back and making them do the work. They get sloppy or nervous, and they get eliminated. Prevent defense is also easier than position defense because it's not zone oriented. It's more aggressive as well: you hide less and being mobile is emphasized.

I was in Chicago once, and had the opportunity to talk to some guys from Thunderstruck. They were telling me about a tournament field in Vegas some years ago in which they zoned out one bunker at extreme range down a main trail. One guy from the start would take three steps and start laying paint just over that bunker. He made three eliminations in the first two minutes. This is a perfect prevent defense. Other players on his team were making aggressive moves, but this one shooter made the plan work—*controlled aggression is where it's at!*

Most of your defense should be geared towards a "prevent" style. It's very flexible in response to what the other team is doing, but it's not just reactive. If you've done your job before the games start, you should have scoped out the bunkers your opposition is likely to see as advantageous. Dedicate a defense player to preventing them from getting in and/or using that position. Even if someone makes it in, rain paint on their heads so they won't even look up. Now *that's* effective prevention.

Delay Tactic

The other side to a prevent is a **delay tactic** in which you aren't stopping the other team as much as you're stalling the inevitable or forcing them to deal with you. A good friend of mine calls this tactic "The Human Speedbump." We do this in big games all the time. The entire offense is getting routed hard, and we figure that they need a few more seconds to get away. So we stop hard behind a tree and start shooting at the attackers. They always stop to return fire, and we always get eliminated. But we always get our teammates a few hundred more feet of running room in the trade, and they can be more effective. You may also have seen a tournament player crash a front bunker and just hug it. The opposing team is forced to deal with that player, because he's a threat in their path. You may not consider this a defensive maneuver until you realize this one player is stopping the entire other team from pushing a side by just sitting there. Again, this is controlled aggression—doing just enough to stop the 'bad guys' and help the 'good guys' without getting hit.

Reserve Player Defense

The **Reserve player tactic** is a different defense mostly used in recreational play. The general idea is to hang back and wait to see what the opposing team does. Your time interval for this is up to you. For example, I've been playing a lot of speedball style games lately (no deer ticks, and none of this hiding stuff...). Earlier this summer I played at a field in Wisconsin that was preparing for a tournament, so the speedball field was all nice and dolled up. We were also playing the older speedball style of

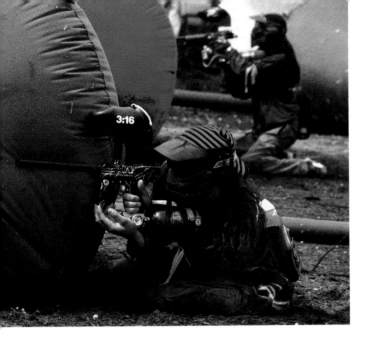

face the back and turn around on the horn. From the break I spun and saw where people were pivoting to move to. I knew where my guys were going, and I didn't have a plan right off the bat. The other team sent most of their players left, while we had a balanced offense. Within three seconds I decided I needed to go on the left to bolster the offense. It worked. Within a minute or two we had held, then cleared the left side. I didn't do it by myself, but my presence was a big help. A few seconds in the "reserve" slot helped the overall offense of the game. I could have slanted right to attack the off side. I could have stayed back and long-balled. I could have sat in the backfield and directed traffic. All of these decisions were opened up to me because I waited to react to the other team. And they were all made in three seconds.

In an outdoor game, I'll wait a few minutes if need be, listen for the shooting and figure how we're holding. If it seems static, then I'll flank or reinforce. In some cases I'll launch myself up a tapeline and sneak around the shooting. If everyone is too busy to look my way, I can make it all the way behind the flag station.

The idea is to be a 'spare player' with intentions to move up on a flag or objective. *Again, controlled aggression is what you're going for.* The key to your move can be timed in minutes or seconds. You can also count the eliminated players and move up when half the other team is eliminated. The main thing is you're not going to sit down the whole

game and wait for the opponent to come to you. It also makes the other team cocky when they make it to your flag after they think they eliminated everyone already. Free shots.

Team Defense

The last category is a ***team defense***. This actually crosses all the previous three categories, but usually sacrifices the defender. The tactic I've already mentioned as "Human Speedbumps" can also be used on a flag return. You run back with the flag runner. If there's any trouble, the runner keeps going but you turn around and return fire. Again, they stop to shoot at you. But your flag runner has a clear path into the station. Any time you make a trade-off like this, think of it as a defensive maneuver. In chess, sacrificing a pawn for a positional advantage that is virtually impossible for your opponent to overcome is a brilliant move.

On the same note, a takedown ("bunkering" or "mugging") can be defensive in nature as well. I can hear you sighing in disbelief from here. But consider: Let's say one player is holding your team in one place. That player's goal is to prevent your team from advancing or keep you preoccupied. To prevent him from achieving his goal, you may want to send in a guy to take him out. Often times you get a trade-off. You and he walk off the field together. But that one move opens up your side and the offense can take control. In this case, bunkering a guy goes from a highly aggressive maneuver to a tactical team-oriented defensive maneuver. This is yet another example of *controlled aggression*.

Sacrificing yourself isn't the only team defense option. Enter the art of an ambush. Often misunderstood, a good ambush should leave an attacking force saying "What in the world just happened?" A good ambush involves three players, requires good setup time, and demands patience to execute well. In an ambush, it is key to cover the attackers in paint as fast as you can. Speed is the key; otherwise, they will find cover, regroup, and give you a hard time. Use your cover, stay low, keep your cool, and when they walk into your zone, let them have it all at once. Of course, this can be very nerve-wracking, but it can also rattle your opponents and cause them to stop an attack. I could write a whole article on the ambush alone—it's more versatile than you think.

Team defense also covers people in your back-field—the heavy shooters who should be working in sync with the team. A guy in the way back long-balling the other team, feeding information to his front crawler is very common, and the easiest to see in action. But it can go further. There's been a lot of talk about "set up plays" recently, and your back players are the best judges as to when you should launch one. So they're a lot like quarter-backs, calling the plays and supporting them to make sure they can happen.

The Bottom Line

I've talked a lot about being an aggressive defender, and controlling that aggression in a way that bene-fits the team. Always consider the team when plan-ning your defense. A solid defense, or at least a planned one, can hold the other team to a points loss or prevent them from organizing that one solid push they need to win the game. Too many teams undermine their best efforts on offense by sacrific-ing their commitment to defense. This neglect is behind the fact that most teams aren't that great. If you want your team to be invincible, take a bal-anced approach to the game. Explore the possibili-ties of dedicating a few players to defensive postures. One guy suppressing the center could make the difference between winning and losing in rec play or a tournament.

—RR

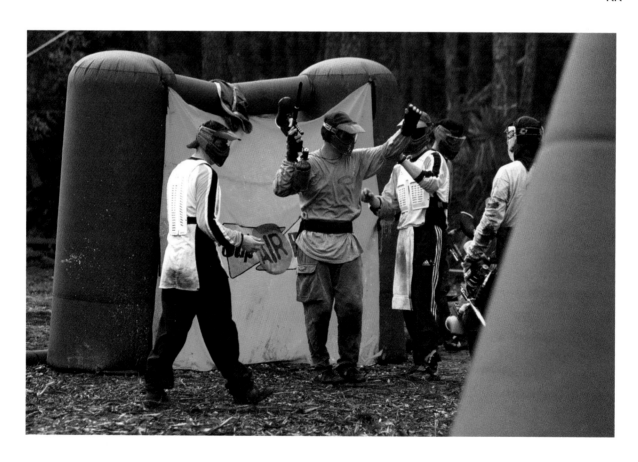

Getting Down to Earth

At the outset, you need to know something about me. I am 6'4" and 250 pounds of big, fat, artery clogging American mass. This makes me quite the atypical "crawler." Your stereotypical crawler is a guy 5'5" with sticks for limbs, and a pat of breakfast butter that slipped onto his shoe representing body fat.

But, since I do crawl, I maintain that anyone can. Crawling can be worked into anyone's game; it's just a matter of how and to what degree. A little floor work can enhance your game by making the impossible likely.

Let us start with a situation most likely to pop up in your game. Say you are in a shootout where nothing is happening. Neither you nor your opponent is moving forward. You have a choice: spend all game in a one-on-one "pop-up-and-shoot" scenario, or try the following.

Swing to your left and release a string. Then quickly roll right and crawl ten feet, and then up three to a different tree. Do not run. Crawl. Assuming you did not run, your opponent, who was likely concentrating on your left side, did not see you reach your new spot. When they pop up to shoot your old bunker, tag them on the head. Crawlers hit the turf just at the right times, not all the time. Crawlers try to fool their opponents by stealth, misdirection, or a combination of the two. A ten foot sideways maneuver is a crawl although it does not appear to be.

Successful crawling begins with the right equipment. Contrary to your assumption, "camouflage" is not a top priority for the crawler's kit. Knee and elbow pads are, however. Technically, I can crawl naked, but it would be painful for me and traumatizing for any witnesses. Pads should allow you to feel the ground when you move but still give protection. I use Redz pads and have never regretted it. Next, you need gloves to serve as padding for your hands. Having a good pair of cleats, a stopwatch, and a stick squeegee in your pads is helpful. You'll need to get streamlined and keep all loose equipment off your body. Once you have acquired these priorities, look into camouflages. You can overcome those big, juicy white logos on your chest with a crawl.

Your chest is already on the turf, who's going to see it?

Crawling is a combination of patience, skill, and time management. Bob Long once gave me the metaphor that when you commit to a crawl (or anything in paintball), you need to see the door opening, decide when to go for it, and gauge how long you have before it slams in your face.

Although every situation must be treated uniquely, I have found two basic techniques for crawling suitable for different occasions. The first is the "Leopard Crawl," which is useful for low or dense cover. The whole time you are moving, you are on your toes, knees, elbows, and hands, and your belly is literally just over the ground. Most of your forward power comes from digging your spikes into the ground and pushing off of them. While you do this, raise your body over the ground and steady yourself on your elbows and hands. Do this in the manner most comfortable for you. For a long time I used my toe spike, but then I switched to Diggers cleats and changed to a side spike on the ball of my foot. If you are doing it right, it should be like rock climbing on flat terrain (except you don't get jackhammer foot or use carabiners). Using five times the energy to move a quarter of the distance, the disadvantage to the Leopard Crawl is energy expenditure. But in heavy cover and places where the only way to cross to a key position is to dig your nose in dirt, the Leopard Crawl is the best option. It is quite a rush to crawl up the middle of a field, cross a ravine unseen under rays of paint shooting above you, and attain a key spot.

The second basic technique is the "Three-Point crawl". As the name suggests, you crawl forward with both knees and one hand on the ground while the other hand holds your paintgun. Keeping an Autococker level as you crawl isn't easy, but do not point it at the ground. If you get surprised, shooting the ground is inef-

fective and pointless. While you're crawling, do not continuously put all your weight on an open hand; you don't want to hurt your wrists. I crawl on a closed fist parallel with my forearm to minimize injury potential. The Three Point Crawl is a very fast crawl, but it is less stealthy, and, therefore, more perilous. From these two basic techniques you can accomplish a lot of maneuvering. A variation of the Leopard Crawl would be moving more like a snake—making more noise, but crawling faster and

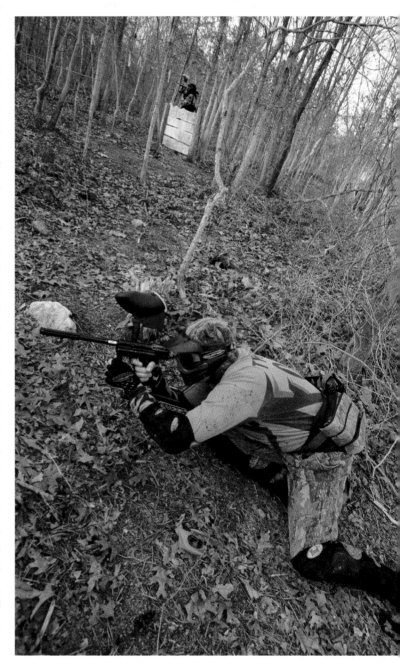

lower to the ground. A Three Point can become a Four Point or even a Two point. Adjust the maneuver to the specific situation. Be mindful of your feet; a beautiful crawl can be easily defeated if your foot becomes a target.

When should you take a chance on crawling? Not all the time. You would gain little from crawling all the way from flag to flag. Getting half way up the field would take the whole game. Instead, crawling should be used to gain an advantage, either with your teammates or on your own. The field—tree roots and shrubs included—looks different when you're a foot off the floor. There are many holes that are only visible at ground level.

The best teacher is experience, so here are some team plays to try.

The "Low-man approach" is a classic. One teammate shoots over your head at an opponent they can not reach due to cover. You start a Three point crawl towards the covered opponent. Speed is the key. Your teammate over you, the High Man keeps signaling you information: "50 feet, on left! 11-o'clock!" or whatever team codes you use. As the crawler, don't say a word. That would defeat the purpose and destroy the surprise attack. Your back player should shout a code word (e.g., "now" will suffice) as a signal for you to pop up and put a string on the opponent. When it works, it's so sweet.

Using the same set up, you can make a "sacrifice" move. The High Man makes a lot of noise, and does a lot of shooting. He will eventually fall back or get eliminated, leaving the crawler, or the Low Man, in the field deep in cover. The crawler waits for the other team to overrun his spot and then fires at them from behind. Either that or run for their flag; they won't expect you to be covering their flag station, will they?

In both cases an aggressive team could argue that you should just make a takedown. This does

not work all the time, and circumstances like heavy overgrowth or a bad trail create a difficult situation for "running up and mugging the bum." Besides, a crawl like this only takes a minute or two. Patience to make a takedown gradually and wisely is rewarding.

Out on a paintball field you have to make quick decisions that can affect the outcome of the game. Crawling may not always be the best thing to do, but it's worth having in your arsenal as part of an overall plan.

For example, assume that you have a good bunker position, but you spy a better one. There is enough cover to work, so you set up a crawl about 30 feet from the new bunker, going low but fast. You will cover that last 30 feet, the "Three Second" point, by running. Here is the general "Three Second Rule" for sprints: it takes a second to see you, a second to comprehend who you are, and what team you are on, and another second to raise a paintgun and shoot. The three seconds of comprehension are three seconds of sprinting you get for free without the risk of getting shot. So crawl to that "Three Second" point and take them by surprise. You can reach the new bunker unseen by slithering right to it. The effect will be the same. Once you get there you have a few free shots, equivalent to those three seconds of sprinting, before the other team adjusts to your new position.

Another field strategy is crawling under a fire-lane, as long your opponent's line of sight does not extend that low. Imagine a line that begins at your opponent and travels straight out along their line of sight. They can not see you as long as their position does not enable them to look over and down. You can crawl literally under their barrel if you possess the nerve.

Stealth is covered extensively in my Fieldcraft chapter, but it bears a quick repeat. Basically, move quietly, clear your path, and set up for a one-shot "Bingo." Crawling makes stealth easier, as being on the ground makes brushing noisy obstacles out of your path easy. The bragging rights for getting "Bingos" is beautiful (and they save money on paint, too).

Crawling is an important paintball tool among many. Knowing when and where to go to ground can be an asset to your game. Even if you are tall and chunky.

—RR

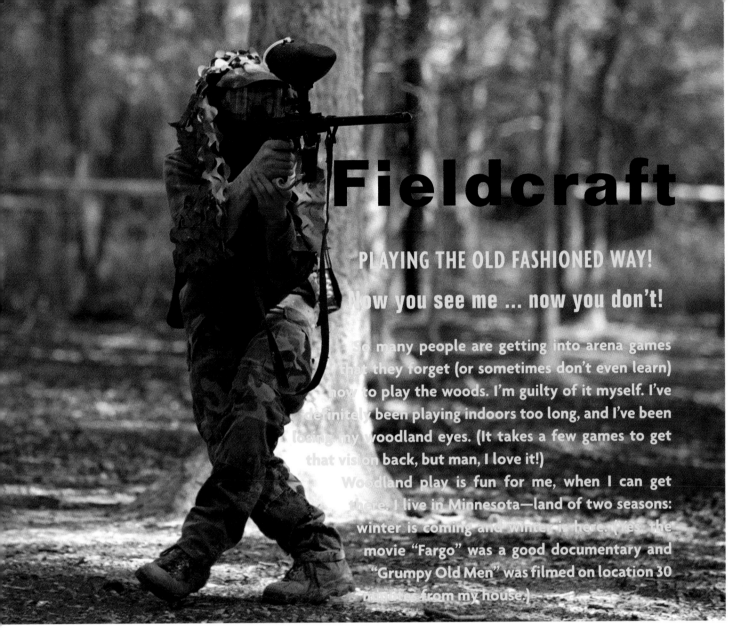

Fieldcraft

PLAYING THE OLD FASHIONED WAY!

Now you see me ... now you don't!

So many people are getting into arena games that they forget (or sometimes don't even learn) how to play the woods. I'm guilty of it myself. I've definitely been playing indoors too long, and I've been losing my woodland eyes. (It takes a few games to get that vision back, but man, I love it!)

Woodland play is fun for me, when I can get there. I live in Minnesota—land of two seasons: winter is coming and winter is here. (Yes, the movie "Fargo" was a good documentary and "Grumpy Old Men" was filmed on location 30 minutes from my house.)

Personally, the best part of woodland paintball is the stalking. I don't want to sound like some kind of wacked-out, back-country, weird-beard here. I'm just saying that when you're outside, closer to nature than usual, successfully stalking your friends (or whoever your opponents happen to be that day) is a thrill! I'm a big guy, and somehow I can do it.

What is Fieldcraft?

Fieldcraft is mainly the art of trickery. The use of camouflage and concealment is a dying art in paintball. Crawlers use a little 'fieldcraft' on tournament fields, but it's virtually obsolete because fields are increasingly *postage-stamp-sized.*

It's a real skill to use terrain to your advantage. It encompasses a number of skills that we either take for granted or don't take seriously as modern players. These days paintball players laugh at people using face paint; back in the eighties, when I started playing, face paint was the norm. The original paintball players used fieldcraft because the game was played outside exclusively. The time has come to modernize the use of fieldcraft to suit the evolution of our sport.

Know your opponents!

What you need to do is *trick* your opponent. How? The first thing you have to understand is your opponent. To begin with, he or she is a human being. However noble in reason and spirit they may be, humans are fallible. In paintball, their imperfections are often relatively easy to spot, if you're paying attention.

Paintball tricks work by understanding the general nature of and specific inclinations of your opponents. Generally speaking, most players today are impatient. Instead of waiting for you to walk on top of them, most will shoot as soon as they see you. Most are also deadlocked on the opponent they see in front of them and less likely to check their sides as they advance.

Here's where using your camouflage comes in handy. For example, I was playing at Stalker Paintball Games, a field in Wisconsin that has a dense canopy and not many light patches. I dove into a thicket bush and sat for a few minutes. Basically, I was out in the middle of nowhere, with no solid

cover for 50 feet other than this thicket. But, the other team was making a push up the center. One player in a JT jersey came screaming up the center. I leveled my gun, waited for him, and hammered down as he made a turn into the spool right in front of me.

Sitting still in your cover, and using your camouflage to your advantage is the essence of fieldcraft. My opponent was so focused on making his bunker that he got sloppy. I understood that he would do just that, and I acted accordingly. I had control of the situation, he just never realized it.

So with that story in mind, let's start with your camouflage.

The Invisible Advantage

We all wear camouflage, but hardly anyone uses it correctly because of a lack of control or understanding. It's ridiculous that so few people really take advantage of their camos. Many players want to shoot their gun as many times as they can. Fine, go ahead! Don't be surprised that someone saw you from the other side of the field. You're making noise, and now we know where you are.

In order to use camouflage, it's important to understand why it works. There are a few different styles that work in different ways in different terrain. I had a long chat with Tim Schloss of Pursuit Products about camouflage. That's his business, he sells "Tiger Stripe", "Realtree" and "Advantage" styles of camouflage, as well as color blocked styles. Great stuff. He told me there's two basic types of camouflage, and two basic ways they work.

Types of Camouflage

Aggressive camouflage works by fooling the eye into thinking it's a part of the background. Good examples of this type would be US Woodland, Belgian dots, Auscam, and so on. It's made to match a background's overall colors. This stuff works best behind shrubs and shadows. Camouflages like

"Tiger Stripe" fall into this category, but for a different reason. You see, the human eye is lazy. When we scan for opponents, we scan horizontally. Aggressive camouflage, like Tiger Stripe, encourages the eye to "slide over" it. There's a few other camouflages like this. US Woodland was actually created for a European military theater by the United States government. Tiger Stripe was originally made for the Vietnam conflict, but was modified slightly for paintballers. You don't want to know how much the Australian government spent on developing Auscam, but it's the best stuff for hiding in Australia that I've found.

Passive camouflage works in a different way; it's made to convince the brain it's part of the foreground, and totally natural. This would include Advantage, Realtree (and it's derivatives), Mossy Oak, and so on. Each of these types is perfect for specific uses. "Advantage" looks like the forest floor, while "Realtree" looks like a tree. These camouflages started as hunting patterns. They are supposed to enable a hunter to stand in front of a tree to get a better shot. That's why they try to be photo-realistic. They're not really meant for other terrain. In their elements, these highly specialized camouflages are excellent.

Then there's a third kind of camouflage, which I call "Weirdo-Flage." These types fit mostly into the "Aggressive" camouflage category. They include, but aren't limited to, JT, Scott, Renegade or Venomwear printed jerseys, Splash clothing. Any of the "Non-Camo" stuff also falls into this category. The idea behind these patterns is simply to bring paint-

ball into the 'mainstream'. Paintball garb as fashionable accessory...you get the picture. They work toward that end, and, occasionally, as partial camouflage. I love the guys who wear off-the-shelf JT Jerseys. Big, juicy white target in center of their chest and on their forearms. Easy target from across the field. Love it.

Some of the non-camo works, but not as well as true camouflage. If you're wearing it to look like a team, cool. If you're wearing it as a true camo... well... umm... yeah...

Whatever you're wearing, the golden rule of camouflage is not to move. The human eye is lazy, but it's also naturally drawn to motion. Motion is perceived as something worth watching.

Paintball players, of course, have to move. Given that fact, note that "Aggressive" patterns allow you more freedom of movement than "Passive" patterns. Aggressive patterns aren't specific to one spot or terrain, and allow you to take a "camouflaged" position anywhere in a broad spectrum of places. If you're wearing a Realtree and you're lying down, it doesn't "look" right and you're more apt to be spotted. A "Tiger Stripe" looks more appropriate in any given place you stop.

As a player, you can also use different patterns in different terrain. I have a set of Realtree I've used in the desert. It worked well. This isn't brain surgery, people. The key is simply to match your camouflage as accurately as possible to your surroundings. I've seen pictures of UK players in Tiger Stripe in which the green just blares out against a brown background; we're talking total absence of greenage on the ground level. I've made boo-boos like this before, mostly in my paintball youth. And if it happens by mistake these days, I just change my outlook on the game and adapt. I'll look for colors where I'm close to blending in and go from there.

Camouflage—All or Nothing!

Use a visor on your goggles or at least a hat brim. Goggle flare is a dead giveaway to your position. Don't use chrome or bright, splashy stuff that may glare as well. Matte Black is still your best bet for color. Wear a full mask. Skin tones aren't nature tones and will give you away. Better yet, paint your mask for camo colors or mottle it somehow to break up the "Black Blob" on your face. My favorite trick is hiding your brightly colored armband by burying your arm into a tree or the ground and using your body as a "cloak" over it.

BEHAVING INVISIBLE

There's a time and a place for battle cries and open charges down the middle, but this ain't one of'em!

Wait your opponent out. They panic when nobody is shooting at them. Take your time and you'll absolutely freak 'em out.

You don't need cool camos or anything like that to hide, however. I could be wearing stark white, and you won't see me if I'm totally behind hard cover (see the Cover chapter). It's that easy. Let's say I'm wearing a really bright jersey and I've got a bright red paintgun. If I'm trying to hide, I'll get behind a rock, a dirt berm, or a hill. Anything I can put my whole body behind relative to an enemy position will hide me.

Nature is one big free camouflage factory!

Use Reference Points and the World Around You

Having a reference point is good as well. I'll often use cover from one angle, knowing that the other team or another player will be coming from that or another angle and crossing my barrel. I can expose myself to one side if I know that side is *safe*. That's

why I run the tape as often as I do, I can expose that whole flank as I wait for you to walk into my dot-sight. Pop, "HIT", Bingo. Thank you.

Terrain is a big part of fieldcraft. Your fieldcraft skills come from learning how to use what's ahead of you and see what's to the side of you. Lining up trees to conceal your movement toward your opponents is always a good idea. You can't plan on things like shadows, wind, and so on to mask your movement. You just have to do it.

But when it all falls together, you have to recognize it for what it is. If I'm stalking a tape (either by crawl or by crouch), I'm constantly aware of my surroundings. I'm looking ahead for the clearest line in the path that requires minimal effort and noise. Leaves are bad, dirt is good. If I have a choice between twigs or dried leaves, I'll take the twig route. I can push twigs out of my way quieter and faster than I can leaves by just dragging my hand along them and not lifting my knees too far.

I'm always listening to the wind. When it picks up, I move. When it dies down, I slow or stop. I listen for airplanes, cars, trucks, trains, people shooting in the center... anything that makes enough noise to mask my movement.

Moves are made quickly and deliberately, and planned 2 steps ahead when possible. The thought process is: "Big Tree to fort. Fort to spool. Spool to shrubs."

I'm always looking ahead. I'm also looking down the field to where opponents *should* be hiding. I can't predict everything, but if I'm coming up on a big tree or an outcropping of barrels, odds are someone is either in there or wants to be. *I'm looking through cover for background shadows.* If I don't see any light behind twigs or shrubs, it's either a rock, a tree, or a player.

Sounds play a very important role, too. Especially nature sounds. Most things in nature that produce noisy sounds will stop when something big comes by and scares them. If the birds and crickets stop chirping, someone spooked them and you should get ready. In some cases, an animal may start making a lot of noise if you approach. Listen for any and all audible changes; they're the best early warning system you'll have in the wild.

A bit of fieldcraft also goes into using nature to fool people. These are old school tricks, but they're still good. Here are some examples from my experience. I'm lying on the ground while two guys are looking for me. They know I'm out there, but not sure where. With one foot I'll wiggle a small tree or a thick shrub away from me. That will get their attention long enough for me to come up and take 'em out. There's also the "Throw a rock away from you so it makes noise over there" trick, but I stopped doing that out of fear of pelting a ref or well-hidden player. You'd be well advised to throw only relatively light things. I've also been stalking, been spotted, and swayed matching the tree in front of me for movement. The player looked away, and I got moving at the flag. (I was able to get the flag, and not make a single elimination that game.) Then there's the 'ballsy' approach. Someone thinks they see me, and they open a barrage at me. I don't flinch or move. After a few moments, they stop shooting. Why? Nothing shot back, obviously nobody's there. One burst later, they're gone.

CLAIM THIS LOST ART AND PUT IT IN YOUR GAME

To a paintball player who uses fieldcraft, tactical possibilities are virtually infinite. I've crawled through a path with no cover in front of me and made it, and I've sat in front of a tree and remained unseen. But if you think this is all there is to know, you're wrong.

I talked to a friend of mine; he plays in ratty old BDU's, uses a pump gun, and wears no mask. He's one of my favorite wire players, because he can just vanish after taking a guy out and pop up thirty paces to the right of where he just was. He's very good. When I started writing this piece, I asked him for help. "Sure!" he said. "Who's gonna read it?" I said new players and tournament competitors. "No way, man!" he said. "I'm not gonna tell 'em all my secrets! I've earned *some* advantage over them!"

I agree. Some secrets are meant to be discovered rather than shared. Besides, I learned from the best. I can't let out all our trade secrets. Ninja Union Local 151 won't let me.

—RR

"ALL-AMERICAN" THINGS YOU CAN DO TO IMPROVE YOUR GAME

"When you attack, you want to attack from the highest heights of heaven. And when you defend, you want to defend from the deepest resources of the earth."
LAO TZU, THE ART OF WAR

BILL GARDNER: First, we'll talk about individual tactics, then we'll talk about squad tactics and team tactics. When I say individual tactics, I mean aspects of the game that improve the individual's play.

And a lot of this comes down to the simple things. For example, there are different ways to load. Obviously, if you stick your elbow out, it becomes a target. You need to learn how to load with your elbow tucked in. These are the little things that make the difference between winning and losing.

You have to develop certain basic skills. First, you have to learn to shoot. You also have to realize that you're not going to be afforded the opportunity to just aim and slowly pull the trigger. You need to work on your snap shooting—the ability to stay within a bunker, then snap out and shoot a target, and then get back behind cover quickly.

Almost every player that achieves any level of skill in this sport gets comfortable with shooting a target at 40 yards or so with a quick snap and a couple of shots. So, from an individual standpoint, you must work on accuracy.

Then, there are bunker tactics—the ways you work a bunker. During a game you often end up behind some structure, either a speed ball bunker or a stick bunker in the woods.

Never look from the same place twice in a row. You bring your head up at the same place every time, and the other guy watches your head come up at the same spot, two times before. So he aims at that spot. As you bring your head up again the paint is on its way, and you're wet before you know where it came from. So learn to peek around left, take two shots, then peek around right and take two shots. Keep your opponent off guard.

Paintball is an aural game, too. You can hear your opponent's gun go off. You can hear paint fly through the air; it whizzes. So, you can and should use your ears to determine when to come up and where to shoot.

ADAM GARDNER: People get shot just because they stay up too long. They want to watch their paint fly and then yell about it. Remember, you can call for a paint check just as effectively from behind a bunker. You saw the ball far enough on it's path that you have a pretty good idea of whether you were on line or weren't. If you didn't get him, you can adjust.

You want to come up, take your shots and immediately duck down, Inexperienced players watch their paint fly through the air as if that's the best part of the game. When they get a hit, they freak out and make themselves an easy target.

BILL: Blind shooting is another excellent tactic. If you're playing in a wooded field, look beyond your opponent for reference points you can zero in on from a better, protected position, and put paint in that direction. For example, get a fix on a branch right over the guy's head. You have a good chance of getting a hit and you minimize your risk of being shot. That's the beauty of blind shooting.

BILL: Different people are interested in different skills. You have your bunker players. You have your back players. People fall into different categories. They may know their orientation towards playing the back positions, and they'll gravitate towards shooting paint a long distance.

So, instead of running down the field, getting as close as they can to the other players, which is an aggressive, front line mentality, their mentality is..."I don't want to get closer,

Some of the best players we've seen will do strange things in the bunker. They'll kick the right side of the bunker as a diversion, then move left. Meanwhile, everyone's thinking that the player is coming out the right side, so that's where they are looking.

We call this working the bunker. Of course, given your athletic ability, there are only so many things you can do. One of our best players is extremely flexible. With his degree of flexibility, he can work a bunker in ways that other people just can't.

It's also good to be skilled at left-handed shooting; this opens up the entire left-hand side of the bunker. So practice shooting with both your left and right hands.

ADAM G: A lot of people will take the first shot they can get. You need to practice patience. There are times when you're far better off letting a guy get closer, especially if he doesn't know where you are.

When people don't see you, you want to make sure that the first thing they hear is your paint hitting them. Learn to breathe, relax, and be patient... not too patient, though.

I'm going to shoot them at a mile and a half. I'm going to take a ton of paint and just dump it."

If you do this, you're shooting by volume, trying to get one of 50 shots to hit. You have to practice shooting long range targets. I bet a guy here once $10 bucks in one shot I could hit him at 100 yards. I shot one shot and hit him at 100 yards. You can definitely shoot 70–100 yards and eliminate players.

If you wear glasses, get goggles that will hold

the glasses. Better still, wear contact lenses. A lot of people say, "I can't wear contact lenses, they're the most uncomfortable things in the world." In paintball, you'd be amazed at how many people finally wear contacts. When you're out on the field, it makes all the difference in the world.

Now there's a thing called being tight in a bunker. Being tight in a bunker means your elbows aren't sticking out. You tuck your harness around the back so it's not exposed. You bring your knees in. You crawl up underneath sections of the bunker, take the harness off completely and lay it on the ground.

ADAM G: You can even lay flat on your back and watch the paint fly by. It's a lot easier to see it as you're watching it fly over. Find your best angle and determine where the shooter is.

BILL: The back player is exposed to many different angles of shots, and it is imperative that he survive because he's the eyes and ears and the communication center of the team. If he dies, the team's ability to win is significantly compromised.

ADAM G: You have to learn to focus on the most immediate danger. For example: Let's say you have an opponent who's positioned with a couple of trees in between him and you. This makes it hard for him to get a shot. Then, you've got another opponent 30 yards away who can either run at any time and bunker you, or has a clean shot. That's the guy you have to stay focused on. He's the greater threat. If you concentrate on the guy who doesn't

have a very good chance of shooting you, the guy who does will blow you away.

People get impatient and forgetful. They look the other way and get caught up in other action. Before they know it, they're out.

If opponents are getting really close or you know that if one of them pops up and you're not looking, he's going to have a good shot at you, you must focus on the immediate danger. Even if it means just pointing your barrel right at that guy and not moving it. *Remember that you're on a team. Tell your teammates to keep the other guys off you.*

BILL: To summarize, individual tactics and techniques: Know how to shoot, know how to live in a bunker, know how to identify the most dangerous target, be patient. Learn to load, squeegee, and other things you do when you're not shooting so that you don't expose yourself. Be tricky, be sly, and be unpredictable.

SQUAD TACTICS

The next level is *squad tactics.* The first thing that comes into play when you have two people is communication. Great communication is the most powerful tool in paintball.

ADAM G: A lot of new players start off with five men. So, there's five of them and there's five of you. At the start of the game, say you shoot two of their guys off the left and you lose one of your guys.

You see all of this and call out, "21," which means "two of them are dead, one of ours." It also conveys that they lost their guys on the left side.

If you look downfield and see there's two guys on your right and one guy in the center, you know there's a very good chance that they are weak on the left. You can quickly run behind the other team, take them where they're weakest, and win the game.

BILL: People tend to play in squads, just like special forces. The most important element of squad level tactics is coordinated shooting and moving.

Teams come up to me and say, "The time was right, everything was great. We all ran right down to bunker him, and we got killed. What did we do wrong?"

My response is usually, "Well, it's pretty simple. You were all running, no one was shooting."

Only by bringing together the shooting and the moving, do you end up with the squad performance that you're looking for.

One of the hardest things to teach players who are moving from the intermediate recreational level to the beginning of tournament play is that you all can't just move at once.

You have to realize that unspoken versus spoken communication comes with experience and effort. I realize, as I run up to this bunker, he's just going to get me if I take one more step. So, I sit down and start shooting, and Adam comes over and does him from another angle. We win because we act to support one another in scenarios that are familiar to us.

A squad that understands shooting and moving works together like clockwork. You get absolute dominance with that combination.

ADAM G: Making a good squad or team is about developing that level of trust. I've got to trust the fact that my teammate is going to be there dropping and firing when I'm making my move.

BILL: The squad must combine individual tactics, communication and the aggressive, coordinated movement we've been describing. Now, a good squad of three that has excellent movement will do just tremendous damage to an uncoordinated, non-communicating team of five. It's the way teams play together that decides who wins or loses.

Team tactics bring together all the squad tactics. Now you have to make the squads work. And to be honest with you, we struggle with this to this day. Teams that come together with the trust factor, the right mix of people, that understand it all, have perfect faith in each other, and make it happen. They're unbeatable.

It's a constant struggle to develop that chemistry. You don't just find it. It's almost like managing a business. You start by picking people not only for their playing abilities but for their personalities and their ability to motivate other people.

Young teams often ask me "How can we get to be the best team?" My reply is, "Make sure that when you go out and play every weekend, you have fun. Don't pick guys that are jerks." Put people together who will work together, who don't need to be told to be helpful and supportive.

Another team tactic involves learning the fields. You start to walk fields as a team. Identify the vulnerable positions and dominant bunkers. Figure out what positions you need in order to win.

ADAM G: We spend a lot of time learning where we want to be and trying to figure out where the opponents are most likely to be. We want to have a game plan. We want to know in advance how the game should go. It takes work, but it pays off tremendously. Once you set that game plan, all your other tactics start to come together—team, squad, and individual.

BILL: We should mention sweet spots. Sweet spots are situations where there's a really nice

offensive or defensive advantage. I remember a time where there were thick pines on both sides of a trail that our opposing team had to run about 35 yards through before they could break out their positions. We lined all 10 guns up on the trail. As soon as the whistle blew, our paint was in the air. Ten guns firing 10 balls a second. We took four out before the game even started. We discovered this sweet spot by walking the field in advance of the game.

Another tactic is to break the opponent's line. When you break lines, Adam's done it very successfully, you can come up behind the other team. You come into their line to shoot them all as if you're one of their players. It happens all the time.

ADAM G: I snuck behind these guys once and two of them turned around and looked at me. They said, thinking I was one of their team: "Hey Jim!"

I went along with their case of mistaken identity and said, "Yeah, what's up?"

"Jim, we got two of them off the front!" They were pretty worked up.

"All right! Way to go!" I replied.

And as they turned back to me I raised my gun and took them out. "Oh, by the way, I'm not Jim." They were shocked!

BILL: And *that* was a team of U.S. Marines!

To wrap this up, I want to quote from a book that I love, *The Art of War* by Lao Tzu. I consider it recommended reading for anyone interested in tactics, even emotional tactics. "When you attack, you want to attack from the highest heights of heaven. And when you defend, you want to defend from the deepest resources of the earth," says Lao Tzu.

I interpret it this way: When you attack, your adrenaline is pumped. You attack with such vigor and force that the enemy cannot defend itself. But, when you defend, you don't take stupid chances. You dig in so deep that there's no way that they can shoot you or eliminate you."

Knowing the Game, Playing to Win

I have always believed that understanding leads to success. Many players play paintball without ever truly understanding the underlying concepts, which is the only way that a person can advance in this sport. As a result of this, many people misinterpret what happens during a game and learn nothing from watching them. Case in point...

After my team, Aftershock, won a game at the World Cup in Orlando, I heard one kid tell his friend, "Oh yeah, you should have seen them. They just mowed the other team down. Aftershock just got up and went at'em. They smoked'em, dude." He was referring to Aftershock winning the game impressively. But he had completely missed the true nature of what had happened. He seemed to be implying that the win was wholly attributable to Aftershock's attack; it wasn't. He couldn't differentiate between what looked dramatic and what had actually transpired.

Witnessing a team dominate and demolish the opposition, without a doubt one of the most exciting and memorable aspects of paintball, sticks in the mind because it is so dynamic. But it does not tell the whole story. Not by a longshot.

The bottom line is that if you want to progress in this sport, you need to learn how to understand what is going on!

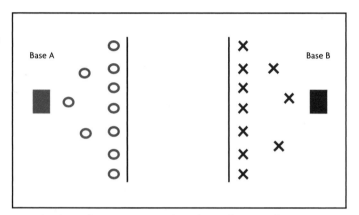

The above illustration is a rough guide to what 99% of tournament paintball teams do when they position themselves at the start of the game. If you look at any tournament game, you will see each team run out to initial positions on the first third of the field, as shown above. The teams will sit in these positions and duke it out until one side gets a few more kills than the other. At that point, the prevailing team will make their move. Only after a significant number of eliminations have been made does the end game unfold. Obviously, the team that gets the most kills in this part of the game normally wins.

Paintball can be broken down, like chess, into three parts: the opening, middle, and the end.

THE OPENING GAME

This is best described as the part of the game where your teammates run out to their primary cover points: the bunkers or trees that you have selected to be your first stopping points.

Now this part of the game, unlike the other two, is completely under your control.

Before the game, your team should have agreed on a selection of bunkers that were not only the

safest to attain, but also provided the best angles for eliminating the opposition.

When the game starts, you should know where you and your teammates are headed, and the path you will use to run to your primary position.

Your team's entry into primary positions should be accomplished without any losses if you have done your prep work correctly.

Having control is important because if you control proceedings then you can predict outcomes (e.g., the victories you aspire to). Without control, you are a hostage to fortune. Luck will smile on you one day and not the next.

With one hundred percent control, you can do whatever you want with no real interference from the other team. But once you get in this position, the middle part of the game begins, and this is where paintball games are won and lost.

THE MID GAME

Ninety-nine percent of paintball games at tournaments follow similar patterns. Both teams run out to their respective primary positions and start firing their guns. As soon as the mid game progresses, people begin to walk off the field.

The stronger team starts picking off the weaker team one by one. This is where the real damage is done. The determinant of who will actually win the game is generally who gets the most kills off the basic line format. This is one of the fundamentals of tournament play.

All tournament teams try to play this way. They run out to their positions, which roughly extend across the width of a field in a line. In this way, all the bases are covered. Both defensive and attacking capabilities can be optimized across all areas of the field.

The basic layout of a field is the length of it divided into three sections. The first third line is where each team lines up. The middle third line of the field is the *killing ground*, and the final third line is where (from your perspective as a player) the opposition resides.

The Mid-Game is the Pivotal Phase

As I alluded to earlier, the perspective of the side line observer is limited because the truly decisive and key eliminations are achieved immediately before the *exciting* finale. Indeed, the reality is that by the time you see five or six tournament players get up and run down the last vestiges of the opponents' defense, the most decisive part of the game is already over. A controllable end game results from a successful mid-game.

> Since the mid game is so
> important, what can we do
> to make sure that
> it's successful?

Technique is the answer. If you are better than your opposition technically, then the killing ratio will be in your favor. If not, more of your team members will be eliminated and you will lose control of the end game. Lost control means defeat. Period.

> Paintball can appear very complex to many people when
> it is actually very simple. Once you understand the
> underlying concepts of it, everything makes sense.

There are no secrets in Paintball; everything is common sense.

THE END GAME

After a successful mid game, the end game should be yours. You began the game in control of your primary positioning. You used your technical prowess to acquire a high killing ratio, which left your opponents at a numeric disadvantage. Now you have control. But it isn't over yet; you still have to take advantage of your supremacy.

Almost everyone has heard of heroic last stands

from players who have killed five or six incoming players alone. It happens, but it shouldn't.

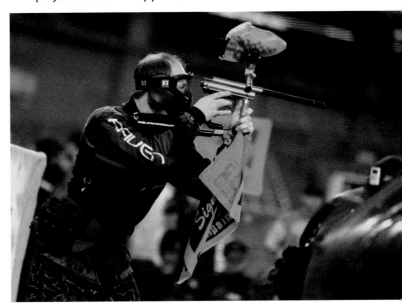

Superiority in numbers should mean victory, but there are exceptions when a field bias will sometimes confer an advantage to the team with fewer players. Not everything always goes exactly as planned in the end game. Sometimes the disadvantaged team wins. This sport is inherently unpredictable, but you must give yourself the best possible chance for success.

These are the basic concepts behind the game, but in order to increase your chances of winning, you must have an idea of the other available styles and strategies.

PLAYING STYLES

There are three basic playing styles in paintball: **defensive**, **technical**, and **aggressive**.

The Technical Style

Historically, the All-Americans exemplify the *technical* approach.

They sit on their line format and eliminate the other team's members with their superior techniques throughout the entire game.

As you watch an All American's game, you will notice a procession of their opponents toward the dead box for no reason other than that the All Americans shot them first. The trick is to do it consistently. That's what they do. If you want this to be your style, then you need to become an extraordinary sharp-shooter, drill regularly, and practice patience.

The Defensive Style

One of the reasons for playing a defensive game is to counter-attack the other team's offensive attacks. It is not very accepted on the tournament circuit because it is seen as a way of compensating for lack of skill and aggression.

Another reason for playing defensively is when the opposing team is believed to be better than your own. It's safer to move only when you are attacked instead of making an offensive move and opening yourself up to trouble.

Only a few teams use this strategy, but I won't mention them, since they might be insulted. So I won't mention Bob Long's Ironmen... but they are getting better! (Just kidding guys!)

The Aggressive Style

This is the most exciting and difficult way to play. It occurs when your team hits the wall of the opposing team, which only happens after significant eliminations have been made. Only two or three teams play this way: Aftershock, four-time World Cup champions, and Bob Long's Ironmen of 1991 to 1994, who were the greatest aggressive team of all time. They attacked with a series of line assaults that could and did break every defense.

KNOWING AND PRACTICING ARE DIFFERENT THINGS

Teams generally acquire their style by default, rather than design, which is a direct consequence of who is on their team. Conservative members play defensively, while eager and slightly crazy members play aggressively. The technical components of each style need to be molded to fit with the technical capabilities of each team. Those who are masterful paintball technicians experience paintball at its most exciting and rewarding. If that's your goal, you are aiming high, and better start practicing now. And now that you know what you have to do, you have no excuses.

—PR

More Than Just A Game

THE REWARDS OF PLAYING PAINTBALL

Jerry Braun Puts Paintball in Perspective

As you have seen, paintball is a game, a sport, a business, an escape, a regimen, an avocation, a corporate training device, a bonding experience, and an all around good time. And still, I would contend, paintball is more than the sum of its parts.

Something about paintball gives a great deal to those who play it. Paintball provides a structure within which players of all ages, backgrounds, physical make-ups, and beliefs can experience the thrill of victory. Its rules are simple and winning is accessible. That's especially important to young people.

Paintball's greatest value comes from what it does for young players. Those who never made the first squad of little league baseball, pee-wee football, or local soccer leagues, who often had to sit on the bench in frustration and embarrassment, can participate and excel in this game. They can score a key elimination, make a sacrifice that helps their team win, and hang the flag to win the game.

In paintball, the recognition, support, and congratulations young people receive from peers build a self-esteem few other activities can foster. To children and their parents, this is where paintball becomes more than just a game.

Travis Jenks takes the flag in front of a cheering crowd at Skyball 1999.

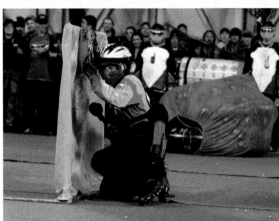

Children who are particularly talented at this game have access to ever increasing levels of difficulty, all the way up to amateur and professional leagues. There are no upper limits for those who seek an extremely challenging competitive experience in this up-and-coming sport.

The game nurtures communication skills, promotes values such as honesty, fair play, teamwork, and goal setting. It also introduces young people to the experience of being decisive, taking risks, and learning from the consequences of their actions. All of this occurs in a safe format and family-friendly atmosphere. In all of these ways, paintball builds character.

Paintball flourishes because it gives so much to its participants in so many different ways. It is an activity that has yet to reach its peak of popularity and its future seems limitless!

Living His Dream

Diagnosed with a rare form of Hodgkins Disease at the age of 16, Travis Jenks is making the most of every moment and taking nothing for granted. Travis seized the opportunity to play with and against the best players in professional paintball in Toronto at Skyball 1999, an international tournament. The Diggers and their owner Jerry Reilly, Operation Paintball, and Mare Island's owner, Matt Crandle, pitched in airfare for the Jenks family, and the Greater Bay Area Make-A-Wish Foundation made hotel arrangements.

Travis was especially grateful to play alongside his personal paintball hero, Bob Long of the Ironmen. This was not their first meeting. The two met initially at the Mare Island fields in California where Travis had his first chance to play with the Ironmen and the Diggers in a scrimmage planned for him by the Greater Bay Area Make-A-Wish Foundation.

"I'd like to get a nice paintball marker and maybe go play with the Ironmen."

The entire paintball industry has rallied around Travis. Bud Orr donated a 98 Autococker and Bob Long gave him a prototype of his new electronic gun, the "Defiant," and a Signature Series Millennium. The Diggers pitched in with a Centerfire AutoMag (complete with Evolution hopper).

WHAT'S NEW AND WHAT'S HOT

BIGGER, BETTER, FASTER, MORE: TECHNOLOGY UPDATES

FROM NITROGEN TO ELECTROPNEUMATICS, NEW MARKERS ARE ROCKING THE FIELD

It would be hard to talk about the recent developments in paintball equipment without talking first about the recent advances in paintball marker technology. Over the past three years, many things have happened to improve the quality and availability of paintball guns on the market. Of note, the largest improvement has been in price.

You're Not Gonna Pay a Lot for This Marker!

On every level, from entry to tournament, the price of high-tech equipment has dramatically decreased. What was once considered unobtainable by the average paintball player has grown easier and cheaper to get. A lot of this has been due to an increase in supply as companies expand their resources and market their products to a larger audience. Probably the most dramatic price change has been in high-end electropneumatic paintball guns. For 50% of what you could spend on a high-end paintgun three years ago, you can buy a piece of equipment today that is equally competitive in terms of high-end performance. The Black Dragun, the BushMaster LCD, the Tippmann 98 Response, the Impulse, the Shocker, and the Spyder LCD are all examples of electropneumatic paintball guns that retail today for less than $600—something unheard of three years ago.

Entry-Level Arsenals

There has been significant technological innovation in the lower end paintball guns as well. One of the most commonly seen midrange semi-automatic paintball guns is the Spyder. Off the shelf, or in aftermarket, you can purchase an electronic trigger frame that fits onto the Spyder, providing an effective and inexpensive instant upgrade. These trigger packs offer the user many of the additional features you see on higher end and electropneumatic paintball guns: several burst modes (three shot bursts, five shot bursts, etc.), shot counters, stopwatch features, and so on. Trigger packs are available for several popular blowback, semi-automatic paintball guns, including the Spyder, the Automag, and the Piranha.

D.I.Y. Designs

Other companies are now providing factory-modified parts to emulate what used to be high-end custom work, available only as aftermarket pieces or air smith specialty creations. Today, anything from vertical feeds to pressure gauges to fancy sight rails is available from the factory. For example, Tippmann Pneumatics currently offers everything from responsive triggers to rear cocking kits as factory modifications.

And still other companies now perform what is called "millwork" to create a more custom look for the players. Millwork is when an air smith sculpts the metal of a paintball gun to make it more pleasing to the eye, instead of a simple aluminum box. Paintball manufacturers are also providing custom anodizing features to create the custom look "out of the box". The paintball industry is trying to give the consumer what they want: something a little flashier than the old-style plain black paintball guns.

The New Wave of Nitrogen

It would also be nearly impossible to talk about the advances in paintball marker technology without bringing up the advances in air tank technology. Most paintball fields are trying to make a switch from CO_2 to nitrogen as a power source. It makes sense from an economic standpoint, as well as environmentally.

In the past, most paintball guns were not designed to shoot at the low pressure and high volume that early nitrogen bottle systems required. This problem was solved some years ago when a preset regulator was placed on nitrogen bottles, regulating their output pressure to 800 PSI—the same output pressure as unregulated CO_2. The early systems were costly, and not many people owned them. Now, for a minimal investment, you can purchase a steel nitrogen bottle with a preset regulator and screw it onto almost any paintball gun that would normally take CO_2.

And for the True Connoisseur...

High-end air systems still do exist, however. The latest offering from W. D. P., makers of the Angel, is an interface between the air tank and the gun, which allows the system to operate at peak efficiency. Many other air systems also exist to allow users to adjust the airflow to their specific paintguns.

If the future holds true to form, you'll see paintball guns becoming more air-efficient and less expensive to purchase as time goes on. Which means that almost anyone will be able to afford the top-level gear. In the meantime, players today can get some fairly high technology for fairly low prices.

BARREL TECHNOLOGY 101

When you first buy paintball equipment, one of the things you will probably look at is a barrel. The barrel is one of the most easily upgraded parts of a paintball gun. Many people do it for looks, or to make the gun sound quieter, while others buy barrels to improve their accuracy or to get more range.

Since this book was first published, there have been a number of improvements to barrel technology that make the range of choices even greater.

Get Your "Freak" On

One of the main reasons to get a new barrel is to match the inside diameter of your barrel to your paintballs. Due to changes in atmospheric conditions, a bag of paint can vary in size from day to day, even game to game. Also, many paintball manufacturers make paint in different sizes. They are all close to being .68 inches in diameter, but there are small bore balls (.678) and large bore balls (.687) The size difference of the paint is miniscule, but if your barrel's inner dimension measures even slightly different from the diameter of the ball, you will lose air efficiency, range, and some accuracy.

Enter Smart Parts. In late 2000 they introduced a barrel system called the Freak. The idea was simple. Why purchase 3 barrels (tight, medium and large bores) when only the inside of the barrel needed to change? So they created a barrel with three main components. There's the front piece, which is the vented portion; the back, which screws into the gun; and an inner sleeve, which fits into the back piece. This sleeve is the working part of the system. Smart Parts makes eight sleeve inserts corresponding to the commonly used bore sizes, from tight to large. When you get to the field, you can choose the sleeve that best fits the paint you will be using that day. With so many inserts to choose from, it's easy to get the one that works best for the conditions. Currently, there are a few more manufacturers making similar products, including ACI. But Smart Parts was the first.

The Freak barrel with assorted inserts. (Courtesy Smart Parts)

Bernoulli and the Flatline

Another barrel that makes use of cutting-edge technology came out a few years ago, when Tippmann Pneumatics offered the market a barrel called the Flatline. When the barrel first came out, Tippmann promised that it could create more range than any other paintball gun in existence. It works on the same principle of aerodynamics that keeps airplanes aloft: the Bernoulli effect. Bernoulli found that if pressure was greater on one side of a surface than on the other, force would be exerted on the side with less pressure. This works on an airplane wing because of its curved surface. Air rushing over the curved top of the wing creates lower pressure than air rushing straight across the flat bottom. This creates lift, and the plane can sustain itself in the air as long as it can keep air rushing over the wings.

So How Does the Flatline Work?

The Flatline barrel is a departure from normal paintball thinking in several ways. Not only is it slightly bent, but it is not polished smooth like a normal barrel. When a paintball is fired out of the Flatline, the paintball rolls against the top of the barrel because of the curve. The ball is given a very great spin as it exits the barrel. This spin creates

Courtesy Tippmann Pneumatics

The Complete Guide to Paintball

lower pressure on the top of the ball than on the bottom. That induces the Bernoulli effect, and creates lift—just like on the wing of an airplane. This lift causes the ball, in theory, to fly farther with a flatter trajectory.

But does it work? Yes, it does create lift. Yes, the ball does fly with a flatter trajectory and it does fly longer. The added range, however, comes with a price. At the maximum range, balls tend not to break. This is true with any paintball gun, and it means that the super-long shots you can get with a Flatline may not be as usable as you may think. The Flatline is also very long, which makes the barrel somewhat cumbersome if you play small bunkers, or if you play in the front all the time.

Fun With the Flatline

That being said, the Flatline has some nifty tricks that make it worthwhile for some. For example, if you tilt the Flatline at a 90 degree angle from true, the spin on the ball will cause it to curve radically to the left or right. In other words, yes, you can literally shoot around trees! Learning how to make the ball curve in such a way takes practice, and balls won't just turn left like at a street corner, but it's a very cool effect. You can also shoot flatter shots, and sneak paint into a hole on the other side of the field. If your game is based on volume shooting, or extreme range, you may want to look into this barrel more.

Other barrels are also out there, and most of the technology and materials have not changed radically. But the Freak and the Flatline were two developments that deserved special notation.

SAFETY GEAR GOES SPACE-AGE

To keep up with improving gun and loader technology, safety standards have evolved rapidly over the past few years. The most dramatic improvements have been in paintball-specific goggles and barrel blocking devices.

Barrel Blockers

When this book was first published, a barrel plug was the industry standard for off-field safety. When properly installed, barrel plugs work. They stop paintballs from exiting the barrel. However, many players were unhappy with standard plugs. They could damage the inside of the barrel. Players kept on losing them. Many players mistakenly assumed that they could use a stick squeegee or a fluffy swab inserted in the barrel and that would be safe.

In 2001, the NPPL (National Professional Paintball League) made a ruling that all players must use a specifically designed "barrel bag" in that season. This bag has an elastic band around the opening, and is reinforced on the closed end to prevent fraying and a blowout in the event that a ball is fired inside it. The bag is held onto the gun with the elastic band, which you place around the feed elbow. Before the game begins, you can either roll the bag up in your pocket or let it hang from the elbow so you can't lose it. The idea is not new—these devices have existed since the mid-1990s—but their widespread application is a recent development. Many companies now make these barrel-blocking devices, and it is not uncommon to see them in use.

The older style of plastic barrel plugs are still around, and they are also still in widespread use today. Which one you decide to use is a matter of personal preference.

The Goggle Brigade

These days, just about everybody is making goggles—and many new companies have emerged just for that purpose. Below are just a few examples of what's new out there in goggle-land:

VForce has introduced a spherical lens and married it to a flexible mask to allow you to shoulder a paintball marker tighter to your cheek. They also have made a lens that the user can remove in seconds without problems.

The VForce Morph Goggle. (Courtesy National Paintball Supply)

Raven created the NuVis system. They created a buckle in the back, so you could put the goggles on around your head instead of over it—which is an especially great feature if you wear glasses. Also, the NuVis lens tints in sunlight, much like some sunglasses do.

The NVX goggle is the latest NuVis product from Raven. (Courtesy Kingman International)

DYE also entered the market recently with their "Invision" series. The major selling point of these goggles is the venting systems, which are designed to let you speak more clearly than with other goggle systems.

DYE's Invision goggles feature multidirectional venting systems. (© 2002 DYE Precision, Inc.)

JT is also making improvements on their basic goggle system. The newest version of their Spectra line is called the "Proteus", and has improved features like fog-resistance and advanced audio capability. They also are making lower-end goggle systems that have vents that can be removed and replaced to match colors. (Red, blue, and white, for example.)

JT's Spectra Proteus™ 2 (Courtesy JT USA)

The panels on JT's entry-level goggles can be replaced with different colors. (Courtesy JT USA)

Several other goggles exist for paintball, and many are viable options, but it is important that whatever goggles you choose are ASTM certified. If they are not certified for paintball use, DO NOT WEAR THEM FOR PAINTBALL! It's that simple. As time goes on, goggles will become more sophisticated and become safer. But it will always be important that your goggles are made specifically for paintball games. Always check, and always check your lenses before you begin playing. Every time. You can't be too safe.

The guy on the right has a Warp Feed under his gun. (Courtesy Airgun Designs)

LOADERS GO ELECTRO

The description of the evolution of the paintball loader from the first edition of this book was complete up to the beginning of the millennium. In very recent times, however, the loader market has really come into the age of electronics.

A few years ago, the loader choices were basic. There were several companies making plastic tubes to hold paint before it went into the gun, but if you were a serious player, you used a Viewloader. More precisely, you used a motorized VL with a paddle to agitate the balls as you shot paint. The reason you did this was that nobody but Viewloader had figured out a system of loading paint from a cylinder to the elbow of a gun without the use of an electronic eye.

All of that changed just a few years ago. Some companies experimented with an "intelliport", a wire that went from the back of an electronic-style gun into a hopper telling it when to feed a ball. At the time, this left a majority of players high and dry, since many blowback semi-autos could not use this technology. Since then, however, with some experimenting and some radical designs, the choices that have become available are amazing.

Warped Minds Think Alike

But, first, one of the predictions we made in this book did come to pass: "force-feed" (see p. 193) was realized in Airgun Designs' Warp Feed. The Warp Feed is a box that can be mounted under the grip frame of any paintball gun. You then attach any kind of loader you like, and it sits to the side of the Warp Feed. The loader is no longer on top of the gun, and is no longer a target when it comes over the top of a bunker.

The Warp Feed box pushes paintballs from the loader into the gun with two discs that spin when there's no paint in the tube. This action pushes paint up from under the gun and into an elbow that already exists in the gun. Cutting-edge technology for the serious pro player.

The Warp Feed. (Courtesy Airgun Designs)

The Latest from Viewloader...

As for what loader the average player should use, as we said before, you have many options to match your needs. Viewloader is still making their impressive VL2000, but it's been improved over the years, and loaders are now available to meet a variety of needs. The standard 9-volt VL2000 is good for most users, feeding paint at 5-7 balls per second. For heavier shooters, a 12-volt model provides a larger paddle and faster response time. It feeds paint at an average of 10-12 balls per second.

The 12-volt model of the VL2000
(Courtesy JT USA)

Recently, Viewloader has made improvements to the basic Revolution system. They replaced the old plastic shell with polycarbonate for extra durability during impacts in close quarters. Viewloader also recently came out with an improved sensor for their clear and translucent loaders called the X-Board, which is less sensitive to light than the old circuit boards that came with VL2000s.

The X-Board sensor
(Courtesy JT USA)

...And Everybody Else

The VL system is patented, so the largest problem facing competitors has been the need for a new way to agitate paintballs in a loader. It took several years to do it, but many companies have finally come up with solutions.

Zap Paintballs recently came out with a loader called the Mach 404, which has the highest capacity out of all the new loaders: over 210 paintballs. Their system uses a central spindle that swings like a pendulum and agitates the paintballs. It works on vibration from your paint gun, agitating at a power relative to the vibrations it's receiving. If you give it a moderately hard tap with your hand, it will agitate the balls at the maximum speed, as compared to the gentler vibration of your gun when you shoot normally.

A more radical approach to loader technology came from Ricochet Engineering, who came up with a loader named the Ricochet-2K. This loader is radical in many ways, most obviously in its appearance, which is something between a stealth fighter and a spacecraft from a sci-fi movie. The Ricochet series was engineered not only to hold paint, but also to deflect paintballs that are coming in to your position. This is important since standard paintball rules say that a hit to the loader counts as an elimination.

The Ricochet series also uses a small switch in the feed neck to move the agitator fingers every

The Ricochet with digital timer/counter
(Courtesy Ricochet Development)

time a ball is fired. There are several models, from a bare-bones one to a fully tricked-out model with an easy to read ball counter and an on-loader timer.

In terms of speed, the fastest-feeding hopper on the market right now is arguably the HALO (Highly Advanced Loader Operation) from Odyssey products. It works like a high-speed egg counter, with a spinning disk to sling paintballs into the open feed neck. But, while it does feed paint very fast, the large size of the HALO may be a turnoff to many people.

With so many choices now available, the modern player can choose a loader to fit any playing style. A back player might need a loader that feeds faster, while a front player might need one that is smaller and more compact. As with all other gear, you can customize your loader to meet your own specific needs.

Some of the information on loaders came from http://www.warpig.com, Copyright Bill Mills

PODS, PACKS, AND PROGRESS

Although accessories, pods, and harnesses haven't undergone the same kind of dramatic technological evolution as guns, barrels, and loaders, there are still plenty of products out there to choose from. In recent years, most pods have held 145 paintballs, and the most recent innovations have made them even faster and more convenient to use.

Slammer SpeedPods™ (Courtesy JT USA)

The Snapp™ speed loader. (Courtesy Allen Paintball Products)

JT, for example, created the Slammer Pod system. These pods have a sliding opening that rides along the outside of the pod. When you push the pod into a "speed collar," it opens like a flower and pours paint into the end hopper. It's the fastest method of reloading made yet. It does have the disadvantage that the pods are never truly closed, so water can get into them. But, for raw speed, you can't beat it.

Other innovations along these lines came from Allen Paintball Products. Their Snapp™ Speed Loader is a pod with a tapered lip and a snapping cap. Among this system's many advantages is the fact that you don't need to buy a whole specialty system to go along with it. They have also developed a curved pod, which fits to the contour of the back and hugs the body when worn in a harness system.

Over the years, style has developed along with function. Planet, a company famous for its various high-end modified guns, has created loaders with a mirror-sheen finish in silver, purple, and a few other colors. In direct sunlight, these pods deflect harmful heat to help keep the paint cool, making reloads easier. But the main advantage is that they look really cool when you have an open harness to put them in.

Packing It In

Harnesses have changed more radically than pods in recent years, becoming more comfortable and easier to use. In some cases, manufacturers have gone back to ideas from the old days of paintball, with results that work as well today as they did in the past. For example, Redz, who built the first truly comfortable pack based on a support belt, have updated their product with the largest breakthrough of the past few years: modular packs. A player can get a few styles of pack and easily interchange them on the basic belt pack depending on what style of game they're playing. If you need lots of paint, get a pack with more pouches. If you need less, get a pack with less. The modular nature makes this pack great for players who change position from game to game. Other manufacturers have made modular systems, too. Jacko makes a pack with zippers, so you can add or subtract sleeves to hold pods. Other companies make similar systems.

Redz also has been using an old idea of stacking tubes in a pyramid style to fit more pods in less space. They do this with a traditional pack, and then use elastic loops between the pods of an additional stack pack. Other companies like Planet and M-Class have been doing this as well. The idea originated back in the days of the 10 round tube harnesses, but has become a way to really carry more.

Flaming bones from Animal Paintball (Courtesy Animal Paintball)

Earlier in the book (see p. 179), we demonstrated how middle players can tape two pods together to carry them. M-Class now makes what they call a 'football', which is a neoprene sleeve that holds two pods for just this purpose. The advantages are very easy to see: no tape, no messes, and you can use any pods you like in them.

Other packs have specifically focused on comfort. JT and DYE have both made packs with a lot of back support in them. Both have a lumbar support, and both are rather comfortable to wear. JT made theirs to fit with the slam pods I mentioned earlier, but they will also fit any brand of pod you wish to use. Other companies like APP have also made more comfortable packs. And, as with all things wearable, it's all about your personal comfort.

FROM CAMO TO DAY-GLO: PAINTBALL FASHION COMES OUT OF HIDING

When this book first came out, paintball was going through a revolution in clothing as more and more events moved out of the woods and into arena settings. With camouflage becoming unnecessary, many players started to embrace the idea of brighter clothing that was made specifically for the paintball market. The paintball industry was more than happy to comply, and a lot of corporations that were previously not involved with paintball are now jumping in with both feet.

Today, you can find paintball jerseys to match any particular. You want dragons? Paintball Junkies. Prefer the flaming skeleton look? Animal Paintball. Something a little more solid in color? Smart Parts. Something you can wear in the woods? JT or Renegade. When this book first came out, there were a few choices, but not nearly as many as there are today!

And something a little more subtle from Smart Parts (Courtesy Smart Parts)

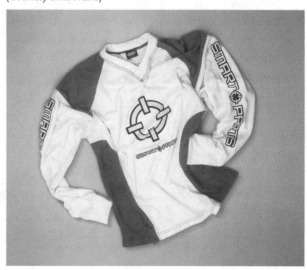

So what are the advantages of a jersey? Today's jersey has more venting in it; in some cases the sides are vented in order to allow players to cool off in the game. The colors are brighter, which appeals to some people. Many jerseys also have built-in elbow guards so you do not need to wear pads. If you play on a team, you can also place your name—or nickname—as well as your team number on the back. These touches have been helping paintball to gain acceptance as a sport.

Woods players, take heart!

Camouflage jerseys or BDUs (Battle Dress Uniforms) are still readily available. Many manufacturers have realized that woods players still prefer their camouflage, and more than happily provide an alternative to the camo everyone else wears.

Pants have also come a long way in the last few years, with manufacturers adding more style, more durability, and more functional features. Sure, you can wear your regular BDUs—but the new pants have paintball-specific features you can't find on surplus shelves. One of the features you find now is squeegee pockets. This solves the problem of where to put a stick style squeegee when you're playing. Some players used a lanyard around their neck. This makes it handy, but if it gets caught or you step on it, you may as well have a noose around your neck! Squeegee pockets put them in the best place possible, right on your leg, and keep them out of the way when you're playing.

"Skid plates" have also gained popularity. These have many names, but all are a layer of cordura mesh or other durable material that protects the knee of the pants from tearing when you slide. Often you'll find that pants and skid plates are of contrasting colors (black and red, purple and black, and so on) which is great for matching up jerseys.

Other pants features include stretch gussets in the crotch, drawstring legs, or even straight leg cuts, pockets, goggle loops, and so on. All of these

Courtesy JT USA

make paintball-specific wear worth the investment. In some cases, BDUs will work fine. But if your style requires more colors, more durability, or just handy pockets, you may want to look into purchasing paintball pants.

One of the more exciting things to happen recently is the introduction of paintball-specific shoes. Since 1996, Diggers has been manufacturing a line of paintball cleats based on a circular sole design and made specifically for paintball. Even more recently, Vans, a company known for its skateboard style, has come out with a paintball shoe. Having used them myself, I can tell you that they're very nice shoes with features that many people wouldn't even think of (like a reinforced toe for the types of slides we make playing paintball.) This is exciting because Vans is the first major shoe company to venture into the paintball market. Hopefully, this is a sign of more things to come in the future.

-Rob Tyger Rubin

Welcome to the Game of Paintball

Tippmann Redux:
They've Come A Long Way, Baby

Three years have passed since we last spoke with Dennis Tippmann, Jr. At the time, the Tippmann 98 was brand spanking new and the choice of players and fields nationwide. Since then, Tippmann Pneumatics—one of the leading paintball marker manufacturers—has led a revolution in product design and innovation. We decided to catch up with Dennis. Take a look.

ANDREW FLACH: Dennis, three years have passed since you spoke with Stew Smith for the *Complete Guide to Paintball* (see p. 154). How has paintball changed since then?

DENNIS TIPPMANN, JR: The entire industry has grown quite a bit in three years. The technology in the guns helps grow the industry, make it bigger, keep it exciting.

Some of the big changes in the last three years would probably be the electronics. There used to be very, very high-end guns offering these electronics. But the price has come down quite a bit and it's a lot more reasonable for the average consumer to afford some of the electronic equipment that they're offering now. Tippmann Pneumatics is also offering some of these electronics options.

ANDREW: In terms of the game itself, the electronics have obviously made the play faster.

DENNIS: Very true. The game actually is being played quite a bit quicker, which makes it more fun to watch. An example is Skyball up in Canada. Paintball is becoming more of a traditional sport in a sense—probably a lot closer to an extreme sport.

ANDREW: With the increased speed and the rate of velocity of feeders and the number of paintballs per minute, is the sport becoming a little more expensive for most people? Are they basically shooting more paint?

DENNIS: Well, no matter what happens, the customer demands more firepower. And I do believe they are spending a little bit more when they go out to play. But it also seems, because the industry is growing, that volumes are going up on everything: the volume of markers that we make, the volume of paint that's being made, everything.

And the prices are actually coming down. The more markers we make, the cheaper we can make them, and the customer is saving in the long run. The same with the paintballs themselves. The price has actually come down quite a bit in the last three years.

ANDREW: Is there any movement toward bigger games or smaller games?

DENNIS: Two things seem to be happening. Ever since the beginning, it seems like the size of the teams has been getting smaller. It used be twenty-man teams, and now you see a lot of tournaments with clear down to three-man teams. Even something like a ten-man team seems to be getting less popular, and three-man and five-man teams are becoming more popular. And I think a big part of that is just the logistics of trying to get that many guys together at once.

ANDREW: What about the players? Do you see a younger demographic, an older demographic?

DENNIS: We've seen the age groups drop since the beginning. The average playing age ten years ago was mid- to upper twenties. And I believe the average age is closer to sixteen now.

And I think the reason for that is the price of the equipment has come down quite a bit. And it's becoming more of a mainstream extreme sport, which is very popular with the younger group. That's one of the reasons the industry has grown quite a bit: because that age group has got a lot more free time and they're out.

They can get out every weekend and go play, where some of the older guys can get out once a month maybe. And we think that's actually helped to grow the sport quite a bit.

ON THE TIPPMANN A-5 AND THE CYCLONE FEED SYSTEM

ANDREW: Let me ask you about the A-5, your new state-of-the-art paintball marker. What's so special about it?

DENNIS: The biggest feature on the A-5 is the Cyclone Feed System. Basically it's a forced feed system. It eliminates the traditional problem of chopping balls, where a ball falls halfway into the gun when the gun's going off and gets cut in two inside your gun. Once that happens, your gun isn't going to work correctly; it's going to be inaccurate. So this feed system pretty much eliminated that problem by feeding quite a bit faster and more reliably.

The balls fall down into what we call a sprocket, and the feed paddles rotate with every shot. So as you pull the trigger, these things constantly index. And they index at a top speed of about sixteen times a second, far faster than any traditional feed system or any gravity feed system. Most of those have a reliable maximum of around ten. And even at ten, gravity isn't really reliable, so you run into this problem of chopping balls.

We're very reliable up to sixteen, which is a huge advantage.

Feed paddle technology has been around for a little while, with one of our previous guns, the Tippmann F/A. But we weren't real happy with the way it worked on the FA because it was a spring-loaded system; you had to wind it up all the time. So we took the opportunity with our new model here to put this feed system back on. We redesigned it so it's air-powered; there are no headaches. It works just like the traditional gun

Inside the Cyclone Feed System. (Courtesy Tippmann Pneumatics)

where you pour your balls into your ammo box and it's ready to go.

ANDREW: What's the hopper capacity on it?

DENNIS: Two hundred.

ANDREW: Do you have any kind of agitation working as well, or is it just gravity feeding into the paddles which are timed with the action of the gun?

DENNIS: The paddles do two things. They act like agitation, and they feed balls into the gun. So you get the benefits of both. Traditional feeders agitate the balls in order to try to get them into a single-file line to be gravity-fed into your gun. This system has a very large feed neck, so several balls fall down onto the paddles, and as those paddles agitate, the balls fall into the teeth or "socket" of the paddles. That loads those balls into the gun directly.

ANDREW: Can you upgrade a variety of guns to include the Cyclone Feed System, or is it only on that A-5?

DENNIS: It's only for the A-5. We looked at possibly making a universal feed system, but to get the best results, we had to design the gun around the feed system. Until this point, most of the feed systems available on the market were battery powered. The Cyclone Feed System is an intricate part of the gun and is air powered, so batteries are not needed. It works off of waste air, so the gun is just as efficient.

Playing With Power: The Tippmann Stealth Line

The Tippmann Proshop is an in-house marker upgrade center offering many GTA (Genuine Tippmann Accessories) and third party add-on upgrades from barrels to double trigger kits and more. The Proshop also offers four customized, factory-built 98 Customs, called the Stealth Line, ranging in price from about $400 to about $500. (Photos courtesy of Tippmann Pneumatics.)

Proshop 98 Sniper

BASE: 98 Custom
BARREL: Flatline Barrel System
ACCESSORIES: Pro Team F/X Collapsible Stock for stability and accuracy.
Pro Shop GTA Remote Line Kit allows the player to choose where the air tank is stored.
BEST FOR: Players that like to shoot from long distances and use sniper-like tactics. Good for crawling and strafing maneuvers.

DENNIS: There's one other feature of the A-5, which is kind of overlooked because the feed system is such a huge step forward. But one of the other features that doesn't get talked about a lot is how easy the gun is to field strip. We've put a lot of effort into that, because with most paintball guns you need a few Allen wrenches to get the gun apart. And with the A-5 you can disassemble the gun by pulling the four push-pins out; it pretty much comes all the way apart from there.

THE FLATLINE BARREL

ANDREW: Let's talk about the Flatline barrel. I think that's one of the real revolutionary innovations since the *Complete Guide to Paintball* was first published.

DENNIS: I believe the idea came from jai alai, where they've got the curved basket where you put the ball in and throw it, and it puts a spin on the ball. And that's where the original idea came from to put a curve in the barrel itself. Just like a golf ball: when the ball has backspin on it and it's flying through the air, it gets some lift. Putting this backspin on the paintball actually takes the arch out of the ball.

We worked on developing that

The Tippman A-5 (Courtesy Tippmann Pneumatics)

barrel for over two years. There are so many variables there: once you put that spin on, it's easy to put on a little too much or too little. We eventually came up with a happy medium where the ball flies as flat as possible. So the big advantage of the Flatline barrel is that it shoots farther.

Maybe an even bigger advantage than that is that it shoots extremely flat. When you aim at a target, you don't have to compensate by aiming high if the target is a hundred feet out there. Instead, you aim right at your target. That's especially useful in the woods, where a lot of times you get trees up above. If you try to arch a ball through the trees and it's not going to make it there, it's going to hit something. When you can actually look down the line of sight and see a clear target, and you can aim right at it, that's a huge advantage.

ON THE PROSHOP

ANDREW: Dennis, tell me about the Proshop. It's new since we last talked. Why did you set it up?

DENNIS: It used to be that a lot of our customers were doing upgrades to their guns, and there were always a lot of questions and our service guys weren't always on top of the latest technology coming from the different parts of the industry. A lot of companies make accessories for our guns now, and we offer some accessories. We set up the Proshop to help the customer with all the accessories that are available on the market. And we do sell quite a few of those accessories through the Proshop.

ANDREW: So these are not necessarily Tippmann manufactured products, but there are other parties involved in manufacturing approved products that can be upgraded to the Tippmann line.

DENNIS: Exactly. What we call our GTA Parts—the GTA stands for Genuine Tippmann Accessories—are parts that we make ourselves. But we do offer quite a few of the other accessories that are made by other companies for Tippmann products. There are three electronic kits that you can put on your marker. Then there's the Flatline barrel system, there are some other barrels made by us, and there are some of the more popular barrels that are on the market. Plus the real velocity adjust-

ment kits, double trigger kits, low pressure kits, drop forward kits.

Just about anything you could imagine that you could put on your paintball marker we offer through the Proshop, and we also install it. We give the customer peace of mind and get the equipment working properly.

A lot of times with these accessories, there are gray areas that the customer gets confused with. You can use this adjuster with this trigger, but you can't necessarily put the low-pressure kit on now. Or say for example a customer wants to know if he should have an expansion chamber on his gun with a compressed air kit. Well, our Proshop guys would tell him no, there's no need to do that, the expansion changer is designed for CO_2 and it's not necessary if you've advanced to the compressed air kit. All these things are available through the Proshop, and this helps our customers do whatever they want to their paintball marker.

ANDREW: What's the average turnaround? Can you deliver most

The basic 98 Custom (Courtesy Tippmann Pneumatics)

Proshop 98 Nitro

BASE: 98 Custom
BARREL: 98 Custom
ACCESSORIES: Comp-Air Low Pressure System for less recoil and consistent shot to shot velocity.
GTA secondary regulator
47 CU in. 3000 psi. GTA Nitrogen Bottle.
GTA Double Trigger Kit for lighter trigger pull
GTA Raised Sight Rail
BEST FOR: Tournament and speedball; however, for the recreational player looking for an upgrade, this marker is recommended by the manufacturer.

Proshop 98 Response

BASE: 98 Custom
BARREL: GTA 14" sniper barrel
ACCESSORIES: GTA Double Trigger kit
Response Trigger for less trigger pull, and adjustable trigger speed for maximum firepower.
Full Bore Rear Cocking Knob
GTA Raised Sight Rail
Psycho Ballistics Drop Forward improves weight distribution
BEST FOR: speedball and recreational games, since its features allow the gun to be held very close to the body.

Proshop 98 E

BASE: 98 Custom
BARREL: GTA 14" sniper barrel
ACCESSORIES: E-Bolt Electronic System
with variable burst patterns and
fully automatic capabilities.
GTA Double Trigger Kit for lighter
trigger pull.
BEST FOR: Tournament play, thanks to
its increased accuracy and lighter
trigger pull for extended use
without fatigue.

upgrades within a certain number of days?

DENNIS: We try to turn everything around, service and Proshop, in twenty-four hours. We feel that the customer needs his paintball marker for the weekend. It takes a couple of days to get it here, it's going to take a couple of days to get it back, so we try to turn it around as fast as possible.

THE HELLHOUND

ANDREW: Now let me ask you, what's the story with the Hellhound? Everybody wants to know.

DENNIS: The Hellhound was originally made for a trade show in Atlanta, Georgia. It was mostly made to be a booth attraction, with the intention of taking it to some of the different paintball shows also. We pretty much sat down and designed the thing from scratch. More than anything it's an attention grabber.

ANDREW: Do you ever put that thing on a paintball field and demonstrate it?

DENNIS: We demonstrate it once in a while, but we never take it on a paintball field. If you took it in a big game, the game would be over. Too much of an advantage.

ANDREW: I think so. What is the quick rundown on the features on the Hellhound?

DENNIS: The number one feature is the Vulcan ten-barrel Gatling gun on the front of the Hellhound. The Vulcan gun is fed by a 600-round capacity ammo box up above the driver's head. So the roof of the vehicle is essentially a large container for paintballs.

The Hellhound does have the Cyclone Feed: it has two Cyclone Feeders,

Courtesy Tippmann Pneumatics

Launcher

one on each side. And two large tubes—they look like vacuum cleaner tubes—come down to each side of the Vulcan gun. The gun itself is run by a cordless electric drill. And it shoots extremely fast. Top speed is around 50 rounds a second.

THE FUTURE OF TIPPMANN PAINTBALL

ANDREW: Let's talk about the future of paintball and Tippmann. Three years ago, the Model 98 was the hot item. Now we're looking at the A-5. Where do you see paintball three years hence?

DENNIS: It's hard to predict what's going to happen with the industry. It always surprises us; it keeps growing and growing. The sport will probably be quite a bit bigger if it keeps growing at the same rate.

The other thing we notice is that it seems like the technology has definitely slowed down since the beginning. In the beginning you couldn't design things fast enough. Now it's getting harder and harder to come up with new and better gun designs.

So I could see a lot of fine-tuning of the current equipment that's on the market. But I don't think there's a need for a lot more firepower. A lot of the tournaments are starting to limit, and obviously they don't allow full auto in most tournaments. Pretty much everyone is putting on a rule that semi-auto is the limit.

But they are allowing the electric triggers, which allow you to shoot very quickly in semi-auto. So I don't see a lot happening on the firepower side of it. But the Cyclone Feed System, for example, makes the firepower that is available more reliable. And I see a lot of the other gun makers and even ourselves concentrating on more reliable, more consistent, more efficient equipment.

I also see some room for more reliability in the paintball itself. It seems like that's one area of the industry that hasn't developed a lot. The balls can be damaged by moisture, or humidity, or if it gets too cold. I see some room for improvement and some new materials, maybe a tighter tolerance on the ball so you get more accuracy.

ANDREW: Are you thinking about doing a sidearm at all?

DENNIS: We talk about it once in a while. The big game is becoming more popular. I think the reason for that is that a big game will accommodate any size group: if you've got two guys that want to go play, or if you've got twenty guys who want to go play. And it's more of a fun day rather than a competition where you're working hard all day. You can go out there and you can play as you want and it's pretty relaxing. A fun day.

We do see the need for a sidearm possibly just for that niche of the market, the guys who just play the big games. Big games are not super-strict on the rules, whereas in a tournament you wouldn't necessarily even be allowed to carry a sidearm. I think they're pretty strict on the one gun per player rule there. But the big games, they just want you to have fun. And if you want to take a pistol or something similar out there on the field with you, they're very happy to let you do that.

We also see some demand for a pistol on the law enforcement side for training. And also—this number is debated a little bit—around seventy percent of players play what we call outlaw. Which means they don't play in an organized field setting; they're just a bunch of buddies getting together in the woods somewhere. And we see a demand for the sidearm in that application also.

ANDREW: Sort of like the original days of paintball, going back to the roots, with fewer shots and more hunting.

DENNIS: Yeah, plus the guys that play outlaw paintball make up their own rules. And if they want to carry an extra gun with them and no one else cares, like I said, they make up their own rules, so we definitely see a demand.

FIELDER'S CHOICE

The appendix in the back of this book provides a list of paintball fields in all areas of the United States and of the world, so you've got plenty of options when it comes to locating a field. If you haven't played for a few years, however, you may be in for the surprise of your life when you get there.

Paintball isn't just that game you play in the woods anymore.

The concept fields used for tournaments are now easily obtainable by field owners willing to set aside space to put them up. There are even parks set up in family fun centers next to go-karts and batting cages! This availability is due to many new companies coming into the arena game market. In addition to the Sup'air system, Ultimate Air has begun to make bunkers that are tubeless, so they can be put up in more remote areas without the pipes Sup'air uses.

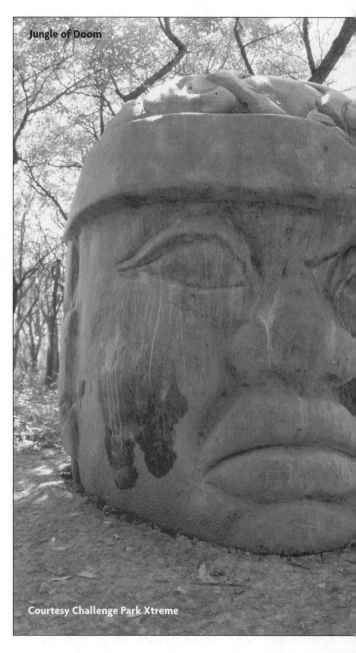

Jungle of Doom

Courtesy Challenge Park Xtreme

Courtesy Challenge Park Xtreme

Many fields have gone even further than that. Although theme fields are not new— SC Village has been doing them since the 1980s—they are home to a whole new kind of theatrics. Probably the most graphic example is Challenge Park, just outside of Chicago, IL. They were an established field for years, then moved in order to facilitate something bigger: a theme park for paintball. Their fields include, among others:

- **Bedlam, IL.** This field is a town. Full buildings, cars parked in the streets, mailboxes, phone booth, streetlights, the works.

- **Jungle of Doom** is a wooded field with a full temple built into it.

- **Armageddon** is a bombed-out cityscape with rubble piles and half-destroyed buildings.

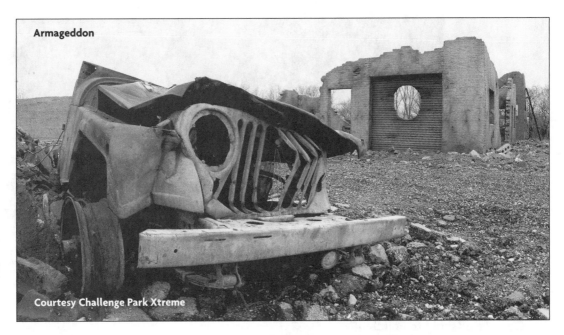

Armageddon

Courtesy Challenge Park Xtreme

Meanwhile, in Canada, a field opened up in Toronto using the abandoned set from "Total Recall". Now called "Area 51", the field has a backdrop that is, literally, something out of a sci-fi movie.

The concept isn't new. EMR has had the "Castle" for years, and holds two "Castle Conquests" every year. Skirmish has several theme fields, like "Hood in the Woods". But the level of theatrics has become so high that, again, paintball fields resemble theme parks more and more.

But what about the good old woods fields? They're still out there. If you just want to play out in the woods, that's still available. But, given what's being done today, look for theme-park field owners to keep trying to top each other in the years to come. The future of scenario paintball is limited only by what field owners are willing to build—and, for the moment, they show no signs of slowing down.

—*Rob Tyger Rubin*

Area 51 recreates *Total Recall* ... the only thing missing is Arnold. (Courtesy Area 51 Paintball)

A WHOLE NEW BREED OF
SCENARIO GAMES

Scenario games have exploded in popularity over the past few years. Scenario games are somewhat different than the big games mentioned in the first edition of this book. They have storylines, as well as characters, plots, and props—more like miniature movies than paintball games. Each player is assigned a character, usually with cards that have abilities or powers, and they're let loose on the field. Teams complete missions for points, and at the end of the game, the team with the most points wins.

There are a few types of players in every game. Most players will be your basic player. Their characters will usually be ground units of some kind, who actually carry out most of the objectives. The minority of players are the "rollers", the role-players. These are the generals, the XO's, the grand pooh-bahs of the game. They achieve mission goals that involve little, if any, actual shooting. Instead, rollers use a lot of talking, diplomacy, and sometimes outright lying in order to carry out their tasks.

One of the big battles at Viper Scenarios' "Texas Revolution VII: The Quest for the Holy Grail" in 2001. The event was held at Paintball USA in Houston. (© James R. Morgan, Sr.)

Whatever level you're on, however, your actions can have a major impact on what happens in the game. If you get a mission that says, "Go get the fuel from the fuel dump and bring it back", your ability (or inability) to do that can affect future missions. You may need the fuel to use a special weapon, or a tank, or any amount of things. The ability to stick to the missions is one of the main factors in determining whether teams win or lose scenario games.

Many people have been playing scenario games in recent years, and, win or lose, they've had fun at it. Right now there are several scenario games that make nation-wide circuits every year, most notably those produced by MXS, Wayne Dollack Scenario Games, and Viper Scenario Series. It used to be that if you wanted to experience a scenario game, you had to go to a home field of the scenario producer. Now, they travel all over the country making scenario games accessible to anyone.

All large scenario games have a few things in common. One is the longer game format. MXS and Dollack both have 24-hour games, meaning they start at noon on Saturday, end at noon Sunday, and are played all through the night. If you get eliminated, you go to a dead zone and jump

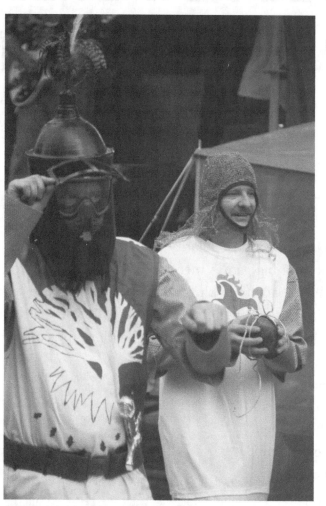

The Foletta brothers as Sir Bedemere and his squire at The Quest for the Holy Grail ((c) James R. Morgan, Sr.)

back into the game after a specific time interval, usually about 15 minutes. The action can be as non-stop or as casual as you like.

Scenario games are also becoming available locally. Many small fields now offer scenario-style games to play on special weekends. These games are great for casual players who want to try out scenario play without investing in a hotel room and a lot of gas money. Sometimes, local venues don't provide the quality of game or staffing that you might get from a larger company, but that's your tradeoff: some quality for a local feel.

If you are in the mood for a road trip, however, there are a lot of field-specific scenario games that are worth the car ride. EMR's "Quest" scenario is still a popular game, attracting players from all parts. There are also some scenario games that they can only hold once. Challenge Park is holding a scenario game during the summer of 2002 that features William Shatner as a guest captain. For obvious reasons, it would be hard to do that game more than once.

With more and more players signing up for scenario games, it's never been easier to find one to suit your needs and interests. Get into the game this season, and try one out for yourself!

—*Rob Tyger Rubin*

The Complete Guide to Paintball

PAINTBALL WITH A TWIST

WHAT EVERY TOURNAMENT PLAYER NEEDS TO KNOW

The Need for Speed

The style and overall feel of today's paintball tournaments, when compared to that of the first games ever played, is a direct reflection of the recent evolution of paintball technology. Today's paintball competitions are dominated by products intended specifically for use in paintball, which represent incredible investments of time and money both in development and in manufacturing by an ever-increasing number of companies.

The technological advancement that has had the most significant impact on the nature of competition is the ability of the paintball marker to shoot high volumes of paintballs both quickly and accurately. Regulator technology, which controls the burst of propellant that hits the paintball and expels it from the marker, has also improved dramatically, allowing players greater control of their markers and greater consistency in shot velocity. Barrels, propellants, loaders, and even paintballs have all improved in quality and cost.

As one might imagine, these technological changes have been accompanied by changes in the style of the game. Whereas early paintball games were dominated by stealth and a "make every shot count" attitude, today's games involve more speed and less stealth; they are held on much smaller fields that are thick with solid cover in the form of "concept bunkers" rather than the relatively sparse cover of woodland fields; and they involve huge volumes of paintballs being thrown continuously across the field from player to player, team to team. "Accuracy by volume" has become an important approach to the game, which is much quicker in every way when compared to the original style of the game.

The New Face of Paintball

The concept fields used for holding today's major tournaments are set up symmetrically from one side to another. Each side has identical cover, identical bunkers, identical advantages and disadvantages, and so forth (at least in theory). The bunkers themselves can be arranged in any number of configurations, and constructed any number of ways. Hyperball fields, for example, have bunkers that are constructed from black plastic tubing of various diameters. This tubing can be cut, nailed together, stood on end, laid on its side, or manipulated in any number of ways to reach a desired end or shape. Inflatable bunkers, by contrast, are made so that each will have a characteristic shape when fully inflated. These individual bunkers can be placed across the field in whatever arrangement is desired, and pro-vide solid cover for players to use as a shield from their opponents' fire.

The lack of trees and brush on today's fields allows players to shoot at one another from basically any point on the field of play, and it also eliminates virtually all hindrances to spectators watching the games. Some venues have even begun to allow spectator participation in the form of coaching, signaling, etc. While opinions on this practice may vary, there is no doubt that the use of concept fields in paintball competitions has made them much more spectator-friendly.

One unarguable characteristic of today's major competitions (i.e. the NPPL series) is that camouflage is no longer of any importance. In fact, most players today wear garments that are quite colorful, often have very flashy designs, and sometimes bear the player's name across the back as well as team sponsors and logos. Even the bunkers themselves are brightly colored. All of this is attractive to outsiders since it does not come across as being "military" or "combative" in appearance, but "legitimate," similar to NASCAR and many other sports. Indeed, competition paintball as a whole embraces the idea that paintball is an extreme sport, and continues to work against the misperception that paintball is in any way connected to violence, warfare, or military training.

All of these factors, when considered together, have helped a new breed of competitive paintballer to emerge on today's circuit: Youth. Whereas paintball was once dominated by self-supporting middle-aged types, the flashy, fast style of today's paintball sport has attracted a growing number of younger and younger individuals. This influx of youth has brought into competitive paintball a new intensity and vigor that was absent in the woods. Speedy players have become a valuable commodity.

Fearlessness is an absolute must, as the games can become incredibly intense.

Courtesy Adrenaline Games

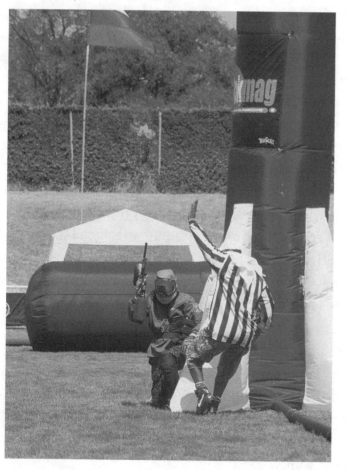

The fast and intense style, smaller fields, and tight cover have increased the physical demands upon the players themselves, requiring greater fitness and endurance over the course of a tournament. In addition, the increased ease with which spectators can observe games is appealing to parents, and the enthusiasm that some youth show for paintball is often matched only by their parents' supportive enthusiasm. Paintball promotes good teamwork, problem-solving skills, and physical development, all of which appeal to parents and have caused many moms and dads to fully support their kids' desires to play paintball competitively.

Overall, today's premier paintball tournaments are characterized by fast-paced games played on concept fields, which are smaller in size than a football field and usually littered with bunkers/cover. Only the "capture the flag" element of the game remains from the early days of the sport, as the objective for teams is not just to eliminate their opponents by marking them with paint, but also to secure possession of a flag and hang it either at their own starting station or their opponents'. Scores are tallied from game to game and tracked through the preliminary rounds, with a set number of teams advancing into the semi-finals and then again into the finals before a champion is crowned.

Tournament paintball is paintball with a twist: the added intensity of competition.

For people interested in playing Tournament paintball, now is an excellent time to get involved. Tournament paintball is quite possibly the fastest growing paintball market at present, and tournaments are regularly being held all across the country on any variety of levels, from local to regional to national to international.

Tips for First-Time Tournament Players

Every paintball player who has ever played in a tournament has one thing absolutely in common: They each had a first-time tournament experience. For anyone, playing in a tournament for the first time can be nerve-wracking. It's hard to know what to expect, and easy to feel intimidated and confused. The important thing to realize is that all this is perfectly normal, and comes with the territory more often than you might imagine—in other

Courtesy Adrenaline Games

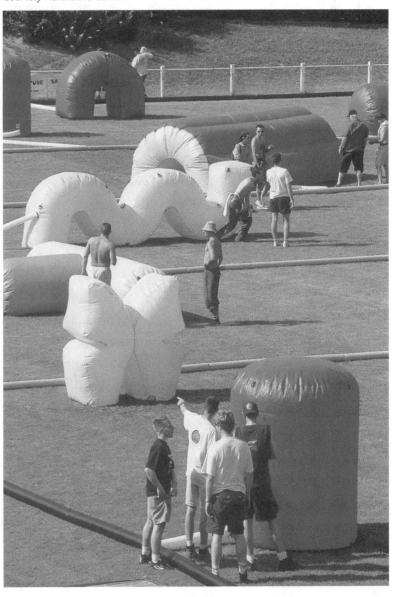

words, you're not the first to feel this way, nor will you be the last. Bearing this in mind, here are four tips for you to remember when you head out for your first paintball tournament:

1) Relax.

You might think this is easier said than done—and you'd be right—but you can still get there. Most people seem to have a hard time relaxing simply because they're afraid: not necessarily afraid of anything in particular, but afraid of confronting the unknown. Some people are afraid of doing something stupid, or wrong, or dumb, or making mistakes, or any combination of the above. Well, the truth is that on your first tournament outing, all of those things *will probably happen.*

Yes, you'll likely make the wrong decision.

Yes, you'll make mistakes. Yes, you'll do something that a seasoned tournament player would call "dumb" or "stupid". And yes, that comes with the territory of being a first-timer, so don't worry about it. You can rest assured that every tournament player in history has been guilty of the same exact offenses.

2) Learn.

Once you've come to peace with the realization that what you fear is not only likely to happen, but is also perfectly normal, you can use it to your advantage by learning from your mistakes. All paintball players learn from experience, and personal experience comes in two basic forms: doing something right, and doing something wrong. The key to developing your potential lies in learning from your mistakes, and this should be your focus. Don't let yourself get so caught up in disgust over making a mistake that you forget to realize the value in such a thing. In addition to learning from your own mistakes, you can learn a great deal from others...so when you're not on the field play-

ing, go watch some other teams play and see if you can pick up on certain things that the better players do, and figure out why they do those things. Don't be afraid to talk to those players as well, to ask them questions about their own tournament experience. If there's one thing you can count on, it's that a fisherman's love for storytelling is eclipsed only by the typical paintballer's, and this can be a valuable resource for your own development in understanding the particulars of Tournament paintball.

3) Don't Get Discouraged.

It is inevitable that you will make the same mistake twice, or three times, or four times, or more. It is inevitable that you will feel like you "should have known better." The competitive nature of those who are drawn to Tournament paintball can make it quite difficult for them to take it easy on themselves. After all, the ultimate goal of playing paintball competitively is to win. If you don't win, don't be discouraged. If you make a mistake that seals your defeat, don't be discouraged. Go back to #2 (above) and apply your feelings there. In time, you will be better as a result of everything you've done wrong, so long as you let your mistakes work for your benefit. So rather than be discouraged, be happy...because you're learning, and that's a great thing.

4) Have One Goal: Enjoy It!

Most importantly, *have fun* on your first day as a tournament paintballer. This is your first step into the realm of the sport of paintball, a realm that has proven time and time again for many, many players to provide the ultimate in excitement and enjoyment. Playing paintball competitively is a bit like a never-ending journey, because there will always be more to learn, new games to play, and new situations to experience. All journeys have a first step, and this will be yours. Enjoy it for what it is, and welcome aboard!

Tips for Continued Development as a Tournament Player

As you grow more comfortable with tournament play, don't forget that there are always areas for improvement, new things to realize, and rough edges to round out. The players who have made the biggest impact in their games, on their teams, and in this sport are those who have striven continuously to improve themselves. There are four basic ideas that are essential to the continued growth of a dedicated paintball player.

1) Learn to be Ambidextrous.

The ability to hold and shoot a marker equally well with both hands is absolutely invaluable in the sport of paintball. It's difficult for most players to embark upon this task simply because it feels uncomfortable at first to hold the marker's grip in your non-dominant hand. The trick to mastering this technique is commitment and repetition, which, in time, will get you over the hurdle of feeling uncomfortable. Once you are able to shoot your marker well with both hands, your success on the field will improve greatly.

2) Develop Snap-shooting Skills.

On today's concept fields, it is guaranteed that at some point you will find yourself pinned behind your bunker by an opponent who has his or her marker aimed at your position (is "posted" on you) from a relatively close range. If you ease out and exchange fire with this opponent, he or she will likely eliminate you. However, if you have developed a good snap-shot, you can pop out, take a quick shot at your opponent, and pop back behind the bunker before your opponent has the opportunity to hit you with a paintball. If you've taken the time to work on your snap-shot, that single 'ball is all you will need to eliminate him or her. If you haven't taken the time to work on it, it's more likely that *you* will be the one to leave the field eliminated from play.

3) Learn to Communicate.

In paintball tournaments, the ability of a team to communicate and work together as a single unit on the field of play is essential. Good tournament players need to be able to communicate effectively with their teammates during the game. It can take a while to get the hang of it, so make an effort always to be aware of it when you're playing, and tell your teammates what you're seeing on the field from your vantage point. It's likely that your team will have some codes worked out for various things (such as eliminations, time, etc.), so learn them well and use them whenever appropriate. If one of your teammates yells a code or says something important, get in the habit of repeating it. Good communication takes practice, but once you've got it down you'll never have to think about it again.

4) Be Open to Constructive Criticism.

A closed mind is a terrible thing because it keeps a player from developing his or her full potential. As you develop as a tournament player, it is important that you remain open to receiving constructive criticism from two sources: yourself and others. Constructive criticism from yourself is important because it teaches you to be aware of your own mistakes. Some players make it a point to find *something* they did wrong after every game, no matter how good the game went or how well they played. The point here is not to be down on oneself, but to find those rough edges that could use some additional improvement. Make no mistake about it: there is *always* room for improvement. With this in mind, do not make the mistake of taking constructive criticism from other individuals as personal attacks. Their input can be invaluable to personal growth, because other people often observe mistakes in ourselves that we are oblivious to.

-—*Justin Owen*

TODAY'S TOP TOURNAMENTS

NATIONAL PROFESSIONAL PAINTBALL LEAGUE

The NPPL (called the "nipple" for short) is *the* premier tournament paintball league, unrivalled by any other series or tournament worldwide. The level of competition that exists at the NPPL tournaments is, quite simply, the highest in the sport of paintball. The NPPL is viewed as the ultimate tournament establishment; it is covered en masse by paintball's press; and success in the NPPL is generally viewed as the most prestigious goal attainable in the sport.

The NPPL series is composed of five separate events spread across the United States, the first of which is in March and the last of which is in October. The 5-player tournaments are held on Wednesday and Thursday, and the 10-player tournaments are held on Friday, Saturday, and Sunday. The World Cup typically adds an extra day to the 5-man, and adds an extra rest day in between the two events. Although the 5-player events are growing, the emphasis of the NPPL is clearly on the 10-player events, for which there are 3 divisions (Professional, Amateur-A, and Amateur-B). Although they are extremely popular, NPPL events are taken very seriously and are viewed as being a professional sports event more than most other tournaments. Teams show up with one thing on their mind: winning. Teams and players in the NPPL make major commitments of time and money in order to play NPPL tournaments, and anyone interested in attending should expect to do the same. Many of the top teams practice once a week or more, and are helped by corporate sponsorships from companies within the paintball circle of businesses. This is a league for those teams and players who wish to play among the best, against the best, and who aspire to be the best.

If you plan to attend one or more of the NPPL events, make your arrangements early. You'll likely need plane tickets, car rentals, hotel rooms, and firm commitment from your entire team's roster. Information is readily available on the Internet. You can bring your own paint if you wish, but most paintball companies sell paint at the NPPL events for better-than-usual prices. The fields are 100% concept fields and generally favor the Sup'air-type inflatable fields, though there are a fair number of Hyperball fields at certain venues.

THE MILLENNIUM SERIES

Though it's been called the "European NPPL," the Millennium Series has established itself as a unique entity among paintball tournaments by pioneering the move toward total use of concept fields, as well as pioneering the regular use of major sports arenas (such as soccer stadiums, etc.) to host paintball tournaments. Consisting of several events held throughout various European countries over the same rough time period as the NPPL season, the Millennium Series enjoys press coverage rivaling that of the NPPL and maintains a similar professional attitude and atmosphere regarding its events.

The Millennium Series is unique in that it embraces the concept of 7-player events, which have been much more successful in Europe than the 10-man events the NPPL holds. Teams and players who play this series make major temporal and financial commitments. Events are "bring-your-own-paint." As in the NPPL, there are three divisions of play. Some top NPPL squads have begun making regular trips to Europe in order to compete in the Millennium tournaments, and as a result a "World Series" has resulting from combining the two series (though very few teams play the full World Series as yet).

The Millennium Series clearly boasts the best play that Europe has to offer, though at the moment NPPL teams who compete in Millennium tournaments still dominate. Teams and players interested in playing Millennium tournaments should be aware that plane tickets, car rentals, lodging, etc.

Courtesy Airgun Designs

will all be necessary, and arrangements are best made early. Information is readily available on the Internet. The fields are 100% concept fields and in the very near future will probably become 100% Sup'air.

MARDI GRAS

The Mardi Gras tournament was originally part of the Gulf Coast Tournament Series but has now taken on a life of its own and basically exists as a stand-alone tournament. It is a 5-player event that is held over a two-day weekend surrounding the Mardi Gras celebration in New Orleans, Louisiana, typically in late January. Many NPPL teams have begun attending it regularly as a sort of pre-NPPL season warm-up, making it an extremely difficult (and prestigious) event to win. The prize package is outstanding, the fields are 100% concept (inflatable) in nature, and the night-life/after-tournament atmosphere is simply incredible as a result of the Mardi Gras celebration itself. People come to this tournament to party first and play second, so it's a unique event in just about every respect.

Information about the tournament is readily available on the Internet, but any teams interested in going should definitely plan ahead in order to reserve hotel rooms, which become increasingly scarce as Mardi Gras approaches. It is appropriate for everyone from the ultra-serious to the ultra-carefree tournament player.

SKYBALL

Though the production of the Skyball tournament has changed hands three times, the initiative demonstrated by its creation has etched it in paintball's history books forever. The Skyball tournament is held annually (usually in late February or early March) in Toronto, Canada, at the Skydome, the home of the Toronto Blue Jays Major League Baseball team. Skyball made its debut in 1998 as the first paintball tournament to be held inside a *major* sports arena, and was wildly successful, drawing

Courtesy Ricochet Development

well more than one hundred 5-player teams from all over the world.

Skyball has seen some problems in the last couple of years, mostly related to scheduling conflicts, but it remains a popular event and the awe of playing paintball under the retractable roof of the Skydome is an experience that is an absolute must for every tournament player at some point in his or her career. Few NPPL teams make the trip to Toronto these days, usually opting for Mardi Gras instead, so the tournament has a much more relaxed atmosphere than when it was first realized. Skyball fills to capacity early, though, so teams interested in attending would be wise to make all arrangements, and *especially* tournament entry arrangements, as early as possible. Information on the event is readily available on the Internet. Fields are 100% concept (inflatable) fields.

THE INTERNATIONAL AMATEUR OPEN

Nicknamed the "Superbowl" of amateur paintball, the International Amateur Open has long been a favorite for teams from all over the world just looking for a great time. Held annually near Pittsburgh, Pennsylvania, near late summer/early fall, the IAO is an amateur-only event that has strict rules governing eligibility. Top NPPL pro and amateur teams and players are expressly forbidden to enter the event, which makes it a very appealing tournament to lesser-known amateur teams who won't have to compete with the "big teams" for the IAO's always-fantastic prize packages. As a result, the IAO has always drawn a huge number of teams for both the 5-player and the 10-player competitions, which are held early and late in the week, respectively.

In addition to the tournament itself, the IAO boasts the world's largest trade show year after year. Many companies choose to debut new products at this trade show, which has taken on a life of its own in recent years. The nightlife of the surrounding area is also grand, complemented by parties thrown by corporate sponsors at local hotel bars and such, as well as numerous players' parties hosted by the IAO staff itself.

The atmosphere of this event is one of sportsmanship and fun, and lacks the rabid seriousness and intensity of the NPPL and Millennium series. It is, however, an incredibly expensive tournament to attend, most of which comes from the overpriced field paint which *must* be used (players are not allowed to bring their own paint). But for up-and-coming teams, this is a great event to take a crack at for one or two years. Information is readily available on the Internet.

-—*Justin Owen*

CODES AND COMMUNICATION

TALK IT UP

In the sport of paintball and *especially* within the ranks of its top tournaments, good teamwork is the key to success. The execution of good teamwork involves the integration of a number of important factors, the single most important of which is communication. Good communication requires commitment and dedication from all members of a team in order to learn how to effectively spread important information during a game. The history of paintball shows us that it is those groups of players who have developed their ability to function as a *single unit* on the field of play, rather than as five or ten individuals playing individually on the same team, that have been most successful.

An integral part of communication on today's tournament paintball fields involves the widespread use of *codes*. Today's tournament teams go to extreme measures in order to learn how to communicate effectively among themselves without giving away important information to their opponents. A full set of codes for a single team usually involves code words to account for any relevant circumstance that might be encountered on the field of play.

Here is a list of codes as they might be within a serious tournament team. *These are merely examples*, and this list is not necessarily exhaustive of the entire range of items for which teams designate specific codes. Different teams' codes can vary greatly depending upon a number of factors, but dedication to learning them and strict adherence to their use is of utmost importance if a team is to succeed on the tournament paintball field.

Code Word	Code Meaning	Code Application
Burn 1, 2, 3…	# of opponents eliminated	Calling out "Burn 1" signifies that you have eliminated one of your opponents; "Burn 2" = two eliminations; "Burn 3" = three eliminations; and so forth.
Down 1, 2, 3…	# of own teammates eliminated	Calling out "Down 1" signifies that you have eliminated one of your opponents; "Down 2" = two eliminations; "Down 3" = three eliminations; and so forth.
Reality	amount of time left in game	"Reality four-fifty" = four minutes and fifty seconds left in the game; "Reality ten-ten" = ten minutes and ten seconds left in the game; etc.
Thunder	provide cover fire	This is a code you might call out if you were preparing to shift from one bunker to another and needed cover fire in order to make it happen. Variations of and additions to this code could further specify where the cover fire needed to be directed, for example.
Rabbit	wanting to move	Variations on this code could specify your plan of action, and this code could be used in conjunction with codes such as "Thunder."
Poison	marker down	Use this code to inform the rest of your team that your marker is experiencing problems during the game, or has quit working entirely.
Fast Food	need to reload	Use this code to inform nearby teammates that your marker's loader is running low on paint and that you need to reload.
Choker	bunkering code	In tournament paintball, there are times when it is necessary to run up on an opponent and eliminate him or her at point-blank range. This is commonly known as a "bunker move," and the code to direct teammates to do it or to alert teammates that you are about to do it is one of the most important ones to have.
Wolverine	push upfield	This code is sometimes used near the end of a game when there is danger of time running out. When a team calls it out, the entire team will move upfield at once in an attempt to overrun their opponents and win the game.
Shadow	opponent is across the bunker from you	To warn a teammate that he occupies the opposite side of the same bunker as one of his opponents, call out "Shadow" along with his name.

In addition to learning code words for communicating actions and circumstances effectively across a team, the nature of today's concept fields (especially the inflatable fields) has made it possible for teams and players to give specific names to bunkers with characteristic shapes. By giving specific names to these bunkers, teams are better able to communicate positions and locations on the field.

Can

Can: A cylindrical bunker set on its end, standing approximately seven feet tall with a diameter of roughly four feet. "Cans" are most commonly found in the backfield, nearest each team's respective starting stations.

Steamroller: A "can" that has been laid on its side.

Dorito: This bunker resembles a pyramid, is roughly eight feet in height, and is one of the most popular Sup'air bunkers made.

Baby Dorito: Just as it sounds, a smaller version of the "Dorito."

Dorito

Wing Nut: Looks like a "can" which has been cut in half, with two fins that stick out from the sides of the bunker.

Wing Nut

Snake: There's no mistaking this bunker; it looks exactly like the name implies and is typically found across the midfield running near the out-of-bounds line. "Snakes" are low bunkers and the players who have become most comfortable using them are those who have learned how to crawl and snapshoot very well.

Snake

Nessie: This bunker resembles a miniature snake, very short in length and displaying a characteristic "S"-curve.

Car Wash: An arch that forms a long tunnel when set up on the field—hence the name "car wash." It is typically found along the midfield line and can easily provide cover for two or more players from each team, even at the same time!

Cone: Looks like a pointed ice cream cone (a "sugar cone") which has

Cone

been turned upside down and sits on its circular surface, pointing towards the sky.

Carrot: A "cone" that has been laid on its side.

Submarine: This is a large bunker that will almost always be found on the midfield line next to one of the tapelines (out-of-bounds borders). It roughly resembles the long-tube appearance of a submarine.

Fish: There is no mistaking this bunker when you see it; it looks like a fish.

Rocket: As is the case above, there is no mistaking the "rocket"; it looks exactly as one would expect a "rocket" to look.

Octopus: This bunker is typically found in the exact center of the field, and resembles a large X laid on the ground with a single cone pointing straight up from the center of the X.

Tombstone: Like the snake, rocket, and fish, the "tombstone" looks exactly as its name implies.

X: When laid down and viewed from above, this bunker forms an "X" on the ground.

T: Resembles a "T" on the ground when viewed from above.

Piggie: This is one of the most interesting bunkers in paintball. It is a low-to-the-ground tube that stands on two triangular "legs," one on each end of the tube. The resulting shape is similar to the appearance of a "Weiner dog," but the cosmetic accents of a face on one side of the tube and a curly-Q tail on the other side give it the unmistakable look of a pig.

Taco: This is another no-brainer; it almost perfectly resembles the shape of the typical taco.

—*Justin Owen*

Cheese: Resembles the shape of a thin, tall, triangular slice of cheese standing on end.

Wedge: Somewhat resembles the "cheese" with its top half cut off.

HANDY HAND SIGNALS

Visual signals are used when it's time to be stealthy and quiet. You and your buddy may be crawling to the flag station unnoticed. Why give away your position by talking? Using visual hand signals, you can communicate to each other silently as you plan your attack.

The following hand signals have been adopted from Navy SEAL small unit tactical signals. Of course they've been slightly modified to meet the challenges of the paintball experience.

Stop
Fist held in air.

Hear
Hold your hand up next to your ear as if you are listening.

Go
Arm up, sweeps from back to front.

Down
Arm forward, sweeps down.

Cover Me
Tap your head with your hand.

See
Point to your eyes.

Go Faster
Fist in air, pumps up and down rapidly.

Out of Air
Fast movement of the hand back
and forth across the throat.

Gun Down
Point "thumbs down" at your gun.

Bunker
Open grip. Fingers point downward.

Flag
Palm vertical.

Take Bunker
Thumb up, index finger extended, pointing ahead.
As in, "Full speed ahead—bunker that guy".

Gun Working
Also known as the universal "o.k." symbol. As in,
"Whatever was wrong is now o.k."

Out of Paint
Make zero with your thumb and fingers.

Flag Station
Inverted bunker

···

Crawl
Wave index and middle finger in opposing up/down motion.

Affirmative
Thumbs up! Another universal symbol for "understood."

Put them together and see how they work.

Here's the message: "I see a bunker. Cover me. I'm going to "bunker" them".

Here's how it looks:

—*Andrew Flach and Stew Smith*

The Complete Guide to Paintball

THIRD EDITION UPDATES:

NEW TECHNOLOGY AND TACTICS

GUNS, GEAR & GADGETS

Tac One Marker (Courtesy of Airgun Designs)

VT Tactical Autococker® Marker
(Courtesy of Worr Games Products)

Excellerator™ 3.5E (© JT USA 2004)

Since our last update, lots of new products have come onto the market. Paintguns themselves have changed in small, but important ways. The focus of the new guns has been on speed, or more accurately, higher rates of fire. We'll cover that a bit later in this update. The other innovation has been their weight.

For example, the Shocker you see on page 122 has come down considerably in weight and size. Other manufacturers, like WDP and Airgun Designs, have also decreased the weight with such innovations as the UltraLight Engineering (ULE) body or the Angel Fly. Many players want the intense rates of fire, but they also want it on a light and easy to maneuver platform. The industry has responded, creating lightweight markers what are very easy to carry sprinting.

So what if you're not into the "flashy paintgun" market? Fear not. The industry has also seen that many players are still hard-core woods players, and have catered to your needs. Airgun Designs has also come out with the "Tac One," Worr Games Products developed the VF Tactical Autococker, and several other paintball manufacturers are making scenario specific paintguns

What's so special about these? Both the Tac One and the VFT have several rails to mount scopes, sites, night vision equipment, and so on. "Under the hood" you're still getting a lot of horsepower, but the body is meant to work. You can also buy lots of after-market parts for such paintguns as the Spyder and the Tippman A-5 from places like LAPCO to get a more military theme to your particular paintgun.

Spyder Adapter (Courtesy of Lapco)

Protect Your Gear

Many manufacturers are also starting to make protective gear for paintguns, specifically the nitrogen air tanks used to power them. Many still make the basic neoprene protective sleeve, but other manufacturers are making true armor. Redz, for example, produces a bottle cover with a pad on the front to protect the bottle from impacts when you slide into cover. JT and DYE both make bottle covers with padding that acts like armor for players that slide a lot. A bottle cover has always been a good idea for players who use fiber-wrapped nitrogen bottles, and the modern tank covers protect better than ever.

Redz Protective Bottle Covers (Property of Redz International, Inc.)

Protect Yourself

Protective gear has become the norm to protect the players in the fast-paced world of arena paintball. Clothing is being designed with player's safety in mind, too. Slider shorts have extra padding for hip bones and the tail bone, and even a pocket for a protective cup. Many companies make an elbow-to-forearm guard, which helps when you're sliding across grass or dirt. They're even better when you're crawling from one position to another in the deep woods. Gloves are even being designed with a miniature skid plate on the heel of the hand, to allow players to slide with more control.

Tactical Full T-Shirt (Courtesy of Under Armour Performance Apparel www.underarmour.com)

All of that may sound nice for the guys who play in the arenas, but what about the woods players? Fear not, you haven't been forgotten. There is more than enough gadgetude to keep you drooling over catalogs for a long time. And, yes, some of it is protective. You need to step a little out of the paintball mainstream, but it's well worth the time. A company called Under Armour has been well known by football and baseball players for its performance apparel. What you may not know is that it also makes a tactical line in all your favorite subdued colors. We know how much you sweat in the woods, at least now you can stay cool while doing it.

Protective Gear (Photo © Nexed Paintball)

Nice Duds

Other innovations have come in the clothing department. In the main portion of the book we talked at length about getting clothing to match what you're doing. We also talked about the "new" clothing. Just like everything else in this game, it's evolved, too. You still have the skid plates and the colors, but now it's about comfort and durability.

Manufacturers from outside paintball are applying what they've learned from other sports to paintball. Nexed is a company that specializes in roller hockey gear. It introduced a trouser line that has stretch gussets in the crotch, the knees, and the hips. The result is apparent when you slide into a bunker. The pants have more give, and they won't bind when you find yourself feeling more like a pretzel than a player. Nexed also introduced a first into paintball pants: pockets on the sides that will hold 140 ball pods. They also double nicely to hold water bottles.

WDP went another route, making clothing designed to contour the body and wick away sweat to keep you cool. It may sound like a lot of hype,

but they're pretty comfortable. Most of the pants and jerseys being made now are durable, and have comfort in mind for hot summer play days. To that end, jerseys are being made of materials that wick sweat away as well.

Customize

But if you want something unique, you can get that as well. Custom Sports Gear makes jerseys and other apparel with your team's logo dye sublimated into the material. What this means is that your team can have its own custom look, which no other team will have. The best part is that the price is competitive with other manufacturers who make regular jerseys.

Accessories

We've also got some great gadgets for scenario players. JT USA has what it calls a Sports Com unit. It attaches to almost any existing JT product. What it does is add a headset ear piece and microphone onto your existing JT goggles! You simply plug it into a FRS radio, and you can communicate hands-free for hours. JT USA also sells a version of its popular Proteus with this modification already attached.

The Ultraback Emissary Paintball Vest (Courtesy of Flurry Industries)

Sportz-Comm™ Kit (Courtesy of JT USA)

Several other companies are making scenario-specific gear as well. Companies like Cops911.com and Flurry Industries make paintball-specific vests that hold all the gear scenario players need to carry. You can order the gear to fit your custom needs, like a hydration pack or more pods on your back.

No matter how you play, you're going to want to carry some extra paint with you. Most companies have adopted the "stacked tubes" idea to pack construction. So when you buy a pack, you see "3x2" or "5x4." What "5x4" means is that the pack holds five pods in sleeves, and another four pods in elastic loops between the sleeves. This almost doubles the paint you can carry onto the field. This isn't to say you will carry more, but it's nice to know you can.

Packs are being made to collapse as you empty them. This creates a smaller target for your opponent to hit, and makes it easier to move as the game progresses. Packs like those made by JT, Redz Comfort, or WGP can hold up to 17 pods,

Paintball Packs
(Property of Redz International, Inc.)

Pro Harness™
(Courtesy of JT USA)

but almost collapse into the width of the basic belt. Other systems like one from Mantis angled the pods out, so you could reach them easier without exposing a lot of your arm when you reached for them.

All of the gear we touched on here is just a small sampling of what's available now. You don't need to go out and buy everything you read about here. It's all about your comfort level, and what will help you play a better game. Experiment a little, and try everything. You may be surprised what you do and don't like.

(Courtesy of Cleo Fogal)

Guns, Gear & Gadgets

RATES OF FIRE

Since our last edition, paintball has been slowly creeping up in technology levels. The boom of the electronic semi has pretty much taken over the industry, and become the "must have" on every paintball marker. If you're serious about the game, you probably own an electronic paintball gun, or at least one with an electronic trigger.

Using Electronic Triggers

The main advantage to electronic triggers is the rates of fire you can produce. This is from the light trigger pull that, in some cases, feels like clicking a mouse button. If you can imagine being able to launch one paintball with the click of the mouse, you can begin to imagine what these triggers feel like. Since most of the electronic paintguns have two-finger or extended length triggers, the players have come up with several techniques to allow you to utilize this technology in ways that are a radical departure form normal shooting mechanics.

Electronic Trigger (© JT USA 2004)

First we'll talk about walking a trigger. In this, you alternate the pull of a trigger between your index and middle finger. It's similar to rapidly typing the numbers 1 and 2 on a keyboard with two fingers. The result with a light trigger is that you tap it faster, and your rate of fire increases.

Second is a technique called Raking. To perform this, you rub your index finger up and down the front of a two-finger trigger, tapping all the bumps on the trigger. With practice, each rake can produce multiple shots. With a properly set-up electronic semi-auto paintgun, you can easily achieve over 15 shots per second, sustained.

Photo by Rigo Ramirez, © JT USA 2004

As of this writing, electronic semi-autos can easily reach 20 shots per second. With loaders like the Halo and the Evolution 2 being made faster, and the electronic interface of the Warp feeder to electronic triggers, the limit of how fast the rates of fire can go is regulated only by physics. And why do we need such radical rates of fire? The new speedball.

Smaller fields and faster players add up to the need to shoot streams of paint into a specific area in an attempt to lock out opponents from reaching the position. This is usually called lane shooting or sweet spotting. To do this effectively, you have to fill an area with paintballs. It goes back to the Running Man Drill mentioned earlier in the book (page 220) and Shooting Lanes (page 238), but now the paintballs are in a much tighter grouping as they fly through the air.

One key to winning on smaller, more open fields is dominating the mother team. Once they are effectively shut down, your teammates can move up on them and eliminate them with better angles. High rates of fire allow your team to dominate shooting lanes.

Do you absolutely need the highest rate of fire semi-auto out there? Probably not. If you play in the woods most of the time, or you play only occasionally, you won't need something that can throw a one-person-volley-of-balls. And even if you play on arena-style courses on an occasional basis, you won't absolutely need anything that fast. But if you're playing high-level competition, it can't hurt to go with the "big guns".

ROB "TYGER" RUBIN ON THRIVING IN CHAOS

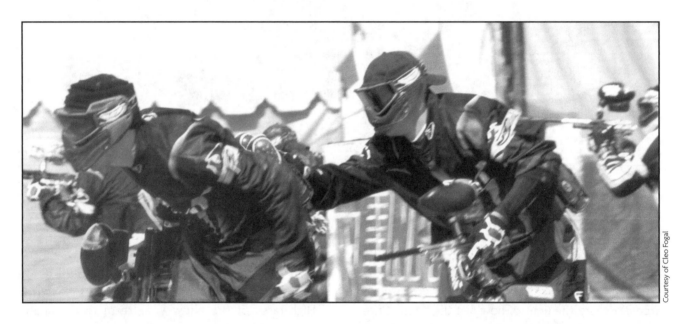

I want to relate something that happened to me a while ago. I was playing in a local trophies-only tournament on a throw-together team. We finished respectably, but not in the finals. So, the field decided that while the finals were being held on the airball field, the tubes field would be open to anyone who wanted to just play. And, considering that only six teams out of 18 advanced, that was a lot of people to jump in for some extra-curricular play.

What's important here is that only one variable was different. The field was the same five-man hyper-pipes field we'd been playing all day. The tech was the same that we had all been used to all day. The players were the same. The paint was the same. The only variable that changed during the "for fun" games was the numbers on the field. Instead of five on five, we started playing a monstrous 12 on 12. It grew up to a huge 15 on 15 at one point on a field built and designed for five on five play.

The one thing I noticed, over and over, was a total mental lockup of the players. It was as though their brains couldn't handle the numbers. What was a somewhat predictable five on five encounter was now a working example of chaos theory. The well-oiled machine had a liberal number of monkey wrenches thrown in there to kill the machinery.

Now for me this isn't anything new. Every paintball field that has a concept area that I've ever played feels a need to cram the walk-ons into it for a good game of Speedball. The most amazing game I've ever played was 21 on 22 on a five-man hyperball field. And I've played woodland fields that felt more crowded than a Tokyo subway. So how do you deal with these walk-on numbers? Simple, really. Make order of chaos. Simply become one with the universe by listening to TJ Lambini's relaxation tapes before the games begin. You don't have TJ's tapes handy? No problems. We'll just start with making sense of the mess you're getting dumped into.

Pre-Game Planning

A friend of mine, Kennedy How, has a T-shirt that reads "Never underestimate the power of stupid people in large numbers." It's true. Mob mentality rears its ugly head in big games, and to a lesser degree in large walk-on groups. But once you know the nature of people, you recognize the patterns.

First of all, realize that the game does not change drastically with the inclusion of large numbers of people. Walk-on play is the basic game. You shoot your opponent, they get hit, and they walk off. No goofy rules of reincarnation, or reinsertion, or wounds, or anything like that. So the basic terms of engagement apply. If you're used to tournament play, this is important to know.

Second is basic human nature. A poignant joke applies: Two men are hiking in the woods. They round a bend and see a large bear on his hind legs, fangs and claws exposed, looking ready to attack. One hiker throws off his pack, removes the sneakers from the side, and starts pulling at his boots. His

Photo by Rigo Ramirez, © JT USA 2004

Rob "Tyger" Rubin on Thriving in Chaos

friend says, "What are you doing? You can't outrun a bear!" The first hiker, having already removed the first boot, looks up and says, "I don't need to outrun the bear. I just need to outrun you."

The point is that in walk-on play, it's every person for themselves! Every player there is paying to play for the day, and their main interest is not necessarily in the team, but to shoot paintballs and have a good time doing it. Translated loosely, "Look out for number one." Oh, sure, you can jump in with your five-man team, but the vapor lock I mentioned before happens every time. Which brings me to my third point: the numbers.

If you're used to counting to five or seven, you are in for a shock when you realize there are three people behind that "back 45" you didn't count on. This is probably the number one cause for the vapor lock I keep talking about. You can have a great five-man team in the arena, but it takes only one guy to zone out and get fixated on the count to expose himself to one angle to ruin a good push.

And fourth is the lack of cover. A typical five-man arena has probably six to eight bunkers on one side of the field to use as cover, not counting the stuff in the center. In a five-man game, this is more than adequate. When the numbers start to get to the absurd, 15 people divided by 6 bunkers equals some very strange bedfellows. Not to mention that some of these bunkers are designed to hold one person, barely. So you get a lot of doubling, and sometimes quadrupling up in bunkers.

These fairly simple principles are always lost to people who don't know what to do in what my friends and I call TREs (target rich environments). But once you step back and understand all this, you can prepare yourself for the insanity.

Organization

Off the break, you get your first problem: getting 15 people behind bunkers set for five. Having a pregame plan is good, so you all know at least where

you're going. Nothing fancy, just "Ok, how many are going that way?" is perfectly acceptable. Anything more complex than that and you'll lose your teammates fast.

Once you know who's going right, left, and center, you can work in your small groups to get a more detailed plan. "I'm going to that back can there." "Okay, I'll go to the laydown in front of that." "Sounds good, I'll go with him to the can, and bump up when you move up." Three players now have a loose game plan. They can now work together to make the first five seconds work.

Don't be afraid to plan to have three guys behind a large bunker. In fact, this can be a major plan of your game. One guy gets knocked out and the other team thinks it's a clear bunker. They move up, and run directly into your barrel. I've done that to a few people before, too. Plan this out in advance. Having no surprises in the first few moments is a good thing.

The other reason you want a plan is to avoid stumbles; literally, two players bumping into each other at a full paced sprint trying to dive behind the same small can together. Don't laugh, I've seen it too many times to count them. Even if your plan includes moving up, let the guy you'll be sharing a space with know what you're up to. Avoids a lot of confusion and a lot of headaches when you bump into the guy.

I want to specifically talk about sweet spotting as well, especially in an opening move like this. If only one guy is running across your stream, you might get one. Great. But now if there's four, one may get hit, the rest will make it through. That's the nature of the numbers. I'm not saying you shouldn't sweet spot off the break, I'm just letting you know you the odds are against you shutting down a side off the break. But getting the numbers in your favor in the first five seconds, it's worth the risk.

Mid-Game Strategy

Mid-game, a lot of your strategy is normal game strategy. Play as you always would, but throw your count out the window. Unless you know for sure that the teams are 14 on 14, don't bother counting. And, even if you do, don't expect your teammates to pick up on the count, let alone the fact you're keeping track of that kind of thing.

If you're just a solo player, you would be ahead to buddy up with someone. They don't even have to know you're doing it. Ask the guy in the bunker next to you what he's shooting at. If you can see a name on their jersey, use it. "Hey! Hamburger Head! Where are they at?" It's why I wear vanity jerseys! If someone wants to ask me something, my name is right there for them to use. Stick with this system for optimal results. Also, don't always believe a total stranger. Sometimes, their interest is to see if you get lit up from the left or right, so take things with grains of salt.

If you're playing with your team, play as you normally do. Just, like I said, toss the count out the window. Work more with a 'feel' for the field. If no-

body is shooting at you from the left, odds are it really might be cleared out. Remember the first principle from before. The game does not radically change, just the numbers of bodies.

The other thing you can do is teach. Grab a few of the walk-on players and give them a crash course in codes and communications. "We break the field into red, white, blue." Taking a few moments to teach could give you a code that would be very important down the road from the player you take some time with. And if it goes horribly right, then you can find someone new to get into your team later.

I've always been a fan of the idea "the more the merrier." And as long as fields insist on stuffing 20 on 20 in a 5 man field, I'll get to experience that. It's not anything that can not be handled. It's a matter of knowing a few things, relaxing a little bit, and taking the game as it comes to you.

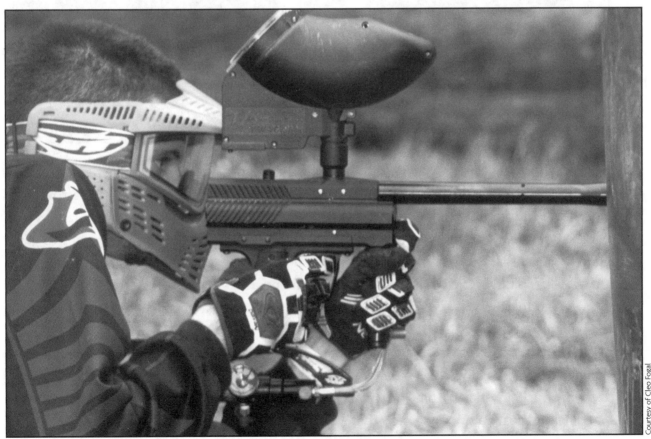

Courtesy of Cleo Fogal

Rob "Tyger" Rubin on Thriving in Chaos

PAINTING THE TOWN

Paintball is an interesting game. Unlike any other game, we can play anywhere. What we play on an airball field can be taken into the woods, or a junkyard, or even into a town setting. It's the latter that we're going to review now: Doing it under urban terrains.

Urban play can take many forms, including everything from an old auto bone yard to glitzy Hollywood sets. But the most basic way to play urban terrain is building to building. One thing that you'll find is that there is no way to take a building with a 100 percent success ratio. It won't happen. No matter how cool your SWAT fatigues look, you will not be able to do it perfectly every time.

The true key to success is being prepared for the urban play environment. If it's paved, it will hurt to play on unless you have knee and elbow pads. We also recommend neck guards, a cap of some kind, and anything else you can think of. Some think it's weak to wear that much padding, but it's really only a sign that you don't want to get unnecessarily injured. Most players have no problems with that.

Now, on to the urban sprawl: let's take a look at any given field that is building to building. Most share a few common items besides buildings. Most are clear cut, meaning the fields are kept to grass and not overgrown. In this case, playing a building field isn't much different than playing any given airball field except you can get into the bunkers as well as hide behind them. Another thing they all share in common is the style of buildings. Most are four walls with windows and roofs. The style may change, but the basics never do.

So right there you can get a few of the techniques down, just by knowing that there are a few constants in how they play.

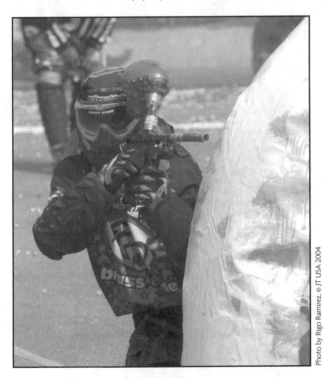

Photo by Rigo Ramirez, © JT USA 2004

Defending

We'll start with defense, or playing in or around a building to hold it. Sometimes you can do more good for your team by going into a building, putting out the unwelcome mat, and moving in. A building can offer a sense of security that other structures may not, but that can come back to hurt you.

So let's start by going into a building. When you go in, get an idea of your surroundings before you

start to go to town. Check the angles of the doorways and windows and how they relate down the field to your opponents. You want to avoid being "locked in" at all costs. Translation: they keep your head down and you can't come up for air without tasting paint.

As a bunker, look at a building as a place you can work with. One way is to stay outside a building. If you're outside the building, you can line up shooting lanes through windows of a building. It's harder to thread the needle from 70 feet away than it is to shoot from the same "needle" when you're inside it. You also want to work all sides of a building, left and right. Buildings are big structures, usually. So you can go from one side to another without any problems.

Once you're inside a building, don't stop moving around. On more than one occasion, I've held off numbers I usually would never have a chance with because I move around in a building. Two shots out the left door, two shots from the right side of a window, back to the left door, then the right door, then the window again... Mix it up. For the most part, you have unrestricted movement in a building. Use it all.

You want to come out of windows and doorways at odd heights. The average person, kneeling, is about 3 feet tall. Standing, it's a little less than six feet. Come out of a door at one foot, poke the barrel out and shoot. They'll never see it coming. For protection, use the corners of windows rather than the sides or bottoms. The advantage is you can conceal more of your paintgun and body from the corner of a window than you can from the bottom or sides.

If that doesn't work, move to the opposing wall of the building, and kneel down. In this case, it's like playing a loose bunker. You can control more angles of the field without exposing yourself unnecessarily. I like to do this in order to snapshoot from windows. It gives me more room to breathe, and also offers an opportunity for me to slide to

a doorframe or wherever if the window angle is too much.

Speaking of windows, watch your angles. You may be inside a building, and protected from the whole right side, but your left could be exposed to one guy who can thread the needle and hit you. Keep an eye on doorways you're not at currently, and most important, be mindful if the bad guys run up on your building. Point blank exchanges happen, and are not fun.

One more thing: When you're inside a building, have an escape route. Sometimes you go into a building knowing your trip is one-way. You either get eliminated or you own the field. But normally, you want to look at the doorways for a route to exit, if you need to.

Courtesy of Cleo Fogal

Attacking

Now we'll discuss attacking a building. If it's unavoidable, if it's a part of the scenario you're playing, if it's where the opponent's flag is, you're going to have to go in. But before you do, you want to do all you can to soften it up a bit. From long range, pour in the long ball. You may not be a fan of high volume shooting, but in this case it's probably the best thing you can do. When you rain in paint, you make it dangerous for the defenders to poke a

head up. By doing that, you make it possible to approach a building from one side without the defenders in the building seeing the move.

Assuming you can do this, and it's easier than you may think, you can pretty much run up to a building. Unless you're Superman, you can't see through walls. Neither can your opponents inside the building. Flatten out against the wall, away from the windows and doors. You don't want them to see any part of you from in the building. If they as much put the barrel out the window to shoot, put a ball on it. A barrel hit is just as good as a goggle hit in my book. I've knelt under a window to shoot up and hit someone's hopper when they stuck it out of a window.

Watch your profile too. If a defender is on the ball, and they're playing the building as hard or harder than you are, they can make a fast move into a corner, see some of your harness, and shoot it. And don't try to pop through the window yourself. The defender is set up, and waiting to do the same thing. At best, you'll trade you for them. At worst, you'll get shot a dozen times point blank because you just scared the blazes out of someone by magically appearing in front of them in a window frame.

Even if you can't get up close to the building, you can play mind games with a defender in a building. Shoot a few balls, then stop. Stay on your position, and when you see movement, put a ball into there. You want to let them feel it's safe to come out the window again, and then put paint on them. You'll get more eliminations by letting the other team run into your paint than any other way.

If you're working a field of buildings, the field boundaries may be a good way to take the field. Depending on the boundary itself, you may be able to work in an alley way, a room to room scenario, or some cover outside the actual town. Keep an eye into the buildings, and move it up. You can also use any natural cover on the boundaries like trees, scrub brush, and so on. Just realize that you may not be able to see inside a darkened building, but they can see out just fine.

Driving

And now, the fun part. Driving. When you're going to enter a hostile enclosure, it's called "driving a building" or "driving through a building." It's a very messy affair, and not a pleasant thing to do from either side of the equation. Even the most highly trained members of a SWAT team drill this over and over, eventually getting it down after hundreds of dry runs.

Ideally, you want at least two people entering a building. Four to five attackers are actually better, but if it's all you have, two will work. Realize that since two people can't usually make it through a door at the same time, the first one in has to be gutsy and trust his partner totally. It's all about knowing a role, trusting your teammate completely, and then doing your job. You want to set up your move by standing against the wall with everyone lined up, ready to push into the building. The lead attacker is the one who decides the moment.

The first one in the building is at the most risk, obviously. But the job of this player is to check the area right inside the doorway, sweeping the barrel toward the inside of the room. So if the door is along the right wall of a room, the lead man steps in, sweeps 90 degrees to his left, makes sure it's clear of bad guys, then sweeps 45 degrees to face the opposing corner.

At the same time, the second in is pointed straight ahead to clear everything from the back wall to the corner of the room. The second will enter the room as soon as the first steps to the side, but he's over the shoulder of the first before he does this. If you need to, put the barrel literally on his shoulder so the muzzle tip is past him. You don't want to shoot someone in the back of the head point blank if you don't have to, especially your own teammate.

If you have more than that, the next in the room will sweep the room as they enter, and ideally the last in line is watching behind the group. That's the ideal. The reality is that the first guy enters the room, a defender panics and starts shooting. And in the chaos that follows, paint is shot in anger and it can be a mess. If you're going to take a building like that, here's a recommendation: If you've got them, paint grenades are a great tool for clearing a room. You want to throw it in so it hits the opposite wall, and bounces back towards the door. That way you get the maximum coverage of spray with minimum exposure. Just toss it in like a hook shot, hard enough to set it off, and bring your hand back fast while keeping your body completely on the other side of the doorway. It's not the ultimate answer, but it certainly can make taking a room of a building easier if it's already been "softened up." (Of course, it never quite works like that. You're lucky to get an organized move through a doorway, let alone a well choreographed dance of paintballs and players moving like a well oiled machine.)

Urban play is a nice break from the woods style we're all used to. And with many fields building sets, or villages, or even castle structures, odds are you'll be on one sooner or later.

VISUALIZATION TECHNIQUES

Visualization Techniques

Albert Einstein once said that imagination was more important than knowledge. "Knowledge is limited," he said. "Imagination encompasses the whole universe." With that in mind, let's talk about your imagination, and how to harness it for sports performance. Lately it's been termed "sports psychology," but what it really comes down to is the use of visualization techniques.

Visualization techniques equire that you use your imagination. Before you write it off as being stupid, put this into your brain: Baseball players, football players, downhill skiers, martial artists, and most other serous athletes use visualization as a part of their training. In some cases, it's a matter of being cheaper (sky divers and sky surfers perform what's called a "dirt dive" to practice formations they will do in the air before they jump from the airplane). In others, an athlete can be out of commission due to injury and unable to actually play.

Training Your Mind

To begin, here's a brief introduction to the techniques you'll be using later on. The first is the ability to see things with your mind. Everybody has this ability. For example, if someone told you to picture a pencil in your mind, you would not have a hard time doing it. More than likely, you'll see a long cylindrical object used to mark paper. The trick to using visualization techniques is to be able to visualize the same pencil, but change the eraser's color to yellow, or green, or blue, or any other color for that matter.

CELEBRITY SPOTTING

One of the more interesting developments of late is the ability to spot the celebrity who plays paintball on occasion. Not to drop names, but many of Hollywood's premiere stars not only play, but play competitively.

Last year's National Professional Paintball League (NPPL) circuit featured a team named the Stoned Assassins featuring B-Real and Everlast, from the musical group House of Pain. They even performed in concert after one of the events.

Before he died, Maurice Gibb was an avid paintball player. He even owned a series of paintball shops named Commander Mo's in Florida. The NPPL renamed one of its events the Commander's Cup in his honor.

If that's not enough, high profile movie stars have been seen on the fields, not the least of whom is William Shatner. In the last few years, Shatner, "SPPLAT," nationally broadcast morning radio personality Eric "Mancow" Muller, and Airgun Design's president Tom Kaye, have been the force behind a scenario game called SPPLAT Attack, renamed to Shatnerball in 2004. This game has been held with proceeds going to a charity called Ahead with Horses (a thera-peutic riding organization that works with children who are very badly disabled). Thousands of people have played in the first two events, and even more have been planned on every Labor Day weekend in the foreseeable future.

So don't be surprised if the next time you play paintball, you suddenly find yourself sharing a bunker with someone famous. Hey, it could happen!

Photo by Rigo Ramirez, © JT USA 2004

Photo by Rigo Ramirez, © JT USA 2004

What I'm trying to get you to do, is to play with your own imagination a bit, and get used to manipulating things in your minds eye without actually touching them. If you can get to the point where you can mentally tie pencils into knots, you'll have something. The reason this is important is that once you can manipulate things in your mind, you can also start to play in the realm of "what if" and "how can I..." Starting with basic items like pencils is a good way to begin.

Seeing the Shot

But the true power of visualization is the ability to play games or game segments in your mind. The logical question is "Why?" It's a fair one. Why would you pretend to play paintball when you can really play paintball? The best way to answer that is with an example provided by Rob "Tyger" Rubin.

"Playing with Palmerized last year at the Knoxville indoor was a real treat. The first day of the five-man event, I had the chance to walk the field along with everyone else. Up until then, I really had never seen a purpose to walking a field. I always play cold, I preferred to play cold. The 'Point me to a bunker and I'll get there' kind of thing. But I was there, I figured I may as well walk the fields.

"I took some time looking over the corner bunkers, and where my moves would be once I started to move up. From one layer back of the corner bunker I stood to the outside, and visualized the view from the other side of the field into my current position. And in my mind's eye, I could see the view from the other side of the field. I visualized the angle at which you would have to lean out in order to stay mostly protected from the flag area and still shoot into the center dish at the opponent. Even though my view was blocked physically from that angle, I visualized where that spot would be.

"Then I looked up field into the barricades, and saw a small gap. It was like kicking a field goal. The

left and right poles I had to shoot through were separate bunkers, and I would have to just barely clear the top of both bunkers to land the paint where it needed to go, but there it was. It was a hole about 6 inches wide that ended up putting paint on the outside of that key bunker. I could visualize the range of the Stroker, and the arc of paint it would take to hit a kneeling player that I couldn't see. I figured it could work, and I kept it in mind. In the first game I played that morning, I took out an opponent who had stuck his body into my gap, trying to shoot at our guy in the center. I never saw my paint hit him, but I saw a referee get all excited because a player right in front of him took one to the head. All these angles were seen before shooting a single ball on the field."

What he did was play a game segment in his head, visualizing the outcome based on what he knew already. Some would call it good field walking, and in fact, a lot of field walking is visualization with the visual aid of being able to stand behind what you want to visualize. It's the easiest way to take the idea of visualization and put it into your game immediately. Before a single ball is fired, you can try plays and angles. It also has the advantage that you can do all this without showing your opponents what you have planned.

The key to doing this type of visualization is having the ability to see both ends of the field at once, or at least having a sort of overhead view of a field in your mind. Many of the arenas now have a way to physically stand over the field, and look down on it. If you can keep this kind of overhead map in your mind's eye while walking a field you can see angles on one side of the field while standing on the other.

Doing this kind of visualization also helps you find bunkers that really offer you minimal protection or offer no advantage in field position for your team. While walking the fields, you need to visualize your angles of shooting out at your opponents while sitting or kneeling in a bunker, and who can

shoot at you. While in there, try to see it from the other side of the field; are you an easy target? This is a lot of head work, I know, but when you hit your spots perfectly, it's all worth it.

Playing the Scenario

Another type of visualization you can use before you play is running through set plays in your mind. Robbo keeps on talking about "set plays" being the wave of the future, so let's implement it to a degree. To do this, you need to envision your favorite field. You know, the local field that you go to all the time and could probably play blindfolded. Yes, that one. Now we're going to design a set play using visualization techniques.

I may go way over all of your heads here, but stay with me. Right from the break, picture going up to a bunker on the left side of the field that's about half way up the field. How would you get there? Are there any barricades further up the field to block your opponents from shooting at you? Can you run behind any bunkers on your side of the field to mask your movement?

Now for the more interesting concepts and questions: Are there any opportunities to run a path or a route that isn't usually taken? This is what takes a lot of practice on your part. Can you place in your mind's eye positions that are off the beaten trails of that field in order to make it to that central bunker? On concept fields this really is hard to do, but in the woods it's always an option.

Off the break is easy to visualize, but trying to see where you can go while in game is always more difficult. There are a lot of variables, most of which you can't really control. Where did the other team set up? Which way are they looking? Where are your teammates at any given moment? You can't predict every variable, no matter how well you can visualize things. Instead, use visualization to see a more complete view of the field when a game is over. Part of paintball is the BS sessions between games. Even if you don't believe half of what you

Photo by Rigo Ramirez, © JT USA 2004

hear, listen to where people were. What bunkers did they take? What about their teammates? This is important because it will help you visualize more of the overall game. Once you know where everyone was, you can then figure out what you could have done, and then implement it the next game. Could you have made that move to the next position? Was the snake really cleared? Knowing there was only one person in front of you, would you have made that move on him?

You can also use visualization techniques like this to practice moving up as well. For example, some players like to think of how they can move up to a bunker position using someone else's move. They visualize how fast they can run, the distance between bunkers, and the likelihood they'll get shot at while running. Those players do that to make moves automatic in their minds. They don't have to think about making those moves, they just do it. This is part of building an instinct for the game that will help you overall. Some say you can't train for instinct, but you can by becoming more accustomed to moving in response to things happening on the field. And the easiest way to train your mind to respond is to visualize scenarios and play them out in your head.

All of this sounds like heady stuff; but when you see some guy looking up field before a game, and you can see his hand moving like a guide, or his head slightly nodding left to right, he's visualizing his opening move. It's really easy to pick up, and it can help your game with a minimal effort. You just need to open your mind to something intangible, and use your imagination.

PAINTBALL VIDEO UPDATE

Another of the largest leaps in the paintball world has been in the video medium. When this book was first published, we had lofty ideas of what we wanted to see, but we couldn't imagine the explosion of video that has come out in the last few years.

The first is the home video market. Several companies are making direct-to-home-video releases of big events and tournaments. Such video series as Jawbreaker or 720 and even Force of Nature are common staples of the paintball event scenes. Even the larger events, like SPPLAT Attack, have been released as a home DVD.

But it doesn't stop there. Before being released to the home market, SPPLAT Attack 1 was released as a Pay Per View event viewed by thousands of people across the United States. SPPLAT Attack 2 was aired as a special on the Outdoor Life Network (OLN). Other cable television channels have also picked up the paintball fever as well. FOX Sports Net has been covering the NPPL Super Seven as it's been played

Photo by Rigo Ramirez, © JT USA 2004

around the country. OLN will also be airing tournament action through the season.

This isn't to say that you'll only see it as a sport. For example, in the UK they produced a show called X-Fire, a game show using paintball. Arguably, it was a cheesy game show, but it proved to a lot of people that paintball has, in fact, gone mainstream. Even now, you can see television commercials featuring paintball as a medium to sell things like automobiles and beer. Nobody would have thought of this several years ago.

If your need is more immediate, and your Internet connection is fast, there are many sources for on-demand videos. Tournament action can be found on such sites as www.pigtv.net and www.forceofnature.com. Other sites, such as www.webdogradio.us, feature clips to improve your game. Several paintball fields also have videos online showing how much fun you can have playing at their field.

Visualization Techniques

Paintball Glossary

ACTION

1. The mechanism by which something is operated, as that of a gun.

2. A military encounter, as a battle or skirmish.

3. Actual combat with enemy forces.

AGITATOR

1. A machine or device for agitating and mixing.

2. In reference to paintball, it is a device that is attached to a paintball hopper or incorporated into the design of the hopper. It has a shaft that enters the inner enclosure of the hopper with some type of impeller attached to the end of it. When activated the agitator rotates the impeller which moves the paintball around inside of the hopper allowing them to align with the feed port, located at the bottom of the hopper, and fall freely into the hopper feed nipple.

ASA

The abbreviation for Air Source Adapter. See "ASA Adapter".

ASA ADAPTER

Also referred to as CA Adapter. A device that is designed to allow a constant air tank to screw into it and let the Co_2 gas in the tank pass through it. In most cases, the ASA Adapter is designed with a actuating pin. When used with a constant air tank that has a pin valve, the ASA Adapter pin actuator presses in the pin valve's pin and allows the flow of Co_2 gas from the tank into and through the ASA Adapter. The gas then goes to the paintguns valve mechanism either directly or indirectly via some type of gas line.

AUTO, FULL

Continuous firing and reloading of paintgun as long as the trigger is held down.

AUTO, SEMI

1. Partly automatic.

2. Automatically recocking of paintgun and loading the next paintball but requiring a squeeze of the trigger to fire each shot.

AUTO TRIGGER

A trigger and sear design used with pump action paintguns, that allows the user of the paintgun to have the gun fire each time the pump handle is pulled back allowing gun mechanism to be cocked and then pulled full forward. The gun will fire automatically when pump handle is returned to full forward position each time the pump handle is cycled from front to rear and back as long as the trigger is being held down.

BACK BOTTLE SYSTEM

Refers to a constant air system design whereby the gun's ASA adapter is located at the rear of the paintgun and that is where the constant air tank is attached. The constant air tank is used as the gun's shoulder stock and may or may not have a butt plate attached to it. Pump action paintguns usually have the ASA adapter in-line with the barrel and cocking mechanism. Semi Auto paintguns usually have the ASA adapter in-line with cocking mechanism.

BACK BOTTLE ADAPTER

An ASA adapter which is attached to the rear of a paintgun, that is used to connect a gas supply to the gun and is usually in line with either the barrel/cocking mechanism or just the cocking mechanism.

BARREL PLUG

A safety device that is inserted into the front end of a paintgun barrel to prevent a paintball from exiting the barrel.

BARREL, RIFLED, INTERNAL

A barrel that has internal grooves, either straight or in a spiral pattern.

BOLT

The internal part of a paintgun that is common to Stock, Pump Action and Semi Auto paintguns. The bolt usually has a O-ring(s) at the front end of it. The O-ring acts as a seal between the bolt and the inner wall of the paintgun barrel when the bolt is in the full forward position. The bolt performs two functions

1. It is the device that moves the paintball from where it is loaded into the chamber of the paintgun, to the bore of the paintgun barrel.

2. It is the device by which CO_2 gas is transferred from the paintgun valve system to the rear of the paintball via the front of the bolt.

BOLT (closed)

One of two design criteria by which semi auto paintguns are manufactured. The closed bolt design means that the bolt is in the full forward position with the bolt O-ring sealing against the inner wall of the paintgun barrel when gun is ready to be fired via the trigger. This is with respect to the paintgun being connected to a CO_2 gas supply (constant air tank or remote air system) and fully pressurized.

BOLT (open)

One of two design criteria by which semi auto paintguns are manufactured. The open bolt design means that the bolt is in the full rear position with the bolt just behind the feed nipple port (the port that allows the paintballs to flow into the paintgun body) when paintgun is ready to be fired via the trigger. This is with respect to the paintgun being connected to a CO_2 gas supply (constant air tank or remote air system) and fully pressurized.

BOLT, VENTURI

A bolt with a concave face. The face of the bolt will have multiple holes in it. These holes are known as thrust ports.

BORE DROP LOADING

Guns using bore systems load into a receiver the same size as the barrel or directly into the barrel itself. This keeps the ball from having to load over any large seams or steep angles.

BOTTLE

1. Slang for tank.

2. A portable container for holding liquids or gases, having a neck and mouth.

3. In paintball it is the container part of a constant air tank.

BLOW BACK

paintball gun's leakage of CO_2 gases between the bolt and the inner barrel wall and/or leakage of CO_2 gases from the cocking mechanism between the gun's hammer and inner wall of the gun's housing. Blowback may occur for two reasons. First, and easiest to fix, is that the O-rings on the gun's bolt and/or hammer need to be replaced. The second reason for blowback is more complex. It has to do with the positioning of the gun's components at the time that the CO_2 gas is released into the gun's barrel.

BOTTOM LINE

A style of constant air system where the ASA adapter is located at the bottom of the paintball gun's grip frame. This ASA adapter is where the constant air tank is connected to the paintgun. The ASA adapter may be designed into the grip frame so as to be part of the grip frame or it may be a after market ASA adapter that is mounted to the bottom of the grip frame. If it is a after market ASA adapter it will have to have a gas line connecting it to the paintgun in order to allow gas to flow from the tank into and through the ASA adapter to the gas line and then to the paintgun.

BREECH DROP LOADING

Guns using breech loading systems load into an area larger than the inner diameter of the barrel. The ball must then be up into the barrel.

BREECH LOCK SYSTEM

A design that prevents the paintgun from being accidentally pumped twice before it is fired once. Breech locking guns must be fired before the gun can be pumped again.

BUTT PLATE

A device that fits on to the end of a tank allowing it to be used as a shoulder stock.

CALIBER

With respect to a paintball the diameter of a circular section. With reference to a paintgun the diameter of the bore of a gun taken as a unit of measurement.

CALIFORNIA STYLE

A style of constant air system developed in California in the late 1980's that consisted of a paintgun, a 'L' shape shoulder stock with a constant air tank holder located on the bottom side of it, a constant air tank of either 7 or 10 ounce in size with a Thermo on/off valve that would be held in the shoulder stock's tank holder and a hose with fittings that would connect the tank to the paintgun.

CARBON DIOXIDE

Also known as CO_2. A colorless, odorless, incombustible gas that has many purposes such as dry ice, the carbonation in carbonated beverages, and in fire extinguishers. CO_2 is present in the atmosphere and formed during respiration. CO_2 is a compound gas made of oxygen and carbon. CO_2 stores it's energy when it is in a liquid state and releases it into a usable force through expansion into a gas. Used in paintguns as a pressurized gas (power source) for shooting paintballs out of the paintgun's barrel. With respect to semi auto paintguns, CO_2 is also used for recocking the paintgun.

CGA

Denotes Compressed Gas Association. Usually used to refer to a cylinder valve outlet connection detailed in the CGA pamphlet V-1.

CHECK VALVE

Allows substance (such as gas, liquid or solids) to flow in only one direction. Once passed the check valve the substance cannot flow back through check valve.

CHRONOGRAPH

Electronic device that measures the speed of an object directed across it.

CO_2

The abbreviation for Carbon Dioxide.

CONSTANT AIR

A terminology developed in California in the late 1980's. It refers to the use of a refillable gas tank that is connected to a paintgun and supplies the CO_2 gas necessary to power the operation of the gun. The term "Constant Air" was derived from the fact that the paintgun would have a prolonged supply of gas and would be able to get 300–1000 shots per tank of gas, depending on size of tank and type of gun. This was opposed to paintguns that used 12 gram CO_2 cartridges and only got 15–25 shots per cartridge on the average.

CRITICAL TEMPERATURE

The temperature above which liquid phase cannot exist.

CRITICAL PRESSURE

The saturation vapor pressure at the Critical Temperature.

CYCLE RATE

Indicates the number of cycles a paintgun can perform per second.

DETENT, BALL

Sometimes call Ball stop, anti-doubler, wire nubbin. A device that keeps no more than one paintball from loading into the chamber of a paintgun when the paintgun is executing one cycle. It does this by maintaining the paintball in a stationary position until the paintguns bolt pushes the paintball into the barrel of the gun.

DEW POINT

The temperature and pressure at which the liquefaction of a vapor begins.

DIRECT FEED

A system by which paintballs are fed directly into the paintgun chamber or barrel via a feed nipple. The feed nipple is usually fastened to side of the paintgun at a 45 degree angle. Feed nipples on pump action guns are usually 1" in diameter and feed nipples on semi auto paintguns are usually 7/8" in diameter.

DISK, RUPTURE

A small copper disk in the valve of a tank that is designed to rupture if the pressure in the tank becomes too great. The rupture disk is usually held in place by a safety plug that has vent holes in it.

DONKEY

Slang for ASA Adapter.

DOT

Abbreviation for Department of Transportation whose Title 49, Code of Federal Regulations regulate the movement of hazardous materials.

DOUBLE ACTION

Requiring only one pull of the trigger to cock and fire.

ELBOW

Slang for hopper adapter.

EXPANSION CHAMBER

A device which conditions CO_2 gas by allowing it to expand before it enters the paintgun's valve system.

FEED NIPPLE

Also known as Feed port. The feed nipple is a short tube that is connected to the paintgun housing at an angle of 45 degrees. It provides the passage by which paintballs move from the paintball hopper, through the hopper adapter, which attaches to the feed nipple, and into the chamber of the paintgun. Commonly, feed nipples for pump action paintguns are one inch in diameter, while semi auto paintguns have seven eighths inch feed nipples.

FEED PLUG

A plug at the bottom of a power feeder that angles the balls into the feed port. It can also be turned to stop the balls from feeding into your gun.

FEED TUBE

A paintball storage container tubular in form, closed at one end and open at other end with some type of lid covering the opening. When playing paintball the player uses the feed tube to reload his paintgun's hopper.

FEEDER

Slang for hopper.

FILL STATION

An apparatus consisting of at least one valve used for exhausting pressurized fill hose, a fill hose and some type of fill adapter for connecting a constant air tank to one end of the hose. It is used for filling smaller constant air tanks with liquid CO_2 from larger siphon fill tank. The large siphon fill tank is usually 50 to 60 pounds in volume weight.

FITTING, ELBOW, (90 DEGREE)

A fitting that allows the connection of two items at a 90 degree angle to each other. Such as a CA hose to make a ASA adapter or paintgun.

FLAG STATION

With reference to the game of paintball, this is a team's base camp and is the location where a team's flag is kept. It is also the location where a team must return the opposing team's flag in order to win the game.

FLANK

1. The extreme right or left side of an army or fleet.

2. To stand or be placed or posted at the flank or side of.

3. To defend or guard at the flank.

4. To menace or attack the flank of.

FOGGING UP

This refers to those times when a person's breathing and lack of movement will cause the lenses of a persons goggles to fog over, severely reducing visibility.

FORE GRIP

A horizontal grip generally located on the front of a gun. This grip is generally grasped with the players off hand; i.e. the hand not on the trigger frame; to stabilize the gun for shooting.

F.P.S.

Abbreviation for 'feet per second'. This is the standard method in the U.S. for determining the speed at which a paintgun is shooting.

GAS EFFICIENCY

Refers to the amount of shots a gun gets in relation to the amount of liquid CO_2 it uses. Similar to miles per gallon; i.e. getting 350 shots from a seven ounce constant air tank.

GOGGLES

Eye protection worn by players to prevent eye damage. Paintball goggles are specifically designed for the sport of paintball and should not be substituted with goggles made for any other application other than paintball.

GOING LIQUID

Refers to liquid CO_2 entering the paintgun before it has had a chance to expand into a gas or vapor.

GRIPS

Components that fit on the paintgun grip frame and provide surface area by which the shooter may grip the gun. Grips are replaceable on many types of paintguns. Different styles of grips can provide greater comfort and ease of use for the individual paintball player. Different styles of grips include rubber, wood, and wraparound types.

HAMMER

Also known as the lower bolt or the striker. This component, when released from the cocked position, strikes the valve assembly and forces it open. When this striking of the valve assembly by the hammer occurs, CO_2 is allowed to pass through the valve assembly from the gas source to the paintgun barrel.

HAMMER (DOWN)

Refers to pulling the trigger, putting paint on someone is a sudden and intense manner, seizing the moment on offense by showering a target with paint.

HAMMER SEAR

The part of a gun that retains the hammer in a fixed position, usually under main spring pressure. When the trigger is pulled by the shooter's finger, it pushes against the sear allowing it to release the hammer and thus allowing the hammer to strike the valve assembly.

HARNESS

The combination of straps, pouches and other parts forming the working gear worn by a paintball player to carry paintball, CO_2 cartridges, tanks, squeegee and anything else he/she requires to play the game of paintball.

HOSE

In paintball a hose is used to transfer gas from one component to another. Such as from a constant air tank to a ASA adapter on a paintgun.

HONE

A tool that is mechanically rotated and has abrasive tip(s) for polishing or enlarging holes to precise dimensions.

HOPPER

A container used to hold paintballs, usually with a lid that covers the opening where the paintballs are loaded into it, and has a feed nipple at it's bottom.

HOSING

Refers to consistent rapid firing. A tactic typically used when pinning down an opposing player.

HYDROSTATIC TEST

A container test required at definite intervals by DOT to determine the wall thickness via measuring elastic expansion. Purpose of the test is to assure the container is safe for continued use.

I.D.

Abbreviation for inner diameter.

IN-LINE CONFIGURATION

Refers to the manner in which the bolt and hammer of a paintgun are positioned in relation to each other. An in-line configuration indicates that the bolt and hammer are in line with each other one behind the other.

LENSES, THERMAL

A dual lens system. The outer lens is made of a super hard polycarbonate material. The inner lens is made of a different polycarbonate composition that allows anti fog jell coat to stick to it. The two lenses are attached to each other by means of a rubber gasket that makes an air tight seal between the two. The space between the two lenses is called a thermal barrier and helps to reduce fogging on the inner lens.

LOADER

Slang for hopper feed tube.

LIQUID

Slang for CO_2 in liquid form.

MUZZLE

The mouth, or end for discharge, of the barrel of a gun, pistol, etc.

MUZZLE BREAK

1. A pattern of holes or slots machined into the end of a barrel that act as exhaust ports.

2. A machined add on part with a pattern of holes or slots machined into it that fastens to the end of a barrel either by press fit or set screw fatteners.

MUZZLE VELOCITY

The speed at which a paintball is traveling when it leaves the muzzle of a paintgun barrel.

NELSON BASED

Refers to pump guns (most pump guns) that were designed after the original 007. Nelson based guns have an in-line bolt and hammer system.

NITROGEN (N₂)

Refers to Nitrogen gas. A colorless, odorless, relatively non-reactive gas which is compressed to high pressures. The difference between Nitrogen gas and Co_2 is that Nitrogen is measured by pressure while Co_2 is measured by weight.

N.P.T.

Refers to normal temperature and pressure which is defined as 700 F and 14.696 PSI.

O.D.

Abbreviation for Outer Diameter. Outer diameter refers to distance across an object.

O-RING

A ring of pliable material, as rubber or neoprene, used as a gasket.

OFF SET SIGHT RAIL

A sight rail that is mounted at an angle away from top dead center of paintgun body. The off set sight rail allows a sight to be mounted so that it is unobstructed by other parts of the paintgun.

PAINTBALL

A round capsule filled with brightly colored water based dye that is designed to break upon impact leaving a splat mark on the object it hits. Paintball sizes are .50 Cal., .62 Cal. and .68 Cal., the last being the most current size and readily available. The .68 caliber paintball offers much better range, accuracy, and breakability due to its' size and mass.

PAINTBALL GUN

A mechanical device, usually powered by Co_2 gas, used to propel paintballs.

PAINT CHECK

The time at which a player is checked for splat mark(s). A paint check may be called by referee or player, but may be only invoked by a referee and game may only be restarted by referee. Misuse of the paint check rule by a player is cause for that player to be removed from current game.

POWER FEED

A feed nipple design that incorporates the blow-back from the paintball gun to increase the rate at which paintballs are fed into the paintgun. Most power feeds are designed into the paintguns, but there are some after market bolt on power feeds available for guns like the VM-68 series of paintgun and others.

POWERLET

An icon developed by the air gun industry for Co_2 cartridge. In paintball, it refers to 12 gram Co_2 cartridge.

PRESSURE REGULATOR

Regulates the pressure of gas flowing through it. Some regulators are preset to p.s.i., and some are adjustable.

PSI

Abbreviation for pounds per square inch.

PULL PIN

A pin fastener which can be removed quickly to speed disassembly of a player's paintgun.

QUICK CHANGER

A device that is either a part of the paintgun or a separate unit that connects to the gun, usually via the ASA adapter. It allows the rapid loading and unloading of a 12 gram CO_2 cartridge.

QUICK DISCONNECT

Usually made of stainless steel or brass, this unit is composed of two parts, a male fitting and a female coupler that connect together to form a air tight connection. In paintball the quick disconnect is used by the player to quickly disconnect the CO_2 source, such as a remote system, from the paintgun.

RECEIVER

The main body of a paintgun where the bolt and hammer are usually housed. A gun's feed nipple is typically a part of your receiver.

REMOTE SYSTEM

Also known as a "Remote" or "Remote Set-Up". The system usually consists of a constant air tank that is carried on the player's body, usually in a pouch or fanny pack, and a high pressure gas line with quick disconnect and all the fittings required to connect it to the paintgun.

RESTICLE

A network of fine lines, wires, or the like placed in the focus of the eyepiece of an optical instrument.

RIFLING, EXTERNAL

Also know as External porting. With reference to paintball gun barrels, it is a spiral hole pattern which is drilled into the barrel. When a paintball is shot through a ported barrel, the ports allow the air in front of the paintball to escape as the paintball pushes forward. The loss of air restriction in front of the paintball allows the paintball to shoot straighter and further. The barrel porting also breaks up the sound made when the gun is fired, thus the paintgun operates much quieter.

RIFLING, INTERNAL

Grooves or raised points in a barrel that are either straight or spiraled in pattern.

SHERIDAN BASED

Refers to those guns that are based on or are similar to the original Sheridan family of guns. A Sheridan based gun is generally discernible by its stacked design. The hammer and valve system are in the lower section while the bolt is in the upper section.

SIGHT RAIL

Allows the mounting of a sighting system to a paintgun.

SIGHT RAIL, RAISED

A sight rail that is raised up off the body of the gun. The purpose for this is to allow the shooter a better field of view.

SIGHT, RED DOT

An optical sighting device powered by a battery that produces a red dot reticle. Red dot sights do not project a dot on target.

SIGHT RINGS

Adapters to mount your sight to the sight rail. (Note. Different rings are required to mount different sights to different guns.)

SKIRMISH

1. A fight between small bodies of troops.
2. Any brisk conflict or encounter.

SKIRMISH LINE

1. The invisible line between two opposing teams that have confronted each other.
2. A formation taken where by players are positioned beside each other in a line.

SLIMED BARREL

Slang for when a ball has broken in the barrel of a paintgun and coated it with paint. A slimed barrel will not shoot straight.

SPECIFIC HEAT

Amount of heat required to raise a unit mass of substance one degree of temperature at either constant pressure or constant volume. Usually expressed in BTU per pound per degree F.

SPECIFIC VOLUME

Volume of a unit mass of substance at a given temperature. Expressed as cubic feet per pound at 700 F.

SPLATTER

The residue sprayed on a player by a paintball when it makes impact with a object close to that player.

SPRING, MAIN

The spring that drives the hammer.

SPRING VALVE

The spring that closes the valve after it has been opened by the hammer.

SQUAD

Any small group of persons engaged in a common enterprise; a team or sub-group within a team.

SQUEEGEE

A device used to clean the barrel of a paintgun.

STACKED CONFIGURATION

Refers to the manner in which the bolt and hammer are positioned in relation to each other inside the paintgun receiver. A stacked configuration indicates that the bolt and hammer are stacked one on top of the other.

STICK FEED

A gravity feeder, usually made out of PVC material, which holds the balls stacked in a line one on top of the other.

STOCK 'L'

A shoulder stock that is shaped like an 'L' laying on its side. This stock usually fastens to the bottom of the paintgun's grip frame and may have a constant air tank holder attached to it.

STOCK 'T'

A shoulder stock that is shaped like a 'T' laying on its side. This stock usually fastens to the bottom of the paintgun's grip frame and may have a constant air tank holder attached to it.

SUPPRESSOR

A tubular device that is press fitted onto the front end of a paintgun barrel designed to reduce the amount of sound that is made by the gun when it is fired. Also known as Silencer.

TANK, CHILLED

Refers to a tank that has become very cold due to rapid pressure loss. This may be caused by rapid firing or purposefully releasing the remaining air pressure in a tank. (Note, a tank must be chilled before it can be filled with Co_2).

TANK, CONSTANT AIR

A container or structure for holding a liquid or gas. In paintball a tank is made up from two components, a valve and a bottle.

TANK, ANTI-SIPHON

A tank designed to allow only vaporous CO_2 gas to exit the tank through the tank valve.

TANK, SIPHON

A tank specifically designed to draw liquid CO_2 from the bottom of the tank. This is accomplished by a gas line that is attached to rear end of the tank valve and weighting down the other end of the gas line so that it remains located in the bottom area of the tank.

THREAD SAVER

Also know as Bottle cap. A protective cap that screws onto a tank valve. This keeps the valve from being damaged while not in use.

TOOL, VELOCITY ADJUSTING

Also called Adjusting tool. A tool used specifically for adjusting the velocity of a paintgun.

TOURNAMENT CAP

A cap which covers a gun's velocity adjuster so that the velocity cannot be adjusted during game play, Normally required for tournament play.

TRIGGER SHOE

After market product that fits on the trigger of a gun to provide the trigger finger with more surface area to grip the trigger and comfortable feel.

TWELVE GRAM

Slang for 12 gram CO_2 cartridge.

TUBE, PAINTBALL

A small cigar-like tube used to carry 10 paintballs.

TUNNEL VISION

Refers to a player who has focused so intently on the player or players directly in front of him that he is not aware of players moving to the side of him.

UN (United Nations) Number

The DOT (Department of Transportation) Number found on the Cylinder (bottle) label. For example UN1066, the "UN" prefix to this number indicates that 1066 is recognized throughout the world as identifying nitrogen. Sometimes "NA" (North America) will appear as a prefix. NA numbers are recognized in the USA and Canada.

VELOCITY ADJUSTER

A component of a paintgun (usually a set screw) that when turned in either clockwise or counter clockwise direction will increase or decrease the paintguns muzzle velocity.

VALVE

Any device for halting or controlling the flow of something, such as a gas or liquid, through a pipe, out of a bottle neck, or other passage.

VALVE PORTING

The enlarging or drilling of additional holes in a valve body so that more gas will be released when valve system is opened.

VALVE SYSTEM

All the internal parts in the paintgun which control the flow of gas through the paintgun.

WRENCH, ALLEN

A hexagonal tool which comes in various sizes and is used to turn screw fasteners such as hex or button head screws. They are also used to turn anything that has a hexagonal hole. In paintball they are used to adjust the paintball gun's velocity as well as disassemble it.

Where to Find the Game You Love

A state-by-state and international listing of fields, manufacturers, distributors and shops involved in the paintball industry

U.S.A. PLAYING FIELDS & SHOPS

ALABAMA

Advanced AL Adventures
7880 Bear Creek Rd.
Sterrett, AL 35243
205-672-2860

Paintball Pro Shop
7880 Bear Creek Rd.
Sterrett, AL 35243
205-967-8661

Splat Alley
705 McKinley Ave.
Huntsville, AL 35801
205-539-5959

ARIZONA

The Command Post
1432 N. Scottsdale Rd.
Tempe, AZ 85281
602-970-6329

The Command Post
2734 West Bell Rd. #1346
Phoenix, AZ 85053
602-863-2569

Desert Fox Paintball
9651 S. Houghton
Tuscon, AZ 85747
520-574-9232

Survival & Army Surplus
15231 N Cave Creek Rd.
Phoenix, AZ 85032
602-482-6663

Westworld Paintball
2920 W. Thomas Rd.
Phoenix, AZ 85017
602-447-8200

ARKANSAS

First Assault
Route 51
Arkadelphia, AR 71923
501-245-3549

Paintball Arkansas
Mayflower, AR 72106
501-470-4400

CALIFORNIA

ABC Paintball
535 Salmar Ave., Unit B
Campbell, CA 95008
408-866-9222

Action Paintball
240 North Broadway
Escondido, CA 92025
760-738-1097

Adventure Game
3604 Ross Ave.
San Jose, CA 95124
408-723-1455

Adventure Game Supp
17618 Sherman Way
Van Nuys, CA 91405
818-708-3384

American Canyon Pball
Jungle, Vallejo, CA
www.paintballjungle.com
707-552-2426

Auction Surplus
512 South Blosser Rd.
Santa Maria, CA 93454
805-928-7408

Bear Creek Pursuit Pball
584 Cestaric Dr.
Milpitas, CA 95035
408-946-7676

Bud Orr's Pro Shop
13517 Alondra Blvd.
Santa Fe Springs, CA 90670
310-407-2898

Cambrian Surplus
2059 Woodard Rd.
San Jose, CA 95124
408-377-6953

Central Coast Pball Park
4765 Santa Margarita Lk
Santa Margarita, CA 93453
805-481-1476

Central Coast Pball Park
1554 West Beach Street
Arroyo Grande, CA 93420
805-481-1476

Check Yourself Paintball
5708C Hollister Ave.
Goleta, CA 93117
805-967-6190

Delta Archery's Splat Div
1820-D Arnold lnd. Way
Concord, CA 94520
510-685-7141

Eagles's Nest
PO Box 1788
Valley Center, CA 92082
619-749-0281

Gramps & Grizzly
7203 Arlington Ave.,
Riverside, CA 92503
909-359-4859

Gramps & Grizzly
2085 River Rd. #B
Norco, CA 91760
909-278-0173

Hobby World
18575 Valley Blvd.
Bloomington, CA 92316
714-824-1747

Indoor Speedball
15000 Avalon
Gardena, CA 90248
213-323-1021

I & I Sports Co., Inc.
1524 W. 178th St.
Gardena, CA 90248
310-715-6800

I & I Sports Co., Inc.
15349 A Los Gatos Blvd.
Los Gatos, CA 95032
408-358-9774, 358-9864

I & I Sports Co., Inc.
18232 E. Gale Ave.
Industry, CA 91748
626-810-5523

I & I Sports Co., Inc.
2957 S. Sepulveda Blvd.
Los Angeles, CA 90064
310-444-9988

I & I Sports Co., Inc.
19751 S. Fugueroa St.
Carson, CA 90745

I & I Sports Co., Inc.
5637 Cottle Rd.
San Jose, CA 95123
408-224-6800

J&S Surplus
Highway 1 & Struve Rd.
Moss Landing, CA 95039
408-724-0588

Jungle Island Pball Pk
Lake Elsinore, CA
Lake St. @ 15 FWY
1-800-5 JUNGLE

Jungle Supply
2840 E. College
Visalia, CA 93292
209-636-3128

KAPP Paintball
65 Brockwood Ave.
Santa Rosa, CA 95405
707-571-1077

KAPP Paintball
57 W. Barham Ave.
Santa Rosa, CA 95407
707-571-8068;571-81497

Kingsmen Shop
201 North Hill St.
Oceanside, CA 92054
619-722-5108

Finding Paintball

Maximum Pball Supp.
4741 N. Blackstone Ave.
Fresno, CA 93726
559-222-3814

North County Paintball
San Marcos, CA 92069
619-440-5944; 273-4444

Outdoor World
1440 41st Ave.
Capitola, CA 95010
408-479-1501

Outdoor World
3903 Santa Rita Rd.
Pleasanton, CA 94566
510-463-3221

Outdoor World
222 No. Freemont St.
Montery, CA 93940
408-373-3615

Pacific Paintball Supply
3181 Cleveland Ave. #C
Santa Rosa, CA 95403
707-571-1077

Paintball Paradise
260 Shotwell St.
San Francisco, CA 94110
415-552-5335

Palmer's Pursuit Shop
3951 Development Dr.
Unit #3
Sacramento, CA 95838
916-923-9676

SC Village
River Road & Hellman St.
Corona, CA 91720
949-489-9000

Skan-Line Game Supp
1677 Superior Ave, Unit H
Costa Mesa. CA 92627
714-645-LINE

Skirmish. Inc.
7361 Reseda
Reseda, CA 91335
818-705-6322

Spotcha Paintball
828 N. 2nd St.
El Cajon, CA 92021

Strategic Game Supply
10680 Katella Ave.
Anaheim, CA 92804
714-772-6422

Surplus City
4106 Franklin Blvd.
Sacramento, CA 95820
916-485-1120

Survival Sports
4800 Minnesota Ave.
Fair Oaks, CA 95628
916-965-1770

Tagline
9077 Arrow Route 100
Cucamonga, CA 91730
909-481-7753,
481-7754 fax

T.A.S.O.
15950 Downey Ave.
Paramount, CA 90723
310-531-0515

Unique Sporting
10680 Katella Ave.
Anaheim, CA 92804
714-772-6422

Velocity Paintball
4248 B Bonita Rd.
Bonita, CA 91902
619-470-3533

Velocity Paintball
12623 Poway Rd.
Poway, CA 92064
619-513-2778

Warped Sportz
11919 W. Pico Blvd.
Los Angeles, CA 90064
310-914-9222,
914-9511 fax

COLORADO

Adventure Game
425 Thames Dr.
Colo. Springs, CO 80906
303-893-4263

Dragon Man's Pball Pk
1225 Dragon Man Dr.
Colo. Springs CO 80929
719-683-2200

Pro-Star Sports
PO Box 1280
Littleton, CO 80160
303-972-4113

Rocky Mountain Pball
430 W. Fillmore
Co. Springs, CO 80907
719-473-3725; 473-3576 fax

Rocky Mountain Pball
7500 So. University #110
Littleton, CO 80122
303-689-7608

RMT Sports
PO Box 1280
Littleton, CO 80160
303-972-4113

Warped Sportz
3970 S. Broadway
Englewood, CO 80110
303-806-9721

CONNECTICUT

The Gun Rack
240A Rt. 21, Cnty. Home
Rd. Thompson, CT 06277
203-928-1512

Hogan's Alley Paintball
445 State St.
North Haven, CT 06473
203-288-2746

Hogan's Alley Paintball
998 No. Colony Rd.
Meriden, CT 06450
203-238-2875

Paintball Plus
5 Padanaram Rd.
Danbury, CT 06811
203-730-8850

Splattown, USA
223 Merrow Rd. Rt. 195
Tolland, CT 06084
860-870-9737

DELAWARE

Paintball Adventures LLC
1438 Woodmill Dr.
Dover, DE 19904
302-736-5777

FLORIDA

Elite Forces Field
Cowcreek Road
Edgewater, FL
904-767-2131

Extreme Rage Al Sports
3598 Fowler St.
Ft. Myers, FL 33901
941-939-0911
939-5141 fax

Florida Paintball Center
8440 Ulmerton, #500
Largo, FL 34641
813-538-9946

GI Jeff's
5257 S Ridgewood Ave.
Allandale, FL 32123
904-767-2131

G&H Sterling LTD
8362 Pines Blvd., #290
Pembroke Pines, 33024
305-438-7571

Guerrilla Games
111 W. Olympia Ave.
Punta Gorda, FL 33950
813-627-8865

Hi-Tec Paintball Park
PO Box 301
Bradenton, FL 34206
941-746-5866

Holly Army Navy
3440 Ave. G, N.W.
Winter Haven, FL 33880
813-967-5920

Paintball Experts
70 W. 49th St.
Hialeah, FL 33012
305-823-6892

Paintball Park
8240 Durrance Rd.
Ft. Myers, FL
941-939-0911, 598-1015

Pursuit Paintball Games
5132 Conroy Rd., #918
Orlando, FL 32811
407-843-3456

Paintball World
3445 Vineland Rd.
Orlando, FL 32811
407-648-8404

South Florida Paintball
7232 S.W. 8th St. Ste. 2
Miami, FL 33144
305-267-1122

**South Florida
Indoor Pball**
2801 SW 31st Ave.
Pembroke Park, FL 33009
954-893-8284

Space Coast
3600 Garden St.
Titusville, FL 32796
321-264-4484

Splat Attack
10129 SW 72nd St.
Miami, FL 33173
305-412-9991

Sunny's at Sunset
Sunrise, FL 33322
305-741-2070

Survival City
111 W. Olympia Ave.
Punta Gorda, FL 33950
813-639-1100

Tropic Trades
9696 S.W. 40th St.
Miami, FL 33165
305-221-1371

Wayne's World of Pball
4841 S. Pine St.
Ocala, FL 34480
352-401-1801

Xtreme Paintball
3561 NW 9th Ave.
Oakland Park, FL 33309
305-564-5451

GEORGIA

A-1 Pball Forest & Supply
W. Pine Chapel Rd.
Calhoun, GA 30701
706-625-0072

Appalachian Paintball
1116 S. Thornton Ave.
Dalton, GA 30720
706-226-1765

Bay's Paintball
501 Eve St.
Augusta, GA 30904
706-733-1055

Georgia Paintball
1289 Roswell Rd.
Marrietta, GA 3062
770-971-8040

Indoor Paint Games
285A Lake Mirror Rd.
Forest Park, GA 30050
404-361-6740

Insane Paintball
986 Battlefield Pkwy.
Ft. Oglethorpe, GA 30742
706-866-2121

**Mountain Adventure
Games**
123 So. Campus Rd.
Lookout Mtn., GA 30750
706-820-4419

Outer Limits
220 Holbrook Dr. SW
Rome, GA 30165
706-234-9896

Splat Zone Indoor
5050 Jimmy Carter Blvd.
Norcross, GA 30093
404-441-9333

Wildfire Paintball
1989 Tucker Ind. Rd.
Tucker, GA 30084
770-493-8978

Wildfire Paintball
7301 Campbellton Rd.
Atlanta, GA 30331
770-493-8978

Wildfire Paintball
2641 Hesterton Rd.
Madison, GA
770-493-8978

Wildfire Paintball
2191 Rabbit Hill Cr.
Dacula, GA 30211
770-493-8978

HAWAII

Xlent Services
PO Box 2271
Ewa Beach, HI 96706
808-671-1110

IDAHO

Winders
5515 E. Iona Rd.
Iona, ID 83427
208-523-2475

Walter Middy's MMOV
6759 Supply Way
Boise, ID 83705
208-429-1276

ILLINOIS

Air America
2275 S. Mt. Prospect Rd.
Des Plaines, IL 60018
847-545-9999

Bad Boyz Toyz
888 So. Rt. 59, #104
Naperville, IL 60565
630-355-8808

Bad Boyz Toyz
17913 Torrence Ave.
Lansing, IL 60438
708-418-8888

Bad Boyz Toyz
15160 LaGrange Rd.
Orland Park, IL 60462
708-460-1122

Bad Boyz Toyz Skokie
7135 Central Ave.
Skokie, IL 60077
847-679-9125

Bad Boyz Toyz
700 N Milwaukee, #133.
Vernon Hills, IL 60061
847-362-4848

Challenge Games-Aurora
2256 Fox Valley Ctr D21A
Aurora, IL 60504
630-499-1025,
499-1045 fax

Fox Paintball
737 Soute Route 31
West Dundee, IL 60118
847-426-1041

Fox River Pball Sports
1891 N. Farnsworth
Aurora, IL 60505
630-585-5651

Operation Paintball
15N850 Brier Hill Rd.
Hampshire, IL 60140
630-736-9107

Pursuit Adventure
956 S. Bartlett Rd. # 282
Bartlett, IL 60103
630-736-9107, 736-9132

Rockford Pball
7821 No. 2nd St.
Macheseney Park, 61115
815-282-2992

Strange Ordnance
914 Greenwood Ave.
Glenview, IL 60025
708-998-8312

Video Smideo
10408 Rte. 47
Huntley, IL 60142
847-669-3225

INDIANA

Adventure Zone
8641 E. 116th St.
Fishers, IN 46038

Apocalypse Paintball
302 W. Gilmore
Angola, IN 46703
260-668-1022

Blast Camp
608 Third Street
Hobart, IN 46342
219-947-7733

Blast Camp
109 9th St.
Michigan City, IN 46360
219-947-7733

Dark Armies
2525 N Shadelands Ave.
Indianapolis, IN 46219
317-353-1987

Fantasy Fields Paintball
PO Box 194
Denver, IN 46926
765-985-3068

Gator Joe's Pball Supp
1223 S. Girls School Rd.
Indianapolis, IN 46231
317-247-0410

Indianapolis Army & Navy
6032 E. 21st
Indianapolis, IN 46219
317-356-0858

Indy Extreme
9508 Haver Way
Indianapolis, IN 46240
317-566-9115

Michiana Paintball Club
In&Outdoor Fields, Store
Scottsdale Mall, S Bend
219-291-2540

Paint Ball Sports
821 W. Coliseum Blvd.
Ft. Wayne, IN 46808
260-471-4334

Warped Sportz
1515 W. 81st Ave.
Merrillville, IN 46410
219-736-6111

IOWA

ICU Paintball Worgamz Inc.
4489 N.W. 2nd Ave.
Des Moines, IA 50313
515-282-9080

North Iowa Arms
810 N. 8th Street
Clear Lake, IA 50428
515-357-3545

Total Paintball
324 E. 4th St.
Davenport, IA 52801
319-324-0276,
322-4262 fax

Velocity Paintball
1324 5th St.
Coralville, IA 52241
319-351-4245

KANSAS

Drop Zone Extreme Sports
5849 S.W. 21st St.
Topeka, KS 66064
1-785-228-9200

Drop Zone Extreme Sports
811 East 23rd St. Ste. E
Lawrence, KS 66046
785-841-1884

Drop Zone Extreme Sports
407 So. Parker St.
Olathe, KS 66061
913-768-0200

Victory Paintball
95th & Renner Blvd.
Lenexa, KS 66212
913-397-0966

KENTUCKY

American Pball Games
8471 US 42, Box #6
Florence, KY 41042
888-440-1088

Crossfire Paintball
4111 Dixie Highway
Elsmere, KY 41018
606-342-9FUN

Corssfire Paintball
128 Mill St., Rte. 50
Milford, OH 45150
513-576-1112

Jimmy Elliott Firearms
Box 156, Poorhouse Rd.
Gravel Switch, KY 40328
606-332-7728

Relentless Pursuit Pball
1603 W. Douglas
Wichita, KS 67213
316-264-5455, 5255

LOUISIANA

**OFF Limits
Extreme Sports**
608 Robinson Rd.
Elm Grove, LA 71051
318-987-2696

MAINE

Blast'em Paintball
54 New Country Rd.
Saco, ME 04072
207-284-8205

**Crossfire Pball
Adventures**
452 River Rd.
Mexico, ME 04257

**PG's Adrenaline
Sports Park**
Jumpsight Rd.
Lebanon, ME
603-765-3984

Van Houten Army/Navy
Lower Cross Rd. Box 130
E. Lebanon, ME 04027
207-457-1224

Woodland Warriors
PO Box 130
E Lebanon, ME 04027
207-457-1224

MARYLAND

The Company Store
13015 Wisteria Dr.
Germantown, MD 20874
301-515-2680

The Company Store
2303 K E. Forest Dr.
Annapolis, MD 21401
410-571-1156

MD Surplus & Outdoor
Route 301 & Mermarr Rd
White Plains, MD 20695
301-645-0077

Paintball Discounters
10176 Balti Nat'l Pike #215
Ellicott City, MD 21042
410-750-1502

Paintball Wholesalers
2400 Bear Run Rd.
Taneytown, MD 21787
410-756-1006

Paintball Wholesalers
205 C Bucheimer Rd.
Frederick, MD 21701
301-624-4399

Paintball Wholesalers
38 West Main St.
Westminster, MD 21157
410-840-8669

Timber Ridge Pball Club
14432 Tollgate Ridge
Hancock, MD 21750
301-678-5451

Warped Sportz
118 Shawan Rd. #281
Hunt Valley, MD 21031
410-527-1522

MASSACHUSETTS

Action Games
Tewsbury, MA 01876
508-459-8699

ADCO Sales Inc.
4 Draper St.
Woburn, MA 01801
781-93501799

Boston Paintball Supp
131 Beverly St.
Boston, MA 02114
617-742-6612, 4530 fax

Boston Paintball Supp. W
50-60 Worcester Rd. #9E
Framingham, MA 01701
508-879-6621

Cape Cod Paintball
173 Claypond Rd.
Bourne, MA 02532
508-759-5130

Horror Show Paintball
946 So. Washington St.
So. Attleboro, MA 02703
508-399-1111, 399-6311
horrorshowinc@aol.com

Paintball Heaven
1221 Bedford St.
Bridgewater, MA. 02324
508-697-5808

P&L Paintball
159 Bay Rd.
No. Easton, MA 02356
508-238-1365

P&L Paintball
436 Bay Rd.
Taunton, MA 02780
508-880-8822

P&L Paintball
491 W Main St.
Avon, MA 02322
508-897-0022

P&L Paintball/Apache
Spring Lane
Holbrook, MA 02343
508-897-0022

P&L Indoor Paintball
45 Emerson Ave.
Brockton, MA 02301
508-897-0022

Randolph Paintball
410 South St.
Randolph, MA 02368
781-986-2255; 986-2254

Ultimate Adventure
7 Sweetwater St.
Saugus, MA 01906
617-231-0114

MICHIGAN

Action Outdoors
1622 E. Michigan
Jackson, MI
517-783-4434

Action Sports Paintball
710 S. Main.
Cheboygan, MI 49721
616-627-3474
fax 627-7477

Atomix Paintball
1020 Decker Rd.
Walled Lake, MI 48390
248-926-9980

Big Time Sports
26 1/2 So. Monroe St.
Coldwater, MI 49036
517-278-2770

Bullseye Army Surplus
4907 South Division
Grand Rapids, MI 49548
616-530-2080

Chaos Paintball
409 Upton (Field)
Battle Creek, MI 49015
616-968-6399

Colors Field
12874 N. Maple Island
Fremont, MI 49412
616-924-6561

Exotic Sportz Eazt
23944 Eureka Rd.
Taylor, MI 48180
734-287-6460

Exotic Sportz Wezt
125 Pearl St.
Pinckney, MI 48169
734-878-2002

Exotic Sportz Splatz
5312 Highland
Waterford, MI 48327
www.exoticsportz.com

Exotic Sportz Pro Shop
619 Pearl St.
Pinckney, MI 48169
734-878-2002

Harry's Army Surplus
201 E. Washington
Ann Arbor, MI 48l04
313-994-3572

**Hell Survivors Inc.
PlayField**
619 Pearl St.
Pinckney, MI 48l69
734-878-5656, 878-6540

Hole in the Wall
68111 16th Ave.
South Haven, MI 49090
616-637-8749

Hole in the Wall
8126 W. Main St.
Kalamazoo, MI 49009
269-353-2978

Killer Paintball
19590 Middlebelt Rd.
Livonia, MI 48334
248-615-0000

Lone Wolf Creek Pball
45129 Cass Ave.
Utica, MI 48317
313-739-1790

**Michigan Paintball
Outlet**
111 W. Genefee
Lapeer, MI 48446
810-245-1914

Outpost Pball Supplies
340 Morgan Lane
Lansing, MI 48912
517-332-1332

Outsiders Paintball
2341 S. Dort Hwy.
Flint, MI 48529
810-742-5057

R.J. Performance
1444 N. Irish Rd.
Davison, MI 48423
810-658-5274

Swan Creek Paintball
9550 Swan Creek
Saganaw, MI 48609
517-781-1416

MISSISSIPPI

Brass Eagle Retail Store
Mossy Oak Outlet Center
West Point, MS 39773
601-494-4500, 9544 fax

Warped Sportz
2752 Bienville Blvd.
Ocean Spring, MS 39564
877-WARPED1

MISSOURI

Dragon Arms Paintball
30845 Copperfield Rd.
Gravois Mills, MO 65037
573-372-2409

**Drop Zone Extreme
Sports**
7711 No. Oak Traffic Way
Gladstone, MO 64118
816-436-9994

Express Paintball Supp
3656 Hwy 61 S
Festus, MO 63028
314-937-4321

Jaegers Subsurface Pball
9300 Underground Dr.
Kansas City, MO 64162
816-452-6600

National Pro Shop
11142 Lindbergh Busi.
St. Louis, MO 63123
314-845-7079

**Owens Outpost
Field/Shop**
Hwy. 50
Warrensburg, MO 64063
816-850-6338

Paintball Mania Supplies
PO Box 528
Arnold, MO 63010
314-296-0964

Wacky Warriors
PO Box 414
Arnold, MO 63010
314-296-0964

MONTANA

Crossfire Paintball
PO Box 2255
St. Cloud, MN 56302
320-253-5630

NEBRASKA

Warped Sportz
108 E. 11th St.
Kearney, NE 68848
308-234-9277

NEVADA

National Pball Supp W
#102 750 Freeport Blvd.
Sparks, NV 89431
803-458-7221;
609-464-1068

NEW HAMPSHIRE

**Adventure Games Pball
Park & ProShop**
158 Deering Ctr. Rt 149
Weare, NH 03281
603-529-FLAG

**Adventure Games Pball
Supply Outlet**
297 S. Willow St.
Manchester, NH 03103
603-647-BALL

Beauia's Army/Navy
24 Canal St.
Laconia, NH 03246
603-524-1018

Boston Pball Supp North
101 Main St.
Salem, NH 03079
603-894-6359

Canobie Paintball
47 Roulston Rd.
Windham, NH 03087
603-893-1863

PG Xtreme West
140 Main St.
Keene, NH
1-866-749-8736

NEW JERSEY

ABC Pball Supp & Field
1745 Greenwood Lake Tpk.
Hewitt, NJ 07421
973-728-1762

ABC Pball Supp & Field
1216 Rt. 17 North
Ramsey, NJ 07446
201-327-6600

Del Hobbies Paintball
322-Artillery Ave.
Pedricktown, NJ 08067
856-299-6000

**Fireball Mountain
Old Bridge**
1959 Englishtown Rd.
Englishtown, NJ 08831
732-656-9566

Fireball Mountain No. H.
281 Meany Rd.
No. Hanover, NJ 08562
609-758-0855

Fireball Mountain Rt.1 SS
2819 Business Rte. 1
Lawrenceville, NJ 08648
609-219-1911

Impact Paintball
2037 Woodbridge Ave.
Edison, NJ 08817
732-339-0820

Indoor Pball Planet
107 Pleasant Ave. & Rt.
17N
Up. Sad River, NJ 07458
201-934-1100

N'tnl Pball Supp East
570 Mantua Blvd.
Mantua, NJ 08080
609-464-1068

On Target Sports Pball
505 No. White Pike
Lindenwold, NJ 08021
856-784-9130

**Outdoor Haven
Sport Goods**
Rt 206
Columbus, NJ 08022
609-267-0119

Paintball Depot Inc.
1451 Rt. 46
Ledgewood, NJ 07852
973-584-2220

Paintball Depot Inc.
Rt. 57, 3 miles west of
Hackettstown, NJ
www.paintballdepot.com

Ramsey Outdoor Stores
226 Rte. 17
Paramus, NJ 07652
201-261-5000

Stop Gun Paintball
567 Monmouth Rd.
Cream Ridge, NJ 08514
732-928-2810

NEW YORK

3 Guys Games & Pball
968 Rte. 9.
Queensbury, NY 12804
518-793-4587

3guysgames.com
3 Guys Games & Pball
175 Canada St. (Seasonal)
Lake George, NY 12845

3 Guys Games & Pball
331 Cornelia St #2A
Plattsburgh, NY 12901
518-561-6607

Adirondack Pball Games
PO Box 4550
Queensbury, NY 12804
518-792-8845

Army Navy Surplus
1158 George Urban Blvd.
Cheektowaga, NY 14225
716-684-8728

**Blizzard Paintball
Pro Shop**
95-D River Rd.
Harriman, NY 10926
845-782-9438

Cousins Deer Park
1912 Deer Park Ave.
Deer Park, NY 11729
631-243-1100

**Cousind Field Long
Island**
Granny Rd. (Outdoor)
Coram, NY 11727
1-800-FLAG-007

Cousins Field New Jersey
750 Route 539 (Outdoor)
Manchester, NJ 08759
1-800-FLAG-007

Cousins Field Plattekill
Camp Sunset Rd.
Plattekill, NY (Outdoor)
1-800-FLAG-007

Cousins Franklin Square
1157 Hempstead Tpke.
Franklin Sq., NY 11010
516-616-0520

**Cousins Indoor
Field&Pro**
114 Parkway Dr. South
Hauppauge, NY 11788
1-800-FLAG-007;
631-864-4776

Cousins Medford
2900 Route 112
Medford, NY 11763
631-698-3657

Cousins Mt. Kisco
159 East Main St.
Mt. Kisco, NY 10549
914-241-3294

**Cousins Paintball
Headquarters**
956 So. Second St.
Ronkonkoma, NY 11779
631-588-0366

Dragons Den Pball Supp
Poughkeepsie Plaza
Poughkeepsie, NY 12601
914-471-1401

GRC Paintball
VanAllen Rd.
Belfast, NY 14711
716-365-2470

HeadRush Paintball
6255 E. Taft Rd.
Syracuse, NY 13212
315-725-RUSH

HeadRush Paintball
State Rte. 49
Rome, NY 13440
headrushpaintball.com

High Velocity Paintball
239 S. Fehrway
Bay Shore, NY 11706
631-242-2096

Hudson Valley Paintball
15 Grand St.
Kingston, NY 12401
845-331-6777

Island Paintball
770 E. Jericho Tpke.
Huntington Sta., NY 11746
877-PAINTNY

Mark's Cycle Corner
154 Wickham Ave.
Middletown, NY 10940
914-343-4480

Mid Hudson Hobbies
2 North St.
Middletown, NY 10940
914-342-8697

Montgomery Sport. Goods
32 Union St. (Rt. 211)
Montgomery, NY 12549
845-457-4678

NYC Paintball Supply
l37 Ave. T
Brooklyn, NY 11223
718-714-0575

Outdoors Cabin
3211 Transit Rd.
Elma, NY 14059
716-656-9944

Paintball Adventure
10865 Wilson Rd.
Wolcott. NY 14590
315-587-4995

Paintball Game Supplies
160 Dispatch Dr.
E Rochester, NY 14445
716-383-5662

Paintball Madness
998 Wolf Lake Rd., Rt. 17E
RockHill, NY paint-
ballny,com
845-794-9365

P'ball Survival Game HQ
945 Coney Island Ave.
Brooklyn, NY 11230
718-462-9731

Palenville Paintball Games
Route 23A
Palenville, NY 12463
800-362-9695

Pro Paintball
10 Railroad St.
Victor, NY 14564
716-924-9930

Recon Challenge
390 Columbia Tpk.
Rensselaer, NY 12144
518-477-7156

Splatball The Game
PO Box 25351
Farmington, NY 14425
716-742-1486

Staten Island Pball Ctr.
2727 Arthur Kill Rd.
Staten Island, NY 10309
718-317-0101, 227-1400

NORTH CAROLINA

Black River Paintball
559 N. Raleigh St., Ste. D
Angier, NC 27501
910-639-9700
305-832-3892 fax

Gotcha Paintball
4339-C Falls of the Neuse
Raleigh, NC 27609
919-501-7770

Gotcha Parts Pball
176 Darius Pearce Rd.
Youngsville, NC
919-271-3367

Idol's Adventure Sport
Rockingham, NC 28379

NC Paintball/Midway
Hwy 52 S.@Hickory Tree
Winston-Salem, 27284
910-764-2701

No. Carolina Paintball Supp
1702 Spring Gordon Rd.
Greensboro, NC 27403
336-292-1102

Paintball Central
1814 Spring Garden St.
Greensboro, NC 27403
336-274-4002

Paintball Central
2602 Eric Ln.
Burlington, NC 27215
336-228-3800.

Paintball Central
6106 Burlington Rd.
Sedalia, NC
336-274-4002

Turbo Paintball
PO Box 12294
Jacksonville, NC 28546
910-324-6862

Wolverine Pball Adventures
441 N Lousisanna, #T
Asheville, NC 28806
828-254-4371

World of Paint Ball
6422 Wilkinson Blvd.
Belmont, NC 28012
704-825-5444

OHIO

Action Enterprises
5860 Lewis Ave.
Toledo, OH 43612
800-552-3089

Adrenaline Zone
810 West 13th St.
Lorraine, OH 44052
216-681-4445

Alternative Sports Supp
Valley Loop Rd.
Springfield, OH 45503
937-399-2403

Bull Creek Paintball
9703 Greensburg Pk.
Portage, OH 43451
419-266-4799

C0 Paintball Pro Shop
3069 Silver Dr.
Columbus, OH 43224
800-536-1104,
614-784-1104
www.copaintball.com

CO Pball Supp MailOrder
3069 Silver Dr.
Columbus, OH 43224
800-536-1104,
614-784-1104
www.copaintball.com

CO Pball Cleveland/Parma
5755 Ridge Rd.
Parma, OH 44129
440-842-8035
www.copaintball.com

CO Paintball Lima
1910 W. Robb
Lima, OH 45805
419-222-8892
www.copaintball.com

Combat Adventures
295 S. Second
Middleport, OH 45760
614-388-8601

Combat Zone
7060 S. TWP. Rd. 131
Tiffin, OH 44883
419-447-8424

Deer Run Paintball
17124 Harmon-Patrick Rd.
Richwood, OH 43344

JONT Enterprises
1396 New Garden Rd.
New Paris, OH 45347
513-437-7195

Jungle Jim's Paintball
152 S. Main St.
Miamisburg, OH 45342
513-859-0916

Miami Valley Shooting
7771 S. Cassel Rd.
Vandalia, OH 45377
513-890-1291

Mohawk Paintball Field
453 Country Rd. 2000
Jeromesville, OH 44840
419-368-4089

Paintball Discounters
3069 Silver Dr.
Columbus, OH 43224
800-536-1104
paintball-
discounters.com

Paintball Field of Fun
Columbus, OH
614-784-1104

Paintball Games Coliseum
3621 State Rte. 273
Belle Center, OH 43310
513-464-4480

Pinnacle Woods
8752 East Ave.
Mentor, OH 44060
216-974-0077

Queen City Paintball
5961 #4 Boymel Dr.
Fairfield, OH 45014
513-942-BALL

R&B Games
113 E. North St.
Fostoria, OH 44830
419-435-4225

R&B Games
178 So. Main St.
Bowling Green, OH 43402
419-353-2176

R&B Games
528 So. Main St.
Findlay, OH 45840
419-427-2176

Richland Paintball Supply
888 Laver Rd.
Mansfield, OH 44905
419-589-5577

Splatland Paintball
Wrightway Road N.
Dayton, OH
513-293-5560; 461-4486

Splatterpark Pball Games
5560 CR 109
Mt. Gilead, OH 43338
800-536-1104,
419-946-4964
www.splatterpark.com

Toldeo Indoor Paintball
5860 Lewis Ave.
Toledo, OH 43612
419-478-2221

Xtreme Paintball Sports
3081 Dryden Rd.
Moraine, OH 45439
937-298-5138

OKLAHOMA

Adrenaline Paintball Supp
1280 Interstate Dr.
Norman, OK 73972
405-579-3500

Boot Hill Pball Field
1m. N 1/2m. E. Fair-
grounds
Stillwater, OK
405-269-6001

Cedar Ridge Pball Games
306 N. 1st
Henryetta, OK 74437
918-652-8891

Dodge City Pball Field
9601 N.E. 63rd St.
Oklahoma City, OK
405-771-5229

Paintball of Tulsa
6390-H E. 31st St.
Tulsa, OK 74135
918-665-7856

Shaggy Bros. Paintball
5575 N.W. Expressway
Oklahoma City, OK 73114
800-320-7277

OREGON

Adrenaline—Sportz
9921 S.E. Stark
Portland, OR 97216
503-251-0065, 251-0068fx

Paintball Games
1820 W. 7th Ave.
Eugene, OR 97402
541-465-4766; fax 4776

Splat Paintball Sports
2880 Ferry S.W.
Albany, OR 97321
541-928-0957

Warpaint Pball Supply
2304 E. Adams Ave.
Lagrande, OR 97850
503-963-6947

Whack'm & Splak'm
PO Box 58
Keno, OR 97627
503-884-8942

PENNSYLVANIA

Boyd's Front Line
420 Butler Mall
Butler, PA 16001
724-285-8740

Double D Paintball
933 E. Market St.
York, PA 17403
717-699-5738

E.M.R. Paintball Park
PO Box 728, Rt. 706 & 601
New Milford, PA 18834
570-465-9622

Kuba's Surplus Sales
231 W. 7th St.
Allentown, PA 18102
215-433-3877

Sgt. York's
900 Market St.
Lemoyne, PA 17043
717-761-3819

Wanna-Play Pball Supp
725 North Rte. 15
Dillsburg, PA 17019
717-432-7997

RHODE ISLAND

Boston Pball Supp North
1428 Hartford Ave.
Johnston, RI 02919
401-351-2255

Paintball Wizards of NE
682 Broadway
Pawtucket, RI 02860
401-724-3751

SOUTH CAROLINA

Adrenaline Heaven Pball
1310 Whiskey Rd.
Aiken, S.C. 29801
803-643-8199

Paintball Inc.
155 Verdin Rd.
Greenville, SC 29607
803-458-7221

Paintball Charleston
178 Irby Dr.
Summerville, SC 29483
843-819-7070

The Paintball Store
5131 Dorcester #14
N Charleston, SC 29418
843-552-1115

Pro Fox Paintball
1200 Woodruff Rd.
Greenville, SC 29607
803-458-7221

SOUTH DAKOTA

Big Jim's Feud Ranch
HRC30, Box 17
Spearfish, SD 57783
605-578-1808

TENNESSEE

Paintball Park
9640 Davies Plantation E.
Memphis, TN 38002
901-372-3383

TEXAS

Adventure Expeditions
1308 Chestnut St.
Commerce, TX 75248
903-886-7691, 886-3014

Awful Ventures Pball&More
4309 W. Pipeline
Euless, TX 76040
817-282-3636

C.M. Support/ViewLoader
4921 Olson Dr.
Dallas, TX 75227
214-381-3075; 388-6743

Centrex Paintball
Route 7, Box 192
Killeen, TX 76542
817-628-7076

Command Post
8635 Long Point
Houston, TX 77055
713-827-7301

Command Post
10607 I-10 East
Houston, TX 77029
713-675-3221

Command Post
2843 SE Beltway 8
Pasadena, TX 77503
281-998-3233

Constant Action
1701 W Ben White #120
Austin Texas 78704
512-326-1109, 326-4072fx

Constant Action
1319 Rutland
Austin Texas 78758
512-837-3787, 837-4274fx

D.A.M. Games of E Texas
PO Box 5270
Longview, TX 75608
214-297-2075

Green Beret
2213 N. 10th St.
McAllen, TX 78051
210-687-1147, 1148

Hit & Run Pball Park
Rt. 2, Box 156D
Mansfield, TX 76063
817-453-8914

Lone Star Paintball
23214 Baneberry
Magnolia, TX 77355
713-356-2158

Olympic Paintball Sports
712 N. 31st
Temple, TX 76504
254-791-5050, 5051 fax

Olympic Paintball Sports
3601 Parmer Ln.
Austin, TX 78727
512-834-9290, 834-1934

Olympic Paintball Sports
15010 Fagerquist Rd.
Del Valle, TX 78617

Olympic Paintball Sports
36 White Flint Park Rd.
Temple, TX 76510

Outpost Paintball Field
2341 Murdine Rd.
Aransas Pass, TX 78336
512-758-2181

Paintball Bonanza
S. Main at Chimney Rock
Houston, TX 77035
713-935-0552

Paintball Games of Dallas
3305 E J Carpenter Frwy
Irving, TX 75062
214-554-1937

Pball Game Supp of TX
1101 Royal Pkwy, #117
Euless, TX 76040
817-571-1177

Paintball Gear
7979 N. Eldridge #3018
Houston, TX 77041
281-897-8678

Paintball Gear
12121 NW Freeway
Houston, TX 77092
713-935-0552

Paintball Maxx
5829 W Sam Houston N. #601
Houston, TX 77041
713-983-9190
849-3232 fax

Paintball of Waxahachie
507 No. Hwy 77 #614
Waxahachie, TX 75165
972-937-2468

Paintball Player's Supp
7024 Jacksboro Hwy.
Fort Worth, TX 76135
817-237-0299

Paintball Store
9220 FM 1960 W.
Houston, TX 77070
201-469-9777

Pball Supp of Lewisville
1081 W. Main St., #107B
Lewisville, TX 75067
972-221-9036

Survival Games of Dal/Ft.W
105 Waits Circle
Garland, TX 75043
817-267-3048

Survival Game of TX
2309 Aldine Meadows
Houston, TX 77032
713-370-GAME

Unicam
2624 Elm St.
Dallas, TX 75226
214-651-1350

West Texas Paintball
2235 19th
Lubbock, TX 79401
806-744-4000

Wolfe City War Games
Rt. 2, Box 267
Wolfe City, TX 75496
903-450-1006

UTAH

CCS 1Air Assault
175 East 400 St #1000
Salt Lake City, UT 84111
801-350-9102

Straight Shooter Pball
3940 Washington Blvd.
Ogden, UT 84403
801-394-2916

VERMONT

3 Guys Games & Pball
1236 Route 4 E.
Rutland, VT 05701
802-775-1548

First Downhill
W. Dover, VT 05356
802-464-7743

Mike's Hobbies & Raceway
162 N. Main St.
Rutland, VT 05701
802-775-0059

VIRGINIA

B.C.B.G. Paintball
11501 Washington Hwy.
Ashland, VA 23005
804-798-1551

B.C.B.G. Paintball
7540 West Broad St.
Richmond, VA 23294
804-755-4388

Hobby Town of VA
1218 Blue Ridge Ave.
Culpeper, VA 22701
703-825-8729

Pev's Paintball Pro Shop
11204 Lee Highway A-1
Fairfax, VA 22030
703-273-7732; 273-1807fx

**Pev's Pball Pro
Shop/Games**
13932 Jeff. Davis Hwy.
Woodbridge, VA 22191
703-491-6505

**Pev's Pball Pro
Shop/Games**
2594 Hanco Center Dr.
Woodbridge, VA 22191
703-897-0989

Pev's Paintball Pro Shop
50-A Pidgeon Hill Drive
Sterling, VA 20165
703-709-7387

Pev's Pball Pro Shop
556 Garrisonville Rd.
Stafford, VA 22554
540-720-1319

Splathouse Inc.
946 Grady Ave., Ste. 8
Charlottesville, VA 22901
804-977-5287

WASHINGTON

A.M.S.
18144 Woodinville Sno-
homish Rd.
Woodinville, WA 98072
425-483-8855

AWOL Sporting Supply
PO Box 55398
Seattle, WA 98155

AWOL/Splat Mountain
7018 NE Bothell Way
Bothell, WA 98011
206-487-9158

Boomers Paintball
3807 E. Sanson
Spokane, WA 99207
509-483-1879

The Jolly Soldier
902A N.E. 65th St.
Seattle. WA 98115
208-524-2266

Mobile Tactics Pball
1829 Hwy. 20 Unit E
Burlington, WA 98233
360-755-9020

Paintball Products NW
205 S. 4th Ave.
Yakima, WA 98902
509-453-4963

Semper Fi Paintball Supp
5373 Guide Meridian #E-3
Bellingham, WA 98226
360-398-8081

Shadow Lake Paintball
22237 196th Ave SE
Renton, WA 98058
206-852-7105

West-Side Pball Supply
6325 Evergreen Way #3
Everett, WA 98203
425-513-6211

West-Side Pball Field
17305 Old Mill Rd.
Snohomish, WA 98290
425-513-6211

Western Paintball
419 B. W. Entiat Ave.
Kennewick, WA 99336
509-585-8353,585-9695

WISCONSIN

**Casanova's Outdoor
Adventure Store**
13735 W. Capitol Dr.
Brookfield, WI 53005
262-783-6456;
783-6065 fx
www.casanovaadven-
tures.com,www.adven-
turezones.com

JD Paintball Supplies
7045 Hwy. 70 E.
St. Germain, WI 54558
715-479-5838

Paintball Dave's
203 N. Broadway
Milwaukee, WI 53202
414-271-3004

Paintball Sam's
Highway K
Racine, WI 53185
414-534-3197

WORLD WIDE WEB

AAA Paintball Park
www.aaapaintballpark.com
Charlie@aaapaintball-
park.com

Wayne's World
Scenario Paintball Games
wd24hour@atlantic.net

CARIBBEAN

Caribbean Water Craft
1747 Central Ave.
Rio Piedras, PR 00920
809-793-8345

Hunters Paintball Field
O' St. #129 Ramey Base
Aguadilla, PR 00604
787-890-2064

Kings Jewelers
Munoz Riviera, #105
Fajardo. PR 00648
809-863-0909

Seven Seas Bike Shop
53 Union
Fajardo, PR 09648
809-863-8981

TBT Inc.
PO Box 1557
Luquillo, PR 00673
809-889-3685

VIP Paintball Supplies
One De Diego
502 Puerto Nuevo
San Juan, PR 00920
787-793-6741

INTERNATIONAL PLAYING FIELDS

UK

ENGLAND

Activ 8 Paintball
62-63 Worcester St.
Wolver Hampton West
Midlands WV2 4LQ, 1901
835444, 1902 835442

Activate-UK Paintball Arena
Booking Office
PO Box 36
Dawlish, Devon EX7-9EU
0870-220 0765,
www.activate-uk.co.uk

Adventure Sports Ltd.
Wedgenock Rifle Range
Wedgenock Lane, War-
nick
Warwickshire, CV35 7PX
01926-491-948

Ashcombe Valley Centre
Ashcombe, Dawlish,
Devon EX7 0QD, 01626-
866766

Belsales
60 Peabody Rd., N. Camp
Farnborough, Hants,,
GU14 6HA; 01252-376827

Bridgehouse Survival
51 Caldervale Ave., Charl-
ton-Cum-Hardy, Man-
chester, M21 7PN,
0161-445-8804

CCS Leisure
20 Griffith St, Rushden,
Northampton, NN10 0RL
01933-314805

Cheltenham Paintball
Unit 3, The Vineyards
Glouchester Rd, Chel-
tenham
Glouchestershire
01242-245504

Global Leisure
95a Nutwick Road
Havant, Hamshire, PO9
2UQ
01705-499-494

Grizzley Sports
11 St. Margarets Crescent
Putney, London, SW15
6HL
0181-780-0480

Hook Gun Company
399 Hook Rd., Chessing-
ton
Surrey, KT9 1EL

Lodge Bushes Pball
49 Salisbury Grove
Giffard Park, Milton
Keyes
B'hamshire, MK14 5QA
01908-618-386

L.S.E.
20 Mt. Vernon Rd, Barns-
ley, S. Yorkshire, S70 4DJ

London Paintball Co.
3 Kirkdale Close
Chatham, Kent, DA1 5BH
01634-864-173

Marksmann Paintball
22 HorseCroft Place, The
Pinnacles, Harlow, Essex,
CM19 5BX, 01279-626135

Mayhem Megastore
Pryors Farm, Patch Park,
Abridge Essex
014028-424; 014028-517

**Mayhem Pball Pow-
erGames**
The Power House Lewes
Rd. Blackboys Nr. Uck-
field
E. Sussex, TN22 5LG
01825-890-033

Mayhem Paintball
Midlands,172 Argyle St.
Cuckoo Bridge Ind'lEstate,
Nechells, Bham B7 5TE,
01435-866-189

Operation Paintball
Unit 23C,
Hagh Ln Ind East, Hexham
N Cumberland, NE46 3PU

Paintball Experience
27 Sidmouth St, Devizes
Wiltshire, SN10 1LD
01380-728-982

Paintball Planet
251 Deansgate
Manchester M34EN
44 (0)-161-839-2789

Paintball Planet
Unit 11 Millside Trdest.
Lawson Rd. Dartford Kent
DA1 5BH 44 (0)-1322-
222270

Paintball Sports
291 Deansgate
Manchester M3 4EW
0161-839-8493

Paintcheck Epsom
16 Beaconsfield Pl, Epsom
Surrey, KT17 4BD
01372-726-224

Pidley Paintball
49 Craitherne Way
North Arbury
Cambridgeshire, CB4 2LZ
01223-67665

Predator Paintball
14-16 Holbeach Rd.
Catford, London, BR2
9NY
0181-690-7717

Pro-Line
8a Midas Bus. Cntr, Wantz
Rd, Dagenham, Essex,
RM10 8PS; 0181-595-7771

QED Leisure
166 Lynne Road
Downham Market
Norfolk, PE38 9QG
01366-384-778

**Sheffield Paintball Cen-
tre**
Unit C4, Main St Haken-
thorpe
Sheffield S12 4LB

Skirmish-Kent
The Holt, Church Ln,
Chelsham, Surrey, CR6
9PG 01883 627376

Skirmish-Nottingham
Unit 1, Wellbeck Ind Est,
Alfred Close, Notting-
ham, NG3 1AD
01602 410 454

Survival Game
Canterbury, 52 Swale
Ave., Rushen-den, Isle of
Sheppey
Kent ME11 5JX, 01795-583-
303

Survival Game/Frome
14 Arcacia Dr, Frome
Sommerset, BA11 2TS
01373-471-035

Survival Game (Staffs)
Painley Hill Farm
Bramshall, Uttoxeter
Staffordshire, ST14 8SQ
01889-502-508

Survival Game (SW)
Southdown Farm
Yarnscombe nr. Barnstable
N. Devon, EX31 3LZ
01271-858-279

Survival Game West Midlands c/o Daystate
Newcastle St., Stone
Staffordshire, ST15 8JU
01785-819-609

Survival Game (Yorks)
Moore Farm
Elsham near Brigg
S. Humberside
01652-688-912

Wigan Birds and Pets
80 Ormskirk Rd, New-town
Wigan, WN5 9EA, WDP

Unit 5 Metro Triangle
221 Mount St, Nechells
Birmingham, B7 5QT
0121-328-2228

SCOTLAND

Aberdeen Profields
Cullerlie By Skene
Aberdeenshire AB3 6XA
0133-08414

Alternative Leisure
East Woods Bus. Center
Green Hill Ave.
Glascow, G46 6OX
01416 382-811

Edinburgh Profields
136A St. Johns Road
Edinburgh EH12 7SB
0131-316-4004

Maxamillion Events
Overton Cottage
Kirknewton
Midlothian, EH27 8DD
01506-884-088

Mayhem-Edinburgh
14 Ochiltree Ct., Mid
Calder Livingstone
W Lothian, Scotland EH53 0RU

SimulateD ActivitieS
4 Lochrin Place, Tollcross
Edinburgh, EH3 9QY
0131-2299827

WALES

Leisure Pursuits
Langrove Country Club,
Fairwood Common
Swansea, S. Wales
0144-128-2410

Paintball Consortium
53 Station Rd., Deeside,
Clwyd, N Wales
01244-821490

SimulateD ActivitieS
19 Seymour St., Aberdare
Mid Glamorgan, CF44 7BL
01685-875-633

CANADA
Alberta

Alan Kerr/Ty Cale Security Equip.
10769 99th St., Ed, Ata,
T5H 4H6, 403-424-8851

Edmonton Survival Game
4968 98th Ave., Edmonton Alta, T6B 2Y7
403-469-4263

Pball Adventure World
1912 Mackay Rd. NW
Calgary, Alb, T3B 1C7
403-289-8887, 4904 fax

Pursuit Supplies Int'l
5809 118th Ave, Ed.
Alberta, T5W 1E5
403-477-9252

Tactical Adventure Game
Box 344, Red Deer,
Alberta, T4N 5E9,
403-347-4444

Unique Outdoor Supplies
4968 98 Ave, Edmonton
Alberta, T6B 2Y7
403-469-4263

BRITISH COLUMBIA

Adrenaline Sports
1050 Saskatoon Ave.
Prince Rupert, BC V8J 4P1
604-627-7644

BC Elite Adventure Sports
16492 104th Ave.
Surrey, BC, V4N 1Y5
604-951-0988

Frontline Paintball Supp
13377 72nd Ave.
Surray, BC CD V3W 2N5
604-501-0903

MANITOBA

Paintball Paradise
St. Laurent, Man. CD
204-338-1535

NOVA SCOTIA

Banshee Paintball
122 Portland St.
Dartmouth, NS, B2Y 1H8
902-469-6926

L & M Surplus
1823 Sackville Dr.
Mid. S'ville N S, B4C 257
902-865-6794

Spike's Action Games
416 Robie St. Truro, NS,
B2N 1L8, 902-893-8377,
897-7700

Wizard Paintball
11 Riverside St.
N Glasgow, NS, B2H 3S1
902-755-9904

ONTARIO

CD Paintball Supp
6 Brucedale Ave. West
Hamilton, Ont, L9C 1C2
416-383-9614

Flag-Grab Paintball
PO Box 30 RR#1
Lansdowne, Ont, K0E 1L0
613-659-4145

Premium Paintball
6083 Kingston Rd.
Scarborough Ont. M1C 1KS
800-236-6090

RLD Games Ltd.
350 Brawley Rd. West
Brooklin, Ont. CD L0B 1C0
1-800-668-5809

Superior Paintball
94 Megginson Dr.
Sault Ste. Marie, Ont. P6A 6A9, 705-946-8773

Triangle Computer&Hobby
6 George St.
Pt Colborne, Ont. L3K 3S1
905-834-4341

Finding Paintball

Ultimate Adventures
76 Cardish St.
Kleinburg, Ont L0J 1C0
905-893-1815

QUEBEC

Adventure Division Ltd.
860 Bernard Pilon
McMasterville, Qc, J3G
5W8
514-441-1129; 464-5639

Le Jeu Survival I
Mansonville, Quebec
514-295-2706

Le Jeu Survival II
Iberville. Quebec
514-346-2709

PBLAction Games
7155 Transcanada W
St-Laurent, Qc, H4T 1A2
514-595-5993

Quebec Paintball
800 Chemin de la
Canardiere, Qc. G1J 2B7
418-623-4496

**Survie Commando
Games**
474 Chemin Covey Hill
Hemmingford Qbc
514-949-8736

SASKATCHEWAN

Adventure Co. Paintball
2713 45th A Ave.
Lloydminster, Sk., S9V 1A6
306-825-7902

Moosehorn Pball Games
Box 278
Maidstone, Sk, S0M 1M0
306-893-2912

AUSTRALIA

NEW SOUTH WALES

Adventure Quest Games
19 Sommerset St.
Epping, Sydney 2121
02-876-6382

**Aussie Paintball Game
201 Canterbury'**
Bankstown, NSW 2200
02-790-1401

**Hamsta Where? Action
Apparel**
18 Brunker Rd.
Greenacre NSW 2190
02-796-8536

Impact Paintball
102 The Esplanade
Ettalong Beach 2257
02-43-413-829

Phantom Zone
93A Argyle St.
Parramatta 2150
02-891-1848

Skirmish Adventures
Head Office
Level 2, 18 Brunker Rd.
Greenacre NSW 2190
02-796-7955, 02-796-8397

Skirmish Adventures
Pinch Hill Hume Hwy.
Gunning, NSW 2581
1-800-63-62 -61

Skirmish Adventures
Lawrence Hargreave Dr.
Helensburgh, Sydney
N.S.W. 2190 Australia
1-800-63-62-61

QUEENSLAND

Pball Australia Pty. Ltd.
Gold Coast War Museum
Springbrook Rd., Mud-
geeraba Gold Coast 4213
07-5-305222

Samford Skirmish
Samford Rd. Samford
4520
07-289-1820

Skirmish Adventures
Bowhunters Rd.
Townesville, Qld. 4810
02-796-2671

Skirmish Sunshine Coast
Ettamogah Pub Aussie
Village, Bruce Hwy,
Palmview, Sunshine Coast
07-4-94-5566

Top Gun Paintball Fields
Glengarry Rd.
Keperra 4054
07-392-0022

Top Gun Paintball Fields
Cedar Creek Lodge
Thunderbird Park, Mt.
Tamborine Qld.
07-392-0022

SOUTH AUSTRALIA

Skirmish
Mary St., Unley 5061
08-371-0776

VICTORIA

Pball Skirmish Games
1175 High St.
Armdale, Victoria 3143
03-822-1100

Skirmish Survival Games
200A Evans Rd.
Cockatoo 3781 (map 10
Melways) 0419 122 204

WORLDWIDE

BRAZIL

**Mercenarios Pball
Supply**
Shopping Center Lapa
Rua Catao, 72-Lj. K-18
05049-901 S. Paulooo-SP
01155-11 3871 1468

Wargames Paintball
Target Emp. Com. Field &
Supply, Av. Brig. Luis
Antonio 478 5° and Sao
Paulo, 01426
01155-11 232-5470

CURAÇAO

Canoa Paintball
Roud to Canoa
Curacao
5999 6677350, www.cura-
caopaintball.8m.com

CZECH
REPUBLIC

Survival Games Bohemia
Jana Masaryka 26 Praha 2
Czech Republic 120 00
042 2 691 0843

DENMARK

Action Pursuit Centre
Nybrovej 304 C5, DK-
2800, Lyngby
8781211 31535511

Arms Gallary City
Nybrogade 26
1203 Kobenhavn K
33-118-338

Danish Paintball
østerbro 37A
9000 Aalborg, 98 124277

Danish Paintball
Frederiksgade 72 Kld
8000 Aarhus C, 86-98937

Shoot to Thrill
Amagerbrogade 220 B
DK-2300 Copenhagen S
45-32-97-44-04

Proline Scandinavia A/S
Yderlandsvej 25
Kobenhavn S 2300-45-
3154-2045

FRANCE

CAMP
64 rue des mathurins
75008 Paris France
01-42-68-10-00; 01-42-68-
12-96 fax

F.L.A.G.
1 rue du Rocher
78610 St-Leger-En-
Yvelines
34-86-33-14

Skirmish France
Domaine de Bousserain
71320 Toulon
Sur Arroux,France
01033 85795148

GERMANY

Brass Eagle Germany
Rainer Ehrig-Braun
Siegfried-Leopoldstr. 5
5300 Bonn-Beuel
0228-473205

Doc's Paintball Shop
Myhler Straße 19
27711 Osterholz-
Scharmbeck
04791-89-136

**Farbdschungel Furth
P'ball Gear**
Elsternstr. 3a
Tuch-enbach 90587
0911-7568-212

HarBur Marketing Inc.
Auf der Pick 5
D-66849 Landstuhl 49
Germany 06371 60291;
06371-912310 fax

JM SchieB-Sport-Bedarf
Postfach 5843, D-8700
Wurzburg 09302-846

**Kaiserslautern Rod &
Gun Club**
86 SVS SVBH, Unit 3240,
Box 535, APO, AE 09094
49-631-57484

Kotte & Zeller
Industristr. 415 65, W-
95365 Rugendorf
092-21-84034

OPM Paintball Supplies
Ronsdorferstr. 143,
Tor 11 40233 Dusseldorf
0211-733-3155

Paintball Consortium
Holderlinsallee 6
2000 Hamburg 60
40-279-45-65

Paintball Special Sports
PO Box 6532, D 4400
Munster, 0251-55503

**Paintball Sports Ger-
many**
Kleine Pfaffengasse 3
67346 Speyer
06232-620571

Venom, The Toxic Toys
Lohbecker Berg 18
45470 Muhlheim an der
Ruhr
0208-380280

GREECE

**Voyager Adventure
Games**
25 Sigala Street
542 48 Thessaloniki
30-31-325833

HOLLAND

ASCO Sports-Inc.
Hoefblad 12
1911 PA Uitgeest
0-2513-20420

**ASCO Sports Paintball
Games Ned.**
Hoefblad 12
1911 PA Uitgeest
0-2513-14870

ASCO Paintball Games
1e Middellandstraat 104b
3021 BH Rotterdam,
010-4778979

Euro Pball Adventures
Marimbastraat 6
5802 LW Venray
04780-87087

Jobs Paintball Shop
William De Zwijgerlaan
71-73
1056-JG, Amsterdam
020-850-700

The Old Man Hardware
Damstraat 16
Amsterdam 1012 2M
020 627 0043

Realistic Fantasies Pball
Erasmusgracht 5, 1056BB
Amsterdam, Holland
020-683-6474

Splat Attack
Schenkkade 293-294
2595 AX's-Gravenhage
31-0-70-385-6699

**Stichting Paintball Lim-
burg**
Dwarsstraat 27, 6361 XM
Nuth. 31-45-244385

IRELAND

Escarmouche Paintball
Belfast 327500, SimulateD
ActivitieS
Cork, Ireland
150-4624

**Skirmish Ireland
Cranwell**
Rockville Crescent
Blackrock, Dublin Eire
010353 12819009

ISRAEL

Israel Paintball Games
PO Box 53052
Tel Aviv, Israel 61530
972-3-482653

ITALY

**Associazione Giochi
Sopravvivenza**
PO Box 38
21020 Casciqago-Va

**Survival Game Sport
Adventures**
F.I.G.P., Via Strada del
Trombone, 14, 44013 Con-
sandolo FE
39-532 858145, 337 590589

JAPAN

International Paint-ball Game Federation Japan
1024 Kamikasuya Isehara,
Kanagawa 259-11
81-463-87-5895

J.P.P.L.
7-1 Yama Iwadecho Naga-gun, Wakayama 649-62
81-736-61-6322

KOREA

Asia Pacific Int'l
Keoyang Bldg. Rm. 202
#51-8, Susongdong,
Chongno Gu, Seoul,
Korea 110-140
82-2-734-9130

MEXICO

Chango's Army
Aeropuerto Atizapan
Distrito Federal, Mexico
525-519-0303

NEW ZEALAND

Super Splat (NZ) Ltd.
241 Blenheim Rd.
PO Box 22662,
Christchurch
64 03 343-3055

NORWAY

IB Paintball
Vogts Gate 39
0444 Oslo 4
47-22-718102

Paintball Centre
Ostifaret 10
1476 Rasta, Norway
47-2-700-130

PANAMA

Sports International
Via Brasil, Building #38,
Local #24, 6-9425 El
Dorado, Panama 265-0625

PHILIPPINES

Gotcha, Inc.
291 P. Guevarra Ave.
San Juan Metro Manila
011-63-2-70-64-47

ROMANIA

Mercenars Club
B-dul 1 mai nr. 29
B.PF9 ScB. Ap.35
Constanta cod 8700
004041587592; fax
004041545226;
GSM 092752454

RUSSIA

Action Paintball Games
20-2 Panfilova Str.
Moscow, 125080, Russia
095-785-1762
095-796-4646

Paintland Paintball Sports Club
Kalashny pereulok, 10,
Moscow, 095-918-4580,
291-2259

Russian National P'ball Assn
5 Kozuhovskaia
Moscow 22-1-60
095-277-7424, 166-6200

SLOVENIA

Soberl d.o.o.
Rosinova 3
Maribor, Slovenia 62 000
62 413 946

SOUTH AFRICA

IMEXO
PO Box 7216, Roggebaal
Cape Town 8001, SA
021-701-5941

Indoor Paintball City
7 Du Preez Street, Knights
1413 Johanesburg, So.
Africa
011-828-7583

Paintball Supplies
PO Box 3090, Symridge
1420 Johanesburg, So.
Africa
011-828-7583

SWEDEN

Paintball Sports
Bispmotalagaten 7
591 30 Motala
0141-55550

Tradition Sturegallerian
114 46 Stockholm
08-611-45-35

Tradition Femmanhuset
411 06 Goteborg
031-15-03-66

THAILAND

International Paintball Club
437-118 Soi Yodsak
Pattaya, Thailand
(66) 01-919-2635

VENEZUELA

Estrategia
C.C. Multicentro 1er Piso
Local 26 Cagua, Aragua,
2122
044-960455, 044
99577970

Paintball Sport de Venezuela Ave. Francisco di Miranda
Centro Plaza, Niveo
Jardin, Local CC-322-A,
Los Palos Grandes, Cara-cus, Venezuela 582-286-4483

Survival Games Club, CA
Calle Baruta con Los
Cerritos
Res. Paso Real #18 Caracas,